Third Edition

Tourists
and Tourism

A tourist shares his photographs with villagers in the Urabamba Valley, Peru. (Photo by Sharon Gmelch)

Third Edition

Tourists and Tourism

A Reader

Sharon Gmelch
University of San Francisco
and
Union College

Adam Kaul
Augustana College

WAVELAND
PRESS, INC.

Long Grove, Illinois

For information about this book, contact:
Waveland Press, Inc.
4180 IL Route 83, Suite 101
Long Grove, IL 60047-9580
(847) 634-0081
info@waveland.com
www.waveland.com

Cover photo: George Gmelch
Cover design: Katherine Beal

10-digit ISBN 1-4786-3622-X
13-digit ISBN 978-1-4786-3622-9

Printed in the United States of America

7 6 5 4 3 2 1

Third Edition

Tourists
and Tourism

Contents

Part III:
Tourism's Many Implications and Dilemmas   225

Tourist photography outside the Sun Yatsen Memorial Hall in Guangzhou, China. (Photo by Sharon Gmelch)

Preface

Tourists and Tourism was first published by Waveland Press in 2004 with a second, substantially revised edition appearing in 2010. In this third edition, three-quarters of the content is new. Important areas in tourism studies including dark tourism, medical tourism, photography and film, nonvisual sensory experiences of tourism such as taste and sound, the material culture of souvenirs, and student and volunteer travel are covered.

New voices are included as well. In recognition of the international scope of the study of tourism, half the contributors live and teach outside the United States. Given the global reach of tourism and travel, the chapters also cover a wide geographic range.

Like earlier editions, *Tourists and Tourism* is organized for the classroom. We surveyed past readers and instructors to find out which chapters should be retained and then "field tested" the new selections with students. Special thanks to University of San Francisco students Maya Barba, Jackie Cepeda, Maria Delgado, and Gaelle Mondestin and to the students in Adam Kaul's 2016 "Global Connections" class at Augustana College in this regard.

The chapters are arranged thematically, each taking a critical and analytical approach to their subject. They vary in length and style, with some providing deeper context while others are written to spark debate in the classroom. This gives instructors flexibility when designing their courses, and students a variety of ways to learn. A number of pieces specifically address issues that relate to the student experience, including study abroad, service learning, social media, and the ethics of travel. Finally, an introduction to the use of film in teaching and a link to an important film resource from the Anthropology of Tourism Interest Group is provided.

We are grateful to Tom Curtin at Waveland Press who shepherded us through the editorial process, and to Jeni Ogilvie for her careful copyediting, patience, and good cheer. We also wish to thank Katherine ("Kat") Beal for the cover design.

Part 1: Tourism and the Tourist Experience

Tourists and guide above the Colca Valley, Peru. (Photo by Sharon Gmelch)

Tourists on a university alumni trip to the Amazon. (Photo by Sharon Gmelch)

1

Why Tourism Matters

Sharon Bohn Gmelch

Why would anyone study tourism? People lie on the beach, swim, drink rum punch. . . . Why does it matter?

It matters for many reasons. To begin, tourism is one of the world's largest industries, directly employing over 100 million people and supporting one in eleven jobs globally (WTTC n.d.). There are well over a billion international tourist arrivals each year. That's a lot of people traveling around the world to experience other people and places, and a lot of foreign exchange for the countries they visit. Many governments, regions, and cultural groups view tourism as a positive force for economic development, while others worry about its impacts on society and the environment. More will be said about these later. Clearly, tourism is more than its frivolous sun, sand, and sea stereotype.

When anthropologists study tourism, they look at many things: what motivates people to travel and how they decide where to go, the experience and practice of being a tourist, the lives of tourism workers, tourism's benefits and costs for host populations, and much more. The possible topics are almost as broad as anthropology itself. While many researchers have proposed analytical frameworks or examined the theoretical debates about tourism, including several of this volume's authors, my intent here is to provide a broad overview of the topic and its many ramifications.

I first became interested in tourism in the early 1980s when I began taking students to Barbados for a semester-long anthropology field school. Although important work had been done on the topic by social scientists like Dean MacCannell (1976), Valene Smith (1978), and Dennison Nash (1981), tourism was not widely studied. Yet its impact was impossible to ignore. Tourists, arriving by air and aboard cruise ships, more than tripled Barbados' population each year. Because most locals are Afro-Caribbean (90 percent) and most visitors to the island were white Europeans or North Americans, they automatically stood out. Many also stood out because of their dress or behavior, which included visiting stores and banks clad only in bikinis or swim trunks, prompting one Bajan shopkeeper to post the following quaint request: "We value your business and we know that you're cool, but please leave exposed tummies around the pool."

All vacations represent a "time out" during which tourists occupy a liminal status—removed from their everyday routines and responsibilities, if not their home society, yet not really part of the places they visit. For many visitors, Barbados represents a fantasy isle, which is an image promoted by the country's tourism industry. Resorts have names like Crystal Cove, Royal Pavilion, Discovery Bay, and Treasure Beach. Whenever my students were treated as tourists, they quickly attempted to disassociate themselves. They were appalled by most tourists' ignorance of the island and its people (a point elaborated on by Kaul and Kim later in this volume) and by the rudeness and misbehavior of some. Moreover, they reasoned, they were living in villages with local families and studying the culture, not just there to have fun.

A Brief History of Tourism

The impulse to travel for more than necessity—subsistence or trade—is very old, but it has not always been possible. At one time, travel outside of a person's home locale could be dangerous—the terrain, the absence of reliable maps, bandits, anything could happen. Religious pilgrims were some of the earliest "tourists." Most traveled by foot to holy sites like Mecca and Jerusalem to fulfill a lifetime goal and, perhaps, to secure a better afterlife. For the medieval pilgrims in Chaucer's *The Canterbury Tales*, the trip to martyr St. Thomas Becket's shrine combined a spiritual quest with pleasure and adventure. Along the way, they enjoyed new sights and experiences and each other's sometimes ribald companionship.

Travel has long been associated with education. The Roman statesman Seneca recognized as early as the first century that "travel and change of place impart new vigor to the mind."[1] In the seventeenth and eighteenth centuries young English and American elites, usually men, polished their education by taking the "Grand Tour" in the company of a tutor to the great sites of European architecture, art, history, and culture. Today, international exchange programs, which combine structured learning with touristic travel, are an important part of college curricula.

People have also traveled for health. Destinations boasting hot springs, pure mountain air, or warm water and salubrious sea breezes promised both mental and physical recuperation. In 1751 George Washington took his half-brother Lawrence to Barbados hoping he would recover from his tuberculosis there; he died on the voyage home. (The place they stayed, however, is now a heritage tourism site.) In the eighteenth century spa resorts sprang up throughout Europe and remain popular there and elsewhere today. Medical tourism is one of the newer trends, with people traveling to distant locales to receive more economical treatment but, in many cases, also pampered care and the opportunity to recover in an interesting place. Brazil is currently popular for cosmetic surgery, India for heart surgery and reproductive services, as discussed by Amit Sengupta (this volume).

Tourism for the average person only became possible with advances in transportation. Thomas Cook, a Baptist minister and temperance worker, used Britain's new railway system in 1841 to transport factory workers from Leicester to Loughborough, just 19 miles away, for a temperance rally. He soon began organizing excursions throughout England and later went on to develop elaborate journeys via railway and steamship to the Continent, Egypt, and the Holy Land, combining people's fascination with the novelty of new modes of travel and their emerging curiosity about new places. He issued tickets at favorable rates, hired local guides, and even handled their lodging and currency changes. The travel agency he built still bears his name.

The place where Washington stayed in Barbados is now a heritage tourism site. (Photo by author)

The transportation industry itself has played a key role in promoting tourism: American railways encouraged people to travel to the Southwest; steamships lured early visitors to Alaska with images of glaciers, totem poles, and Native people. In the 1970s travel for the masses literally took off with the growth in jet travel (particularly the Boeing 747 jumbo jet) and the introduction of charter flights and all-inclusive holidays. Today, other technologies like the smartphone are radically transforming the tourist experience. Now the selfie (see Kohn this volume) brings the traveler's social world along for the tour.

Where and Why People Travel

The reasons people travel and where they decide to go are complex. While some people travel primarily for a change of scene or simply to find a place to relax, others seek out different people, places, and experiences. They travel to marvel at Iceland's glaciers or the Galapagos' unique wildlife, to walk the Inca Way or go whitewater rafting in Nepal, or to visit an exotic culture or an iconic heritage site. Others pursue special interests. Culinary tours of France and Peru are currently popular as is "voluntourism" to a host of locations where visitors can help restore a coral reef, teach computer coding, or work on an organic farm or archaeological site (see Garland this volume).

Cost and safety are important considerations for most people when deciding where to go. After that, much depends on how well a destination has been marketed through websites, brochures, advertisements, and feature articles. In 2013, the Barbados Tourism Authority launched a sexy social media ad campaign starring Barbados native and R & B star Rihanna. Destinations are advertised like any other "product" through pictures, words, and music, which create appealing images: idyllic beaches, majestic vistas, glamorous resorts, remote cultures, and unique experiences. Countries seek to differentiate themselves from others. Recent international ad campaign slogans include, "It's More Fun in the Philippines" and "There's Nothing Like Australia."

Individual tourists also have preestablished ideas about certain places. Many sites are famous for being famous. The iconic tourism sites in the early twentieth century were the Taj Mahal, the pyramids of Giza, Victoria Falls in Zimbabwe, and Old Faithful Geyser in Yellowstone. Today, they include Peru's Machu Pichu and Cambodia's Angkor Wat.

Other sites become desirable based on word-of-mouth recommendations or the mental associations created by books and films. Since 1989, American baseball enthusiasts have traveled to a cornfield in Iowa to see the "field of dreams" made famous by the movie of the same name. Tourists from all over the world visit Anne Frank's house in Amsterdam. Japanese tourists travel to Prince Edward Island to visit the fictional home of Anne Shirley, the beloved Canadian heroine of Lucy Maude Montgomery's 1908

Huayna Picchu looms behind the fifteenth-century Incan city of Machu Picchu, Peru. (Photo by Frank Otto)

novel *Anne of Green Gables* (and later a television miniseries). Anne's spunk and determination first made her a popular character in Japan in 1954 when the book was translated and introduced into Japan's junior high school curriculum. Status considerations can also determine where tourists go: some destinations have more cachet than others based on their distance, expense, challenge, perceived exclusivity, associations with "high culture" or celebrities, and a host of other factors.

A Unique Form of Globalization

Unlike most forms of globalization, tourism brings consumers (i.e., the tourists) and producers (e.g., local service providers, ethnic "Others") into direct contact with one another. When we buy bananas at our local grocery or a pair of jeans at the local Gap, we seldom think about who harvested them or the conditions under which they were made. Today, most of the things we buy at home are made by the people we visit aboard—by workers in China, Vietnam, Indonesia, or Mexico. As tourists, we experience their home countries' standard of living, meet individuals—if only tourism workers—and develop some empathy for and interest in their lives.

Globalization is usually viewed as a homogenizing force. Countries' increasing economic and political ties and the accelerating flow of information, goods, and people worldwide are seen as diminishing cultural differences. The tourism industry, however, has a vested interest in preserving difference. Government tourism boards, travel services, resorts, and the like, aggressively promote aspects of local heritage, culture, cuisine, and place in order to emphasize a destination's uniqueness and to distinguish it from other places tourists could visit (see Timothy this volume). Consequently, despite the uniformity imposed by the spread of international standards in accommodation, hygiene, food, and travel and hospitality services, tourism does not necessarily destroy cultural differences. Folk dances and festivals, historical events, ethnic and regional dress-styles, indigenous arts and crafts, vernacular architecture, and local markets and foods are just some of the cultural differences and crafted "authenticity" that tourism promotes. New "traditions" are also created.

Tourism's Many Impacts

Tourism affects not only the people who travel but also the people and places they visit. Exactly what happens and the scale of the impact depends on many factors, including the number of tourists who come, whether they visit during a single season or arrive year-round, the size of the country and its population, how developed the local economy and infrastructure are, and who controls the industry and profits from it—multinationals, local elites, or the average resident.

When large numbers of tourists visit a place, especially if they visit year-round, residents often feel overwhelmed. In Barbados, three times the total population of the island visit as tourists each year. Yet because most people arrive on cruise ships and don't stay long or else come primarily to enjoy the beach, some parts of the small island remain relatively untouched. In many popular European destinations the swelling number of tourists, the result of cheap flights and apartment rentals, has led to protests and antitourist graffiti that make it clear how locals feel. Venice now receives 30,000 cruise ship passengers *a day* during the high season. When those who arrive by air or land are added, its total tourist numbers stand at 22 million a year. Antitourist protests by residents have become commonplace, and the United Nations Educational, Scientific, and Cultural Organization (UNESCO) has warned the Italian government that the city must control tourist numbers or risk irreparably damaging its buildings and cultural heritage in addition to its citizens' nerves.

Tourism can be especially intrusive when tourists visit places primarily to see "native" people, observe their ceremonies, take photographs, and shop for indigenous arts and crafts. Some Pueblo Indian reservations in the American Southwest control the impact of tourism by making areas of their villages off-limits, by keeping the performance of many ceremonies secret, and by being evasive or uncommunicative when questioned (Sweet 1991). Other restrictions include not allowing photography, audio recording, or sketching of those ceremonies that are open to the public and only allowing tourists onto the reservation when accompanied by a local guide. Similar strategies are used in other parts of the world.

When local people become objects of the "tourist gaze"—when they are watched and photographed even while doing the most mundane things— their lives may be altered. The Inupiaq hunters of Kotzebue, Alaska, stopped butchering their seals on the beach, moving this and similar activities indoors, in order to escape being watched and photographed (Smith 1978). The "love market" at SaPa in Vietnam's northern highlands is another example. Historically the Red Dao sought marriage partners while trading and socializing at the market. Courting couples would serenade one another with mouth harps and personalized songs that revealed their attraction while extolling their own domestic abilities and work ethic. Today, the market has lost this function. Once couples felt too much on display, they began meeting elsewhere. In many parts of the world, residents now post signs explaining local customs and laying out rules for visitors—remove shoes in a temple, do

Red Dao women, Vietnam. (Photo by author)

not photograph or touch religious icons, do not give candy to local children, do not kiss in public, ask permission to photograph local people, do not look at a woman's face, do not touch a person's head, dress modestly.

To attract tourists, destinations often commodify local rituals and celebrations, marketing them as tourist "spectacles." When this happens, their meaning and value for local people can be lost. When the Chambri of Papua New Guinea opened their initiation ceremony to visiting tourists, they unwittingly turned it into a "performance." The presence of a foreign audience combined with the small changes they made in the ceremony in order not to frighten tourists greatly diminished its mystery and meaning for the initiates (Errington and Gewertz 1989). The Alarde ceremony in Spain—a large-scale, elaborately costumed reenactment of the Basque town of Hondarribia's victory over the French in the seventeenth century—declined after Spain's Ministry of Tourism and Information included it in its national advertising in the 1970s. As more tourists arrived, the municipal government decided that the ceremony should be performed twice so that more visitors could watch it, thus redefining it as a public tourist spectacle rather than a local expression of Basque pride. As a result, participation dropped dramatically. Years later, however, the festival acquired new local significance as part of the struggle for regional political rights in Spain (Greenwood 2004).

The Hawaiian hula is another example of an indigenous custom that has been thoroughly commodified for tourism. It was once a sacred temple dance that celebrated the procreative powers of the Hawaiian chiefly class; today it is performed for tourists in entirely secular contexts—the airport, hotel lobbies, theme parks. Yet to most tourists it represents "authentic" Hawaiian culture—an age-old tradition that is real and unmediated. Terms like "authentic" and "traditional" are frequently used to describe aspects of local culture marketed to tourists. Most travelers like to think that what they are seeing is "real"—a historical and largely internally generated part of local culture. Yet new dances, songs, and festivals are created all the time to provide visitors with entertaining "cultural" or "folkloric" events to watch. Some of these creations like Barbados's Crop Over festival (celebrating the end of the sugarcane harvest) have become part of local culture. It was developed in 1974 by the country's tourism board to promote tourism during the slack summer season but now has been embraced by residents and Barbadians living abroad who return home to visit at this time. Dances created specifically for tourism in Bali have now been incorporated into Balinese culture; the "frog dance" created for tourists in the 1970s is now performed at Balinese weddings (Bruner 1996).

As Dean MacCannell (1976) has pointed out, authenticity exists whenever people have significant control over their lives and play an active role in determining what changes occur in their society. He provocatively asks which is more real or "authentic," the town that decides on its own to tear down historic buildings to build a golf course for tourists or the town that is prevented by the government from making any changes in order to artificially preserve its ancient townscape? Traditions and culture are constantly reworked and reinterpreted to fit the needs and reality of each generation. Tourism is now part of that reality in most of the world.

Some researchers talk about tourism's "demonstration effects" and the changes these produce. When foreign tourists arrive in less developed countries they bring with them an affluence that can create a sense of relative deprivation and unrealistic desires in local people of modest means for the lifestyle and possessions tourists have. (Of course, television, films, the Internet, and other outside influences also contribute to this.) Raising the expectations of people who do not have the resource base or opportunities to acquire what comparatively wealthy visitors have can result in some locals searching for ways to get rich quick—activities like street crime, hustling, gambling, prostitution, and drug dealing. Tourists provide the opportunity and the market, in the case of sex and drugs, for such activities.

Prostitution is found in virtually every tourist location. Some young women (and men) move to tourist areas intentionally in hopes of finding a foreign lover or marriage partner or to become prostitutes (see Brennan this volume). Others are lured from rural villages under false pretenses—to become performers, dancers, bar hostesses, factory workers—by middlemen and then get trapped into prostitution. Specialized tour operators in Western countries, Japan, and the Middle East offer package sex tours that market the sexual allure of exotic Others and guarantee their availability. Local governments are not entirely innocent here; some like Thailand have in the past actively marketed their population's physical beauty and suggested their availability to tourists in advertising campaigns. Some cities like Bangkok have become bywords for the sex trade and have developed commercial sex sectors. In the Caribbean and parts of Africa, male "beach bums" or gigolos patrol the beaches looking for tourist women to hook up with.

Child prostitution is a growing problem in many tourist destinations (see Montgomery this volume). The Bangkok-based organization End Child Prostitution in Asian Tourism (ECPAT) estimates that a million children are involved. According to the World Tourism Organization (WTO), a study of 100 schoolchildren in Kalutara, Sri Lanka, found that 86 had their first sexual experience at ages 12 or 13, the majority with a foreign tourist. Recent legislation in the United States, Germany, Britain, and Sweden has made it a crime to travel abroad for the purpose of having sex with a minor; prosecutions have been brought against some tourists.

On a positive note, tourism usually creates new markets for local arts. Hotels hire local performers—musicians, dancers, singers, theater troops—to entertain their guests and buy local art to decorate their rooms and lobbies. Tourists also buy local art and crafts (as well as oddities) as mementos and souvenirs of their trip. Although many people bemoan the emergence of what they consider to be degraded and quasi–mass-produced "airport" or "tourist art," the sale of these items creates opportunities for local people of modest means to earn money. It also demonstrates their ability to read the market, that is, to judge what tourists like (e.g., wooden statues of colonial figures in Africa, baskets with novelty shapes in Alaska) and to provide it. Having a more diverse clientele, especially in a small-scale society, also creates room for artistic experimentation.

This brings us back to tourism's considerable economic impact. Tourism will generate 2,000 billion USD worldwide by 2020. Unfortunately, much of this money never reaches the populations of destination countries. One study in Thailand estimated that 70 percent of all the money spent by tourists left the country via foreign-owned tour operators, airlines, and hotels, and through the use of imported drinks and food—a phenomenon called "leakage." Caribbean countries as a whole lose between 70 and 90 cents of every dollar that tourists spend on holiday. All-inclusive resorts, which offer tourists a prepaid package of airfare, accommodation, entertainment, meals, and other services, put little money into the local economy since tourists have no reason to leave the resort to eat in a local restaurant, hire a local guide, or shop in local stores when they have already paid for everything.

Cruise ships, which are in essence floating all-inclusives, likewise contribute little to the countries they visit (see Klein this volume). When ship passengers disembark at a port, many have already purchased their tours through the cruise line and the car rentals, taxi services, helicopters, and tour operator booths they first encounter are often controlled either by multinational chains, local elites, or expatriates. These same groups also own many of the larger retail stores tourists are funneled into. Some cruise ship lines lease or own their own Caribbean islands, a practice that further reduces the time and money tourists spend at destination ports. In an attempt to partially offset this, more destinations now charge cruise lines a passenger head tax.

Tourism also drives up the cost of living for local people, often forcing them to move away. Venice's population has been declining for years, and tourism is largely to blame. The need for tourist lodging has given property owners a strong economic incentive to convert apartments and houses into short-term holiday rentals that bring in far more money than having long-term tenants. In the Napa Valley, as I discuss in more detail in a later chapter, most of the people working in tourism—in hotels, restaurants, and wineries—cannot afford to live there because tourism has raised the cost of living, including housing. Most live elsewhere and commute in and out of the valley each day, clogging its two arteries each morning and late afternoon.

To encourage tourism, less developed nations usually have to spend large sums of money upgrading their infrastructure—building international airports, excavating deep-water harbors, laying miles of paved road, building new electricity generating plants, increasing the capacity of their water supply and service, and so forth. Major construction projects are often financed with loans from the World Bank or regional development banks and come with preconditions that often fail to take a country's specific circumstances into account. They are usually paid back through local taxes and reduced spending in the public sector, which siphons money away from local schools and libraries, hospitals, and other organizations and services that directly benefit residents. When services like water or electricity are in short supply, priority is given to maintaining the comfort of tourists (to help guarantee their future business) rather than to locals.

While tourism clearly creates new jobs especially during the construction phase, the downside is that these jobs last for only the duration of the project, and most of the later-phase jobs that are created (e.g., hotel maids, waiters, gardeners, bartenders) are seasonal and low-paying; they provide little in the way of benefits, long-term security, or opportunities for advancement. Despite these limitations, many tourism workers are grateful for the jobs they have and like the work they do. Some local people are able to become independent entrepreneurs by opening small guest houses or shops, becoming tour guides, or making crafts to sell. It is the local elites, however, who benefit the most since they are the ones that have the capital, connections, and know-how to take real advantage of emerging opportunities.

When large-scale tourism projects are undertaken—building international airports, deep-water harbors, resorts, and golf courses or establishing game parks and nature preserves in the name of conservation *and* tourism— local people are often displaced, while large swathes of their former agricultural or grazing land and hunting and fishing grounds are lost (see Dowie 2009). About 70 percent of the national parks and game reserves in East Africa are on former Maasai grazing land. In the 1990s, hundreds of Filipinos were resettled to make room for the huge Samal Island tourism estate adjacent to Mindanao (Ness 2003). The Philippine government projected the creation of hundreds of replacement jobs, but the job-training programs promised to displaced locals were minimal and the construction of the huge complex was repeatedly delayed and scaled back. This left most relocated residents without jobs, without access to their old agricultural land and fishing grounds, and with few of the new services that had been promised. Too often, tourism's positive and negative impacts are grossly asymmetrical.

Because tourists often seek beautiful places or unique landscapes to visit, which are ecologically fragile, local environments are easily degraded. Imagine the impact 300,000 hiking boot-clad tourists have on the paths and stone buildings of Machu Pichu each year compared to the 500 or so Incas who once lived there. Japanese geologists have reported land slippage at Machu Pichu of nearly a half inch a month. Many coral reefs have been damaged by tourism, both by locals who harvest coral to sell or make into jewelry and by tourist dive boats and cruise ships. A single anchor dropped from a cruise ship over a coral reef for just one day can destroy an area half the size of a football field. The building of hotels, yacht and cruise ship harbors, and other tourism infrastructure in the Caribbean and parts of Central America

Maasai woman in Tanzania sells handicrafts from a *boma* (livestock enclosure and encampment) created for tourism. (Photo by author)

has destroyed wetlands and mangroves, which provide habitat and nurseries for many species of birds, fish, and crustaceans and help protect shorelines, often with serious consequences during hurricane season.

Tourists use a lot of water, usually many times more than do locals. Think of all the water used each day by guests taking showers, by hotels to launder sheets and towels, and by resorts to replenish swimming pools and to maintain lush landscaping and golf courses. A single golf course in a tropical country like Thailand can use as much water in a year as 60,000 rural villagers. In places where fresh water comes from wells, overpumping can cause salt to intrude into the groundwater. The heavy water usage required by tourism also produces a lot of waste water, and even when treated it usually contains a large amount of phosphates and nitrates. When these are released into the sea, living corals are stressed and die over time, causing the reef to break down. Without a reef barrier to absorb wave energy, there is nothing to prevent beach erosion, and the habitat for many creatures is lost. Some resorts also release their sewage directly into the ocean.

Tourism accounts for at least 60 percent of air travel and, therefore, of the fuel and ozone-depleting emissions that jets emit. It also accounts for many other unexpected environmental impacts like noise and visual pollution. As a result of the noise caused by helicopter tours over the Grand Canyon, natural stillness—one of the things visitors expect to find in an area of such scale—can be found in only one third of the Grand Canyon. In Yellowstone National Park in the winter of 2000, so many visitors used snow mobiles that researchers found that engine noise was heard 90 percent of the time at eight popular sites including Old Faithful geyser. Today, the number and size of snowmobile groups allowed in the park each day are limited, and snowmobiles have to pass stringent tests for noise and air pollution.

Visual pollution occurs when tourist developments are built without architectural sensitivity to the surrounding landscape or to local building styles, when their sheer size overwhelms the landscape, or when their location on mountainsides or coastlines considers only the tourists' and not the locals' views.

Slowly people are becoming more aware of the environmental impact that tourism can have. Ecotourism is one attempt to address the problem. It refers to travel to places of relatively untouched natural beauty where a serious effort has been made to minimize tourism's environmental impact and to promote sustainable development. Ecotourism developments are typically small-scale and their building methods and architecture are low impact and convey a sense of place (e.g., by using local materials and styles). Here tourists are given the opportunity to experience and learn about special ecosystems, like Belize's tropical rain forests and Costa Rica's cloud forests and both countries' coral reefs, and enjoy low-impact environmental adventures (e.g., forest floor and canopy walks, river rafting, snorkeling, and scuba diving). Ecotourism also promotes conservation ethics and is committed to improving the local environment and the lives of local people. Yet it only appeals to some tourists and can only cater to relatively small numbers. There is also the phenomenon of "eco-light." Since tourism is a poorly regulated industry, it is easy for destinations to claim to be "green" when they are not.

"Responsible tourism" asks all of us to examine why and how often we travel as well as the kind of tourism we engage in. It encourages tourists to do their homework—to learn something in advance about the people and cultures of the places they plan to visit and about the business practices of the tour operators they plan to travel with. Such tour operators should be committed to generating economic benefits for local people and enhancing the well-being of host communities as well as minimizing the negative social, economic, and environmental impacts of the tours they offer. The next time you travel, enjoy yourself but be a good global citizen and think about the bigger picture and the impact of your travel. Be responsible. Tourism does matter.

Source: Written expressly for *Tourists and Tourism.*

Note

[1] Ancient Romans toured Athens and collected artifacts from the Parthenon as souvenirs. Local people apparently lined the base of the Acropolis with other items for the Romans to see and buy.

References Cited

Bruner, Edward M. 1996. "Tourism in the Balinese Borderzone," in *Displacement, Diaspora, and Geographies of Identity*, eds. Smdar Lavie and Ted Swedenburg. Durham, North Carolina: Duke University Press.

Dowie, Mark. 2009. *Conservation Refugees: The Hundred-Year Conflict between Global Conservation and Native Peoples*. Cambridge, MA: The MIT Press.

Errington, F., and D. Gewertz. 1989. "Tourists and Anthropologists in a PostModern World." *Oceania* 60:11, 37–54.

Greenwood, D. 2004. "Culture by the Pound: An Anthropological Perspective on Tourism as Cultural Commoditization," in *Tourists and Tourism*, 1st ed., ed. Sharon Bohn Gmelch. Long Grove, IL: Waveland Press.

MacCannell, Dean. 1976. *The Tourist: A New Theory of the Leisure Class*. Berkeley: University of California Press.

Nash, D., et al. 1981. "Tourism as an Anthropological Subject." *Current Anthropology* 22(5): 461–81.

Ness, Sally Ann. 2003. *Where Asia Smiles: An Ethnography of Philippine Tourism*. Philadelphia: University of Pennsylvania Press.

Smith, V. 1978. *Hosts and Guests: The Anthropology of Tourism*. Philadelphia: University of Pennsylvania Press.

Sweet, L. 1991 "'Let 'Em Loose': Pueblo Indian Management of Tourism." *American Indian Culture and Research Journal* 15(4): 59–74.

WTTC (World Travel and Tourism Council). n.d. See https://www.wttc.org/research/policy-research/human-capital/ (accessed June 25, 2017).

2

Secular Ritual: A General Theory of Tourism

Nelson H. H. Graburn

Tourism, defined by the sentence "a tourist is a temporarily leisured person who voluntarily visits a place away from home for the purpose of experiencing a change" (Smith 1989:1), may not exist universally, but in many ways it is functionally and symbolically equivalent to other institutions—calendrical festivals, holy days, sports tournaments that humans use to embellish and add meaning to their lives. In its special aspect—travel—tourism has its antecedents in other seemingly more serious institutions such as medieval student travel, the Crusades, and European and Asian pilgrimages.

It is my contention that tourism is best understood as a *kind of ritual*, one in which the special occasions of leisure and travel stand in opposition to everyday life at home and work. This general theory applies to all forms of tourism. Therefore, we have to understand the nature of tourist travel and experience in terms of the *contrasts* between the special period of life spent in tourist travel and the more ordinary parts of life spent at home while working. Tourism experiences are meaningful because of their difference from the ordinary and they reflect the home life from which the tourists stem. Thus, any one kind of tourist experience (e.g., a week in Paris) can mean something very different in the life of tourists from, for example, urban New York, metropolitan Tokyo, or rural California. Indeed, for some people a week in Paris would be too ordinary and boring, whereas for other people, from very different social backgrounds, it might be too daunting and exciting and they would never undertake such a vacation. Thus, we can see that the tourists' gender, class, occupation, and life stage are all significant in determining where tourists choose to go and what they think of the experience when they have been there.

Tourism: Rituals of Reversal

The ritual theory of tourism proposes that the motivations and compensations of tourism involve "push" and "pull" factors. Tourists leave home because there is something that they want to get away from, and they choose to visit a particular place because they believe that they will experience something positive there that they cannot easily experience at home. This kind of explanation involves the "ritual reversal" or "ritual inversion" of some aspects of life. Simple examples would include the winter migrations of eastern Canadians to the Caribbean and of Scandinavians to the Mediterranean, when these northerners seek some warmth away from home, or when lower-middle-class Californians go to large hotels in Las Vegas or Reno at any time of the year and "live it up" by occupying large, well-appointed rooms and being served lavish meals (Gottlieb 1982). Middle-class Japanese who vacation in the hotels of Southeast Asia in the wintertime seeks both touristic goals: seasonal warmth and a luxurious style of life (Beer 1993)—inversions of their cramped lives in cold Tokyo.

The felt needs of tourists, the things that they look for and forward to in their travels, are never the complete opposites of their home class position and lifestyle. For instance, erudite people don't want to become ignorant, although they may want a relaxing break, and good athletes don't try to become physically incompetent. The felt needs are indeed the product of, or an inherent part of, the values of the home class and lifestyle. Scandinavians and Canadians value sunshine and warmth; American college professors value culture and history and may seek more of it on their vacations; many obese people value thinness and may visit a special reducing establishment; and gourmets may partake of simple foods in their travels, but never bad foods—not willingly! So the temporary reversal sought is rarely an antithesis of their values but is a product of their cultural background, and the promised reward is supposed to satisfy the need in a direction of further enhancement of these values, not turn the tourist into an entirely different kind of person.

The claim that tourism is a secular ritual, embracing goals or activities that have replaced the religious or supernatural experiences of other societies, was strongly suggested by a recent television advertisement in the San Francisco Bay area (1997). It showed exciting scenes of young, fit people diving off cliffs into the sea, skiing down steep slopes, bungee jumping, and so on. At the end of these came a voice-over, "If you want a religious experience, why don't you try a religious experience!" as the scene moved to a shot of the Protestant evangelist the Reverend Billy Graham, who was about to bring his crusade to the area.

Tourism, Ritual, and Time

Tourism in the modal sense emphasized here is but one of a range of choices or styles of recreation or vacation. All of these ritualized breaks in routine define and relieve the ordinary. There is a long tradition in anthropology of the examination of these special events and institutions as markers of the passage of time. Vacations involving travel (i.e., tourism) are the modern equivalent for secular societies to the annual and lifelong sequences of festivals and pilgrimages found in more traditional, God-fearing societies. Fundamental is the contrast between the ordinary/compulsory work state spent "at home" and the extraordinary/voluntary metaphorically "sacred" experience away from home.

The stream of alternating contrasts provides the meaningful events that mark the passage of time. English anthropologist Edmund Leach (1961) suggested that celebratory events were the way in which people without clocks and calendars used to measure the passage of time, implying that those who have scientific calendars and other tacit reminders such as newspapers, TV, and radio rely only on the numerical calendar. I believe that even "scientific, secular" Westerners gain greater meaning from the personal rather than the numeric in life. We are more satisfied and better recall loaded symbols marking the passage of time: for example, "that was the year we went to Rome" or "that was the summer our dog drowned at Brighton Beach" rather than "that was 1988," because the former identify the nonordinary, festive or sorrowful, personal events.

Our two lives—the sacred/nonordinary and the profane/workaday/at-home—customarily alternate for ordinary people and are marked by rituals or ceremonies as should be beginnings and ends of lives. For instance, after a period of work we celebrate with TGIF (Thank Goodness Its Friday), "happy hours," and going-away parties, to anticipate the future state and to give thanks for the end of the mundane. The passing of each year is marked by the annual vacation (or by Christmas or a birthday); something would be wrong with a year in which these events didn't occur, as though we had been cheated of time! These repetitive events mark the cyclical passage of time just as in traditional Christian societies weeks would be marked by Sundays and churchgoing and the year would be marked by Easter, Harvest Festival, Advent, Christmas, and so on. These rituals have been called rites of increase or rites of intensification in agricultural or forager societies (Durkheim 1912), but are generally better thought of as *annual cycle rites*. The types of holidays and tourism that fill these may be family occasions at home, but when they involve travel (e.g., weekends spent skiing or fishing, weeks spent on the beach or even longer trips traveling abroad), they are usually of the seasonal or "annual vacation" type, a form of re-creation, renewing us and making the world go round.

Life is not only cyclical with the same time-marking events occurring again and again, but it is also progressive or linear, as we all pass through life by a series of changes in status, each of which is marked by different but similarly structured rituals. These life-stage marking events are called *rites of passage* and were first analyzed by French folklorist Arnold Van Gennep (1960); it is his model that we shall follow in our analysis of tourism as ritual. Just as rites of passage (e.g., births, graduations, marriages, and funerals) are usually more significant rituals than ordinary cyclical events such as birthdays, Thanksgivings, or *Días de los Muertos*, so rites-of-passage-type tourist experiences may be unusually intense (e.g., semesters abroad, honeymoons, or retirement cruises). But in the relatively individualistic, informal lives of the contemporary Euro-Americans, many rites of passage as kinds of tourism may be purposely self-imposed physical and mental tests (e.g., college-aged people trekking across continents trying to go as far as possible with little expenditure) (Cohen 1973, Teas 1988) or when recently broken-up, divorced, or laid-off middle-class persons take "time off" for long sailing, walking, or cycling trips or other adventures (Frey 1998, Hastings 1988).

The Structure of Ritual and Tourism

For the present discussion our focus is consciously on the prototypical examples of tourism, such as long-distance travel to famous places or to visit exotic peoples, all in unfamiliar environments. However, even the most minimal kinds of tourism, such as a picnic in the garden, contain elements of the "magic of tourism." The food and drink might be identical to that normally eaten indoors, but the magic comes from the movement and the nonordinary setting. Conversely, a very special meal in the usual but specially decorated eating place may also, by contrast with the ordinary, be "magic" enough for a special celebration.

The alternation of sacred and profane states and the importance of the transition between them were first shown by the French sociologists Hubert and Mauss (1898) in their analysis of the almost universal ritual of sacrifice. They emphasized the sequential process of leaving the ordinary, that is, the sacralization that elevates the participants to the nonordinary state where marvelous things happen, and the converse of desacralization and return to ordinary life. "Each festival [each tourist trip, we contend] represents a temporary shift from the Normal-Profane order of existence into the Abnormal-Sacred order and back again" (Leach 1961:132–136). The flow of time has a pattern, represented in figure 1.

Each festive or tourist event is a miniature life, with a happy anticipation, A–B, an exciting middle, C–D, and a bittersweet ending, D–F. The periods before A and after F are the mundane, everyday life, expressed in "That's life." The period C–D, the metaphorically "sacred," the "liminal" (see below) out-of-the-ordinary period, is the time of pilgrimage, travel, and tourism. These holidays (formerly "holy days") celebrated in vacations and tourism

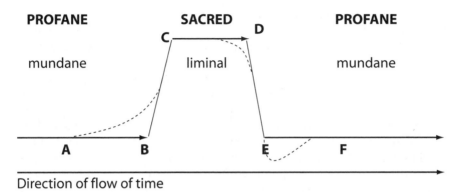

The Ritual of Tourism (modified from Feyerabend 1997:11)

might be expressed as: "I was living it up, really living . . . I've never felt so alive." These changes in moral and spatial states are usually accompanied by aesthetic changes and markers. This is most obvious in the case of religious rituals and rites of passage, where colorful dresses and strikingly decorated settings are accompanied by chanting, singing, and music. In tourism, too, there may well be aesthetic and sensory changes, in clothing, settings, and foods, and even in touch and smell in the case of tropical beach holidays or Japanese hot springs tourism (Graburn 1995b).

Entries and Exits

The experience of being away on vacation (or going on pilgrimage) has important effects on the life of the traveler *outside* of the actual time spent traveling. Just as there are rituals of preparation, cleansing oneself, changing garments, perhaps putting on perfumes, or getting into the right frame of mind before undertaking religious rites such as pilgrimages, sacrifices, or Christian communion, so for the tourist and travelers there are rituals of preparation. These routinely involve not only planning, booking, and getting new clothes, gear, or luggage, but also social arrangements such as getting someone to water the garden, to look after the house and pets, to collect the mail, to leave numbers for emergencies, and often having parties for saying goodbye.

All of these necessary actions produce the pleasure of anticipation in the period A–B and the weeks and months before the actual takeoff B–C, but the feelings are also ambivalent. There may be misgivings about having made the right decisions, having laid out so much money, or having chosen the right traveling companions. There is also the remote possibility that one is saying goodbye forever, especially for long journeys to more distant places for greater lengths of time, as well as for the elderly or infirm either as travelers or those left behind. [For instance, when I went to graduate school in Canada (by ship), my mother at home in England died unexpectedly before I had my first trip home.] Nevertheless, this period of anticipation is extremely important: the pleasure being looked forward to itself shines on many of the preparations and is often what people "live for" in their workaday lives.

Going home, the journey D–F, the reentry process coming down from the "high" C–D, is equally important and fraught with ambivalence. Most people are reluctant to end a vacation, to leave the excitement and new friends, and to have to go back to work. In fact, a desire to get home and end the vacation might be seen as an admission that it didn't turn out to be as good as expected—that the recreation did not recreate. Some travelers even have twinges of sorrow during the period C–D, for instance on reaching the furthest point away from home (Frey 1998), as they anticipate "the beginning of the end," the loss of new friends, or of the "paradise" visited.

The work of Berkeley undergraduate Amanda Feyerabend (1997) on the rituals and experience of the reentry and the reincorporation into normal society explains what is called *reverse culture shock*. The term is a corollary to the notion of *culture shock*—the feeling of strangeness and inability to cope—that travelers feel when first in unfamiliar environments, such as tourists at point C in figure 1. The reverse of this is the unhappiness felt when the tourist first gets back into his/her home and working environment (the period E–F in figure 1). Feyerabend's informants suggested that while their normal home and work lives might be quite satisfying most of the time, life suffered by comparison with the excitement, the out-of-the-ordinary special experiences that they had just left behind; thus, the lowered state of feelings at E–F is a relative measure of happiness.

Feyerabend also found that, in general, the length of time this ambivalent reverse culture shock lasted was approximately *half the length of time* the traveler had been away. For instance, after a two-day weekend of skiing in the nearby Sierra Nevada range, Berkeley students felt the next day (Monday) was a real letdown, but they would feel okay by Tuesday. On the other hand, a student who returned from a year abroad in a foreign country might feel ill at ease and not quite at home for the whole next semester back in the United States.

The Tourist Experience: Liminality and Communitas

Van Gennep (1960), building on the work of Hubert and Mauss, gave us the model commonly used for the analysis of rituals in general. While Hubert and Mauss emphasized the micro-rituals of preparation, separation, and reincorporation in their look at sacrifice, Van Gennep focused on the central period of the ritual, C–D, and the nature of the participants' experience. In his analysis he labeled the "sacred" out-of-the-ordinary period "liminal," meaning "on/over the threshold," following the European custom where a groom has to carry his bride over the threshold of their new home. At this liminal point the participants are neither in nor out, or as Victor Turner (1974) put it, they are "betwixt and between." In some societies this special period is likened to a temporary death; the person in their old status dies, then follows the liminal period where they are bracketed off from ordinary time (or their ordinary place in the case of tourism), out of which they are reborn with their new status, e.g.,

Bachelor → [groom at wedding ceremony] → husband
Single   → [bride at wedding ceremony]   → wife

Victor Turner (1974) and Edith Turner (Turner & Turner 1978) further examined this period of liminality in African rituals and Christian pilgrimages, and they noted: "If a pilgrim is half a tourist, then a tourist is half a pilgrim" (1978:20). Turner stressed that for the participants (those to be transformed in the ritual or the travelers as pilgrims and tourists), the normal social structure of life, work, and family roles, age and gender differences, and so on tends to become looser or disappear. This leveling he called "anti-structure" though, of course, these participants are always surrounded by others carrying out their usual structured roles (e.g., priests or shamans at rituals, and guides, hoteliers, and food workers for pilgrims and tourists). Turner suggested that this leveling of statuses ideally sought outside of home and work structures produces a special feeling of excitement and close bonding among the participants, which he called *communitas*. This state is often signaled by a reduction in marked differences, with all pilgrims wearing the same clothes or all Club Med clients in their beachwear, and with people addressing each other as equals and sharing the same foods, drinks, accommodations, pleasures, and hardships. While consulting for Club Med, I explained this ritual model to a number of *chefs de villages* and GOs *(gentils organisateurs)* who replied with a flash of understanding: "Of course, and the hard part of our job is to keep our customers 'up' in the state of communitas for their seven days nonstop!"

This liminal state, this special human feeling of communitas, may be examined and understood in a variety of ways. In lay language, "going on a trip" usually refers to a journey but it can refer to an "altered state of consciousness" (ASC) brought on by drugs or alcohol, and a special religious or magic experience; "trip" literally means away from the ordinary. Such experience may be called a "high" after which there is a "letdown" or a "come down" (i.e., period C–D followed by D–F in figure 1), and a "high" is opposed to a feeling of depression or a "low," the negative ASC experienced in period E–F. The special state of consciousness experienced during a "trip" was illuminated when I was discussing Feyerabend's findings with my undergraduate class on tourism. Some students pointed out that the reverse culture shock (E–F), lasting half as long as the period of absence (C), paralleled the students' common belief that the time it takes to get over a serious love affair or a broken friendship is half as long as the relationship lasted, putting the "magic" of tourism and pilgrimage into the same emotional category as love and friendship!

Variations on a Theme: Different Strokes for Different Folks

Our analysis of tourism as ritual and the equation of the feelings and meaning of the trip with other human experiences does not mean that all tourism experiences are the same any more than all rituals are the same. Turner and others have characterized the state of communitas as being "high," "liminal" (or liminoid when not part of a truly religious experience), a state of homogeneity, equality, and humility among the participants, a period of transition, magic, or otherworldliness. For today's tourists, the vacation away from home might be described as above, but also may be described as "away," "timeless," a time of freedom, play, mindless spending, and attention to the past or the future (cf. Dann 1996).

The range of tourist experiences has best been outlined by Israeli sociologist E. Cohen in his "Phenomenology of Tourist Experiences" (1979a). Here he takes into account the equation I have suggested between today's tourism and more spiritual pursuits such as pilgrimage, by placing such serious pursuits at one end of his continuum. At this serious end, the traveler is seeking a very important or "sacred" experience or place "out of this world," a sacred center spiritually more important than anything at home. These "existensional" tourists or pilgrims are on a true exploration and many are so moved by the experience attained or the place visited that they stay there and never go home or, in a more practical sense, they never want to go home. Thus, American Jews, having visited Israel, may emigrate there; North American mainlanders may retire to Hawai'i or San Franciscans to the Mendocino County coast. The nature of such tourists' experiences may well be spiritual rather than patently religious; one may feel deeply moved by "communing with nature." Others, atheist or agnostic, might follow the old European pilgrimage way through northern Spain, the Camino de Santiago, and have profoundly moving, even life-changing experiences both along the way and on reaching the cathedral in Santiago (Frey 1998).

At the other end of Cohen's continuum are the mere diversionary or recreational tourists, who never seriously doubt their commitment to their home lifestyle, but just want a simple change—perhaps a change of climate or season, a temporary change of recreation or sports—and have very little desire to explore or seek new experiences. And in the middle of the continuum are the more exploratory tourists, who may make considerable efforts to go to out-of-the-way places, may try to learn foreign languages, or may live temporarily like foreign peoples. These "experiential" and "experimental" tourists are fascinated by difference, like to get close to others, and like to immerse themselves in different environments (e.g., jungle ecotourists, Middle Eastern *souks*, or visitors to remote Nepalese villages). Such people, often young adults without much money or work experience, but probably well educated by their home standards (Cohen 1973, Teas 1988), have the exploratory urge and the *cultural self-confidence* (Graburn 1983) to get out of their shell and experiment with different lifestyles.

Plus ça Change, Plus c'est La Même Chose (The More Things Change, the More It's the Same Thing)

This chapter claims that tourism is a manifestation of a need for a change, and that the change the tourist seeks depends on what perceived touristic attractions would satisfy something not fully met at home. In this concluding section, this general proposition is explored by some specific cases, pointing in particular to the social historical contexts.

In the contemporary Western world and in modern Japan, tourism is the opposite to work; it is one kind of that recent invention: re-creation. It is a special form of play involving travel and "getting away from it all" (i.e., from work, including homework and housework). There is a symbolic link between work + staying and play + travel. Most people feel they ought to go away when they have holidays, and never to go on a vacation might be an indication of sickness or poverty, or extreme youth or old age. Able-bodied adults who don't take holidays might be thought of as poor, unimaginative, or the "idle rich." For the middle classes, this going away on holiday is supposed to be a worthwhile, even a stimulating, creative, or educational experience (see below); for such people, staying at home can be "morally excused" by participating in some creative activity, such as remodeling the house, redoing the garden, or seriously undertaking painting, writing, or sports.

Sociologist Dean MacCannell (1989) has powerfully expressed another instance of this theory in *The Tourist: A New Theory of the Leisure Class*, claiming that the educated middle classes are the sector of our present population who are the most alienated, contrary to Marx's nineteenth-century assertions. MacCannell shows that the urban and suburban middle classes feel that their lives are overly artificial and meaningless, lacking deep feelings of belonging and authenticity. These are thought to exist elsewhere, especially in the simpler lives of other peoples such as family farmers, manual workers and craftsmen, and "primitive peoples." This missing authenticity is thought to lie, above all, in the past, as indicated by English geographer David Lowenthal (1985) in *The Past is a Foreign Country*. Thus, historical, cultural, and ethnic forms of tourism have become increasingly popular, all of them catering to one form or another of modernity's nostalgia for the pre-modern (Graburn 1995b). MacCannell also shows us that the producers of tourist packages and displays understand these longings and are capable of "manufacturing" authentic Others and Pasts, so that the unfortunate tourists are once more faced with the artificial and commercial in their quest for "reality" and the untouched. One popular arena for getting in touch with the true and the pure is Nature itself, which is often sought in its wilder forms by Euro-American campers, backpackers, and ecotourists, and in more managed versions by the equally alienated urban Japanese (Graburn 1995a). The world's tourist industry, in its advertising and its packaged offerings, must paradoxically create the illusion that the tourists are, by purchasing their services, getting satisfaction of their needs.

While MacCannell's work is a brilliant analysis of educated Western-ers, it is not a universal theory. Many people in Europe and North America are not necessarily seeking the particular ritual inversion from "fake to authentic culture"; indeed, it has been shown that this "moral" concern with authenticity correlates with years of education. This search for the pure and the Other, which Urry (1990) has called the "Romantic" gaze, is supple-mented by a more direct, communal, and, some would say, unsophisticated (perhaps a better term is unpretentious) kind of enjoyment he calls the "Col-lective" gaze. The latter is typical of the "working classes," who are more gregarious and derive as much pleasure from the company they keep as the places they visit. Indeed, R. Campbell (1988) has shown that city bus drivers often return to their places of work on their days off, just to socialize with their coworkers. Similarly, Japanese *salarymen* and other groups of male workers often go on trips together, leaving their families at home. Hence, Japanese women often travel in single-sex groups, and children travel in school groups.

The research focus on the "gaze"—the visual practice of sightseeing—has also been challenged by those whose research shows that the changes desired may be sensual or tactile. Selänniemi (1994) found that Scandina-vians wintering in the Mediterranean or elsewhere in the "south" want a thor-oughly Scandinavian vacation, but one in which they can soak up the sun, lie on the beach, or play simple sports. Jokinen and Veilola (1994) have criti-cized tourism theorists in general for overemphasizing the visual, the sight-seeing quest, because that is the touristic goal of the educated class to which the tourism theorists themselves belong.

In conclusion, this chapter has taken care in using the ritual model not to see all tourism as one individual might experience it, nor should it be expected that ritual reversals are all-encompassing. In fact, tourists on holiday are seeking specific reversals of a few specific features of their workaday home life, things that they lack or that advertising has pointed out they could better find elsewhere. Other than obtaining some straightforward goals, whether they be warmth for northerners, weight loss for the overweight, his-tory for the culturally hungry, or immersion in nature for bored urbanites, tourists generally remain unchanged and demand a lifestyle not too different from that at home. Rarely do the timid become bold, the neat become messy, the educated become dumb, the monolingual be come polyglot, the frigid become sexy, or the heterosexual become gay, except when these are the specific goals of the trip. Gottlieb (1982) has shown how tourists may play "Queen [Peasant] for a Day" with temporary changes in life or class style, and E. Cohen (1973, 1979b) and Frey (1998) have described some of the more rigorous touristic choices for the young or the alienated moderns, but most tourists on their seasonal and annual vacations want to enjoy their own chosen pursuits and come back refreshed as better versions of their same old selves.

Source: From *Hosts and Guests Revisited: Tourism Issues of the 21st Century*, Valene Smith and Maryann Brent (eds.), 2001. Reprinted with permission of the author and Cognizant Communications.

References

Beer, J. 1993. *Packaged Experience: Japanese Overseas Tourism in Asia.* Doctoral dissertation, University of California, Berkeley.

Campbell, R. 1988. "Bushman's Holiday—or the Best Surprise is No Surprise." *Kroeber Anthropological Society Papers* 67/68: 12–19.

Cohen, E. 1973. "Nomads from Affluence: Notes on the Phenomenon of Drifter Tourism." *International Journal of Comparative Sociology* 14:89–103.

———. 1979a. "A Phenomenology of Tourist Experiences." *Sociology* 13:179–201.

———. 1979b. "Sociology of Tourism." [Special Issue] *Annals of Tourism Research* 1–2.

Dann, G. 1996. *The Language of Tourism.* Wallingford: CAB International.

Durkheim, E. 1912. *Elementary Forms of Religious Life*, trans. J. Swain. London: Allen and Unwin.

Feyerabend, A. 1997. "Coming or Going: An Examination of Reverse Culture Shock in the 'Tourism as Ritual' Theory." (unpublished paper) Berkeley: University of California.

Frey, N. 1998. *Pilgrim Stories: On and Off the Road to Santiago.* Berkeley: University of California Press.

Gottlieb, A. 1982. "Americans' Vacations." *Annals of Tourism Research* 9:165–187.

Graburn, N. 1983. "The Anthropology of Tourism." [Special Issue] *Annals of Tourism Research* 10.

———. 1995a. "The Past in the Present in Japan: Nostalgia and Neo-traditionalism in Contemporary Japanese Domestic Tourism," in *Changes in Tourism: People, Places, Processes*, ed. R. Butler and D. Pearce, chapter 4. London: Routledge.

———. 1995b. "Tourism Modernity and Nostalgia," in *The Future of Anthropology: Its Relevance to the Contemporary World*, ed. A. Ahmed and C. Shore, pp. 158–178. London: Athlone Press.

Hastings, J. 1988. "Time Out of Time: Life Crises and Schooner Sailing in the Pacific." *Kroeber Anthropological Society Papers* 67/68: 42–54.

Hubert, H., and M. Mauss. 1898. *Sacrifice: Its Nature and Functions*, trans. W. Halls. London: Cohen & West.

Jokinen, E., and S. Veilola. 1994. "The Body in Tourism: Touring Contemporary Research in Tourism," in *Le Tourisme International entre Tradition et Modernité*, ed. J. Jardel. Nice, France: Actes du Colloque International, Laboratoire d'ethnologie.

Leach, E. 1961. *Rethinking Anthropology.* London: Athlone Press.

Lowenthal, D. 1985. *The Past Is a Foreign Country.* Cambridge: Cambridge University Press.

MacCannell, D. 1989. *The Tourist: A New Theory of the Leisure Class.* New York: Schocken Books.

Selänniemi, T. 1994. "A Charter Trip to Sacred Places—Individual Mass Tourism," in *Le Tourisme International entre Tradition et Modernité*, ed. J. Jardel, pp. 335–340. Nice, France: Université de Nice, Laboratoire d'ethnologie.

Smith, V. 1989. "Introduction," in *Hosts and Guests: The Anthropology of Tourism*, 2nd edition, ed. V. Smith, pp. 1–17. Philadelphia: University of Pennsylvania Press.

Teas, J. 1988. "'I'm Studying Monkeys; What Do You Do?'—Youth and Travelers in Nepal." *Kroeber Anthropological Society Papers* 67/68: 35–41.

Turner, V. 1974. *Dreams, Fields, and Metaphors: Symbolic Action in Human Society.* Ithaca, NY: Cornell University Press.

Turner, V., and E. Turner. 1978. *Images and Pilgrimage in Christian Culture.* New York: Columbia University Press.

Urry, J. 1990. *The Tourist Gaze: Leisure and Travel in Contemporary Societies.* London: Sage.

Van Gennep, A. 1960 [1909]. *The Rites of Passage*, trans. M. Vizedom and G. Caffee. Chicago: The University of Chicago Press.

3

Staged Authenticity: Arrangements of Social Space in Tourist Settings

Dean MacCannell

When I published the following article in 1973 I was an assistant professor of sociology, recently out of graduate school. I had no idea that it would eventually become one of the most frequently referenced articles in the tourism research literature, continuing to incite comment and controversy down to the present day. (See, e.g., Lau 2010, 2013; Knudsen and Rickley-Boyd 2012; MacCannell 2008, 2014.)

A number of subsequent studies have provided empirical verification of my concept of "staged authenticity" (see, e.g., Gable and Handler 2005).[1] But there are also published accounts that seek to dismiss the whole idea of "staged authenticity" claiming that tourists are not interested in "authenticity" but only want to have fun or be entertained. (See, e.g., Bruner 2005:5 ff.)

As you read "Staged Authenticity" I would like for you to bear this criticism in mind but with a caveat. It was not my intention to write an article about tourists' psychological motivation. My article is about the ways "authenticity" is socially constructed and "staged" for tourists. I had discovered a ubiquitous arrangement of space in places designed to attract tourists—a strategic revelation of "authentic" back-region activities and "secrets." Please give a second glance at my subtitle, "arrangements of social space in tourist settings." It is not a study of the psychological motivation of tourists. Many, perhaps most, tourists are attracted to the authentic. The real Mona Lisa attracts far more visitors than the millions of its copies combined. Nevertheless, I readily accept that there are tourists who are not interested in the authenticity of the things they visit and others who are not disappointed even when they know that the show they are witnessing is fake.

But this does not change the essential structure of tourist settings. Tourists are still bombarded by strategic revelations of back regions ranging from real to artificial. Near the end of "Staged Authenticity" I give voice to tourists who have seen through the staging and are able to laugh about it.

In all my writing about tourists and tourism, I have tried to focus on social and cultural structuring of the tourist experience while allowing the tourists to think and feel for themselves. I do not believe there is any special category of "tourist psychology" beyond the diverse psychic manifestations of humanity in general. The tourist can grab hold of "staged authenticity" any way he or she sees fit. My only point is that wheresoever the tourist goes, staged authenticity will be found there for the taking. For more elaboration see my (2008) article "Why It Never Really Was About *Authenticity.*"

Staged Authenticity: Arrangements of Social Space in Tourist Settings

A theme in Talcott Parsons's work (1937, 1964) is his insistence on the necessity of integrating social scientific understanding of belief, action, and social structure. By the end of the 1950s, there was some agreement in sociological circles that Parsons's own theoretical system had not succeeded in bringing off this integration. (See the discussions in Gouldner [1970] or Friedrichs [1970].) But this is not the important point to be grasped from Parsons's total project. He left us all with a clearly defined problem to solve. During the 1960s, Berger and Luckmann (1966), Erving Goffman, Harold Garfinkel (1967), and others began constructing bridges that permit analytical passage from social structure to the structure of behavior and beliefs. Now, in the 1970s, we can, I think, begin to study the relationship of social structure and beliefs in specific social situations, using more refined conceptions than have previously been available.

This paper is part of my study of tourism. The central finding of the larger study is that sightseeing is a form of ritual respect for society and that tourism absorbs some of the social functions of religion in the modern world. The dimension of social life analyzed in this paper is its authenticity or, more exactly, the search for authenticity of experience that is everywhere manifest in our society. The concern of moderns for the shallowness of their lives and inauthenticity of their experiences parallels concerns for the sacred in primitive society. Each contributes to the structural solidarity of the society in which it is found. The solidarity of primitives depends on every individual's keeping his place, and this is guaranteed by the sacralization of functionally important aspects of individual behavior such as gift exchange and mate selection. Primitives may, but they need not, worry about the authenticity of their rituals. The very survival of their society stands as internal proof of the victory of good over evil and real over false. By contrast, individual morality is only indirectly linked to the solidarity of modern society in which functionally important relationships are among bureaucracies, communities, and other complex organizations. Under modern conditions, the place of the individual in society is preserved, in part, by newly institutionalized concerns for the authenticity of his social experiences.

I began the analysis of the problem of authenticity by starting across one of the bridges between structure and consciousness that was built by Erving Goffman, and, in the course of the study, I found it necessary to extend his conception a little to make it to the other side.

Social Space and the Structuring of Beliefs

Paralleling a commonsense division, Goffman has described a structural division of social establishments into what he terms "front" and "back" regions. The front is the meeting place of hosts and guests or customers and service persons, and the back is the place where members of the home team retire between performances to relax and to prepare. Examples of back regions are kitchens, boiler rooms, and executive washrooms, and examples of front regions are reception offices, parlors, and the like. Although architectural arrangements are mobilized to support this division, it is primarily a social one, based on the type of social performance that is staged in a place, and on the social roles found there. In Goffman's own words: "Given a particular performance as the point of reference, we can distinguish three crucial roles on the basis of function: those who perform; those performed to; and outsiders who neither perform in the show nor observe it. . . . [T]he three crucial roles mentioned could be described on the basis of the regions to which the role-player has access: performers appear in the front and back regions; the audience appears only in the front region; and the outsiders are excluded from both regions" (1959:144–45). The apparent, taken-for-granted reality of a social performance, according to Goffman's theory, is not an unproblematical part of human behavior. Rather, it depends on structural arrangements like this division between front and back. A back region, closed to audiences and outsiders, allows concealment of props and activities that might discredit the performance out front. In other words, sustaining a firm sense of social reality requires some mystification.

Social reality that is sustained through mystification may be a "false" reality, as occurs in conning. Equally interesting is the case wherein mystification is required to create a sense of "real" reality. Once social structure differentiates into front and back in the movement from primitive to modern arrangements, the truth can no longer speak for itself. It must always be announced and revealed.

A recent example of a mystification designed to generate a sense of real reality is the disclosure that chemical nitrates are injected into hams for cosmetic purposes to keep them more pink, appetizing, and desirable, that is, more ham-like (Minz 1971). Similarly, a respondent of mine reports that some of the go-go girls in San Francisco's North Beach have their breasts injected with silicones in order to conform their size, shape, and firmness to the characteristics of an ideal breast. Novels about novelists and television shows about fictitious television stars are examples on a cultural plane. In each of these cases, a kind of strained truthfulness is similar in most of its particulars to a little lie.

Mystification, then, can be the conscious product of an individual effort to manipulate a social appearance, as occurred in the ham and breast examples. It can also be found where there is no conscious individual-level manipulation. Social structure itself is involved in the construction of mystifications that support social reality.

Examples are found in avoidance behavior surrounding back regions. The possibility that a stranger might penetrate a back region is one major source of social concern in everyday life, as much a concern to the strangers who might do the violating as to the violated. Everyone is waiting for this kind of intrusion not to happen, which is a paradox in that the absence of social relationships between strangers makes back-region secrets unimportant to outsiders or casual and accidental intruders. Just having a back region generates the belief that there is something more than meets the eye; even where no secrets are actually kept, back regions are still the places where it is popularly believed the secrets are. Folklorists discover tales of the horror concealed in attics and cellars, attesting to this belief.

Back Regions, Intimacy, and Social Solidarity

An unexplored aspect of back regions is how their mere existence, and the possibility of their violation, functions to sustain the commonsense polarity of social life into what is taken to be intimate and "real" and what is thought to be "show." The beliefs supported by this division of society into front and back center on popular ideas of the relationship of truth to intimacy. In our society, intimacy and closeness are accorded much importance: they are seen as the core of social solidarity, and they are also thought by some to be morally superior to rationality and distance in social relationships, and more "real." Being "one of them," or at one with "them," means, in part, being permitted to share back regions with "them." This is a sharing which allows one to see behind the others' mere performances, to perceive and accept the others for what they really are.

Touristic experience is circumscribed by the structural tendencies described here. Sightseers are motivated by a desire to see life as it is really lived, even to get in with the natives, and, at the same time, they are deprecated for always failing to achieve these goals. The term "tourist" is increasingly used as a derisive label for someone who seems content with his obviously inauthentic experiences.

The variety of understanding that is held out before tourists as an ideal is an authentic and demystified experience of an aspect of some society or other person. An anonymous writer in an underground periodical breathlessly describes her feelings at a women's liberation, all-female dance where she was able, she thought, to drop the front she usually maintains in the presence of men:

> Finally the men moved beyond the doorway. And We Danced—All of us with all of us. In circles and lines and holding hands and arm in arm, clapping and jumping—a group of whole people. I remember so many other dances, couples, men and women, sitting watching, not even talking. How could I have consented to that hateful, possessive, jealous pairing? So much energy and life, and sensuality, we women have so rarely and ineffectively expressed. But we did, on Saturday. The women in the band were above performing and beyond competition, playing and singing together and with we who were dancing. And We Danced—expressing for and with each other. [Anon., no date, p. 33; all punctuation and capitalization as in the original]

An earlier, one-sided version of this connection among truth, intimacy, and sharing the life behind the scenes is found in descriptions of the ethnographic method of data collection. Margaret Mead has written: "The anthropologist not only records the consumption of sago in the native diet, but eats at least enough to know how heavily it lies upon the stomach; not only records verbally and by photographs the tight clasp of the baby's hands around the neck, but also carries the baby and experiences the constriction of the windpipe; hurries or lags on the way to a ceremony; kneels half-blinded by incense while the spirits of the ancestors speak, or the gods refuse to appear. The anthropologist enters the setting and he observes . . . " (Mead 1955:31). These writers base their comments on an implicit distinction between false fronts and intimate reality, a distinction which is not, for them, problematical: once a person, or an observer, moves off stage, or into the "setting," the real truth begins to reveal itself more or less automatically.

Closer examination of these matters suggests that it might not be so easy to penetrate the true inner workings of other individuals or societies. What is taken to be real might, in fact, be a show that is based on the structure of reality. For example, Goffman warns that under certain conditions it is difficult to separate front from back and that these are sometimes transformed one into the other:

> [W]e can observe the up-grading of domestic establishments, wherein the kitchen, which once possessed its own back regions, is now coming to be the least presentable region of the house while at the same time becoming more and more presentable. We can also trace that peculiar social movement which led some factories, ships, restaurants, and households to clean up their backstages to such an extent that, like monks, Communists, or German aldermen, their guards are always up and there is no place where their front is down, while at the same time members of the audience become sufficiently entranced with the society's id to explore the places that had been cleaned up for them. Paid attendance at symphony orchestra rehearsals is only one of the latest examples. (1959:247)

Under the conditions Goffman documents here, the back-front division no longer allows one to make facile distinctions between mere acts and authentic expressions of true characteristics. In places where tourists concentrate, I am about to show, the issues are even more complex.

Authenticity in Tourist Settings

Everett C. Hughes has suggested to me (in correspondence) that the original tours were religious pilgrimages. The connection between the two is not merely one of organizational similarities. The motive behind a pilgrimage is similar to that behind a tour: both are quests for authentic experiences. Pilgrims attempted to visit a place where an event of religious importance actually occurred. Tourists present themselves at places of social, historical, and cultural importance.

It is worth noting that not all tourists have regarded back regions as socially important places. On occasion, and for some visitors, back regions are obtrusive. Arthur Young, when he visited France in 1787 to make observations for his comparative study of agriculture, also observed the following:

> Mops, brooms, and scrubbing brushes are not in the catalogue of the necessaries of a French inn. Bells there are none; the *fille* must always be bawled for; and when she appears, is neither neat, well dressed, nor handsome. The kitchen is black with smoke; the master commonly the cook, and the less you see of the cooking the more likely you are to have a stomach to your dinner. The mistress rarely classes civility or attention to her guests among the requisites of her trade. We are so unaccustomed in England to live in our bedchambers that it is at first awkward in France to find that people live nowhere else. Here I find that everybody, let his rank be what it may, lives in his bed-chamber. (Young 1910:332)

Among some, especially some American tourists and sightseers of today, Young's attitude would be considered insensitive and cynical even if there was agreement that his treatment of the facts was accurate, as apparently it was. One finds in the place of Young's attitude much interest in exactly the details Young wanted not to notice.

A tourist's desire to share in the real life of the places visited, or at least to see that life as it is really lived, is reflected in the conclusion of one tourist's report from a little Spanish town: "Finally, Frigliana has no single, spectacular attraction, such as Granada's Alhambra or the cave at Nerja. Frigliana's appeal lies in its atmosphere. It is quaint without being cloying or artificial. It is a living village and not a 'restoration of an authentic Spanish town.' Here one can better see and understand the Andalusian style of life" (Pearson 1969:29). There are vulgar ways of expressing this liberal sentiment, the desire "to get off the beaten path" and "in with the natives." An advertisement for an airline reads: "Take 'De tour.' Swissair's free-wheeling fifteen day Take-a-break Holiday that lets you detour to the off-beat, over-looked and unexpected corners of Switzerland for as little as $315. . . . Including car. Take de tour. But watch out for de sheep, de goats and de chickens" (Advertisement 1970:42).

Some tourists do make incursions into the life of the society they visit, or are at least actually allowed to peek into one of its back regions. In 1963 the manager of the Student Center at the University of California at Berkeley would occasionally invite visitors to the building to join him on his periodic inspection tours which was, for them, a chance to see its kitchens, the place behind the pin-setting machines in the bowling alley, the giant blowing fans on the roof, and so forth, but he was probably not a typical building manager. This kind of hospitality is the rule rather than the exception in the areas of the world that have been civilized the longest, a factor in the popularity of these areas with Anglo-Americans. A respondent of mine told me she was invited by a cloth merchant in the Damascus bazaar to visit his silk factory, and she answered "yes," whereupon he threw open a door behind his counter exposing a little dark room where two men in their underwear sat on the floor on either side of a hand loom passing a shuttle back and forth between them. "It takes a year to weave a bolt of silk like that," the owner explained as he closed the door. This kind of happening, an "experience" in the everyday sense of that term, often occurs by accident. A lady who is a relative of mine, and another lady friend of hers, walked too far into the Canadian Rockies near Banff and found themselves with too much traveling back to town to do in the daytime that was left to do it in. They were rescued by the crew of a freight train, and what they remember most from their experience was being allowed to ride with the engineer in the cab of his locomotive. A young American couple told me of being unable to find a hotel room in Zagreb, Yugoslavia, and, while discussing their plight on the sidewalk, being approached by an old woman who led them by a circuitous route to a small apartment where they rented a black-market room, displacing the family of workers who slept on a couch behind a blanket hung as a curtain in the living room.

Touristic openings into society's back regions are ubiquitous. A certain amount of what is called "personal style" is a product of the way the individual relates to touristic opportunity. Some individuals are always on the lookout for a touristic opening. They are said to have an "adventuresome attitude."

A report from the Caribbean suggests that a taste for adventure can be culti-vated: "'But tourists never take the mail boats,' said the hotel manager. That clinched the matter. The next afternoon, I jumped from the dock at Potter's Cay in downtown Nassau to the rusted deck of the *Deborah K.*, swinging idly at her spring lines. . . . [The writer describes island hopping on the mail boat and ends his account with this observation.] The next day, while aloft in a Bahamas Airways plane, I spotted the *Deborah K.* chugging along in the sound toward Green Turtle Cay. She is no craft for the queasy of stomach and has a minimum of the amenities that most people find indispensable, but she and her sister mail boats offer a wonderfully inexpensive way to see life in the Bahamas—life as the natives live it, not the tourists" (Keller 1970:24). Given the felt value of these experiences, it is not surprising to find social structural arrangements that produce them.

Staged Authenticity in Tourist Settings

A common reason for taking guided tours of social establishments is that the tour organizes access to areas of the establishment that are ordinarily closed to outsiders. School children's tours of firehouses, banks, newspapers, and dairies, for example, are called "educational" because the inner opera-tions of these important places are shown and explained in the course of the tour. This kind of tour, and the experiences generated by it, provides an inter-esting set of analytical problems. The tour is characterized by social organi-zation designed to reveal inner workings of the place; on tour, outsiders are allowed further in than regular patrons; children are permitted to enter bank vaults, to see a million dollars, to touch cows' udders, etc. At the same time, there is a staged quality to the proceedings that lends to them an aura of superficiality, albeit a superficiality that is not always perceived as such by the tourist, who is usually forgiving about these matters.

An account from Cape Kennedy provides illustration:

> No sightseers at the Manned Spacecraft Center ever had a more dramatic visit than those who, by design or accident of time, found themselves touring the facility last month during the unforgettable mission of Apollo 13. . . . In a garden-like courtyard outside the News Bureau in Building 1, a group of tourists visiting the Manned Spacecraft Center here stared at the working correspondents through the huge plate-glass windows. The visitors, too, could hear the voice of Mission Control. A tall young man, his arm around his mini-skirted blonde girl friend, summed up the feelings of the sightseers when he said, half aloud, "Being here's like being part of it."
>
> "Dear God," his girl whispered earnestly, "please let them come home safe." (Gordon 1970)

The young man in this account is expressing his belief that he is having an almost authentic experience. This type of experience is produced through the use of a new kind of social space that is opening up everywhere in our society. It is a space for outsiders who are permitted to view details of the inner operation of a commercial, domestic, industrial, or public institution. Apparently, entry into this space allows adults to recapture virginal sensations of discovery, or childlike feelings of being half in and half out of society, their faces pressed up against the glass. Also, it can be noted that what is taken by some political radicals and conservatives to be indices of a general relaxation of society's moral standards ("swinging," "massage therapy," wide-screen cunnilingus, etc.) are only special cases of reality displays, public orgasm worked up in the interest of social solidarity.

Other basic (that is, biological process) examples of staged intimacy are provided by the tendency to make restaurants into something more than places to eat:

> The newest eating place in Copenhagen is La Cuisine, strategically located on the Stroeget, the main strolling street of the city. Everyone is flat-nosing it against the windows these days watching the four cooks.
>
> In order to get to the cozy, wood-paneled restaurant in the back of the house, the guest must pass the kitchen. If he is in a hurry he may eat in the kitchen, hamburger joint-style.
>
> "The kitchen" bit is a come-hither, actually, admits Canadian-born, Swiss-educated Patrick McCurdy, table captain and associate manager. "A casual passer-by is fascinated by cooks at work, preparing a steak or a chicken or a salad." (Sjöby 1971:5)

What is being shown to tourists is not the institutional "backstage," as Goffman defined this term. Rather, it is a staged back region, a kind of living museum for which we have no analytical terms.

The Structure of Tourist Settings

A student of mine has told me that a new apartment building in New York City exhibits its heating and air conditioning equipment, brightly painted in basic colors, behind a brass rail in its lobby. From the standpoint of the social institutions that are exposed in this way, the structure of their reception rooms reflects a new concern for truth and morality at the institutional level. Industry, for example, is discovering that the commercial advantages of appearing to be honest and aboveboard can outweigh the disadvantages of having to organize little shows of honesty. An interesting parallel here is with some of the young people of the industrial West who have pressed for simplicity and naturalness in their attire and have found it necessary assiduously to select clothing, jewelry, and hair styles that are especially designed to look natural. In exposing their steel hearts for all to see, and staging their true inner life, important commercial establishments of the industrial West "went hippie" a decade before hippies went hippie. Approached from this standpoint, the hippie movement is not, technically, a movement, but a basic expression of the present stage of the evolution of our industrial society.

The current structural development of industrial society is marked by the appearance everywhere of touristic space. This space can be called a stage set, a tourist setting, or simply a set depending on how purposefully worked up for tourists the display is. The New York Stock Exchange viewed from the balcony set up for sightseers is a tourist setting, as there is no evidence that the show below is for the sightseers. The exhibitions of the back regions of the world at Disneyland in Anaheim, California, are constructed only for sightseers, however, and can be called "stage sets." Characteristics of sets are: the only reason that need be given for visiting them is to see them—in this regard they are unique among social places; they are physically proximal to serious social activity, or serious activity is imitated in them; they contain objects, tools, and machines that have specialized use in specific, often esoteric, social, occupational, and industrial routines; they are open, at least during specified times, to visitation from outsiders.

A "front region" organized to look like a "back region" at a carpet factory and showroom, Kusadasi, Turkey. (Photos by S. Gmelch)

Touristic consciousness is motivated by its desire for authentic experiences, and the tourist may believe that he is moving in this direction, but often it is very difficult to tell for sure if the experience is authentic in fact. It is always possible that what is taken to be entry into a back region is really entry into a front region that has been totally set up in advance for touristic visitation. In tourist settings, especially in modern society, it may be necessary to discount the importance, and even the existence, of front and back regions except as ideal poles of touristic experience.

To return to Goffman's original front-back dichotomy, tourist settings can be arranged in a continuum starting from the front and ending at the back, reproducing the natural trajectory of an individual's initial entry into a social situation. While distinct empirical indicators of each stage may be somewhat difficult to discover, it is theoretically possible to distinguish six stages to this continuum, and here is a place where the exercise of a little theoretical license might eventually prove to be worthwhile.

Stage 1: Goffman's front region; the kind of social space tourists attempt to overcome, or to get behind.

Stage 2: a touristic front region that has been decorated to appear, in some of its particulars, like a back region: a seafood restaurant with a fish net hanging on the wall; a meat counter in a super-market with three-dimensional plastic replicas of cheeses and bolognas hanging against the wall. Functionally, this stage (two) is entirely a front region, and it always has been, but it is cosmetically decorated with reminders of back-region activi-ties: mementos, not taken seriously, called "atmosphere."

Stage 3: a front region that is totally organized to look like a back region: simulations of moon walks for television audiences; the live shows above sex shops in Berlin where the customer can pay to watch interracial couples copulating according to his own specific instructions. This is a problematical stage because the better the simulation, the more difficult it is to dis-tinguish it from stage 4.

Stage 4: a back region that is open to outsiders: magazine exposés of the private doings of famous personages; official revelations of the details of secret diplomatic negotiations. It is the open characteristic that distinguishes these especially touristic set-tings (stages 3 and 4) from other back regions; access to most non-touristic back regions is somewhat restricted.

Stage 5: a back region that may be cleaned up or altered a bit because tourists are permitted an occasional glimpse in: Erving Goff-man's kitchen, factory, ship, and orchestra rehearsal cases; news leaks.

Stage 6: Goffman's back region; the kind of social space that motivates touristic consciousness.

That is theory enough. The empirical action in tourist settings is mainly confined to movement between areas decorated to look like back regions, and back regions into which tourists are allowed to peek. Insight, in the everyday, and in some ethnological senses of the term, is what is gotten from one of these peeks into a back region.

Tourists and Intellectuals

There is no serious or functional role in the production awaiting the tour-ists in the places they visit. Tourists are not made personally responsible for anything that happens in the establishments they visit, and the quality of the insight gained by touristic experience has been criticized as less than profound. David Riesman's "other directed" (1950) and Herbert Marcuse's "one-dimensional" men (1964) are products of a traditional intellectual concern for the superficiality of knowledge in mass industrial society, but the tourist setting per se is just beginning to prompt intellectual commentary. Settings are often not merely copies or replicas of real-life situations, but copies that are presented as disclosing more about the real thing than the real thing itself discloses. Of course this cannot be the case, at least not from technical standpoints—from the standpoint of ethnography, for example. The Gray Line guided tours of the Haight-Ashbury when the hippies lived there cannot be substituted for the studies based on participant observation that were undertaken at the same time: the intellectual attitude is firm in this belief. The touristic experience that comes out of the tourist setting is based on inauthenticity, and as such it is superficial when compared with careful study; it is morally inferior to mere experience. A mere experience may be mystified, but a touristic experience is always mystified, and the lie contained in the touristic experience, moreover, presents itself as a truthful revelation, as the vehicle that carries the onlooker behind false fronts into reality. The idea here is that a false back is more insidious and dangerous than a false front, or an inauthentic demystification of social life is not merely a lie but a superlie, the kind that drips with sincerity.

Along these lines, Daniel Boorstin's (1961:77–117) comments on sightseeing and tourism suggest that critical writing on the subject of modern mass mentality is gaining analytical precision and is moving from the individual-centered concepts of the 1950s to a structural orientation. His concept of "pseudo-event" is a recent addition to a line of specific criticism of tourists that can be traced back to Veblen's "conspicuous leisure" (1953:41–60), or back still further to Mark Twain's ironic commentary in *The Innocents Abroad*. In his use of the term "pseudo-event" Boorstin wants his reader to understand that there is something about the tourist setting itself that is not intellectually satisfying. In his own words: "These [tourist] 'attractions' offer an elaborately contrived indirect experience, an artificial product to be consumed in the very places where the real thing is as free as air. They are ways for the traveler to remain out of contact with foreign peoples in the very act of 'sight-seeing' them. They keep the natives in quarantine while the tourist in air-conditioned comfort views them through a picture window. They are the cultural mirages now found at tourist oases everywhere" (Boorstin 1961:99). This kind of commentary reminds us that tourist settings, like other areas of institutional life, are often insufficiently policed by liberal concerns for truth and beauty; they are tacky. Another way of approaching the same observations is to suggest that some touristic places overexpress their underlying structure and upset certain of their sensitive visitors thereby: restaurants are decorated like ranch kitchens; bellboys assume and use false, foreign first names; hotel rooms are made to appear like peasant cottages; primitive religious ceremonies are staged as public pageants. This kind of naked tourist setting is probably not as important in the overall picture of mass tourism as Boorstin makes it out to be in his polemic, but it is an ideal type of sorts, and many examples of it exist.

Boorstin is insightful as to the nature of touristic arrangements, but he undercuts what might have developed into a structural analysis of sightseeing and touristic consciousness by falling back onto individual-level interpretations before analyzing fully his "pseudo-event" conception. He claims that tourists themselves cause "pseudo-events." Commenting on the restaurants along superhighways, Boorstin writes: "There people can eat without having to look out on an individualized, localized landscape. The disposable paper mat on which they are served shows no local scenes, but a map of numbered super highways with the location of other 'oases.' They feel most at home above the highway itself, soothed by the auto stream to which they belong" (1961:114, my emphasis). None of the accounts in my collection support Boorstin's contention that tourists want superficial, contrived experiences. Rather, tourists demand authenticity, just as Boorstin does. Nevertheless, Boorstin persists in architecting an absolute separation of touristic and intellectual attitudes. On the distinction between work ("traveling") and sightseeing he writes: "The traveler, then, was working at something; the tourist was a pleasure-seeker. The traveler was active; he went strenuously in search of people, of adventure, of experience. The tourist is passive; he expects interesting things to happen to him. He goes 'sight-seeing.' . . . He expects everything to be done to him and for him" (Boorstin 1961:85). As I have already suggested, the attitude Boorstin expresses is a commonplace among tourists and travel writers. It is so prevalent, in fact, that it is a part of the problem of mass tourism, not an analytical reflection on it.

In other words, we still lack adequate technical perspectives for the study of "pseudo-events." The construction of such perspectives necessarily begins with the tourists themselves and a close examination of the facts of sightseeing. The writers of the accounts cited in the first sections of this paper express Boorstin's disappointment that their experiences are sometimes fleeting and insulated and a desire to get in with the natives, but, more important here, a willingness to accept disappointment when they feel they are stopped from penetrating into the real life of the place they are visiting. In fact, some tourists are able to laugh off Boorstin's disappointment. The account of a trip to Tangier from which the following is excerpted was given by a writer who clearly expected the false backwardness she found there and is relaxed about relating it: "A young Arab pulled a chair up to our table. He had rugs to sell, but we insisted we were not interested. He unrolled his entire collection and spread them out on the ground. He wouldn't leave. I could see beneath his robes that he was wearing well-tailored navy blue slacks and a baby blue cashmere sweater" (Thompson 1970:3). Similarly, the visitor to Las Vegas who wrote the following has seen through the structure of tourist settings and is laughing about it: "[A]long with winter vacationists by the thousands, I will return to lively Las

Vegas, if only to learn whether Howard Hughes, like the Mint Casino, has begun issuing free coupons entitling the visitor to a backstage tour of his moneymaking establishment" (Goodman 1970:11). For these tourists, exposure of back regions is a casual part of their touristic experience. What they see in the back is only another show: it does not shock, trick, or anger them, and they do not express any feelings of having been made less pure by their discovery.

Conclusion

In highly developed tourist settings, such as San Francisco and Switzerland, every detail of touristic experience can take on a showy, back-region aspect, at last for fleeting moments. Tourists enter tourist areas precisely because their experiences there will not, for them, be routine. The local people in the places they visit, by contrast, have long discounted the presence of tourists and go about their business as usual, even their tourist business, as best they can, treating tourists as a part of the regional scenery. Tourists often do see routine aspects of life as it is really lived in the places they visit, although few tourists express much interest in this. In the give-and-take of urban street life in tourist areas, the question of who is watching whom and who is responding to whom can be as complex as it is in the give-and-take between ethnographers and their respondents. It is only when a person makes an effort to penetrate into the real life of the areas he visits that he ends up in places especially designed to generate feelings of intimacy and experiences that can be talked about as "participation." No one can "participate" in his own life, he can only participate in the lives of others.

And once tourists have entered touristic space, there is no way out for them so long as they press their search for authenticity. Near each tourist setting there are others like the last. Each one may be visited, and each one promises real and convincing shows of local life and culture. Even the infamously clean Istanbul Hilton has not excluded all aspects of Turkish culture (the cocktail waitresses wear harem pants, or did in 1968) and, for some Europeans I know, an American superhighway is an attraction of the first rank, the more barren the better, because it is more American.

Daniel Boorstin was the first to study these matters. His approach elevates to the level of analysis a nostalgia for an earlier time with more clear-cut divisions between the classes, and simpler social values based on a programmatic, back versus front view of the true and the false. This classic position is morally superior to the one presented here, but it cannot lead to the scientific study of sightseeing. Specifically, Boorstin's and other intellectual approaches do not help us to analyze the expansion of the tourist class under industrialization, and the development on an international scale of activities and social structural arrangements for tourists, social changes Boorstin himself documents. Rather than confronting the issues he raises, Boorstin only expresses a long-standing touristic attitude, a pronounced dislike, bordering on hatred, for other tourists, an attitude that turns man against man in a "they-are-the-tourists-I-am-not" equation. (For an excellent discussion of this aspect of the intellectual approach, see Burgelin [1967:66–69].) Additional study of sightseeing, using analytical models that are up to the task, will show that the touristic attitude, and the structures that produce it, contributes to the destruction of interpersonal solidarity that is such a notable feature of the life of the educated masses in advanced industrial society.

Daniel Boorstin calls places like American superhighways and the Istanbul Hilton "pseudo," a hopeful appellation that suggests they are insubstantial, or transitory, which they are not, and suggests also that somewhere in tourist settings there are real events accessible to intellectual elites, and perhaps there are. In this paper I have argued that a more helpful way of approaching the same facts is in terms of a modification of Erving Goffman's front-back distinction. Specifically, I have suggested that for the study of tourist settings front and back be treated as ideal poles of a continuum, poles that are linked by a series of front regions decorated to appear as back regions, and back regions set up to accommodate outsiders. I have suggested the term "stage setting" for these intermediary types of social space, but there is no need to be rigid about the matter of the name of this place, so long as its structural features and their influences on ideas are understood.

I have claimed that the structure of this social space is intimately linked to touristic attitudes, and I want to pursue this: the touristic way of getting in with the natives is to enter into a quest for authentic experiences, perceptions, and insights. The quest is marked off in stages in the passage from front to back. Movement from stage to stage corresponds to growing touristic understanding. This continuum is sufficiently developed in some areas of the world that it appears as an infinite regression of stage sets. Once in this manifold, the tourist is trapped; his road does not end abruptly in some conversion process that transforms him into Boorstin's "traveler," "working at something" as he breaks the bounds of all that is pseudo and penetrates, finally, into a real back region. Tourists make brave sorties out from their hotels hoping, perhaps, for an authentic experience, but their paths can be traced in advance over small increments of what is for them increasingly apparent authenticity proffered by tourist settings. Adventuresome tourists progress from stage to stage, always in the public eye, and greeted everywhere by their obliging hosts.

Note

[1] Source: *The American Journal of Sociology* 79(3): 589–603, 1973. Reprinted with permission of University of Chicago Press. The 2017 introduction was written expressly for *Tourists and Tourism*.

References Cited

Advertisement for Swissair. 1970. *New York Times* (April 19): Section 10.

Anon. n.d. "Dear Mom and All Mothers" *Tiohero* 5:32–33. Ithaca, NY: Glad Day Press.

Berger, P., and T. Luckmann. 1966. *The Social Construction of Reality.* Garden City, NY: Doubleday.

Boorstin, D. J. 1961. *The Image: A Guide to Pseudo-Events in America.* New York: Harper & Row.

Bruner, Edward. 2005. *Culture on Tour.* Chicago: University of Chicago Press.

Burgelin, O. 1967. "Le tourisme jugé." Special edition, "Vacances et tourisme," of *Communications* 10:65–97.

Friedrichs, R. W. 1970. *A Sociology of Sociology.* New York: Free Press.

Gable, E. and Handler, R. 2005. "Horatio Alger and the Tourist's Quest for Authenticity, or, Optimism, Pessimism, and Middle-Class Personhood," *Anthropology and Humanism* 10(2): 124–132.

Garfinkel, H. 1967. *Studies in Ethnomethodology.* Englewood Cliffs, N.J.: Prentice Hall.

Goffman, E. 1959. *The Presentation of Self in Everyday Life.* Garden City, NY: Doubleday.

Goodman, J. 1970. "Hitting the 'Freebee' Jackpot without Trying—in Las Vegas." *New York Times* (January 25): Section 10.

Gordon, I. H. 1970. "Space Center Is Open to Visitors Even in a Crisis." *New York Times* (May 3): Section 10.

Gouldner, A. W. 1970. *The Coming Crisis of Western Sociology.* New York: Basic.

Keller, A. 1970. "He Said: 'Tourists Never Take the Mail Boat'—That Clinched It." *New York Times* (May 24): Section 10.

Knudsen, D. C., and J. Rickley-Boyd. 2012. "Tourist Sites as Semiotic Signs," *Annals of Tourism Research* 38:1252–1254.

Lau, R. 2010. "Revisiting Authenticity: A Social Realist Approach," *Annals of Tourism Research* 37:478–498.

———. 2013. "Semiotics, Objectivism and Tourism, an Anti-Critique," *Annals of Tourism Research* 44:283–284.

MacCannell, Dean. 2008. "Why it Never Really Was About *Authenticity*," *Society* 45:334–337.

———. 2014. "Comment on Lau and Knudsen/Rickley-Boyd," *Annals of Tourism Research* 44:283–287.

Marcuse, H. 1964. *One-dimensional Man.* Boston: Beacon.

Mead, M. 1955. *Male and Female.* New York: Mentor.

Minz, M. 1971. "Cancer Link Possible in Food Tinting." *International Herald Tribune* (n.d.).

Parsons, T. 1937. *The Structure of Social Action: A Study in Social Theory.* New York: McGraw-Hill.

———. 1964. *The Social System.* Glencoe: Free Press.

Pearson, E. 1969. "Discovering an Undiscovered Town in Southern Spain." *New York Times* (June 6): Section 10.

Riesman, D., R. Denny, and N. Glazer. 1950. *The Lonely Crowd.* New Haven, CT: Yale University Press.

Sjöby, J. 1971. "Dining Out: International Fare in Danish Restaurant." *International Herald Tribune* (February 26).

Thompson, B. 1970. "Hustled, Harried—But Happy." *New York Times* (August 16): Section 10.

Twain, M. 1966. *The Innocents Abroad: or The New Pilgrim's Progress.* New York: Signet Classics.

Veblen, T. (1934) 1953. *The Theory of the Leisure Class.* New York: Mentor.

Young, A. 1910. "Travels in France," in *The World's Greatest Books,* eds. Lord Northcliffe (Alfred Harmsworth) and S. S. McClure. Vol. 19. No location indicated: McKinlay, Stone & Mackenzie.

4

An Ethnography of Travel in La Réunion

David Picard

Since the emergence of tourism studies about 40 years ago, we have become accustomed to the idea that tourism is governed by social institutions in the form of sign worlds (MacCannell 1976; Turner and Turner 1978), ritualized journeys of escape and recreation (Dumazedier 1967; Graburn 1989), collective gazes (Urry 2002) or socially held meta-narratives (Bruner 2004), and imaginaries of Self and Other (Picard and Di Giovine 2014, Salazar and Graburn 2014). While these approaches have been instrumental for the formation of the field, they have also shaped a way of understanding tourism as a relatively homogenous cultural phenomenon, which makes individual tourist experiences either disappear or be seen as expressions of an intrinsically hollow and meaningless mass-produced consumer culture.

Most approaches in tourism studies heavily rely on the analyses of images, texts, discourses, and spatial representations, and here may well lay the main problem. Graburn (2002) justly stresses that it makes little sense for the researcher to study tourism through one-dimensional or punctual approaches, without being able to articulate the observations made with the wider experiential sequence of the journey and the social contexts of the tourists' everyday lives. Bruner (2004) contents that collective institutions like sign-worlds, conventionalized gazes, or the liturgical order of tourism rituals certainly supply tourists with a meta-narrative frame leading to and through the journey and providing means to articulate and communicate the journey's experiences. Yet, he argues (and I follow him on this point), they are not equivalent, not even in a metaphorical way, to the emotions, transformations, and deceptions that define the actual experience of the journey, whatever its particular format.

Bruner (2005) stresses two fundamentally distinguished dimensions of tourism experience, one defining the highly personal and intimate emotional processes taking place during the journey, the other defining the socially conventionalized techniques and expressions to articulate these processes through images, words, gestures, and other forms of behavior. In a similar approach, Edensor (1998) and Coleman and Crang (2002) suggest we approach tourism as a form of agency between personal experiences—or "inner journeys" (Graburn 2002)—and social institutions in the form of images, texts, and site representations that tourists have become socialized to.

To study tourism in a more comprehensive way, one needs to follow the rhythm of the journey and observe the emotions, silences, exchanges, and subtle negotiations that appear throughout the trip. Tourists, even if they may appear to be part of a large crowd, habitually travel alone or in small groups, as couples or with friends. An ethnographic approach to tourism hence represents above all a huge logistic (and financial) issue. One way to solve this is to gain employment as a tour guide and do participant-observations from within this particular perspective—an approach pioneered by social scientists including Amirou (1995), Cohen (1985, 2004), and Bruner (2004). It is also the approach that I chose to carry out this and subsequent studies (Picard, Pocock and Trigger 2014; Picard 2015, 2016; Picard and Moreira 2018 forthcoming).

Ethnographic Research on Tourism in La Réunion

Between 1998 and 2000 I gained employment with a tourist agency in La Réunion, an island in the Western Indian Ocean popular with European tourists and where I had started a PhD program in 1998. During the four years of the study, I guided twenty four-day round-trips on the island. These always followed the same itinerary, stopped in the same hotels, passed the same sites, and included the same food.

The groups were composed mainly of German nationals who had booked their trip via a well-known German tour operator. Their numbers varied between three and eight. I stayed with these tourists all day long, sharing meals and drinks, drove the minibus, performed a guide discourse, and engaged in informal, often long conversations. I also spent the night at the same hotels, though in a separate room. In the evenings and during breaks, I recorded and wrote up the sequences of dialogues and conversations that unfolded during the daily journeys and during the stopovers in the hotels.

At the end of the round-trip, I left the groups at the airport. However, I stayed in contact through correspondence and, later, visited many of them in their homes in Germany. I also asked them to print and send me what they considered "the ten most significant photos" of their holiday in La Réunion, together with comments and text. I offered to cover the cost of the prints and postage. This particular research approach allowed me to observe in great detail what actually happens when tourists do tourism and what happens when they return home. The major limitation of this approach lies in that the study cannot follow the journey home and the reintegration into the home environment.

The Dialectics of Tourism Experience

During the journey I took the tourists to scenic views, led them into museums and interpretation sites, entered forests, fields, and riversides, and directed them to seashores, beaches, and villages. Most of these sites engaged several senses. The tourists felt the heat of the sun and the coolness of the rain. They watched the land, objects, and people that appeared in front of their eyes. They smelled the odor of the streets, mountains, and forest. They tasted food and drink. They immersed themselves in small lakes, rivers, and lagoons. While thus engaging with their surroundings, they listened—more or less attentively—to my explanations about the island and its populations and about myself.

I noticed that the dialogues and conversations seemed to unfold in very personal, individualistic ways, taking into account personal concerns, tastes, and preoccupations. I also noticed that the ways they unfolded were very similar, as if the participants were following the same cognitive processes.

This involved (usually) several sequential phases:

(1) The Wow Phase

During the first phase, of the first contact with a specific site or story, the tourists were usually speechless. Arriving at a spectacular vista or facing a large waterfall, the sole visible or audible articulations I could record were "ah" and "oh," sometimes also "oh my God" (*oh mein Gott*) or "oh shit" (*oh Scheisse*). Often, their eyes were wide open, and sometimes their mouths as well. On rare occasions, tourists became short of breath, sweated, trembled, felt dizzy, or said they "needed to sit down"—visibly displaying symptoms of shock or extreme awe.

(2) The Amazement Phase

In the second phase, the tourists usually verbally articulated the emotions induced by the encounter in absolute terms. They used exclamations like "beautiful!" or "amazing!" Often they shook their heads, looked at their friends, and smiled; couples exchanged kisses and held hands.

(3) The "It's like" Phase

In the third phase, the tourists typically searched for known analogies, namely by saying, "it's like . . . " ("it's like in Bali"; "it's like on the moon"; "it's like Chinese food"; "it's like nothing I have seen before"; etc.). They were relying on personal memories from previous travels and on images, texts, and representations that typically stemmed from literature or movies.

(4) The "But" Phase

In this somehow antithetic fourth phase, the tourists normally reconsidered the encounter and the analogy they had used, sometimes also introducing a moral judgement ("but in Bali, the site was much bigger"; "but this is so much nicer than the moon"; "but it tastes much better"; "this space is just incredible"; etc.).

(5) The "Me" Phase

In the fifth phase, the antithetic images generated associations with personal memories or preoccupations, which in turn often triggered conversations disconnected from the actual encounter ("We were in Bali with our children last year . . . "; "I feel like a small grain in the universe, though I am not religious like my parents . . . "; "there are lots of Chinese restaurants now in Germany . . . "; "we used to travel a lot when we were young . . . "). In most cases, the encounters were a form of alterity; thus they induced emotions and cognitive processes that would eventually let the tourists talk about themselves. People, sites, and stories acted as triggers or projections to work out personal preoccupations and embed them in narratives, and eventually reconstitute forms of Self. The experience of Other worked as a tool to transgress, transform, and eventually maintain Self.

Variable Time Frames to Work Out Personal Travel Experience

While these phases of touristic cognition followed a similar dialectical sequence, the speed of this sequence and the means by which it was articulated varied largely from one to the other. Some tourists—especially those with a lot of travel experience—often appeared much less impressed by certain sites or stories than others with less experience. For the first category, the whole process was frequently articulated through the uttering of a single phrase. Fabian,[1] for instance, a tourist who had substantial travel experience reacted very quickly when facing a large Hindu temple. "Ah!" he said, "a Hindu temple. With all the colors. Looks a bit kitschy." He took a photo, then explained: "I have seen similar ones in Bali, but there they are even bigger. They have the most beautiful ones I have seen so far." After less than a minute, Fabian was ready to go back to the bus. He articulated his astonishment ("Ah"), then succinctly defined the encounter and gave it a valuation ("a

Hindu temple"; "a bit kitschy"). After taking a photo, he found an analogy from a previous journey ("like in Bali") and linked the encounter to his personal life ("the most beautiful ones I have seen so far").

In other cases, this process took much longer: sometimes hours, weeks, or even months. In one case, representing the other extreme, a woman, Donata, with whom I continued to exchange letters after the journey, seemed to work out the experience of a volcanic caldera over several weeks. At the actual site, she reacted, typically, with an "ah," and then said, after a short while: "This is so beautiful." Later, in the bus, she explained: "This had something artistic; perfect lines and forms. Like on the moon. I had the impression of seeing something prehistoric." Several weeks after the trip, I received a letter from her in which she described a photo she had taken at the same site. "This allows me to imagine how evolution has taken place. While I am not part of any religious community, when facing this landscape I had the impression to be a small grain in the universe," she wrote. The outer journey was accompanied by an inner one that was far from over when this tourist returned home. It took months for her to translate and stabilize the experience into a form of memory, possibly leaving her deeply transformed.

Coming Home as an Essential Part of Tourism Experience

What the last case in the previous section also points to is that the observations during the tour need to be extended beyond the actual journey and be articulated within home contexts. I therefore suggest two further phases as part of the touristic cognition process here observed, which extend into the home environment. I could not observe these phases directly but had to rely on descriptions told to me by the tourists during interviews when I visited them in their homes in Germany several months later.

(6) **The Coming Home Phase**

A sixth phase hence describes the event when tourists come home, integrate their souvenirs into their home environment (by means of incorporating material objects into existing collections, using ingredients in welcome-home dinners, or giving them away as gifts), and talk about their journey among themselves and with friends or relatives. This phase also includes home reappropriation rites, like walking through all the rooms, having a pee, cleaning the house, having a drink, and/or going to the supermarket to fill the fridge.

(7) **The Souvenir Phase**

A later phase occurs several weeks or months later when the encounters of the journey appear transformed into more or less rigid souvenirs that have become part of the tourists' everyday normality. When I met the tourists later, most of what had happened during the journey was reduced to a set of key memories and stories. Paradoxically, while the tourists' conversations during the trip were mainly focused on their home concerns (their children, jobs, partnerships, memories, etc.), in this post-tourist context, the memories where about the actual trip and sites encountered. As the guide, I had become part of these objectifications and was often confronted with funny anecdotes of the trip that I had long forgotten. In this Souvenir Phase, objects acquired during the trip had frequently become part of existing collections. These included often very anodyne-seeming bits and pieces—stones, shells, and small arts-and-crafts objects—whose value seemed to lie less in their specific form or artistry and more in their symbolic quality.

The Multiple Roles of Souvenirs in the Post-Tourism Context

When asked about meanings and usages of such souvenir objects, most of the tourists gave explanations that actually resembled religious relics. The objects were usually displayed in cabinets with glass doors, on shelves, or in shadow boxes, all of which in many ways seemed to constitute contemporary forms of living-room shrines. Photos were framed and put on walls or in photo albums, as if their visual invocation of the island and their actual physicality perpetuated an "authentic link" (Stewart 1984) between the island and the fragment of the island taken home. The tourists and their cameras had actually been on the island where they had captured the sites, creating a sympathetic relation[2] between the spaces of the journey and the images and objects taken home and incorporated into their—thus a little less—mundane worlds of home. What had been captured by the tourist cameras during the journey was a reflection of the realms encountered, as if this process was able to transfer the quality of the visited island onto the photographic memory— similar to Renaissance practices of capturing the sacred aura of a religious shrine via hand mirrors that pilgrims would take to a sacred site and subsequently back to their homes (Robinson and Picard 2009).

Similarly, many tourists/informants explained to me how they had felt their bodies become "recharged," full of energy and sunshine, when they had returned from the journey. Because most tourists considered home and away as evolving in ontologically differentiated realms, once they had returned home these material remnants of the island gained a symbolically and materially heightened quality. In a way, objects' metonymic qualities only became visible once tourists had returned home. In this context, these souvenirs were subjected to different ceremonial usages, once again reminiscent of different forms of religious practice. They were shown to those selected visitors who were granted access to the living room or shown the holiday photo albums, accompanied with stories about the trip. Moreover, they were "activated" at a very personal level in specific moments—for example when the tourists felt down or stressed because of bad weather, difficult work relations, relationship problems, etc.—as a therapeutic means to invoke the good memories of the journey. Many tourists told me that this evocation had happened to them by actually touching small souvenir objects and even photos, as if such acts were able to bring back memories and the marvelous realm of the journey. Others used consumable objects like spices or soap bought while on the trip to prepare a meal or take a bath, which would make them feel better.

Tourism as Re-creation of Social Life

Some of the tourists among the sample appeared to have had a stressful working life in their home contexts, which did not allow them to spend a lot of time together. This was the case for Nicolas and Francesca and also for Valerio and Hisako. The latter were both insurance brokers and explained to me that they often worked for ten hours a day and therefore did not have much time to maintain their couple's life and the love that had once brought them together. Nicolas owned a company and told me he spent most of his time apart from his wife, who would stay at home. Traveling, therefore, seemed a means of escaping these contexts of alienation and spending time together, to "generate shared experiences," as Nicolas explained.

The desire to transform a deficient social life—among couples and friends, but also in a wider sense of felt disconnections between one's existence and the greater cosmos, past or future (see next section)—by means of the journey was usually fulfilled through the way in which these tourists experienced sites and then talked about their experiences. In most situations, they related their encounters to the spaces that marked their everyday life—allowing them to reflect upon, and re-create, the symbolic fabric of their relations. These couples frequently projected themselves, as couples, into the social spaces of La Réunion and wondered about how it would be to live "here." They then eventually usually talked about their common lives back in Germany, for instance that they actually liked their lives there. Nicolas, for instance, tasting a passion fruit found in a forest in the interior of the island, said, "Wow! This is delicious! It tastes like a multivitamin juice, almost artificially. At home, we had these once in a dessert." Francesca, his wife, responded, "Yes, and since recently, you can buy these in the supermarket as well."

In a different context, facing my explanations about local religious practices related to a particular saint, Nicolas defended the "real God" who "had said not to admire other symbols." Francesca responded, with an ironic, but sympathetic smile, that "all these saints are part of Catholic mysticism." She explained that she was a Protestant and wouldn't be "scared by this." In another situation, facing an isolated hamlet in the mountains, she said, "This is so isolated. How can people live here? Is there a school, or a supermarket, or a doctor?" He said, "It looks okay for a holiday house. You can come up here from the coast in less than two hours." She responded, "Never in my life would I want to live here. To go shopping, you will spend an entire day in these mountain roads." I explained to them that with the poverty and competition over land during colonial times, people tended to go further and further away from the coast to have their own land. He responded, "Okay, if you grow up here, if you are used to the solitude, you will surely feel fine here. You wouldn't want to live in the city. If these people here arrived in our town in Germany, they would probably not like it very much either." The observations of these three situations show how Nicolas and Francesca almost always systematically negotiated their encounters in terms of their context back home.

Similar to this case, Valerio and Hisako almost systematically put what they encountered during the journey in parallel with realities that marked their life back in Germany. On top of a mountain, gazing inside one of the island's valleys, Valerio said, "Oh this is magnificent. This depth and these colours. When we were in Colorado, we have been at similar viewpoints, but the land didn't have the same extension. It must be a very different life when you live in a valley like this." Hisako later commented, "Yes, but we are fine where we live. There are all our friends, our parents and the job. Maybe it is sometimes difficult, the bad weather, the stress, but it is our home." Facing this and other landscapes, both frequently talked about "back home" ("we are happy at home"; "at home, it is different . . . ") and thus brought this "back home" back into being. The journey seemed to work as a means to transform meaning and relations that marked their everyday life, both that of the couples and that of their broader life worlds.

When I revisited Valerio and Hisako and also Nicolas and Francesca in their respective homes, I found neatly organized households in which the souvenirs of the journey had been integrated in similar ways. Nicolas had hung prints of the volcano in the corridor, and some smaller material objects had been arranged in a cabinet above the television, together with objects taken home from other journeys. The photos had been put into an album that was arranged in a living-room cupboard, together with other photo albums.

Valerio and Hisako had their photo prints still in the envelope, in a drawer with other envelopes that were waiting to be put into albums— "maybe during the autumn, when we have time," Hisako told me. The movement away from home, the related transgression of quotidian rhythm and practice, and the socially concentrated and emotionally heightened space of the journey in these cases become means to reassemble fragments of social life, re-create affective links among friends and couples, and embed these in personal narratives. Attractions here primarily work as means to evoke and renew memories of past experiences and, from there, to reinvoke memories through which to think and articulate social life at this small intimate scale.

Tourism to Re-create an Existential Order of One's World

Another motif of travel seemed to lie in the hope that the experiences of the touristic journey would transform tourists' lives at a more existential level. In these cases, life back home frequently seemed to be marked by different degrees of boredom or feelings of senselessness. This was, for instance, the case for Lula-Maria who, after divorcing her husband, went through what she called a "psychologically difficult phase" and thus joined the trip, with her best friend, Donata, to "see something else," "without husbands." For Donata, herself in a transitional period of her life, the journey made her engage with ideas of the supernatural and to rethink her relations to a wider cosmos and the religion of her parents. Facing different religious sites, she seemed to engage in a long process of reflection (as mentioned earlier) that went beyond the relationships of her immediate social environment. In her later conversations with me, she questioned a deeper meaning of the world: of evolution, nature, and truth in human life.

At a different level, this existential search for meaning also seemed to underpin Arianna and Sepp's travels: an elderly couple, both retired, who, in their own words, were "bored of life" and "didn't know what to do all day long in their home." They told me they saw life like "a film that would soon be over." During the journey, they hardly engaged at all with what I told them or what they saw but persistently talked about themselves, their "sad life," their youth during the Hitler Regime in Germany, their difficult relationships with their children, the problems their daughter had at work, and the "black people you see more and more in Germany now." They explained to me that they had hoped that traveling would allow them to "leave this sad environment" (*die traurige Umgebung verlassen*) for a while, to "see some colors" and "rediscover their optimism" (*ihren Optimismus wiederfinden*). I am not sure the journey allowed them to find this form of transformation. To the contrary, Carmen, an elderly woman, explained to me that she had a souvenir photo of her father standing in front of the Victoria Falls in East Africa and that she had always dreamt about going there, "as a means to find my father." She told me that she had realized this project the year before, and "a circle had been closed" (*ein Kreis hat sich geschlossen*).

For many of the tourists who had lived in the former German Democratic Republic (GDR) (where travel had been strictly regulated), the fact of being on a tropical island was very frequently put into perspective alongside memories of the suppressive regime of the former Socialist country. Many encounters within the island were here directly related to the lack of freedom to travel before the fall of the Berlin Wall, and the wider circumstances that had led to German reunification in 1991. The particular case of Sepp[3] and Arianna was symptomatic. Both related their encounters—be it of graffiti on a wall, poor neighborhoods, or a dinner beside a hotel swimming pool—to memories of social life in the former GDR and the changes brought about by unification. Entering a poor neighborhood in one of the coastal towns, Sepp said: "Oh, so these are the slums then, aren't they?" (*Dies sind dann die Slums, oder nicht?*) I explained that many people live in sheet-metal houses and that I was not sure if the term "slums" was appropriate. No one in La Réunion would use this or similar terms to describe this kind of relatively common neighborhood. I further explained that life on the island had quickly changed since the 1960s and that many people had difficulties integrating into the new society on the island. He responded with a long reflection about his own life world, saying: "Me as well, I had big problems to integrate myself in the society that had come from the West. Everything went quite fast after the fall of the wall. Before, there was a certain conviviality in our quarters and villages, even at work. But now, everyone fears to lose their jobs." In other contexts, confronting various sites induced violent emotional reactions. For instance, when we arrived at the volcano, he spontaneously started to cry, cursing the former political leaders of East Germany (the GDR). He murmured: "That I can still see this, all this beauty . . . " He later added:

> I had thought I would never see a volcano in my life. If you live in East Germany you cannot imagine that such beauty exists. While there are lots of difficulties following the opening of the wall, this liberty to travel, to see other countries, compensates them all. No one can take these moments away from us any longer, we should live while being alive. An accident can easily happen or you lose your job. But these souvenirs will remain.[4]

In these very different cases the encounters of the journey challenged tourists' life worlds in a deeper, existential way. It made them reflect upon, and re-create, personal life histories by articulating public events that had marked their personal lives, thus relating their belonging to more generic narratives, for example of nation, family, and humankind. It eventually allowed them to become new persons, where memories of a violent past, or of a life that no longer existed, were transformed and objectified into stories. The distance from home allowed them to encompass these existential dimensions of social life and rearticulate them with their present context. It allowed them to move on in life.

Tourism to Re-create Sociability

Another common travel motif seemed to lie in a search for immediate sociability. The act of traveling became the motif for the journey, especially for those tourists living in relative solitude back home. For instance, Carmen, an 82-year-old woman living alone in a major German city, had been going on two "big" journeys, in her words, each year throughout the ten years preceding the trip to La Réunion. She joined group tours, often with a travel companion, another elderly lady from another city whom she had met on one of these trips. According to Carmen, the sociability of these journeys was formed around a shared interest in "different cultures and people."

Fabian, who lived alone and, in his words, had no real friends in his hometown, was a similar case. Traveling had become his *raison d'être*, he told me, as it allowed him to meet fellow travelers and talk about his shared interest in foreign places and tourist destinations. During the trip, both Carmen and Fabian revealed themselves to be highly knowledgeable about a wide range of destinations around the world. Both were excellent dinner-table raconteurs, often focusing on tourism infrastructures. A typical dialogue emerged, for example, when we arrived at the volcano and Fabian said:

> Oh, this is magnificent, the cleanliness, the intensity of the landscape, the forms, the width of the land. There is no comparison with Mauritius. Such landscapes, one cannot find in Mauritius. What a pity that such sites lose their beauty with tourism development, like it has happened in Spain and even in Bali.

One night over dinner, he explained that the hotel we were staying in was "very, very beautiful" and then told a story about a hotel in Morocco, with showers in the corridors and dogs hanging out in the kitchen. This led him to talk about another hotel, somewhere in Africa, where he had to pump water from a well every morning. Almost any story he told situated him as an expert within a wider tourism world; he rarely talked about himself in other terms.

When I later revisited Fabian and Carmen, in their respective homes in Frankfurt and in Berlin, I found surprising similarities in the ways they used tourist souvenirs to decorate their home spaces. The ground floor of Fabian's house was almost entirely filled up with touristic objects. There was hardly any way to get through the living room, which looked like a touristic curiosity cabinet with souvenirs on the floor, in cupboards and glass cabinets, and hanging on the walls. As he had no friends, he enjoyed these on his own. Similarly, the living room in Carmen's apartment was decorated with travel objects wherever I looked, though they were smaller and organized in themed collections. She told me that she took home similar sets of objects from each destination—a small arts-and-crafts sculpture or doll, a stone, and a shell. Additionally, she had images and image-like craft art hanging on the walls, and a neatly organized collection of photo albums, all in the same format, allowing her to recollect images and stories from each of her journeys. Both told me, in their respective ways, that the act of traveling induced a form of social flow with fellow travelers that was rare in their home environment.

Destinations as Projection Grounds

At a different level, it is also important to point out the strong sense of belonging to a German national narrative among the subjects. For instance, I usually told the tourists a popular legend of a slave who escaped from the plantations and found freedom in the mountains, thus evoking a common plot of romantic hero stories. I used this story to talk about wider issues emerging from debates in La Réunion about dealing with the heritage of slavery. While slavery was in most cases not of particular interest to the tourists, many spontaneously made an analogy with debates then dominating the German public media about how to deal with the heritage of the Holocaust.

Similar to a fable that uses animal characters as metaphors to talk about politics and human relations, the story of dealing with slavery worked as a metaphor to evoke events that, for the tourists, seemed in their structure similar. I observed on a different occasion that French tourists would react in different ways, often using stories of slavery as metaphors to talk about the perceived confines brought about by modernity and globalization, topics that were then dominating the French public media.

Many theories of tourism have focused on the structural frames of tourist experiences. Through its focus on the social and societal relevance of individual travel trajectories, this study shows how these broader frames and cultures of tourism are articulated at the level of personal tourist experience. While we can never "fully" access the inner worlds of tourists (or anyone else for that matter), this study demonstrates that, whatever its meta-narrative frame or mass-produced setup, the journey makes tourists feel perplexed, out of place, often speechless, and in search for sense and meaning. Temporarily dislocated outside their social and moral comfort zones of their quotidian environments, tourists are challenged to engage with what they hold to be normal and natural. Many encounters have a highly metaphorical value, representing analogies with issues that preoccupy the tourists in their home contexts. The encounter with the Other becomes a tool to engage and transform these issues from home. The experience of alterity thus enables individuals, couples, and friends to rethink and reaffirm, but also to readjust, the emotional and affective foundations of what makes them individuals, couples, and friends and, at a more existential level, human beings participating in the wider history and nature of the world.

The journey away, which constitutes a transgression of the continuity of the home context, thus enables tourists to transform the circumstances of home—either temporarily, where tourists feel that they can "recharge their batteries" and re-create social links and flow, or permanently, where they return as transformed persons, able to "move on in their lives." While the experience of the journey is always made by an individual person, the best words that tourists find to articulate this experience are often precisely those used in public representations of sites. Tourists often fail to convince others about the authenticity of their experiences when all they say is all that has always been said about a specific site in a tourism advertisement: "It was truly magical!" This should, however, not lull social scientists into believing that the collective reaffirmation of such texts, images, and representations by tourists indicates a mechanical reproduction of mass-produced and inherently hollow tourist products.

Source: For a more detailed discussion, see "What It Feels Like to Be a Tourist: Explorations into the Meaningful Experiences of Ordinary Mass Tourists," *Ethnologia Europaea* 43:5–18, 2013.

Notes

[1] All the names of the tourists are pseudonyms.

[2] Originally developed by anthropologist James Frazer, the notion of sympathetic relations relates to the power objects or entities that had once been in contact with each other and are believed to continue to exert influence upon each other (e.g., a relic of a saint perpetuating the realm of the saint), or the ability of a metaphor or a copy with similar traits to an original to affect the original (e.g., an image of the divine) (Greenwood 2009).

[3] Sepp appears under the pseudonym of Eberhard in two other texts of mine (Picard 2011, 2012).

[4] For a more elaborate treatment of travel syndromes using Sepp's (also known as Eberhard's) case, see Picard (2012).

References Cited

Amirou, R. 1995. *Imaginaire touristique et sociabilité du voyage*. Paris: Presses Universitaires de France.

Bruner, E. M. 2004. "The Balinese Borderzone," in *Culture on Tour: Ethnographies of Travel*, ed. E. M. Bruner, pp. 191–210. Chicago: The University of Chicago Press.

———. 2005 *The Role of Narrative in Tourism*. Paper presented at On Voyage: New Directions in Tourism Theory, October 7–8, 2005, Berkeley: UCB. Accessed online on 26.10.2016: http://www.nyu.edu/classes/bkg/tourist/narrative.doc

Cohen, E. 1985. "Tourist Guides: Pathfinders, Mediators and Animators." *Annals of Tourism Research* 12(1): 1–49.

———. 2004. "A Phenomenology of Tourist Experiences," in *Contemporary Tourism: Diversity and Change*, ed. E. Cohen, pp. 65–86. Oxford: Elsevier.

Coleman, S., and M. Crang, eds. 2002. *Tourism: Between Place and Performance*. Oxford: Berghahn.

Dumazedier, J. 1967. *Toward a Society of Leisure*. New York: Free Press.

Edensor, T. 1998. *Tourists at the Taj: Performance and Meaning at a Symbolic Site*. London: Routledge.

Graburn, N. 1989: "Tourism: The Sacred Journey," in V. *Hosts and Guests: The Anthropology of Tourism*, 2nd ed., ed. Valene L. Smith, pp. 21–36. Philadelphia: University of Pennsylvania Press.

———. 2002. "The Ethnographic Tourist," in *The Tourist as a Metaphor of the Social World*, ed. G. M. S. Dann, pp. 19–40. Wallingford: CAB International.

Greenwood, S. 2009. *The Anthropology of Magic*. Oxford: Berg.

Hennig, C. 1997. *Reiselust: Touristen, Tourismus und Urlaubskultur*. Frankfurt: Insel.

Hom, Cary S. 2004: "The Tourist Moment." *Annals of Tourism Research* 31:1, 61–77.

Jackson, M. 1998. *Minima Ethnographica: Intersubjectivity and the Anthropological Project*. Chicago: Chicago University Press.

Lanfant, M.-F. 2009: "The Purloined Eye: Revisiting the Tourist Gaze from a Phenomenological Perspective," in *The Framed World: Tourism, Tourists and Photography*, ed. M. Robinson & D. Picard, pp. 239–256. Farnham, UK: Ashgate.

MacCannell, D. 1976. *The Tourist: A New Theory of the Leisure Class*. New York: Schocken.

Picard, D. 2011. *Tourism, Magic and Modernity: Cultivating the Human Garden*. Oxford: Berghahn.

———. 2012. "Tourism, Awe and Inner Journeys," in *Emotion in Motion: Tourism, Affect and Transformation*, eds. D. Picard and M. Robinson, pp. 1–19. Farnham, UK: Ashgate.

————. 2015. "White Magic: An Anthropological Perspective on Value in Antarctic Tourism." *Tourist Studies* 15(3): 300–315.

————. 2016. "The Festive Frame: Festivals as Mediators for Social Change." *Ethnos* 81(4): 600–616.

Picard, D., C. Pocock, and D. Trigger. 2014. "Tourism as Theatre: Performing and Consuming Indigeneity in an Australian Wildlife Sanctuary." *Journal of Tourism and Cultural Change* 12(3): 206–223.

Picard, D., and M. A. Di Giovine, eds. 2014. *Tourism and the Power of Otherness: Seductions of Difference*. Bristol, UK: Channel View Publications.

Picard, D., and C. N. Moreira. 2018 forthcoming. "Wine Magic: Consumer Culture, Tourism and Terroir." *Journal of Anthropological Research*.

Robinson, M., and D. Picard, eds. 2009. *The Framed World: Tourism, Tourists and Photography*. Farnham, UK: Ashgate.

Salazar, N. B., and N. H. Graburn, eds. 2014. *Tourism Imaginaries: Anthropological Approaches*. Oxford: Berghahn.

Stewart, S. 1984. *On Longing: Narratives of the Miniature, the Gigantic, the Souvenir, the Collection*. Baltimore, MD: Johns Hopkins University Press.

Turner, V., and E. Turner 1978: *Image and Pilgrimage in Christian Culture: Anthropological Perspectives*. New York: Columbia University Press.

Urry, J. 2002. *The Tourist Gaze*. London: Sage.

5

Let's Go Europe: Students as Tourists

George Gmelch

Writing about the connection between travel and education, Mark Twain declared that "travel is fatal to prejudice, bigotry, and narrow-mindedness . . . broad, wholesome, charitable views of men and things cannot be acquired by vegetating in a little corner of the earth all one's lifetime."

Nearly all universities today encourage students to travel; most have international programs designed to send them abroad. And once abroad, academic schedules are often arranged to allow time for students to tour. In effect, they are encouraged to be tourists. While international program directors may not like to admit it, colleges are some of the U.S.'s largest tour operators.

But what exactly do students do and learn while traveling in other cultures? Twice I have taught in a summer abroad program in Innsbruck, Austria, where classes each week ended at noon on Thursday so that students could travel on their own—three-day jaunts around Europe on rail passes.[1] Like most faculty, I believed that travel offered all kinds of educational benefits.[2] I also believed that my students would learn even more if they kept a journal. Having to write about their daily experiences, I reasoned, would encourage them to reflect upon the people, places, and customs they were encountering as tourists. So, I required the students in my anthropology classes to keep a travel journal.

But when I collected their journals after the first weekend and began reading, I was startled at how shallow their engagements had been with the people and places they had visited. And, on the whole, the few generalized observations they made seemed to be naïve and simplistic. My students didn't appear to be learning much of anything. Yet, it was clear from class discussions that they valued their travel experiences highly; in fact, most believed that they had learned more by being tourists than from their on-campus classes, including my own. The contradiction between what I read in their journals and the students' claims about the educational value of their travel piqued my curiosity and led to the research described in this chapter.

What really happened when they went on the road as tourists? To find out, I asked them to record all their movements and activities in "travel logs." This required making brief notations every 15 minutes—from the time they got up in the morning until they retired at night—about what they were doing (e.g., "on train," "in art museum") and the number of people they were with. At the end of each trip, students calculated how much time they had spent at each activity (waiting for trains, riding trains, sightseeing, shopping, drinking, eating, etc.).

My intent wasn't to collect "data" from my students, as I hadn't yet thought of writing about their experiences. Rather I thought that the logs would help them see the patterns in their journeys (and perhaps the folly in some of it). Only later, as I reviewed the material they turned in, did I begin to think that it revealed something significant about what students really learn when they travel. I then developed a questionnaire to gather additional data, and I also conducted a dozen interviews. In searching through the scholarly literature, I discovered that while much had been written about the educational impacts of study abroad programs,[3] hardly anything existed about what students learn as tourists or travelers. Here I describe what my students did when they traveled, examine the ways in which their travel was transformative, and offer an explanation as to why.

Students on Tour

At the end of classes each Thursday afternoon, the students, packs on their backs, set out for the Innsbruck train station to begin their weekend trips. With Eurail passes in hand, they visited countries throughout Western Europe and parts of Central Europe. Their preferred destinations were places other students had recommended, which also happened to be the places featured in popular guidebooks like *Let's Go Europe*. The most popular destinations were, for example: Italy—Venice, Florence, and Rome; Austria—Vienna and Salzburg; and Germany—Munich and Berlin.

They traveled frequently, never staying long in one place. Their travel logs showed that they visited an average of 1.7 countries and 2.4 cities per weekend.[5] This means that they averaged slightly over a day in each of the cities they visited. (They stayed longest in the resort areas of the French and

Italian Rivieras and at adventure tourism sites.) Their city-a-day tourism can be attributed to several factors. Many wanted to see as much of Europe as they could during their brief time abroad. They were not sure when, if ever, they would come back. There was also some competition among the students, especially the men, to see how much of Europe they could cover with their Eurail passes.[4] Often getting to know a city or place mattered less than being able to say that they had been there. The tendency to "map hop," as some students referred to it, was also motivated by their desire to get maximum value from their Eurail passes.

They moved about hastily despite the program director's advice to get to know the places they visited and "not to run up the mileage." One consequence of their highly mobile form of tourism was that they spent a lot of time waiting in train stations and sitting on trains: an average 18 hours for each three-day weekend journey.

Despite all the time spent in transit, the journey itself was much less important to students than the destination. Few reported spending, or were observed to have spent, much time looking out the window. Annie reflected at the end of the term, "Now that I look back, I wish that I had paid more attention to the places that we were passing through because I think that probably a lot more would have come out of it." But there were an equal number of students who had no regrets. Michelle, who calculated that she had spent five full days sitting on trains since arriving at Innsbruck, wrote: "Some of my most striking moments occurred on the trains—the train strike in Milan, sleeping in couchettes with complete strangers, being hot as hell, the French man that molested Betsy and me, the beautiful scenery in Switzerland, random thoughts, open windows, mountains . . . sleeping with Andrew, not knowing what stop to get off." Decisions about where to go next were often made on the spur of the moment. If students were disappointed with a place once they reached it, they were inclined to return to the train station and pick a new destination, sometimes merely wherever the next train was headed.

As the term progressed, most students slowed down and stayed longer in the places they visited. Some became critical of those who continued to travel excessively. Betsy, who had visited eight countries in her first three weekends in Innsbruck, commented: "Americans approach their leisure activity like work . . . they exhaust themselves running about trying to get in as much as they can. I am guilty of this too, but I now try to spend some time pondering where I am."

"I wonder if we really enjoy the museums and sights that we see," noted Julia in her journal. "It seems that too often we are too concerned about where to go next . . . " At the end of the term she wrote: "I need to go back and stay for a longer period of time in each place. Everywhere we went everyone would ask why we only stayed for one day. And now I am wondering the same thing. For most Americans it seems to be enough to visit a place, take a few pictures and say to their friends and relatives, 'Been there, done that.'"

Travel Companions

Students also recorded the number of companions with whom they traveled. The average group size during journeys was 5.2 students, shrinking to 4.6 once they arrived at a destination. Why such large groups? For most students, this was their first time abroad and they were understandably nervous about traveling alone or even in pairs; they found security in numbers. Over the summer, as they learned their way around and became more confident, the size of their groups declined by a third. The shrinkage was also the result of the frustrations they experienced when looking for accommodation, going to restaurants, and visiting places in large groups. Some students saw another liability to traveling in a group, as Stephanie noted while on a train to Amsterdam:

> I have realized that we create our own little culture here and that may not
> be entirely good. Don't get me wrong. I've had fun. But our student cul-
> ture isolates us from absorbing and trying to fit in to the cultures that we
> are visiting. Even in Innsbruck we tend to go out in flocks, mostly to
> local bars at night and the same bars over and over again. And more often
> than not, the places we choose are tourist magnets where we don't have
> any chance of meeting people in the country we are in. I think it will be
> important for me to come back to Europe with just one or two people.

Some students admitted that they often followed the "herd" rather than deciding for themselves how they really wanted to spend their time. Ben wrote about his companions during a trip to Munich. Though a freshman, he was the only one in the group who had been there before: "I said, 'Let's go to the Hofbrauhaus' and everybody followed. I felt like the Pied Piper."

Walking around European cities in groups limited the students' opportunities to interact with local people. When in groups, they spent most of their time interacting with each other and far less time observing their surroundings. Their conversations, even when standing before great works of European art, architecture, or scenery, were often about people, places, and events back home, rather than where they were at that moment. Local people are also less inclined to start a conversation with a group of students, especially boisterous Americans, than with just one or two individuals. In a comprehensive study of American students studying in Europe, J. Carlson and colleagues (1990) found that "the most important medium for personal experience in the host country was conversation with host nationals."

Daily Routines of Student Travelers

What did students do once they arrived at a destination? Most did what the students who preceded them had recommended. They also consulted their guidebooks and got advice from local tourist offices. In Salzburg, they walked around the old town, climbed the hill to the castle, and took the

Tourists gather and wander in St. Mark's Square in Venice, Italy. (Photo by S. Gmelch)

Sound of Music tour; in Venice they went to St. Mark's Square, rode the canals in a gondola or vaparetto, and visited the glass shops; in Munich they looked at paintings in the Alte Pinakethek or technology in the Deutsches Museum, visited the *Englischer Garten*, and spent an evening in the Hofbrauhaus drinking beer with other tourists; in Florence they went to the Uffizi and the Academic museums (the latter mainly to see Michelangelo's *David*); and in Budapest they visited the castle district, the free museums, and because goods and services were cheaper there than elsewhere, they ate well and the female students went to spas for massages, pedicures, and facials.

The travel logs showed that early in the term the students rushed to the great cities of Western Europe—Paris, Munich, Venice, and Vienna—where they engaged in cultural tourism—visiting museums and galleries and looking at great architecture. Toward the end of the term, the students' interests shifted to recreational sites—the beach resorts of the Italian and French Rivieras, and Interlaken, Switzerland, which offered paragliding, white-water rafting, and horseback riding. The number of museums they visited declined by more than two-thirds during the last half of the term. When I asked students about this in class, some said, with others nodding or murmuring in agreement, that they'd had their fill of museums and churches. About staying on the French Riviera toward the end of the term, Jane wrote: "Laying out seems to be the only incentive these days! Whatever happened to sightseeing?"

Besides going to the prescribed attractions, the students spent their days walking the streets, looking at buildings, stepping into churches to gaze at the art and stained glass windows, sitting on benches and watching people go by, resting in parks, and talking amongst themselves. And like tourists everywhere, they took photographs. Many of their photos were of themselves and their companions posed in the foreground of the places they visited. When I asked why a postcard wouldn't be as good, one student said: "A photograph is proof that you've been there. You took it and it's got you and your friends in it."

There was nothing remarkable about the students' eating habits, except that 1.5 times per weekend they went to an American-style or franchise restaurant (e.g., McDonald's, NY Bagels, and Pizza Hut). Their interest in American franchise restaurants was strongest when they were in countries like Hungary, where none of the students spoke the language and waiters spoke little English, making it difficult to decipher the menu. In Budapest, a group of students took a thirty-minute taxi ride across the city to find a NY Bagels. Food was one of the subjects students were required to write about in their journals, and usually it was the women who wrote the most. They wrote not only about the different kinds of foods they saw but often about what dishes they ordered for dinner. The women were more willing and interested in trying new foods. The men were more inclined to write about European beer and how it differed from American beer than about the food they ate.

College students enjoy their independence. (Photo by Andrea Tehan)

Time was also spent shopping. Female students set aside time specifically to shop, but students of both sexes made a habit of looking at the goods displayed in shop windows as they walked around. For many women, shopping was an integral part of traveling; they could always tell me what the best buys were in each country or city they visited—leather and jewelry in Italy, Hummel figurines in Germany. Many looked for "bargains," which they defined as high-quality goods at lower prices than they would find at home. They also shopped for mementos or souvenirs of the places they visited and for presents to take home to parents and friends. The amount of time spent shopping declined over the summer as their funds ran low and as they purchased the requisite number of gifts or ran out of luggage space.

In the late afternoon, students returned to their hotel or hostel to nap. Evenings, after going out to dinner, were mostly spent drinking and fraternizing in bars. The travel logs showed that only 14 percent of the students routinely did something other than go to bars in the evening. The students stayed out late (after midnight), and often reported going to bed drunk and exhausted.

Education? If So, What Kind?

It should be evident from the descriptions above that most students do not learn much about European history and culture. Certainly not as much as their parents and professors would hope. In the words of one of my Innsbruck colleagues, "Europe is for the students a big shopping mall in which to hang out, not a place to challenge one's cultural categories." Perhaps. But there was also evidence that touring and living in Europe for a summer did have a significant positive impact on students.

At the end of the term, I asked each student to read his or her own journal while imagining that it had been written by someone else and then to describe how the author had changed, if at all, since arriving in Europe. Two broad areas of change emerged from these reflexive accounts. First, a large majority of the students believed that the experience of having gone abroad on their own, and then traveling extensively through Europe without the supervision of parents or other adults, had given them more self-confidence. Some typical declarations were: "I now have the confidence that I can handle any situation I encounter in some way, even if I am alone, unable to communicate easily and unsure of the culture. . . . "

The other change that many students wrote about was having become more adaptable. They believed they were now better able to cope with the surprises, discomfort, and inevitable problems that arise when traveling. The terms they used to describe this change in themselves included being able to "survive," "cope," and "deal" with unfamiliar situations and minor adversity. For example, Emily wrote:

> This trip has made me more laid back. I always tended to need things on time and just the way I like it at home or else I became quite agitated. I suppose that is just part of being American. Here [Europe] you learn that things don't always go your way, and that you simply have to go with the flow. You have to adjust to the differences. Your train isn't always going to be on time; you may not want to go everywhere that your travel companions do; the locals may not speak English or be particularly thrilled to see you; and you will not get ice in your drink. I can deal with that now.

When Emily first arrived in Europe, the limited hours that stores were open angered her, but five weeks later she noted: "I have learned to accept them. . . . I now even think it's great that they close the stores on weekends, as it gives people time to spend with their families."

The students' perceptions of how they had changed were echoed by their parents, whom I interviewed later over the telephone. When I asked if they thought their son or daughter had changed while abroad, most said yes and talked about their being more "mature" and "independent." Typical of many, one mother said about her daughter: "She was just so self-assured when she got back." The phenomenon the students and their parents described is part of what developmental psychologists call "personal development," that is, the "unfolding, growth, evolution, expansion and maturation of the individual self" (Kauffmann et al. 1992:124). Personal development differs from "cognitive development," which has more to do with the acquisition of knowledge (e.g., what students actually learned about European cultures and places).[5]

What interested me even more than how the students had changed was why. After several decades of taking students abroad on anthropology field programs, I already knew that cross-cultural experiences had a big impact on them (Gmelch 1992, 2005). But I was never sure what exactly caused the change until an idea occurred to me while reading the Innsbruck students' journals. The journals showed that from the instant students left the familiarity of their Innsbruck dorm at the beginning of every weekend trip, they were continuously confronted with problems to solve—where to go, how to get there, where to stay, where best to change money, where to find good but reasonably priced places to eat, what sights were worth seeing given their limited time, what places or areas of the city were unsafe and to be avoided, what goods were worth buying and where, and so on. In order to make good decisions, and to satisfy their basic needs, they had to learn how each local "system" worked. And to do so, they had to communicate with local people, asking the right questions and understanding the responses, sometimes given in a foreign language. They often had to ask the same questions of different people to assure the reliability of the information, much as anthropologists do in fieldwork.

As traveling is rarely predictable, I believe students learn much from having to cope with the surprises, unexpected problems, and predicaments, such as missing a train connection, getting lost, and arriving in a town only to discover there is no available accommodation. A dozen students, for example, found themselves stranded in Italy by a train strike. They had to find a way to let the college administrators in Innsbruck know they were safe, learn enough about the strike to assess how long it might last, and look for alternative ways of getting back to Austria. For young adults traveling on their own in a strange culture, often for the first time, these are challenging life experiences.

Because the students travel in so many different countries and move so frequently—almost a new city every day—the challenges they face are multiplied. They have to find and arrange for travel, shelter, food, and local transportation and decide how best to spend their free time, not once but several times every weekend. Such challenges, of course, are compounded when the travel takes them across national borders. When students journey from Austria to Hungary, Italy, France, and Spain, they are not just crossing political boundaries but cultural and language barriers, and therefore new social systems, new customs, and new meanings—the basics of which they must learn in order to get by. In some countries, women students face the additional problem of dealing with unwanted sexual advances from local men. Traveling in a foreign country also requires a certain level of organization. Students have to remember to bring and keep track of their passport, Eurail pass, student identification, and money.

When I returned from Austria, I found support in the writings of development psychologists for the idea that student tourists' personal development arises primarily from their having to cope with change and solve problems. N. L. Kauffmann and his colleagues (1992), for example, found that change and maturation in adolescents occur most often during "periods of discontinuity, displacement, and disjunction." Put differently, individuals acquire new understandings about life, culture, and self when they must deal with changes in their environment and circumstances. This is exactly what happens to student travelers.[6] Conversely, it is argued, as Mark Twain noted over a century ago, that little change occurs when students are in "situations of equilibrium," such as staying at home.

In conclusion, the real education student tourists derive from their travel comes in the form of their own personal development. I think the words Hannah wrote at the end of her summer in Innsbruck are true for many student tourists, "Coming to Europe was a huge experience for me, bigger than anything I've ever done before. I'll never be the same because of it."

Source: Adapted from G. Gmelch "Crossing Cultures: Student Travel and Personal Development," *The International Journal of Intercultural Relations* 21(4): 475–89, 1997.

Notes

[1] The most comprehensive study of American students studying in Europe found that students spent more than one month on the road during their academic year abroad (Carlson et al. 1990).

[2] I had previously taught anthropology field programs in Ireland and Barbados, but not a conventional term abroad before. The Innsbruck program was run by the University of New Orleans, which still operates it today.

[3] A useful review can be found in Kauffmann et al. 1992.

[4] In a similar vein young backpackers often engage in a "one-downsmanship," bragging about how tough their experiences are.

[5] The students' personal assessments of how they had changed are consistent with the research literature on the impact of international study programs on students. For example, a study of 1,260 American Field Service students found that they became "less materialistic, more adaptable, more independent in their thinking, more aware of their home country and culture, and better able to communicate with others and to think critically" than a control group that did not go abroad (Hansel 1998).

[6] Donald Biggs (1992) arrived at a similar conclusion in his attempt to assess the benefits of study abroad for Cypriot students. He uses the term "surprises" to refer to the differences between the students' home culture and the host culture, which they encounter abroad. It is their exposure to these "surprises," "troubles," or enigmas, and the students' attempts at resolving them, that become "potent influences" in their development.

References Cited

Biggs, D. 1992. "The Costs and Benefits of Study Abroad." Mimeograph.

Carlson, J., et al. 1990. *Study Abroad: The Experience of American Undergraduates in Western Europe and the United States*. Westport CT: Greenwood Press.

Gmelch, G. 1992. "Learning Culture: The Education of American Students in Caribbean Villages." *Human Organization* 51(3):245–252.

———. 2005. "Lessons from the Field." *Conformity and Conflict*, eds. J. Spradley and D. McCurdy. New York: Allyn & Bacon.

Hansel, B. 1998. "Developing an International Perspective in Youth through Exchange Programs." *Education and Urban Society* 20(2): 177–95.

Kauffmann, N., et al. 1992. *Students Abroad: Strangers at Home*. Yarmouth, ME: Intercultural Press.

6

"Backs" to Nature: Musing on Tourist Selfies

Tamara Kohn

We stopped to visit the cluster of dramatic limestone stacks called the "12 Apostles" off the Great Ocean Road in Victoria, Australia. It was my third visit, but the first time there during a busy holiday season when the parking lot was teaming with cars and tour buses offloading tourists from around the world, all stopping briefly to visit the major features of the Victorian coast on a sunny spring day. My companion made a comment about the bus tours as we meandered past the visitor center and along a carefully maintained path edged with flowering native bushes. She understood from her work in the Department of Land and Environments in Victoria that the problem with such tours was the way they came out from Melbourne transporting lunches and snacks for their clients so they could maximize profits, while local businesses struggled to sell their wares. "How come people are so *selfish*?" I exclaimed.

And then, turning the corner, all critical thinking dissipated as my gaze was pulled to the dramatic rocks erupting from the rich blue sea—what a glorious sight . . . but wait! I caught my breath and stopped to really see—not the rocks I had come for, but the people who were there before me. Several clusters of tourists—young couples, families with children, and grandparents—all lined the safety barrier of the biggest lookout point with their bums against the barriers, their backs to the Apostles, grinning and posturing at the smartphones perched on the ends of their "selfie sticks." Not a single individual by the barrier was facing the sea. And then there were at least 20 more people on the platform mostly gazing down at their phones and iPads—perhaps sending texts, perhaps flinging their own selfies taken moments before to their social media world—Facebook, Instagram, Snapchat. "Wow," I thought, "how come people are so *selfie-ish*?!" I felt so disturbed by this that I took a picture of the crowd, and I then went with my friend to take in the "natural" view. I took a couple of shots that blocked out all signs of human occupancy, and then I quickly flung one of my pristine iPhone snaps of the Apostles onto my Facebook status page.

[top] A picture of the 12 Apostles that I took that day (4:31 P.M. 9/23/2016) on my iPhone as the sun set, composed to erase all signs of human presence. [bottom] Tourists looking everywhere but out to nature—12 Apostles, 4:31 P.M. 9/23/2016. (Photos by author)

You as reader could have read the above account with a range of thoughts depending on your age, your ethnicity, your relationship (or not) with your smartphone and a social network of others, your experiences of travel and tourism, and your aesthetic sensibilities. Possibly your thoughts are as broad and contradictory as my own. I am lost without my iPhone and its camera eye while at the same time I wish to be free of it and to travel in the world around me with only the senses my body affords me, unmediated by the desire to capture, to compose, and to share with distant audiences. And yet, record I must! The following discussion tries to come to terms with what this selfie[1] tourist trend may tell us and how it connects to what we already know about travelers and photography.

Tourists Photographing Nature

Writers have long thought about how tourists and travelers consume environments through snapshots. In 1954, Walker Percy cynically wrote about a sightseer encountering the view of the Grand Canyon for the first time: "Instead of looking at it, he photographs it. There is no confrontation at all. At the end of forty years of preformulation and with the Grand Canyon yawning at his feet, what does he do? He waives his right of seeing and knowing and records symbols for the next forty years. . . . The present is surrendered to the past and the future" (463). In other words, the captured representation of the view becomes for the traveler the object, the outcome, of reaching a destination, and the images quickly become collected past relics required for consumption in the future. Indeed, having a camera around your neck in many places in the world identifies you as a tourist (Robinson and Picard 2009), and the camera becomes your basic collecting tool. It provides the means to document a journey, and the photos provide proof or ratification that you've done something, that you've been somewhere (Sontag 1977 [1971]:6; Barthes 2000 [1980]: 85). The pictures provide symbolic capital that demonstrates how you have engaged in an "authentic" journey to somewhere special (Tucker 1997:119). Susan Sontag suggested that this desire to document through pictures can be described as a "chronic voyeuristic relation to the world" (1977 [1971]:11). Claude Levi-Strauss ironically opened his iconic travel book *Tristes Tropique* with the header "An End to Journeying" and suggested that for so many travelers and explorers "mere mileage is the thing" that they seek, and photographs are primarily about documenting their success. This fits with the way travelers (particularly from America) often describe their holidays, declaring that they have "done" a place (e.g., "I did Europe this summer") and that they have the pictures to prove it.

What a "meaningful" journey and encounter is, however, can move beyond surveillance and the desire to record and provide future evidence of a journey taken, and it can slip into the realm of art production and aesthetic composition. Those winning snaps that "sing" aesthetically often get blown up as "art" to adorn walls, or, in the present digital age, they are shared online and accrue exclamations of admiration from the traveler's social network—not just for the fact that the photographer had been there, but because of the intrinsic beauty of the shots. Of course, beauty is in the eye of the beholder. We now carry our smartphone cameras everywhere in our hands and take pictures of everyday encounters that also flit easily between mileage documentation, salvage/memory work, and artistic expression—a plate of food posted on Snapchat (popularly called "food porn"—loved and hated in equal measure by those who see it) may appear alongside a particularly stunning sunset or a koala on a tree branch (images unlikely to attract anything but appreciation).

So, these thoughts around image capture, memory making, and art can help me to understand what I was doing when I took those pristine shots of the seascape at the 12 Apostles. I also can understand that posting lovely photos of a dramatic landscape on social media affords a "theatrical stage" and depository for the visual inventory of a trip (see Lewis-Kraus 2016). But what happens when we add "the selfie" into the picture? What does it mean to turn our backs on nature and produce selfies to post to one's social network? What happens, for example, when we convert that story by Walker Percy into one about a sightseer who encounters the Grand Canyon for the first time and, instead of looking at it and collecting snapshots, turns around, takes a selfie, and posts it immediately online? Selfies, ironically, are mostly

A mountain-top selfie with the photographer's back to nature. (Photo by lzf/ Shutterstock.com)

about Others—or at least about ourselves with others. They point to others we know—friends, family and acquaintances who could be anywhere: at home, on Facebook, or traveling themselves.

What's Not to Like?

I'd like to suggest that posting our smartphone holiday photographs on Facebook is so much more than the keeping of an inventory and a reminder to oneself of one's own traveling experiences. It does act, as photos always have, as a record for the future, but it is simultaneously a mechanism to draw a desired absent audience to that spot, to invite distant friends and family to join with us in almost real time through the lens. In other words, the temporality as well as the sociality of the selfie in nature is different from a previous generation's holiday pictures viewed when they get home or from postcards sent to family and friends via snail mail. We no longer take a holiday away from our social world—indeed, we never put our social network down as it is held in our hands and pockets and animated with every notable event whether far from home or just down the road.

Before the advent of the smartphone camera, Urry suggested that tourism in a postmodern age is all about the visual consumption of images as signs (1995:133). But we visually consume images as signs everywhere we go in the current snapchatty age, so by Urry's definition socially networked individuals are always like tourists even when they are at their local café taking selfies with their baked eggs and flat whites. Yes, Urry's ideas are still meaningful today—photography can indeed still be understood as a technology that "gives shape to travel"—that gives one a reason to stop, "snap," and then move on (1990:139). Additionally, he suggests, photographs "appropriate" and "tame" the objects of their gaze (ibid:138–139). However, if we extend these ideas to accommodate our social network connectedness when we travel (far or near) now, we have to adjust our understanding of what the "visual consumption of images" actually means in light of the new affordances (the multiple features and functions) of our digital technologies. For example, the "like" function of Facebook and other social networks stokes our desire to be "liked." We snap to be liked. We now count the accruing "likes" and other "social buttons" our physically absent but socially somewhat present interlocutors offer us in response to the images we only posted moments earlier. The photos we take exert their power not just over the objects of our tourist gaze but also back into our online social worlds where we are vying for attention and appreciation via social buttons in the "like economy" (see Gerlitz and Helmond 2013).

The selfie image is "liked" for many possible reasons. It is liked because you are in it with stunning natural surrounds and perhaps a few other known folk too. Your presence is clearly critical to the viewers' experiences of the picture. Lewis-Kraus suggests that for him the real-time exhibitionism

Young people pose for a group selfie in front of Tower Bridge, London. (Photo by William Perugini/Shutterstock.com)

of Snapchat is particularly amenable to a "generous" feeling and thus invites lots of "likes" (2016). A traveler asking for social media "likes" has made a choice to post the selfie. She could easily buy the high-resolution arty photos and postcards and posters in the local shop, or download professional shots of famous landscapes from Google Images, but the picture achieved with a selfie stick featuring the photographer (alone or with others) in the foreground is more of a social message than an aesthetic sharing of place. It tends to be posted online where it calls out into her social network and says, "Hi! Look at me [and I guess the rocks behind] NOW!" And when the picture ages during the taker's lifetime (presuming that it isn't lost in the ether due to radical changes in technology) the image may still evoke the emotional and locational contexts of the journey—but it will also encourage remarks on the youthfulness of and expression on the selfie-taker's face and the clothes she wore. The backdrop, however spectacular, would just be the same 12 Apostles (or 9 or 6 or whatever remains in the future as the seas rise and erosion continues to nibble away at the rocks).

My musing here is based mostly on my own experience and my incessant people-spotting when I travel. And yet there is a call for such musing. We are at an interesting turning point—a moment when some (older, less networked) people wouldn't dream of taking "selfies" and turning backs to nature and when others wouldn't consider that odd at all. Indeed, I am caught betwixt and between memories of carrying my heavy Nikon camera through early fieldwork experiences in the 1980s, and my iPhone snap-happy present. My observations of tourists in the past considered how some could, over time, come to identify strongly with the places and people that they repeatedly visited (Kohn 1997). Their photographs, as well as my own, would mostly face outwards, destined for future, never present, printing, viewing, and documentation.

Scholarly work has been produced on selfies, but that thinking tends to home in on the rather new phenomenon's historical context, on the shifting media technologies that have allowed for selfies to be taken, and occasionally on the interpretations made by the photographers of the self-images captured in the photos. Rettberg, for example, has published a book that discusses selfies, *Seeing Ourselves through Technology* (2014). What scholars tend to miss, however, is consideration of how those selfies are constructed and move through time and space. They fail to consider the social relationships implicated by the juxtaposition of the image of the self against a particular natural backdrop that is then thrust into a conversation within a social network that consumes the image and relates to it in real or near-real time.[2] To consider the social allows you to consider how selfies, against a backdrop of nature, can capture images and provide fodder for future memories (like any travel photograph) while also acting meaningfully in the present upon others in the social media ether who are invited, in real time, to share the vision of you and your adventure.

Two Different Cases to Consider: James and Annamarie

James was a beautiful young man I had known since his childhood days in the UK and South India. James hanged himself in his room at his university in a desperate act at a very depressed moment. In my grief at his loss, I went to his Facebook page and combed through the hundreds of photos neatly catalogued in separate folders from his travels with friends in India, Africa, and Asia over the previous years. I felt a jolt of shock looking at the reams of group selfies—young faces crowded together, arms often entwined, in front of exotic landscapes—all but one of the faces smiling with the beams of joy that being together in beautiful new lands can produce. Every shot of James revealed sadness and introspection—mouth closed, eyes relatively dull, body somewhat stiff, but a striking face with high cheekbones and perfect complexion. His friends and family were so used to his "arty look"—he was, they said, a gorgeous poser—and he had had numerous modeling jobs. But now, as I looked at those holiday selfies, they appeared to reveal darkness in that young soul. Shouldn't we have seen this?

What can we think now about traveler selfies from my sad discovery? One thing is that the "real time-ness" of any shot that is shared produces a responsibility—it becomes so much more than just a pretty picture; it becomes a meaningful act of communication that has every potential to be read and acted upon as would any face-to-face encounter. After James died, I know I saw his now archived bodily expression in the selfies as so many cries for help that weren't heard. And yet, perhaps because the act of image posting on social media has become so ubiquitous, and the attention given to the images scrolling past our eyes is thus so fleeting, the pain carried in James' travel pictures was not fully communicated during his journeying. I am reminded here of Roland Barthes' essay, *Camera Lucida*, in which he writes: "Photography may correspond to the intrusion, in our modern society, of an asymbolic Death, outside of religion, outside of ritual, a kind of abrupt dive into literal Death" (2000:92). In other words, in this case, the images that celebrate a traveler's life and flit past many others' eyes only come to rest under a meaningful gaze with death.

Annamarie tells me all about how she took an amazing selfie last year at the top of a mountain in East Timor. As she reached the pinnacle she recalled thinking to herself: "I'm so proud right now!" She took the selfie, not only to document herself in the foreground of an amazing mountain view but also to capture that huge feeling of pride. Then, she said, to make the image even more special, she *didn't* post it on social media. *Not* posting made the image capturing that moment personally meaningful in a world brimming over with zillions of relatively meaningless smartphone snaps flung onto social media. In this case, the selfie communicated most to the "self" who took it—and would do so long after the trip ended.

Clearly from this last example we see that we cannot generalize about the selfie being a never-ending call for social network attention, but I'd like to consider Annamarie's celebratory private selfie, James' posthumously considered holiday selfie images, and the initial description of tourists gazing at their cameras on the viewing platform with their backs to the dramatic Victorian coast as indicative of a trend that tells us about a subtle but critical shift in the tourist gaze. The new "selfie" gaze is about a conscious and bodily positioning of ourselves in relation to others who are not present—about communicating with a socially networked world that we can choose to activate attentiveness from in the moments we take pictures of ourselves. The tourist selfie reconfigures what it is to "see" and "be" as a traveler in the world.

Source: Written expressly for *Tourists and Tourism*.

Notes

[1] "Selfie" replaced "twerk" to become *Oxford English Dictionary*'s "word of the year" in 2013. *Oxford Living Dictionaries* defines the selfie as "a photograph that one has taken of oneself, typically one taken with a smartphone or webcam and shared via social media" (https://en.oxforddictionaries.com/definition/selfie).

[2] For an exception, see the following three publications from my collaborative "digital commemoration" work: Kohn et al. (2018), Arnold et al. (2018) and Meese et al. (2015) that include analysis of the Instagram postings of "selfies at funerals" as a form of "presencing"—a legitimate effort on the part of the selfie-taker to communicate grief to a wider social network.

References

Arnold, M., M. Gibbs, T. Kohn, J. Meese, and B. Nansen. 2018. *Death and Digital Media*, London: Routledge.

Barthes, R. 2000 [1980]. *Camera Lucida*, London: Vintage Books.

Gerlitz, C., and A. Helmond. 2013. "The Like Economy: Social Buttons and the Data-Intensive Web," *New Media and Society* 15(8):1348–1365.

Kohn, T. 1997. "Island Involvement and the Evolving Tourist," in *Tourists and Tourism: Identifying with People and Places*, eds. S. Abram, J. Waldren and D. V. L. Macleod, pp. 13–28. Oxford: Berg Press.

Kohn, T., M. Arnold, M. Gibbs, J. Meese, and B. Nansen. 2018. "The Social Life of the Dead and the Leisured Life of the Living Online," in *Leisure and Death: An Anthropological Tour of Risk, Death, and Dying*, eds. A. Kaul and J. Skinner. Boulder: University Press of Colorado.

Lewis-Kraus, G. 2016. "What We See When We Look at Travel Photography." *New York Times Magazine* (September 22).

Meese, J., M. Gibbs, M Carter, M. Arnold, B. Nansen, and T. Kohn. 2015. Selfies at Funerals: Mourning and Presencing on Social Media Platforms. *International Journal of Communication* 9(1):1818–1831.

Percy, Walker. 1954. *The Message in the Bottle: How Queer Man Is, How Queer Language Is, And What One Has to Do with the Other*. New York: Farrar, Straus, and Giroux.

Rettberg, J. W. (2014) *Seeing Ourselves Through Technology: How We Use Selfies, Blogs and Wearable Devices to See and Shape Ourselves*. Basingstoke, UK: Palgrave Macmillan.

Robinson, M., and D. Picard. 2009. "Moments, Magic and Memories: Photographing Tourists, Tourist Photographs and Making Worlds," in *The Framed World: tourism, tourists and photography*, eds. M. Robinson and D. Picard. Aldershot, UK: Ashgate.

Sontag, S. 1977 [1971]. *On Photography*. London: Penguin.

Tucker, H. 1997. "The Ideal Village: Interactions through Tourism in Central Anatolia," in *Tourists and Tourism: Identifying with People and Places*, eds. S. Abram, J. Waldren, and D. V. L. Macleod. Oxford, UK: Berg.

Urry, J. 1990. *The Tourist Gaze: Leisure and Travel in Contemporary Societies*. London: Sage.

———. 1995. *Consuming Places*. London: Routledge.

7

Tourist Photography and the Reserve Gaze

Alex Gillespie

The interaction between tourist photographer and local photographee is a clearly identifiable genre of interaction that is reproduced, in various ways, across the world. Concepts in tourism research, such as Urry's (1990) "tourist gaze," have tended to endow the tourist behind the camera with much power (e.g., Crawshaw and Urry 1997). The tourist gaze, objectified in the camera, is said to have the power to create a cultural revival (Bruner 2005:119), commodify local culture (Philip and Mercer 1999), and cultivate new forms of self-consciousness amongst the local citizens (Tilley 1999). However, the photographer–photographee relation is a complex interaction with at least two sides (Cohen, Nir, and Almagor 1992). It is not only the photographee who is influenced by the interaction, so too is the photographer. The photographee can gaze upon the tourist photographer, and this "reverse gaze" can play an important role in constituting the emerging self of the tourist photographer.

Characterizing the Reverse Gaze

The reverse gaze is evident in an unusual interaction that I observed during fieldwork in Ladakh, northern India. The interaction occurred at a cultural festival that had been arranged by Women's Alliance, a local NGO, in order to display Ladakhi culture to Western tourists. The audience comprised a couple hundred foreign tourists and Ladakhis sitting and standing in a wide

79

circle. At the center of the circle was an open space where troupes of traditionally dressed Ladakhi women took turns singing and dancing. In this type of situation it is expected that tourists will take photographs, and most tourists were availing of the opportunity. However, not all the tourist cameras were trained upon the dancing women. Several tourists were openly photographing traditional-looking Ladakhis in the audience.

Figure 1 shows a picture I took of a Ladakhi woman being photographed by a French tourist with a telephoto lens. This Ladakhi comes from the remote village of Drass. She is wearing a homespun woolen dress, with traditional jewelry and traditional shoes. Adorning her head is an impressive arrangement of flowers. In many ways, she crystallizes tourists' imagination of Ladakh. Tourists visit Ladakh expecting it to be broadly equivalent to Tibet (Dodin and Räther 2001). As with Tibet, Ladakh is imagined to be spiritual and timeless, and Ladakhis are imagined to practice colorful traditions (Bishop 1989; Lopez 1998). The dress and manner of this Ladakhi woman, more than many other Ladakhis at the festival, conformed to these expectations. Accordingly, she was the focus of many tourist cameras. Indeed, during fourteen minutes I counted twenty-one different tourists photographing her. Some of the tourists asked if they could take her photograph, and some even

Figure 1. My photograph of a tourist photographing a traditionally dressed Ladakhi woman.

posed with her, but the majority did not request permission. Overall she was obliging, though noticeably she did joke with one tourist by pretending to dodge the tourist's photographic gaze. The Frenchman in Figure 1 was the most active photographer that I observed. He followed the Ladakhi woman around the festival taking photographs, and when she sat down, he took up his position in Figure 1. By this time, the Frenchman's relentless photographing had been noticed by other tourists.

Shortly after I took the photograph in Figure 1, a female tourist, near the photogenic Ladakhi woman, offered the Ladakhi her camera while pointing toward the Frenchman. The Ladakhi woman accepted it and began pointing the camera toward the French photographer, and me, behind him. Figure 2, another photograph taken by me, shows the amusement on the face of the Ladakhi photographer, her colleagues, and the tourist who lent her camera to the Ladakhi. In terms of the reverse gaze, the interesting outcome of this interaction was in the manifest embarrassment of the French tourist. As the numerous gazes that the Ladakhi woman had been attracting became aware of the camera she held, they followed its line of sight toward the Frenchman. The gaze of the other tourists combined with her mimicry to create a moment

Figure 2. My photograph of the traditionally dressed Ladakhi woman photographing a tourist.

of confusion. As a consequence, the Frenchman's face flushed and his actions became awkward. As Figure 2 shows, he lowered his telephoto lens. While I could slip my camera into my pocket, his large camera became painfully conspicuous. The tourist on the left of Figure 2 had previously been photographing the photogenic Ladakhi woman, too, but unable to hide his camera, he simply began to photograph, or at least pretend to photograph, someone or something else. Shortly after the photograph in Figure 2 was taken, the French tourist briefly pursued a similar strategy, before standing up and then leaving the festival area. Since he could not ignore the reverse gaze, he decided to simply break off the discomforting interaction.

One could argue that the French tourist was perturbed by the disturbing novelty of this interaction, or simply by being caricatured, but such explanations do not go far enough. The origin of flushing is not simply in the individual's physiological response, it is in the social situation, particularly in the individual's understanding of other people's perspectives. The feeling of embarrassment implies a discrepancy between Self's image of Self and Self's image of how Other perceives Self (Edelmann 1987). The embarrassment of the French tourist indicates that his image of himself has altered, not necessarily in a fundamental way, but simply that within this interaction he has been repositioned (Holland et al. 1998). And the manifestly social nature of his discomfort, the blushing, indicates that the mechanism underlying this repositioning is to be found in the social situation.

During twelve months of fieldwork,[1] this is the only time that I saw a Ladakhi take a photograph of a tourist without the tourist requesting it—though noticeably in this case a second tourist had made the request. As such, the interaction I have reported is highly unusual. Yet, this interaction exemplifies the dynamics of the reverse gaze, which in a less dramatic way is a necessary potential in all photographer–photographee interactions. The photographee, by a prolonged stare, a questioning look, or even just a raised eyebrow, can momentarily reverse the relationship between photographer and photographee. In a glance the photographee can, like the Ladakhi woman with the camera, capture and objectify the tourist photographer as a particular type of tourist.

The power and pervasiveness of the Ladakhi reverse gaze is evident in the diverse ways that tourists[2] try to avoid it. For example, some tourists pretend to photograph a landscape or a building that is in the same general direction as the target Ladakhi. The camera is focused upon something roughly equidistant, and then, with a sideways sweep, the target Ladakhi is photographed quickly and unsuspectingly. A development of this method is to take photographs without looking through the lens at all (this is the method that I used when taking the photographs in figures 1 and 2). Using an automatic focus camera, the strategy is to simply, and swiftly, point the camera in the right general direction and take the photograph. With practice this can be done so quickly that it almost dissolves into a fluid motion. Digital cameras greatly facilitate this method because they reduce the cost of wasted photographs. Surreptitiously using a telephoto lens from a distance is yet another popular strategy to avoid the reverse gaze.

One of the most extreme strategies for avoiding the reverse gaze is either to travel without a camera or to hide one's camera. For example, I met one Australian who, when staying in a *gonpa* (Buddhist monastery), and meeting with monks, hid his camera despite his awareness that he was missing some of the best photographic opportunities that he had encountered. When I asked him why he did this, he said: "It's the Ladakhis' perception of me taking a photo—if I have a camera, I am a tourist, whereas if I don't, that thought is not so prominent in their minds. Like say they look at me taking a photo and say 'there is another tourist taking a photo.'"

The reverse gaze has the power to constitute this Australian as "another tourist taking a photo." Being just "another tourist" is an undesirable self-image. This Australian had made an effort not to stay in a guesthouse or hotel and instead had gone out of his way to stay in a *gonpa*. He did not make this effort in order to be constituted as just "another tourist." Accordingly, he engages in self-presentation (Goffman 1959), trying to control the impression that he makes on the Ladakhi monks. By not wielding a camera he hopes that he can occupy a more favorable, and more unique, position within the reverse gaze. Although it was important for this tourist to capture his experiences on film, in this situation it was more important for him to avoid the reverse gaze. Thus the photographic gaze was subordinated to the reverse gaze.

As an initial starting point, we can characterize the reverse gaze as referring to the gaze of the photographee on the tourist photographer. It is evident that the reverse gaze can cause discomfort, in the form of embarrassment, shame, or a spoiled identity. But why does the reverse gaze cause such discomfort for tourist photographers? I address this question here.

Taking the Perspective of Ladakhis?

One way to explain tourist photographers' manifest discomfort when caught in the reverse gaze of Ladakhis comes from the tradition of symbolic interactionism (Blumer 1969). In accordance with the theories of Cooley (1902) and Mead (1913), it has been argued that embarrassment, empathy, self-reflection, and self-presentation arise through people taking the perspectives of others (Charon 1979). Accordingly, one could explain the power of the reverse gaze over tourist photographers in terms of tourists taking the perspective of Ladakhis. This approach would explain the manifest embarrassment of the French tourist as follows: The Ladakhi being photographed has a negative conception of tourist photographers. Tourists, when they are caught in the reverse gaze become aware, to some extent, of this negative image in the mind of the Ladakhi photographee, and it is this feeling of going against the wishes of the Ladakhis that creates the discomfort because it positions the tourist photographer as an ignorant and superficial tourist.

The evidence from the tourist side of the photographer–photographee interaction clearly supports this interpretation. There is some debate amongst tourists regarding what Ladakhis think about tourists. Some tourists argue that Ladakhis idolize tourists' modern lifestyle and wealth, while others argue that Ladakhis resist modernization and are struggling to hold on to their culture in the face of tourism. However, when the focus is narrowed down to how Ladakhis feel when being photographed by tourists, there is strong agreement: tourists think that Ladakhis do not like being photographed. The following excerpt, from a discussion I had with some young English back-packers, clearly illustrates the general perception:

> BARRY: I try not to be, em, to take pictures of the people, though, em, I want to . . .
>
> TOM: I feel embarrassed to do it, because it is like, like making them feel freakish.
>
> BARRY: It's like "look at the freaks there!"—that's just horrible for the people.

Tom states that taking photographs of the Ladakhis makes "them feel freakish," and Barry corroborates this opinion by saying that it is "just horri-ble" for the Ladakhis. From exchanges such as this, one gets the impression that to take a photograph of a Ladakhi is to ride roughshod over Ladakhi sen-sibilities. Assuming that this is how Ladakhis feel when photographed with-out permission, and empathizing with this feeling, could clearly explain why tourist photographers, when caught in the reverse gaze, feel uncomfortable.

However, an examination of the Ladakhi side of the interaction reveals a complication. There is, in fact, little evidence to suggest that Ladakhis feel as oppressed by tourist photographs as tourists suspect. In order to properly unpack the impression that tourist photographers create in the minds of Lada-khis, it is necessary to consider the broad context of tourism in Ladakh.

Due to border conflicts with Pakistan and China, the Indian government did not allow foreign tourists to visit Ladakh until 1974. Up to that point, Ladakh was one of the least developed regions of India. Between the early 1980s and mid-1990s, 10,000–20,000 foreign tourists visited Ladakh annu-ally (Singh 1997); during 2014–2017, over 1,200,000 foreign tourists went to Ladakh (Palkit 2017). Given that in 2011 the population of Ladakh was only about a 133,000, this constitutes a considerable influx. The majority of these tourists come from Western Europe, with France being the most important market for tourism (Palkit 2017), and, by Ladakhi standards, are wealthy. Accordingly, tourism has had a massive impact on developing the financial economy of Ladakh. Jina (1994:136), for example, estimated that about half of the GDP of Ladakh comes from tourists, and that percentage has held in the twenty-first century (Pelliciardi 2010). Tourism has created jobs and economic wealth, both of which are widely appreciated by Ladakhis.

From the Ladakhi point of view, tourists are a means toward economic development. In order to promote tourism, free festivals, such as the Women's Alliance Festival and the Ladakh Festival, are organized. Such festivals, although expensive to organize and do not produce any direct profits (they are free for tourists), are seen to contribute to the overall economic development of Ladakh by promoting tourism. Furthermore, there is a sense in which individual Ladakhis, by welcoming tourists and by posing for photographs, are also contributing to the development of Ladakh. This attitude is reflected in the fact that, unlike elsewhere (e.g., Bruner 2005:117–118), it is rare that Ladakhis ask for financial compensation for posing for photographs. Returning to the Women's Alliance Festival, it is worth pointing out that the Ladakhi photographee had chosen to attend this festival of Ladakhi culture knowing that it was organized for tourists and doing so wearing her traditional dress (i.e., not her everyday dress). Indeed, the Women's Alliance organizers had requested that women come dressed in traditional dress and, by implication, be photographed. Indeed, while at this festival an elderly Ladakhi man, also in traditional dress, encouraged me to take photographs of the Ladakhis. He had noticed that I was more interested in photographing tourists than Ladakhis.

The impression that tourist photography has made on Ladakhis is that they have an important culture that is revered across the world. In discussions with Ladakhis it repeatedly emerged that tourism gives Ladakhis pride in their culture. Before tourists were allowed into Ladakh, in 1974, Ladakhis conceived of themselves as "backward" and undeveloped (e.g., Galwan 1923). Since the mid-1970s, Ladakhis have become increasingly aware of themselves as possessors of a unique "culture." Now Ladakhis feel the need to preserve and represent their "culture." Indeed, there have even been calls for Ladakh to gain independence from the State of Jammu and Kashmir due to having a "unique culture" (van Beek and Bertelsen 1997:52; Wangyal 1997).

Examining the Ladakhi construction of "Ladakhi culture" reveals that it is comprised largely of the things that tourists photograph. It is as if whatever tourist photography has focused upon has become "culture" for the Ladakhis. The traditional dress, the dances, the monasteries, and the religious paintings are all fundamental to "Ladakhi culture." Consider the following excerpt from an elderly Ladakhi woman who has just been asked why tourists visit Ladakh:

> They come here to see our typical dress, *gonchha* and all. They find it beautiful. They take photographs wherever they find an old man with a prayer wheel in his hand, they see who is wearing big earrings, and who has a long beard and they take pictures of them. They don't come here to see the new generation, as they don't take any pictures of them . . . they are here to see our culture.

The tourists, she says, are here to see the "culture," to see the old men wearing the *gonchha* (a traditional maroon overcoat), and not the younger generation. The "new generation" does not wear the *gonchha* or earrings, and the tourists, she says, "don't come here to see the new generation, as they don't take any pictures of them." The point is that photography is essential to her train of thought. The woman uses what tourists photograph to determine what tourists find "beautiful" and are interested to see. Moreover, that which tourists photograph is positively valued, while that which they do not photograph, the young people, is not valued. While the role of photography in constructing local visions of Ladakhi culture indicates an element of "inventing tradition" (Hobsbawm and Ranger 1983) through tourism (Tilley 1999), it would be overly cynical to think of the emerging discourse of Ladakhi culture as a charade. Ladakhis take their culture very seriously because it is a fundamental component of their current identity.

The most negative views toward tourist photography, that I have heard, came from some young male Ladakhi tour guides who, with the help of some Indian rum, were speaking openly. One of the group provocatively stated that tourists visit Ladakh in the same way as tourists visit a zoo. While some of his colleagues agreed, others strongly resisted the idea, arguing that tourists make an effort to learn Ladakhi, that they eat Ladakhi food, and that they are interested in Ladakhi culture because they do not have their own culture. I have also heard reservations about tourist photography from a couple of elderly Ladakhis who voiced concern about whether the photographs portray Ladakhis in a respectful manner. It is disrespectful, they argued, to photograph Ladakhis when they are working or in work dress. However, if the Ladakhi photographee is dressed in his or her traditional dress, then being photographed should be a source of pride for Ladakhis. Accordingly, the suspicion of tourist photographers that has been noted in other societies (Cohen, Nir, and Almagor 1992; Bruner 2005:219), while not absent, does seem to be much attenuated in Ladakh.

Returning to the theoretical issue at stake: whether tourist photographers are taking the actual perspective of the Ladakhis being photographed, it should be clear that it cannot be so simple. Overall, tourists feel the reverse gaze to be critical of tourist photography. For this reason, tourists, as described, fear the reverse gaze. However, the Ladakhis are rarely as critical of tourist photography as tourists fear. Indeed, Ladakhis are often enamored by tourist photography and get a sense of pride through it. Given this attitude amongst Ladakhis it follows that if tourists were taking the actual perspective of Ladakhis they would necessarily sometimes feel good when taking photographs of Ladakhis in traditional dress because they would recognize it as giving a compliment or gesture of recognition, but I have found little evidence of this. Accordingly, the idea that the power of the reverse gaze over tourists stems from tourists literally taking the perspective of Ladakhis must be abandoned in favor of a more subtle interpretation.

Tourists, Travelers, and Post-Tourists

Generally speaking, tourists are quite self-reflective about tourism (MacCannell 2001; Prebensen, Larsen, and Abelsen 2003). In Ladakh they are especially concerned about the way in which tourists interact with locals. Many tourists that I spoke to referred to the history of colonialism and were strenuous in their efforts to compliment Ladakh and Ladakhis. However, when talking about other tourists, especially tourist photographers, they were particularly critical, as illustrated by the following interaction I had with two backpackers:

TRAVIS: One of the worst and most degrading things that I saw, the other day, was an old guy, and some tourists said "can you pose for a photo for us?" and he was like "yeah, I'm having a break why not" and so the girl like went up and said "can you hold your prayer wheel like this, and hold your *mala* [prayer beads] up," she basically made him pose, and he sort of put a fake smile on, and she took the photo, and then he relaxed again.

TONY: That is so pointless.

TRAVIS: I just felt bad for him.

Travis narrates the tourist photographer as getting an elderly Ladakhi man to "pose" so that she could take a photograph. The photographer is portrayed as taking something, a picture, and giving only inconvenience and disrespect in return. However, there is a degree of justice in the narrative, for the tourist photographer does not get a genuine photograph, she only gets a "fake smile." The inauthenticity of tourist experiences is a recurring theme (see Taylor 2001), especially the inauthenticity experienced by other tourists. In the extract one can clearly see Tony and Travis scorning both the intrusiveness of the tourist photographer and the inauthentic outcome.

The stereotypical representation of the ignorant, foolish, consumerist, and duped tourist, one who methodically "does" the sights, enclosed in an insular bubble, has been an object of ridicule since at least the mid-nineteenth century (Löfgren 1999:38). Today a similar image is propagated through the mass media. From *Tintin* to the *National Lampoon's European Vacation*, tourists are a source of humor. It is easy for Westerners to participate in, and cultivate, such a view of tourists while securely situated in one's home country as a local. But a problem arises when these Westerners go on holiday: then Self becomes a tourist and the tables turn. The pejorative representation of Other threatens to return and be applied to Self. Accordingly, tourists are left with the difficult task of maintaining a positive sense of Self, while simultaneously engaging in the usual critique of tourists. The following excerpt illustrates how a Dutch couple negotiate this task:

AG: What pictures have you taken?

MARTEN: Mostly of landscapes! (*laugh*) and *gonpa*! [Buddhist monastery] And a few times of people . . . also of people, em,

> really sneaky, but em, but em, I'm sure they don't know, but it's different from shoving such a lens [gesturing with hands] in someone's face from a meter distance.

AG: If you were going to photograph people, who would you choose to photograph?

KAREN: The old women, of course, and old men.

AG: Why?

KAREN: Because they look nice.

MARTEN: Their characteristics, (*pause*) but when you want to take a picture of an old woman, try to have a little relation with them, not like run through the country and take some pictures, like Japanese! (*pause*) I am afraid to take photos, I can imagine how offensive it would be.

Marten's initial response and laugh to my question reveals the anxiety that probing tourists' photographic practices can evoke. Many tourists seemed to be ashamed of the fact that they had taken photographs of Ladakhis. Like Marten, tourists were more comfortable talking about landscape photographs or the ignorance of other tourists than about their own efforts to photograph Ladakhi people. My asking Marten about his own photographing practices threatens to position him as one of the multitude of scorned tourist photographers. Rather than defend the practices of tourist photographers, Marten tries to differentiate his own practices from those of other tourist photographers. First, he admits to having taken some "sneaky" photographs of local people, and immediately he asserts that this is quite different from the practices of other tourists. Other tourists "shove" long lenses in the face of locals "from a meter distance." It is implied that such intrusive photography is undesirable, and Marten avoids being intrusive by taking "sneaky" photographs. Second, Marten criticizes tourists who "run through the country and take some pictures." The problem with such tourist behavior is that it fails to establish "a little relation" with the locals.

There are several discursive positions that some tourists try to claim when differentiating themselves from other tourist photographers. Some tourists make a distinction between travelers and tourists. Travelers claim to stay for longer, take up a Ladakhi lifestyle, respect the local culture, and establish personal relationships with Ladakhis. In the later part of Marten's excerpt, one can see Marten trying to claim this traveler identity position. Another identity position that tourists try to claim is that of the post-tourist (Feifer 1985). Post-tourists tour the tourists or embrace the usual tourist practices in self-mockery. For example, when I asked one English tourist why he took a photograph of a *gonpa*, he told me, "because that's what you are supposed to do!" Each of these favored positions is constructed in opposition to an image of the "typical tourist." As with ethnographies, one can read the ideal to which Self strives through Self's representation of Other (Vidich and Lyman 1994). Thus, for example, the tourist who has contempt for tourist photographers who do not engage with the local culture or people is implicitly claiming a traveler identity. Equally, the tourist who mocks the naivety of other tourists who see authenticity where there is, they claim, only inauthenticity, is implicitly claiming a post-tourist identity.

Having outlined the ways in which tourists talk about other tourists, I now want to return to the argument by illustrating that the reverse gaze is in fact best understood as tourists' own representation of tourist photographers turned upon Self (Gillespie 2005). Consider, first, the characteristics of the reverse gaze as perceived by tourists. When the reverse gaze catches the tourist photographer, the tourist feels uncomfortable, shamed, and embarrassed. Tourists perceive that Ladakhis find being photographed by tourists "horrible" as it makes them "feel freakish." I have argued that tourists perceive tourist photography to be more undesirable for Ladakhis than it actually is. Next, consider the way in which tourists represent other tourist photographers. There is widespread scorn and derision of tourist photographers because taking photographs is perceived to be intrusive, degrading, and inauthentic. Notice the similarity between the reverse gaze and tourists' own perception of tourist photographers. Tourists' own perception of tourist photographers contains enough scorn and derision to be able to account for the discomforting effects of the reverse gaze upon tourists. This discomfort is arguably compounded by the fact that it simultaneously reveals a contradiction between tourists' idealized Self-position (traveler or post-tourist) and their actual behavior (just another tourist with a camera). The reverse gaze makes salient the tourist's object state as a tourist photographer, it positions him or her as a typical tourist, and thus challenges (from the tourist's own standpoint) any claim to be a traveler or post-tourist.

Conclusion

Urry's (1990) concept of the tourist gaze directs our attention toward the power of tourists in constituting local cultures for consumption (MacCannell 2001). Similarly, much of the literature on tourism is framed in terms of the effects or impacts of tourists on locals. I have tried to rebalance the relationship, arguing that photography (as with any interaction) is two-sided. Specifically, I have pointed to the power of the reverse gaze of locals as a necessary counterbalance to the gaze of the tourist photographer. The reverse gaze plays a constitutive part in the dynamic emergence of the situated tourist Self. The reverse gaze has the power to turn a buoyant traveler into a discomforted tourist.

The mechanism underlying the reverse gaze, I have argued, is not the actual perspective of Ladakhis. Rather, the discomfort hinges upon tourists' own representations of tourist photography, which they in turn attribute to Ladakhis. Accordingly, we must augment the earlier definition of the reverse gaze: the reverse gaze refers to the gaze of the photographee on the tourist photographer *as perceived by the tourist photographer.*

Tourists usually claim, at a discursive level, a position that is superior to that of the "average tourist" or "typical tourist." However, their actions are likely to run counter to these claims; the majority of tourists cannot act in nontypical ways. Thus, there is a contradiction in how tourists position themselves compared to other tourists. Many tourists criticize the behavior of other tourists despite behaving in this same way themselves. The problem is that, in contemporary society, there is a premium on self-presenting as consistent (Holquist 1990). While most of the time these contradictory tendencies coexist within tourists quite peacefully, there are times when the contradiction becomes salient. Part of the peculiar discomfort of the reverse gaze for tourists in Ladakh, I have suggested, is the potential of the reverse gaze to make salient—if briefly—this contradiction.

Acknowledgements

I would like to acknowledge the financial support of the Economic and Social Research Council and Peterhouse, Cambridge, and I would especially like to acknowledge the intellectual support of Tara Sinclair, Flora Cornish, Gerard Duveen, João Salgado, Edward Bruner, Janet Dixon Keller, and a particularly thorough anonymous reviewer. Finally, I would like to thank all the tourists and Ladakhis who were involved in this research, especially Chakdor Spon and Manish Enn.

Notes

[1] The fieldwork, conducted between 1997 and 2005, included ethnographic observation, group discussions with twenty-five diverse Ladakhi groups, and numerous interviews. All of the group discussions and most of the interviews were recorded on audiocassette and transcribed. The group discussions with tourists were conducted in naturalistic settings—restaurants, bars, and guesthouses. The group discussions with Ladakhis were moderated by Ladakhi colleagues.

[2] Writing about "tourists" is problematic for two reasons: First, the category does not refer to a stable group—most people are tourists at some point in time, and nobody is a tourist all of the time. Second, because so many people become tourists at some point in time, the category itself includes a great diversity of people. Whenever one makes a claim about "tourists" there is always an exception. In my use of the term, I knowingly sacrifice subtlety in order to outline general, but not universal, characteristics of the reverse gaze.

References Cited

Bishop, Peter. 1989. *The Myth of Shangri-La: Tibet, Travel Writing, and the Western Creation of a Sacred Landscape.* Berkeley: University of California Press.

Blumer, Herbert. 1969. *Symbolic Interactionism*. Berkeley: University of California Press.

Bruner, Edward M. 2005. *Culture on Tour*. Chicago: The University of Chicago Press.

Charon, Joel M. 1979. *Symbolic Interactionism*. London: Prentice-Hall.

Cohen, Erik, Yeshayahu Nir, and Uri Almagor. 1992. "Stranger-Local Interaction in Photography." *Annals of Tourism Research* 19(2): 213–233. doi:10.1016/0160-7383(92)90078-4

Cooley, Charles H. 1902. *Human Nature and the Social Order*. New York: Charles Scribner's Sons.

Crawshaw, Carol, and John Urry. 1997. "Tourism and the Photographic Eye," in *Touring Cultures: Transformations in Travel and Theory*, eds. C. Rojek and J. Urry, pp. 176–195. London: Routledge.

Dodin, Thierry, and Heinz Räther. 2001. *Imagining Tibet: Perceptions, Projections, and Fantasies*. Boston: Wisdom Publications.

Edelmann, Robert J. 1987. *The Psychology of Embarrassment*. New York: Wiley.

Feifer, Maxine. 1985. *Going Places: The Ways of the Tourist from Imperial Rome to the Present Day*. London: Macmillan.

Galwan, Rassul. 1923. *Servant of Sahibs: A Book to Be Read Aloud*. Cambridge: W. Heffer & Sons Ltd.

Gillespie, Alex. 2005. "G. H. Mead: Theorist of the Social Act." *Journal for the Theory of Social Behaviour* 35(1):19–39. doi:10.1111/j.0021-8308.2005.00262.x

Goffman, Erving. 1959. *The Presentation of Self in Everyday Life*. London: Penguin.

Hobsbawm, Eric, and Terence Ranger. 1983. *The Invention of Tradition*. Cambridge: Cambridge University Press.

Holland, Dorothy, Debra Skinner, William Lachicotte Jr., and Carole Cain. 1998. *Identity and Agency in Cultural Worlds*. Cambridge, MA: Harvard University Press.

Holquist, Michael. 1990. *Dialogism: Bakhtin and His World*. London: Routledge.

Jina, Prem S. 1994. *Tourism in Ladakh Himalaya*. New Delhi: Indus Publishing Company.

Löfgren, Orvar. 1999. *On Holiday: A History of Vacationing*. Berkeley: University of California Press.

Lopez, Donald S. 1998. *Prisoners of Shangri-La: Tibetan Buddhism and the West*. Chicago: University of Chicago Press.

MacCannell, Dean. 2001. "Tourist Agency." *Tourist Studies* 1(1): 23–37. doi:10.1177/146879760100100102

Mead, George H. 1913. "The Social Self." *Journal of Philosophy, Psychology & Scientific Methods* 10(14): 374–380. doi:10.2307/2012910

Palkit, Nawang. 2017, April 21. "Social News." *Reach Ladakh*. http://www.reachladakh.com/30-annual-growth-rate-in-tourist-arrival-in-ladakh/3722.html

Pelliciardi, Vladimir. 2010. *Tourism Traffic in Leh District. An Overview*. https://www.researchgate.net/publication/272474950_Tourism_traffic_volumes_in_Leh_district_an_overview

Philp, Janette, and David Mercer. 1999. "Commodification of Buddhism in Contemporary Burma." *Annals of Tourism Research* 26(1): 21–54. doi:10.1016/S0160-7383(98)00050-4

Prebensen, Nina K., Svein Larsen, and Birgit Abelsen. 2003. "I'm Not a Typical Tourist: German Tourists' Self-Perception, Activities, and Motivations." *Journal of Travel Research* 41(4): 416–420. doi:10.1177/0047287503041004011

Singh, Harjit. 1997. "Ecology and Development in High Altitude Ladakh: A Conflicting Paradigm," in *Recent Research on Ladakh 6*, eds. Henry Osmaston and Nawang Tsering, pp. 239–250. Delhi: Motilal Banarsidass Publishers.

Taylor, John P. 2001. "Authenticity and Sincerity in Tourism." *Annals of Tourism Research* 28(1): 7–26. doi:10.1016/S0160-7383(00)00004-9

Tilley, Christopher. 1999. *Metaphor and Material Culture*. Oxford: Blackwell Publishers.

Urry, John. 1990. *The Tourist Gaze: Leisure and Travel in Contemporary Societies*. London: Sage.

van Beek, Martijn, and Kristoffer B. Bertelsen. 1997. "No Present Without Past," in *Recent Research on Ladakh 7*, eds. Thierry Dodin and Heinz Räther, pp. 43–66. Bonn: Ulmer Kulturanthropologische Schriften.

Vidich, Arthur J., and Stanford M. Lyman. 1994. "Qualitative Methods: Their History in Sociology and Anthropology," in *Handbook of Qualitative Research*, eds. Norman K. Denzin and Yvonna S. Lincoln, pp. 23–59. London: Sage.

Wangyal, Sonam. 1997. "Political Evolution in Post Independence Ladakh," in *Recent Research on Ladakh 7*, eds. Thierry Dodin and Heinz Rather, pp. 485–492. Bonn: Ulmer Kulturanthropologische Schriften.

8

We're All Photographers Now: A Photographic Exploration of Tourist Behavior

Lisa Beth Anderson

The pervasiveness of smartphones has created a landscape in which most people who have the ability to travel internationally for pleasure have, at their fingertips, technology capable of producing high-caliber imagery. The ever-better photographic capabilities of tourists' digital devices have had a profound impact on their travel habits, their choices of destinations, and the lives of the people living in the places they visit.

The ease with which images can be published on social media has shifted the audience for travel photographs. Instead of an end-of-summer slide show for family or a small group of friends or a personal photo album, many tourists now take photographs with a wide range of friends, acquaintances, potential employers or clients, and even weakly tied social contacts in mind. Keeping this broad audience in mind has reshaped tourist photographic practices.

Documentary
Production

Catalyzed by the popularity of the various story-oriented
applications available on smartphones and encouraged by
the ability to take a nearly limitlessness number of digital
images (compared to the previous limitations and expense of
physical rolls of film), travelers now often take photographs
that aren't particularly visually stunning or unique simply
in order to support the narrative they hope to tell.

Hunting

In their attempt to capture iconic or exotic subjects, tourists
may resort to clandestine behavior, making photos
surreptitiously or without a subject's permission.
At other times a small payment may part of the
arrangement. This is usually negotiated in advance
but sometimes takes the tourist by surprise.

Personal Branding

Tourists with an eye on sponsorship seek to make idealized,
marketing-style images and intentionally include an object
or product with the hope of hash-tagging their way into
being noticed by a particular brand.

Postcarding

Some tourists seek to re-create a great photograph they have seen online or in print. To the vexation of locals, one of the most-asked questions residents hear in many tourist destinations is asked with digital device in hand, "Where can I make this photograph?" Christina Godfrey, a shop owner in Manarola, Cinque Terre, says, "I now keep a large photograph of Manarola in my shop to confirm that 'that view' is the one they are looking for. The people who ask directions to 'the photo' do not ask any other questions."

Theming

In an effort to create unexpected or more original work, many tourists cultivate a theme or follow self-generated creative guidelines when making and publishing travel photographs. They may use a particular technique or specific gear or repeatedly insert the same object into their images.

bocce : bocce

knees : ginocchi

rush hour : ora di punta

Self as Subject

Tourists seek destinations and stunning backgrounds as much for the experience as to photograph themselves being there. "I curated our trip via Pinterest," one maker said of discovering enviable selfies online and figuring out how to get herself to those destinations.

In addition to selfies, some tourists hire professional photographers at their destination to photograph them. This increasingly popular approach is now formally facilitated by various tour companies, including Airbnb.

Urban Portrait Session

Paris · Edit your pictures directly after your photo shoot

Entertainment experience
Hosted by Alex

◊ 2 hours total

▤ Equipment

🗪 Offered in English

$103 per person
★★★★★ 173 reviews

See dates

f 🐦 ✉ </> ···   Saved to Wish List ♥

About your host, Alex	I'm a professional photographer living and working in Paris. I studied photography at École des Beaux-Arts and my work has been selected for the Sony World Photography Awards and shown at the Somerset House in London.
What we'll do	We'll meet at a cafe near the Louvre Museum, then walk around the neighborhood to find perfect spots to take photos. You'll have Paris as your background for a series of pictures that I'll shoot. I'll...+ More
What I'll provide	HD digital pictures 🖥 Between 50 and 100 HD digital pictures sent after the editing.
Notes	- the meeting point is outside cafe Le Fumoir. -

Pushing Back

The ubiquity of tourist/photographers in many parts of the world now shapes the daily experiences of the people living there, upsetting their privacy and the rhythms of their everyday lives. In many destinations locals have found ways to push back against these intrusions. In cities from Amsterdam to Beijing, selfie sticks have been banned. In Venice, residents have taken to the streets to protest cruise ships. In the Sistine Chapel, security guards announce ominously every few minutes that there should be "no photo" made. And recently in Barcelona a street artist has taken to marring the spaces adjacent to famous landmarks with graffiti in an effort to air local grievances and ruin tourists' photography.

Part II:
Production and Consumption

A Qalandar man tries to profit from tourism at the expense of India's now threatened sloth bears. (Photo by Sharon Gmelch)

Tourists climb the steep sandstone steps of Angkor Wat, Cambodia. (Photo by Sharon Gmelch)

9

The Maasai and the Lion King: Authenticity, Nationalism, and Globalization in African Tourism

Edward M. Bruner

Early work on the anthropology of tourism documented a variety of tourist experience in terms of a typology of tourism, including ethnic, cultural, historical, environmental, and recreational tourism (Smith 1989:4–6), as well as a typology of tourists, including explorer, elite, mass, individual traveler, backpacker, and charter tourists (Cohen 1979; Pearce 1982; Smith 1989:11–14). All tourism and all tourists were not the same, but scholars in the field tended to reduce the variety by seeking the essence of the tourist experience, as a quest for authenticity (MacCannell 1976), a personal transition from home to elsewhere (Graburn 1989), a form of neocolonialism (Nash 1989), or a particular type of "gaze" (Urry 1990). The typologies of tourism and tourists ordered the data but yielded few insights. Exceptions to the generalizations were common, rendering questionable their usefulness; one was never sure when or where the general propositions were applicable.

More recent field studies of tourism among particular peoples have tended to avoid typologies and monolithic generalizations, but still there is a predilection to homogenize local tourist displays.[1] The Maasai are represented as male warriors (Bruner and Kirshenblatt-Gimblett 1994), the Pueblo as female potters (Babcock 1990), the Balinese as living in a magical world of dance and drama (Bruner 1996b; Picard 1996; Vickers 1989), and the

Tahitians as representing South Seas sensuality (Kahn 2000). In such cases, a single form of tourism becomes associated with one ethnic group in a given locality, similar to the effect that Appadurai (1988) observes for ethnography, where the connection between topic and place becomes the defining characteristic of a people, to the exclusion of other perspectives, for example, caste with India, lineage with Africa, or exchange with Melanesia. Tourism scholarship thus aligns itself with tourism marketing, in that scholars tend to work within the frame of the commercial versions of their sites. Grand statements about the nature of tourism in Bali or Africa or even more broadly in the "Third World" are sometimes the result, to the neglect of more ethnographically based and nuanced analyses of the variety of tourist displays within any one culture area.

My objective in this article is to open up the theoretical dialogue in tourism scholarship, and I do so by applying a method of controlled comparison (based on Eggan 1954), showing how one ethnic group, the Maasai, are exhibited for tourists at three different sites in Kenya. Although all three sites present a gendered image of the Maasai warrior (the personification of masculinity), a controlled comparison enables me to describe three ways of producing this image. Accordingly, I demonstrate how the breadth of meanings, ironies, and ambiguities in tourist performances emerges from a critical comparison of the processes of their production. For example, familiar concepts in the literature (such as authenticity, tradition, and heritage) are relevant in only certain touristic contexts. I emphasize the importance of the distinction—not fully appreciated in the anthropological literature—between domestic and foreign tourism, as well as the wide-ranging impact of globalization on the staging of local tourism.[2] Further, I show that historically forms of tourism are parallel to forms of ethnographic writing. Finally, I examine the sites in terms of what I call the "questioning gaze," my reference to tourists' expressed doubts about the veracity of what they are seeing and the way their questions and skepticism penetrate the commercial presentation, undermining the producer's dominant narrative.[3]

Elsewhere I have offered humanistically oriented descriptions of tourist performances privileging political complexities and local voices (Bruner 1994, 1996a, 1996b). My emphasis in this article is on the production and on the tourists, not on indigenous perceptions. My intention is to discuss each of the three sites so that the comparisons and juxtapositions between them become grist for the theoretical mill. What I say about any one site is designed to contrast with another.

By way of background, Kenya achieved independence from Britain in 1963 and has a population of approximately 30 million divided into about 42 ethnic groups. The tensions between these many ethnic groups have been severe at times. Tourism is a major source of income, the main attraction being safari runs to view the wild animals in the game parks. The Maasai, presented at the three tourist sites I discuss, are a seminomadic pastoral group with a total population of about 400,000 in Kenya; Maasai also live in Tanzania (Spear and Waller 1993).

My three Kenyan field sites are Mayers Ranch (Bruner and Kirshenblatt-Gimblett 1994), a privately produced performance organized by local entrepreneurs; Bomas of Kenya, a public production developed by the national government; and what a tour agency calls an "Out of Africa Sundowner" party at the Kichwa Tembo tented safari camp near the Masai Mara national reserve.[4] A thumbnail sketch of each site follows.

Designed for foreign tourists, the production at Mayers staged Maasai dancing in their warrior compound, chanting and carrying spears, proud and aloof. The production hid all outside influences and manufactured objects, presenting Maasai as timeless and ahistorical. Mayers reproduced a nineteenth-century colonial narrative (Knowles and Collett 1989) of Maasai men as exemplars of an African primitive, as natural man. It depicted Maasai men as brave warriors, tall and athletic, men who, at least in the past, would raid for cattle, kill lions armed with but a spear, consume raw foods such as milk and blood, and (as "Lords of East Africa") instill respect and fear in others. The producers strived for tourist realism (the aura of authenticity), and the site was designed as a series of tableaux, set up for tourist photography. The tourists viewed the Maasai from a colonial subject position, as did early explorers and ethnographers. Mayers began in 1968 and flourished until the 1980s but was eventually closed by the government, as the colonial aspects were offensive to many Kenyans. I will discuss the relations between tourism and ethnography later, but I note here that the critique of colonialism within anthropology (Asad 1975; Hymes 1972; Marcus and Fischer 1986) was part of the same worldwide anticolonial movement that led to the closing of Mayers Ranch in Kenya. Mayers is presented here as a baseline, as a superb example of postcolonial tourism that eventually gave way to newer modes of production.

Bomas is a national folklore troupe that presents the dances of Kenyan ethnic groups, including the Maasai, primarily for an audience of modern urban Kenyans. The mechanisms of production are prominently displayed. The dances are staged in an auditorium, with rows of seats and a bar in the back for the sale of refreshments. The theme of the production is Kenyan nationalism, to show that all the ethnic groups of Kenya are equally valued. Representatives of Bomas say that their aim is the preservation of Kenyan heritage, as if each ethnic culture is in the past and has to be recuperated in a museum-like setting. Bomas is an ethnic theme park for domestic tourists, a genre now found in many areas of the developing world.[5]

The Sundowner presents Maasai men dancing in the context of an "Out of Africa" cocktail party near an upscale tented safari camp on the Mara reserve. The Maasai performers mix with the tourists, who are served drinks and hors d'oeuvres by uniformed waiters. Globalizing influences are apparent, as Hollywood pop culture images of Africa and blackness are enacted for these foreign tourists as they sip champagne, alternately chatting among themselves and dancing with Maasai, all the while on safari in the African bush. These are posttourists (Feifer 1985; Urry 1990:100–102), beyond traditional tourism, who want a gracious African experience, all the comforts and luxury of home, and a good show rather than staged authenticity.

At all three tourist sites, Maasai men perform for an audience, but there are important differences. These differences are evident in the modes of transportation taken by the tourists to each site, and I describe them here, as the journey to a tourist destination is itself an inherent part of the tourist experience. Mayers is located in the Rift Valley about fifty minutes by car from Nairobi. Most tourists reached Mayers over dirt roads as passengers in a van provided by a local tour company. Bomas is located on the outskirts of Nairobi along the public bus route, and a convenient way of going is to drive or to take a city bus. Kichwa Tembo safari lodge is located by the Masai Mara reserve. In 1999, to take one example in which I participated, a group of tourists on the Intrav agency "Out of Africa" tour first visited Ngorogoro Crater in Tanzania, then went by a small charter aircraft directly from Kilimanjaro Airport in Tanzania to the Kichwa Tembo private airstrip in Kenya. The planes did not stop in Nairobi or go through Kenyan immigration or customs.[6] They flew directly from Tanzania to Kenya, over nation-states, in a seamless journey from one game park to another, indeed a transnational experience. From the perspective of the tourists, there was no border crossing, as the "nations" of Tanzania and Kenya were not really experienced. The tour was above borders, traveling not just in airspace but in global space. Travel by van, public bus, and charter aircraft characterize the three tourist attractions.

First, I summarize briefly the material on Mayers and then contrast these data with Bomas and the Sundowner. The latter sites will receive most of my descriptive and analytic attention. Although this study deals with Kenya, I suggest that the different contexts of production may be replicated in many other areas of the world where tourism is prominent. For reasons I explain in the conclusion, my claim is that my approach in this article has relevance beyond Kenya.

Mayers Ranch

Mayers Ranch was built by the Mayers, a British family who became Kenyan citizens. The Mayers came to Kenya early in the twentieth century, eventually went into cattle ranching, drastically reduced their land holdings after Kenyan independence, and in 1968 established a tourist attraction on their land as a way of generating additional income. There have been four generations of Mayers in Kenya. Their current homestead, located in the Great Rift Valley 30 miles from Nairobi, is blessed with a natural spring and features a verdant lawn and English garden. The Mayers hired local Maasai, some from families who had worked on their cattle ranch as herders, to build a Maasai *manyatta* (compound) for young warriors who would perform their dances and enact selected aspects of their culture for tourists. After viewing the Maasai performance, the tourists would then go to the Mayers's lawn for tea and crumpets.

The transition from the mud huts and brown dust of the Maasai compound to the lush green lawn and garden adjacent to the Mayers's main house enacted a key theme in East African tourist discourse, the contrast between the primitive Maasai and the genteel British, which evokes the broader contrast between the wild and the civilized. The tourists at Mayers experienced vicariously the wildness of the Maasai and, by extension, the wildness of Africa, only to return at the end of the performance to the safety of the Mayers's cultivated lawn, to the veritable sanctuary of a British garden in the Rift Valley. The Maasai dancers never spoke directly to the tourists. They carried spears and clubs, wore a solid red cloth, covered their bodies with red ochre, and braided and decorated their hair. On the elegant lawn, the Mayers were gracious, socializing with the guests and telling stories about colonial times, while two black servants (not Maasai) dressed in white aprons and white chef's hats served tea and cookies. As white settlers, the Mayers themselves were part of the tourist attraction, nostalgic relics of a colonial era. The performance was a fastidious and carefully constructed combination of tribalism and colonialism, which the tourists told me they found fascinating and romantic.

Maasai warriors with spears at Mayers Ranch. (Photo by Edward M. Bruner)

The show at Mayers Ranch was carefully edited and produced. The Maasai performers (or actors) were not allowed by the Mayers (the directors of the drama) to wear or display modern clothing, watches, or any industrial manufactured objects. The only souvenirs sold at Mayers were those hand-crafted by Maasai. The entire performance was produced to achieve tourist realism, an ambience of authenticity, and the appearance of the real. The Mayers directed the Maasai to act as if they were what the foreign tourists regarded as nineteenth-century tribesmen, the African primitive. The ritual performed at the Maasai village was made to seem natural, as if the Maasai were dancing for themselves and the tourists just appeared there by chance. The constructedness of the site was masked. Some of the Maasai dancers had been to school and spoke English, but during performance time they remained aloof and mute.

I first gathered data from Mayers in 1984; when I returned in 1995, I learned that the performance had been closed. During lunch at the Mayers's home, Jane and John Mayers explained to me why they had been put out of business, and they did so, of course, from their own subject position, as descendants of a white British colonial family. It was a combination of fac-tors, they said, but the primary reason was that the government felt they were exploiting the Maasai. The Mayers reported that an African-American tour group visiting the ranch to watch the Maasai performance had objected strongly, complaining about its colonial aspects—specifically that the May-ers lived in a big house whereas the Maasai lived in mud huts, and that the Mayers gave food to the Maasai as part of their compensation, which they felt was paternalistic. The Mayers's brochure said that the Maasai were a lin-guistic subgroup of the Nilotic, but other black American tourists objected strongly to the term *subgroup*, which they regarded as insulting. The key fac-tor, however, according to the Mayers and others in the tourism industry, was that many Kenyans felt the performance of Maasai warriors dancing in a European homestead was simply too anachronistic for modern-day Kenya.

After closing the tourist performance, the Mayers remained on their ranch and engaged in other income-producing activities. They missed the income from tourism, but Jane expressed a feeling of relief, saying they had felt "totally invaded" having 150 tourists come to their home on any given day. Jane agreed that a performance about tribalism and colonialism was indeed an anachronism in contemporary Kenya and felt it would be best if the Maasai were producing their own performance. Some of the Maasai who had worked at Mayers went to the hotels in Mombasa and the coast where they found employment as performers in Maasai tourist productions, and a few became involved in the sex industry, catering mainly to European women seeking a sexual experience with a Maasai man.

Rosaldo (1989) coined the phrase "imperialist nostalgia," noting that contemporary Western peoples yearn for the "traditional" cultures that the previous generation of Western colonialists had intentionally destroyed.

Rosaldo's concept is not entirely adequate for my purposes as it refers primarily to a feeling (a yearning). Cultural tourism goes far beyond this yearning, recreating in performance idealized colonial images and other representations of the past, the pastoral, the original, and the unpolluted. Tourism frequently enacts imperialist nostalgia. Tourism performances, throughout the world, regularly reproduce stereotypic images, discredited histories, and romantic fantasies. The past is manipulated to serve the expectations of the tourists and the political interests of those in power, and because the Mayers, as ex-colonialists, had little power in modern Kenya, their operation could be closed. Mayers Ranch, a good example of tourism artfully produced in the postcolonial era for a foreign audience, catered to the darkest desires of the tourist imaginary, fixing Maasai people in a frozen past, representing them as primitive, denying their humanity, and glorifying the British colonialism that enslaved them.

Bomas of Kenya

The second attraction discussed in this article, Bomas of Kenya, constructs a different picture, for a different audience. Bomas, opened to the public in 1973, is a government museum of the performing arts, an encyclopedic presentation of the cultural heritage of a nation, performed by a professional dance troupe whose members are government employees.[7] Their Web site says Bomas "offers Kenya in Miniature" (Bomas of Kenya 2000). Like Mayers, Bomas has regularly scheduled daily shows. The patrons pay admission, move into a 3,500–seat auditorium for the performance, and then exit from the building to walk to the 11 traditional minivillages.[8]

Each village features the architecture of a particular ethnic group—Kikuyu, Kalenjin, Luhya, Taita, Embu, Maasai, Kamba, Kissii, Kuria, Mijikenda, and Luo—and consists of a few houses typical of that group, or as the Bomas Web site says "the original traditional Architecture . . . as built by the ancestors" (Bomas of Kenya 2000). Significantly, there is no claim that the houses are those of contemporary peoples. Handicrafts are available for purchase in each village. The crafts shown, however, are not restricted to those produced by the members of any one ethnic group but are representative of all Kenyan groups, comparable to the crafts that can be found in any souvenir shop in Nairobi. Nor are the sellers necessarily members of the same ethnic group as those in whose village the array is located. A Kikuyu seller, for example, might be found in the Maasai village. Further, no one actually lives in the villages; they are for display purposes only.

National dance troupes have been established in Uganda, Senegal, Mali, and most other African nations as part of government policy, just as performance troupes, ethnic village complexes, nations in miniature, and national museums have been established in many countries of the world. These sites differ, of course, but a general aim is to collect, preserve, and exhibit the art, culture, and history of a nation. To quote from a mimeographed information program distributed by Bomas of Kenya, "We specialize in traditional dancing and preservation of Kenya Cultural Heritage." The word *preservation* is a key. Whereas at Mayers the claim is that the Maasai are still living as they have for "a thousand years" and are essentially unchanged, Bomas talks of preserving, which implies that traditional ways no longer exist, that they are in danger of disappearing, that they belonged to the ancestors. Bomas makes a claim very different from the discourse directed toward foreign tourists. At Mayers, the Maasai occupy space in the ethnographic present; at Bomas they, and the other Kenyan groups, are in the traditional past.

At the top of the Bomas program one finds "REF: NO.BK/15/11," a reference number, typical of government documents everywhere. Other evidence of a nationalistic emphasis is easy to find. For example, the performance troupe calls itself the "harambee dancers." Coined by Jomo Kenyatta, the first president of Kenya, *harambee* is a powerful national slogan that means roughly "all pull together" (Leys 1975:75). In Kenya there are many harambee groups, sometimes called self-help or cooperative groups, and, indeed, there is a national harambee movement. The program distributed at Bomas consisted of six pages, including advertising, and described each act or scene in sequence—there were 22 in all. The last act, called the finale, was described as follows: "This is a salute in praise of His Excellency Hon. Daniel Arap Moi the President of the Republic of Kenya." Such statements render the performance of traditional dancing explicitly nationalistic.

The Bomas harambee dance troupe consists of members of many different ethnic groups, and any member of the troupe may perform the dances of any of the other Kenyan groups. At Mayers, Maasai performed Maasai dancing, but at Bomas a Kikuyu dancer, for example, could do the dances of the Maasai, the Samburu, the Kikuyu, or any group. Bomas creates an ensemble of performers from different groups who live together at Bomas as a residential community in a harambee arrangement, almost as an occupational subculture, apart from their extended families and home communities. The harambee dancers from Bomas are available for hire all over the world and have made overseas tours to the United States, the United Kingdom, Sweden, Japan, and other countries.

The troupe acts as a single functioning unit, detaching ritual dancing from its home community and putting it in a museum, a professional theater, or on the national or international stage. The troupe becomes an explicit model of the nation, melding diversity into a modern organization, disconnecting heritage from tribe. The implicit message of Bomas is that tribal dances belong to the nation. By separating cultural forms from tribal ownership, Bomas asserts that the multiethnic heritage of Kenya is now the property of all Kenyans. As an expression of nationalist ideology, Bomas speaks about tribalism as memory, in performance, where it is less threatening.

Bomas tells a story for Kenyans about themselves and appeals most to urban Kenyans. Their Web site states that visitors can see "rural Kenyan life" (Bomas of Kenya 2000). On Sunday afternoons, Bomas is crowded with local families who come with their children. Whereas the Mayers were hosts to foreign tourists and, on Sundays, to a resident expatriate British community, Bomas is host to a few foreign tourists but mostly to urban Kenyan families.[9] Businessmen meet there for conversation over beer or coffee. It is a place for Kenyans to honor their ethnicity in an urban setting, to see dances that they might not otherwise have an opportunity to witness. Bomas also arranges special shows for schools and educational institutions in the mornings, two days a week, highlighting their educational function.

For purposes of this article, it is important to understand how Kenyan tourist discourse uses such terms as *tribalism, traditional, modern, primitive,* and *civilized.* The six-page program of Bomas does not once contain the term *tribal* or *tribesmen,* and it uses the word *tribe* only twice, and then merely descriptively, as the equivalent of people or group," in contrast, *tribal* and *tribesmen* are crucial terms in tourist discourse for foreigners. The tourist brochures issued by private tour companies advertising trips to Kenya for an American or European audience use *tribal* with the implicit idea that the people so characterized are primitive and representative of an earlier state of existence. Significantly, the term used in the Bomas program is *traditional,* which contrasts with *modern.* The Kenyan audience at Bomas consists of modern urbanites, and what they witness on stage are their own traditional dances, part of a previous historical era, reflecting on their own present modernity in composite ways. Although sometimes used in the Kenyan media, the terms *tribal* and especially *tribalism* have a negative connotation in contemporary Kenya, as they have in many of the multiethnic nations of the world. The Kenyan government has long acknowledged deep-rooted ethnic identifications as a serious national problem (Chilungu 1985:15; Okumu 1975).

In brief, *tribal* is a term for foreign tourists used at Mayers, *traditional* is a term for domestic tourists used at Bomas, and *ethnicity* is a more neutral term, used by some Kenyans and anthropologists alike to avoid the derogatory or misleading connotations of *tribal* or *traditional.* The terms have different associations in touristic, ethnographic, and political discourse. Bomas, in a sense, has taken the concept of the tribe, and put it in the archives or in the museum, where hopefully, it will be safe and out of the way.

The language of the Bomas program is revealing. Here are excerpts describing two of the Bomas acts:

> The background to this item is the assassination of Nakhabuka, a young and beautiful girl of Abamahia clan in Bunyala (Western Kenya). Her jealous boyfriend shoots her with an arrow at the river, because she has married someone else. Her great spirit enters the body of one of the villagers and demands that a wrestling dance be performed occasionally in her memory.

> This item features a Giriama couple who are getting married. Unfortu-
> nately, the bride, having been bewitched just before the ceremony,
> threatens to refuse her man. It takes the skill of a famous medicine man
> to bring her back to agreement before the wedding can continue. The
> events of the wedding are heralded by the Gonda dance (performed
> mainly around Malindi on the Northern Coast of Kenya).

This is the genre of the folktale. Embedded in the Bomas program are
mini folktales, dramatic narratives about everyday life. The stories are culturally and geographically specific. They refer to the Abamahia clan or to a
Giriama couple and to such actual places as western Kenya or the north coast.
These are real places. There is none of the generalized language of much of
the tourist discourse produced for a foreign audience with its vague references to the untouched African primitive.[10] The function of such generalized
references to tribesmen or to primitives is to distance the object, to deperson-
alize, to separate the tourist from the African. The Bomas stories, on the other
hand, tell about the heritage of specific groups, ones with which the Kenyan
audience can identify. That the stories tell about being bewitched, about a
famous medicine man, and about spirits is part of the magical language of the
folktale, but it also reflects a reality of Kenyan cultural life (Geschiere 1997).

Mayers was performed in a Maasai compound, and all Western objects
were hidden from the audience. Bomas is performed in a modern auditorium
that contains a restaurant and a huge bar. Before, during, and after the performance, members of the audience can order drinks. Mayers was characterized
by an absence of signs; at Bomas there are signs everywhere, including ones
that give the price of admission, directions to the auditorium, directions to the
traditional villages, even signs that advertise Coca-Cola. Each of the villages
has its own sign.

Bomas is professionally produced with such technical virtuosity that it
seems like a Kenyan Ziegfeld Follies, with professional lighting, sound
effects, and with the performers in matching costumes. At Bomas, the performers are clearly on stage and they smile at the audience, whereas at Mayers the Maasai were preoccupied with their dancing. At Mayers, toward the
end of the dancing, the audience was invited to come on to the outdoor stage
to view the performers close up, and to photograph them, whereas at Bomas
there is an unbridgeable gap between the actors and the audience. The audience at Bomas does not mix with the actors on stage. Bomas gives one the
feeling of being at a concert or at a theatrical production, and, indeed, Bomas
employed an American producer for a time.

Mayers had a close fit between the performance and the setting and that
was part of the message. Bomas has a lack of fit between the performance
and the setting, and that too is part of the message. The genre of Mayers was
tourist realism. The genre of Bomas is nationalist theater. Although both are
studiously produced, Mayers was made to seem underproduced, and Bomas
overproduced. The aim at Mayers was to mask the artifice of production. The

aim at Bomas is to expose the processes of production so as to create a discontinuity between the production and what it is designed to represent. Mayers denied change. Bomas highlights change. Bomas detaches culture from tribe and displays it before the nation for all to see and share, and in the process Bomas aestheticizes, centralizes, and decontextualizes ritual. Ironically, what Bomas represents is what British colonialism was trying to achieve, the detribalization of Kenya. The British tried, but eventually failed, to turn Kenyans into colonial subjects. Bomas succeeds, in performance, in turning Kenyans into national citizens. Disjunction at Bomas is a rhetorical strategy, whereas at Mayers the strategy was to stress continuity. Mayers was a Western fantasy. Bomas is a national wish fulfillment. Mayers and Bomas are equally political and each tries to present its own version of history. Mayers was not an accurate reflection of contemporary Maasai culture, neither is Bomas an accurate reflection of Kenyan traditionalism.

Out of Africa Sundowner

Kichwa Tembo Tented Camp is described in the brochure as "luxurious enough for even the most pampered traveler," with private sleeping tents, electricity, insect-proof windows, a veranda, and an indoor bathroom with hot showers.[11] So much for roughing it in the African bush. The camp is located near the Masai Mara National Reserve, which is an extension of the Serengeti. The main attraction at the camp is game viewing from safari vehicles, but the Maasai are also prominent. There are Maasai at the private airport welcoming the incoming tourists, Maasai dancing at the camp, a scheduled visit to a Maasai village, and a briefing on Maasai culture by a Maasai chief, who began his talk to the tour group I joined by saying in English, "I think all of you must have read about the Maasai." I choose, however, to discuss the Out of Africa Sundowner party held on the Oloololo escarpment on the bank of the Mara River.

This performance introduces a new note into ethnic tourism in Kenya. The Sundowner is basically a cocktail party with buffet on a river bank in the bush. The Kichwa Tembo staff set up a bar, with a bartender in red coat, black pants, white shirt, and bow tie. The attraction is called the Out of Africa Sundowner, from the 1985 Hollywood movie starring Robert Redford and Meryl Streep, based on Isak Dinesen's (1938) book about colonial days in Kenya. *Out of Africa* (1985) was also shown to the tour group on the airplane en route to East Africa. The brochure from the tour agency describing the Sundowner says, "Standing at the precipice of the escarpment, the sun setting low amidst an orange and pink sky, it is easy to see why Africa so inspired Karen Blixen and Dennis Finch-Hatton." The brochure invites the tourists to experience the Sundowner, not from the point of view of the movie or the actors, or the book or the author, but rather from the point of view of the main characters in the story. It is all make-believe. At the Sundowner, waiters serve drinks and food to the tourists standing in groups or seated together in clusters of folding chairs. Then the Kichwa Tembo employees form a line, singing and dancing for the tourists, and the Maasai men begin their chanting and dancing. The performance is remarkable in a number of respects.[12]

During the dance, individual Maasai dancers come among the tour group, take the hands of tourists, and bring them into the line to dance with them. The other Maasai dancers smile in approval and visibly express their appreciation of the dance steps now also performed by the tourists. The remaining tourists laugh and comment; most nod in sympathy and enjoyment. A few of the dancing tourists look uncomfortable but make the best of the situation, while others rise to the occasion, dancing away, swinging about wildly, improvising, introducing dance steps ordinarily seen in an American disco. After the dance, the Maasai again mix with the tourists, this time passing out free souvenirs—a necklace with carved wooden giraffes for the women and a carved letter opener for the men. These curios are given as if they were personal gifts, but actually the tour agency at the camp buys these items for distribution at the Sundowner. It is all smiles and politeness.

At the Sundowner, the Maasai warrior has become tourist friendly. Gone is the wildness, or the illusion of wildness, or the performance of wildness, to be replaced by a benign and safe African tribesman. In Mayers Ranch, the particular appeal was precisely the tension between the wild Maasai and the cultured Englishman, but at the Sundowner that binary opposition is dissolved. At the Mayers performance, the tourists moved between two distinct spaces, the Maasai manyatta and the Mayers's lawn, the African space and the English space, the wild and the civilized. The Maasai did not enter the Mayers's area, for to do so would be a violation and would destroy the touristic illusion. At the Sundowner, however, the two spaces have merged—there is no separation between the Maasai and the tourists, but only one performance space where the two intermingle. By breaking the binary, ethnic tourism in Kenya is structurally changed (Sahlins 1981).

During the dancing at the Sundowner, the camp employees begin to sing a Kenyan song called "Jambo Bwana," written in the mid-1980s by a musical group called "Them Mushrooms."[13] The song was first performed in a tourist hotel in Mombasa, became an instant hit, and is still known throughout Kenya. Them Mushrooms moved from Mombasa to Nairobi, established their own recording studio, and have performed abroad.

The message of "Jambo Bwana" is that tourists are welcome in Kenya, which is characterized as a beautiful country without problems. One tour agent in Nairobi said it is now the "tourist national anthem" of Kenya, as it is so popular with foreign tour groups. Prominent in the song is the Swahili phrase "Hakuna Matata," which in one version is repeated four times and means "no worries, no problem." The phrase itself has a history. In the 1970s, there was political turmoil in Uganda and in the states surrounding Kenya.

Smiling Maasai dancing with tourists at the Sundowner. (Photo by Edward M. Bruner)

During this time, "Hakuna Matata," although always part of coastal Swahili language, came to be widely used as a political phrase, to say that Kenya is safe; it was reassuring to refugees as well as to the citizens of Kenya. After Them Mushrooms wrote "Jambo Bwana" in the mid-1980s, the phrase "Hakuna Matata" became more associated with tourism.

"Hakuna Matata" is familiar to tourist audiences as the title song from the Hollywood movie *The Lion King* (1994), with music by Elton John and lyrics by Tim Rice. The lyrics repeat the phrase "Hakuna Matata," defining it as follows:

> Hakuna Matata!
> What a wonderful phrase
> Hakuna Matata!
> Ain't no passing craze
>
> It means no worries
> For the rest of your days
> It's our problem-free philosophy
> Hakuna Matata! [14]

The hotel employees at the Sundowner then sang "Kum Ba Yah," an Angolan spiritual, popular in the United States as a folk, protest, and gospel song. Despite its African origins, "Kum Ba Yah" is now established in U.S. popular culture and has taken on new American meanings. The phrase

"Hakuna Matata" has been similarly appropriated and is associated with *The Lion King* (1994).

At the Sundowner, the performers present "Kum Ba Yah" with a Jamaican reggae rhythm, a musical tradition that, to many North Americans, equates good times, blackness, dancing, and Caribbean vacations.[15] In other words, Africans have taken a phrase and a song originating in Africa and have performed it for the tourists with a New World Caribbean reggae beat. This musical tradition and the songs themselves, "Hakuna Matata" and "Kum Ba Yah," have been widely interpreted in American popular culture as expressions of "Africanness" and "blackness," and then have been re-presented to American tourists, by Africans, in Africa. What is new is not that transnational influences are at work, that a song or an aspect of culture flows around the globe, as ethnographers are already familiar with these processes. Nor is it new that a global image of African tribesmen is enacted for foreign tourists, as this is also the case at Mayers. What is new is that, at the Sundowner, the Americans, who have presumably made the journey in order to experience African culture, instead encounter American cultural content that represents an American image of African culture. The Americans, of course, feel comfortable and safe, as they recognize this familiar representation and respond positively, for it is their own.

This is globalization gone wild: Paul Gilroy's (1993) "Black Atlantic," transnationalism as a Lacanian mirror image, and Appadurai's (1991) "scapes" as a ping-pong ball, bouncing fantasy back and forth across the Atlantic. A reggae Lion King in the African bush. Points of origin become lost or are made irrelevant. Old binaries are fractured. The distance is narrowed between us and them, subject and object, tourist and native. Ethnography is transformed into performance, blurring the lines between genres in ways that go beyond Geertz (1983). What is left are dancing images, musical scapes, flowing across borders, no longer either American or African but occupying new space in a constructed touristic borderzone (Bruner 1996b; cf. Appadurai 1991) that plays with culture, reinvents itself, takes old forms and gives them new and often surprising meanings.

The colonial image of the Maasai has been transformed in a postmodern era so that the Maasai become the pleasant primitives, the human equivalent of the Lion King, the benign animal king who behaves in human ways. It is a Disney construction, to make the world safe for Mickey Mouse. Presented in tourism are songs that have African roots but that in North America and probably globally are pop culture images of Africa and blackness. Black Africa in the American imagination has been re-presented to Americans in tourism.

At the Sundowner, tourists receive drinks, food, a good show, an occasion to socialize, a chance to express their privileged status, an opportunity to experience vicariously the adventure of colonial Kenya, and a confirmation of their prior image of Africa. As posttourists in a postmodern era, they may also revel in the incongruity of the event, of dancing with the Maasai, of drinking champagne in the African wilderness. But what do the Maasai receive? The answer must be seen against the backdrop of what the Maasai received at Mayers and receive at Bomas. The Maasai performers at Mayers received a small daily wage for each performance in which they participated, a measure of ground maize, and a pint of milk a day. They derived additional income from the sale of their handicrafts and from the tips they received by posing for tourist photographs. They were wage laborers, as are the performers at Bomas.

The Maasai on the Mara, however, are part owners of the tourist industry and receive a share of the profits from safari tourism, but this is neither readily apparent nor ordinarily disclosed to the tourists.[16] The tourists see only what is exhibited to them in performance, but there is a vast behind-the-scenes picture. The Maasai receive 18 percent of the gross receipts of the "bed nights," the cost of accommodations at Kichwa Tembo per night per person. This can be a considerable amount as there are 51 units at the camp and the cost per night could be US$300 to US$400 in high season, or over US$100,000 per week with full occupancy (Kichwa Tembo 2000). There are a total of 22 camps and lodges on the Mara, some even more luxurious and expensive than Kichwa Tembo. The entrance fee to the Masai Mara Reserve is US$27 per person per day, and Maasai receive 19 percent of that fee. The percentages of 18 and 19 (odd figures) were the result of a long process of negotiation. The funds are accumulated and given to two county councils, and in one of these, the Transmara Council, where Kichwa Tembo is located, the funds are divided among the "group ranches," each based on one of the ten Maasai clans that own land on the reserve.

The Maasai ownership of most of the land on the reserve, as well as the land on which the camps and lodges are built, is the basis of their receiving a share of the gross receipts. Philip Leakey (a brother of Richard Leakey) reports that before the 1980s, Kenyan elite and foreign investors derived almost all of the income from international tourism (personal communication, February 19, 1999; see also Berger 1996). As a result, most Kenyans including Maasai were indifferent or even hostile to tourism, as they did not profit from it. Further, there was considerable poaching in the game parks. The depletion of the wildlife on the East African reserves posed a danger to the national heritage of Kenya and to the natural heritage of the world, not to mention that the deterioration of game threatened the entire tourism industry and with it a key source of foreign exchange. Things changed in the 1980s, as it was widely recognized that the way to gain the support of the Maasai for tourism development was to give them a stake in the industry, which the Maasai had argued for. Since then, there has been a drastic reduction in poaching on the reserve. The Maasai, who do not usually eat wild game, now have a financial interest in protecting the animals and in stopping poaching. Further, a new law was passed stipulating that anyone caught poaching in Kenya may be killed on sight.

The Maasai profit from tourism on the Mara in other ways. There are 170 park rangers on the reserve, and all are Maasai. The Kichwa Tembo package includes a visit to a Maasai village, where the villagers receive the US$10 per person admission fee as well as the profits from the sale of handicrafts. One day I counted 80 tourists, for a total income of US$800. When the Maasai perform their dances for tourists, they receive compensation. One group consisting of about 15 Maasai received US$163 per performance. Again, tourists are not usually aware of these financial arrangements. Some Maasai on the Mara are wealthy by Kenyan standards, but that wealth is not visible to the tourists. Most Maasai have used their income to increase their herds of livestock—cows, sheep, and goats—which are kept away from the tourist routes.

Maasai are employed at Kichwa Tembo not only as waiters, chefs, and security guards, but in management positions as well. Yet, the tourists do not "see" these employees as Maasai. In the hotel context, the Maasai waiters are reserved and deferential in their white uniforms, avoiding eye contact with tourists and speaking only when spoken to. If waiters were to overstep the bounds of appropriate service behavior they would be reprimanded, whereas if the same Maasai performing for tourists as warriors behaved deferentially, they would be a disappointment to the spectators. All parties understand the behavior appropriate in each position, for it is a mutually understood symbolic system, and each party to the drama performs an assigned role. Within the lodge, the tourists are usually polite to the waiters but are disinterested, for they are perceived as service employees. Kichwa Tembo camp is a space that provides the comfort, luxury, and safety on which upscale tourism depends.

In contexts in which the Maasai are performing as "Maasai," on display for tourists, it is tourist time. The Maasai men, adorned with red ochre, wearing red robes, beadwork, and sandals, and carrying sticks, change their demeanor—they become warriors. In performance, in these contexts, the tourists become voyeurs—there is a cornucopia of visualization, and the simultaneous clicking of many cameras. Ironically, in the same day a single individual might be a deferential waiter in the hotel during the serving of a meal, but a Maasai warrior, one of the "Lords of East Africa," during performance time in the evening.

The Maasai, of course, are well aware of the discrepancy between their own lifestyles and their tourist image, and they manipulate it, but there are many complexities in the situation. Some Maasai, who have in effect become performers in the tourism industry, display themselves for tourists, to be observed and photographed, and if asked, they reply that they do it for the money. They play the primitive, for profit, and have become what MacCannell (1992) calls the ex-primitive. This is the case for performers at all three sites, at Mayers, Bomas, and the Sundowner. Tourism for them is their livelihood, a source of income. On the other hand, I knew one Maasai business executive who assumed "ethnic" Maasai traits only during his nonworking hours. He dressed in Western clothing with shirt and tie during the work week in Nairobi, where he spoke English, but on most weekends, wearing jeans and a T-shirt, and speaking Maasai, he would return to his native village to become a pastoralist to attend to his extensive herd of livestock. On ceremonial occasions, he would wear traditional Maasai clothing and dance and chant in Maasai rituals. To put it another way, what touristic or ethnographic discourse characterize as Maasai "ethnic" traits, may, in tourism or in life, be displayed situationally, depending on the context, which is probably the case universally for all ethnicities. Identities are not given; they are performed by people with agency who have choices.

But boundaries are elusive. As de Certeau (1984) suggests, spatial patterns are not composed of rigid unbreakable regulations, flawlessly executed, but are spatial practices, characterized by transgression, manipulation, and resistance, as individuals appropriate space for themselves. I give two examples. While watching the dancing at the Sundowner, I noticed one man, a waiter in black pants and white shirt, who picked up a club and began dancing along with the red-robed Maasai. He was out of place, apparently a Maasai waiter who decided to join his fellow tribesmen, but it was a broken pattern.

At Kichwa Tembo, one of the tourists, an African-American woman, had taken an optional nature walk with Maasai guides. During the walk they came upon a pride of 12 lions. The woman reported that she had never been so scared in her life, but the Maasai guides urged calm and slowly moved the group away from the lions without incident. After that dramatic encounter, while resting and chatting, the woman showed the Maasai guides a picture of her grown daughter, a strikingly beautiful woman. One of the guides announced to the woman that he wanted to marry the daughter, but the woman passed it off and they continued on the nature walk. Later, back at the camp, the Maasai man came to the woman with his father, a marriage spokesman, and offered 25 head of cattle for the daughter, with the implication of a still larger offer, a huge bride-price. The father urged the woman to consult with her own marriage brokers, and then to meet again to negotiate—a Maasai practice. When the woman told me about this incident, I playfully suggested that the least she could have done would have been to transmit the offer to her daughter and let her make her own decision. But the woman replied that her daughter was finishing her studies at a prestigious law school in California, was very driven and ambitious, and would not want to be the second wife of a Maasai villager. Boundaries are not rigid—tourists and natives do move into each other's spaces.

Maasai then are incorporated into the safari tourism industry on the Mara in a dual capacity. First, they are part owners, possibly partners, and certainly beneficiaries. Second, they are also performers in a touristic drama, a secondary attraction to the wild animals on the reserve, but clearly objects of the tourist gaze. As the Maasai receive a share of the profits and a stake in the industry, the question may be asked, to what extent do they control the images by which they are represented? My observations suggest that if the Maasai now have economic and political power, they do not exercise it to influence how they are presented in tourism. As the Maasai say, they are in it for the money and are willing to play into the stereotypic colonial image of themselves to please their clients, the foreign tourists. As one Maasai explained to me, the European and American tourists do not come to Kenya to see someone in Western dress, like a Kikuyu. The Maasai put on the red robes and red ochre and carry clubs so the tourists will be able to recognize them as Maasai.

Who is producing the Sundowner Maasai? Kichwa Tembo tented safari camp was built by the tour agency Abercrombie and Kent, but was recently sold to another company, Conservation Corporation Africa. Regardless of the particular company involved, the Out of Africa Sundowner is produced by tour agencies and, by extension, by international tourism to meet a demand. Tourism is marketing, selling a product to an audience.

The production is skillful because the hand of the tour agency is masked in the presentation of the Maasai. It is the Maasai dancers who distribute gifts directly to the tourists at the Sundowner (with gifts provided by the tour agent), it is the Maasai chief who collects the $10 fee to enter the village (but it is the tour agent who selects the village), and it is a Maasai (hired by the tour agent) who provides explanations of Maasai culture. At Mayers, the entrance fee was given to the Mayers or to their staff, and the staff provided the commentary on Maasai lifeways. It was apparent at Mayers that white Europeans were explaining and producing Africans, with all its colonial overtones. At Kichwa Tembo, however, Maasai explain Maasai culture, but briefly, as most tourists are not really interested in a deeper ethnographic understanding. In Maasai tourism generally, at Mayers, Bomas, and the Mara, there is a master narrative at work, but it is usually implicit, a background understanding. On site, textual content is less prominent than evocative visualizations, songs, dance, and movement. In a sense, the producer is more important in Maasai tourist attractions than the writer. At the Mara, a casual observer might say that the Maasai are producing themselves, but I believe it more accurate to say that the tour agents are the primary producers, with the Maasai at best relegated to a minor role. The role of the tour agent is concealed, which is part of the production.

If the Maasai at the Mara are behaving in accordance with a generalized Western representation of Maasai and of African pastoralists, then tourism in a foreign land becomes an extension of American popular culture and of global media images. The startling implication, for me, is that to develop a new site for ethnic tourism, it is not necessary to study the ethnic group or to gather local data, but only to do market research on tourist perceptions. I know these statements are somewhat conjectural, but is it too speculative to contemplate that the Maasai will eventually become (rather than just appear as) the pop culture image of themselves? I do not believe in the homogenization of world cultures caused by globalization, for local cultures always actively assert themselves, and I would argue for the long-term integrity of the Maasai. But the issue is raised, how well will the Maasai continue to compartmentalize themselves and separate performance from life? The line separating tourist performance and ethnic ritual has already become blurred in other areas of the world with large tourist flows, such as Bali. The Balinese can no longer distinguish between performances for tourists and those performances for themselves, as performances originally created for tourism have subsequently entered Balinese rituals (Bruner 1996b; Picard 1996). Where does Maasai culture begin and Hollywood image end?

Writing Tourism and Writing Ethnography

To summarize thus far, Mayers presented the tourist image of the African primitive, Bomas presents the preservation of a disappearing Kenyan tradition, and the Sundowner an American pop-culture image of Africa. The tourists at Mayers sat on logs facing the performance area in a reconstructed Maasai village, at Bomas they sit in tiered auditorium seats facing the stage, and at the Sundowner on folding chairs on the escarpment as the performance evolves around them. The performance and the setting were concordant at Mayers; are detached at Bomas; and at the Sundowner, the most global message is delivered in the most natural setting, along a river bank in a game reserve. Mayers served English tea, Bomas serves drinks at the bar, while the waiters at the Sundowner pour champagne. The binary opposition at Mayers is between the African primitive and the civilized Englishman; at Bomas it is between traditional and modern Kenyans; and at the Sundowner, the binary is dissolved because the performance presents what the tourists interpret to be their own transnational media image of Africa. The master trope at Mayers was tourist realism, at Bomas it is undisguised nationalism, and at the Sundowner it is a postmodern image.

Mayers, Bomas, and the Sundowner differ in many respects but all three sites combine tourism, theater, and entertainment. All take simultaneous account of the prior colonial status, local politics, national forces, and global international requirements. I have emphasized globalization at the Sundowner site, but there clearly are global dimensions to Mayers and Bomas. Mayers (as tourist realism) and Bomas (as national theater) are examples of transnationalism, and both arose in Kenya as an extension of the postcolonial condition, one for foreigners and the other for locals, for as Oakes (1998:11) says, both authenticity and tradition are themselves modern sensibilities. In the 1960s, Mayers reworked a nineteenth-century colonial narrative for foreigners, and Bomas is a recent variant for domestic tourists of public displays of living peoples. Such displays have a history dating back to European folk museums (Horne 1992), World Fairs (Benedict 1983), and even earlier (Kirshenblatt-

Gimblett 1998:34–51; Mullaney 1983). Bomas most resembles the ethnic theme parks of contemporary China (Anagnost 1993), Indonesia (Bruner 2000; Errington 1998; Pemberton 1994), and other nations (Stanley 1998).

Viewed historically, the three tourist sites parallel three different forms of ethnographic writing. Mayers Ranch can be likened to ethnographic realism—it strived for an aura of authenticity based on a prior image of what was believed to be the authentic African pastoralist. When Mayers was opened in 1968, colonialism was gone in Kenya, a thing of the past, but there were still many British expatriates and a worldwide longing for a colonial experience—an enacted imperialist nostalgia—that Mayers produced for the expatriate community and foreign tourists.

Authenticity has figured prominently in tourism scholarship since Boorstin (1961) and MacCannell (1976). Boorstin characterizes tourist attractions as pseudo-events, which are contrived and artificial, as opposed to the real thing. MacCannell sees modern tourists as on a quest for authenticity, which is frequently presented to them as "staged authenticity," a false front that masks the real back stage to which they do not have access. For both Boorstin and MacCannell, there is a real authentic culture located somewhere, beyond the tourist view. Contemporary anthropologists would not agree with the early work of Boorstin and MacCannell, for as anthropologists now know, there are no originals, and a single "real" authentic culture does not exist. Of course, all cultures everywhere are real and authentic, if only because they are there, but this is quite different from the concept of "authenticity," which implies an inherent distinction between what is authentic and what is inauthentic, applies labels to cultures, and values one more than the other. There is no one authentic Maasai culture, in part because Maasai culture is continually changing and there are many variants. If one were to identify, say, a nineteenth-century version of Maasai culture as the real thing, one could then look further, back to the eighteenth century or to a more distant region, as the locus of the really real Maasai. It is an impossible quest.

The same vision is apparent in ethnographic realism (Marcus and Fisher 1986; Rosaldo 1989; Tedlock 2000), the basic mode of ethnographic writing until the 1960s. The classic monographs in Africa (e.g., Evans-Pritchard 1940) did not describe what the ethnographers actually observed at the time of their fieldwork but were a construction based on the prevailing anthropological vision of a pure unaltered native culture. As in anthropology, where the hypothetical ethnographic present was discredited and colonialism criticized, so too was Mayers Ranch disparaged and eventually closed. Mayers existed historically before either Bomas and the Sundowner, but it was an anachronism, doomed from the beginning.

An effort to influence the political culture of Kenya, Bomas emerged in response to those forces that led to political activism within anthropology during the 1970s, the epoch of the civil rights movement and the emergence of new nations. The genre is ethnographic activism. Bomas depicts traditional Maasai culture as fast disappearing, requiring that it be preserved in museum archives or in artistic performance. As a collective past, Maasai culture as represented at Bomas becomes part of the national heritage of postindependence Kenya. Bomas is a response to the intense nationalism that characterized many newly independent multiethnic Third World countries. The basic problem for the nation was how to express ethnicity yet simultaneously to contain it, a problem not yet resolved in many African states.

The Sundowner is an outgrowth of global media flows, electronic communication, and pervasive transnationalism. It is for foreign post-tourists, produced in the style of postmodern ethnography. Unlike Mayers, it rejects the realist genre. Unlike Bomas, it rejects nationalist rhetoric. Postmodern ethnography describes juxtapositions, pastiche, and functional inconsistency, and recognizes, even celebrates, that cultural items originating from different places and historical eras may coexist (Babcock 1999). Contemporary ethnographers no longer try to mask outside influences, nor do they see them as polluting a pure culture (Bruner 1988).

In performance, the Sundowner is more playful. It intermingles elements from the past and the present, is less concerned about points of historical origin, and does not strive for cultural purity. The comparison is not quite that neat, however, as the Sundowner tourists do occupy a colonial position and do want to view "primitive" Maasai; nevertheless, there has been a shift in the stance of the audience. Post-tourists at the Sundowner are willing to dance with the Maasai and joke with them, and they are not that fastidious about authenticity. But postmodern tourists, and ethnographers, have not entirely overcome the contradictions of their modernist and colonial pasts. Many postmodern ethnographers, it must be recognized, still struggle with an inequitable colonial relationship and vast differentials in wealth and power between themselves and the people they study. Further, ethnographers, as those who write, control how culture is represented.

That the three sites correspond to different genres of ethnographic writing is not unexpected, as both tourism and ethnography are disciplinary practices, products of the same worldwide global forces. Ethnographers are not entirely free from the dominant paradigms of their times. As an ethnographer studying tourism, ethnographic perspectives are reflected back to me by the very tourist performances that I study. The predicament, of course, is not restricted to an anthropology of tourism; it is inherent in the ethnographic enterprise (Bruner 1986).

The Questioning Gaze

I use the phrase the "questioning gaze" to describe the tourists' doubts about the credibility, authenticity, and accuracy of what is presented to them in the tourist production. The key issue is that tourists have agency, active selves that do not merely accept but interpret, and frequently question, the producers' messages (Bruner 1994; Jules-Rosette and Bruner 1994). In Bomas, authenticity both is and is not an issue—it depends on which Kenyan is speaking, as there is no monolithic local voice. Some Maasai are illiterate, others have been educated at Oxford University; some live in the game parks, others in the city; some are pastoralists, others are doctors, lawyers, and businessmen; some have a stake in the tourism industry, others have not. Urban Kenyans I know have told me they enjoy seeing their native dances at Bomas, as they do not travel frequently to their home areas, and even when they do they are not assured of witnessing a dance performance. They respect the ethnic diversity exhibited at Bomas, and they appreciate the performance as well as the entire Bomas experience. In addition to the dancing, Bomas features picnic sites, a children's playground, football, volleyball, badminton, table tennis, and a swimming pool. In other words, it is more than a display of Kenyan ethnic culture for intellectuals, ethnographers, and foreign tourists; it is a family recreational site.

Yet not all local observers share this view. Originally from Uganda, Christine Southall (a scholar specializing in East Africa) suggested to me that many Kenyan intellectuals laugh at parts of the Bomas performance, criticizing the inaccuracies in its representation of tradition and regarding its characterization of the various ethnic groups as inauthentic. In 1999, Jean Kidula, a Kenyan musicologist who has worked with the Bomas performers, explained to me that Bomas is a failed project because the original objectives were not achieved. The aim in the early 1970s was to construct a national dance troupe that would accurately perform the ethnic arts of Kenya. She feels that the dances now performed are not authentic so that Bomas has become a tourist thing, folkloristic, and commercial. The difficulty was that once the dance troupe was formed the performers began to innovate, and over the years the original tribal dance forms were changed. Kenyan people, she says, understand this but keep going to Bomas primarily because it is entertaining. To these two scholars, authenticity is important, and they criticize Bomas for not achieving it.

Commenting to me on Bomas, Jane Mayers said that "it's not true in any respect," meaning that the Maasai dance at Bomas is not necessarily performed by Maasai, that no one lives in the villages, and that their dance troupe is professional. The questions become, what is seen as true, and how does a performance derive its authority? There are different meanings of authenticity (Bruner 1994), but from my perspective, Mayers, Bomas, and the Sundowner are not authentic in the sense of being accurate, genuine, and true to a postulated original.

Anthropologists, at least in the past, have tended to regard tourism as commercial, even tacky. From the perspective of realist ethnography, tourism is a disgraceful simplification, an embarrassment, like an awkward country cousin who keeps appearing at cherished field sites (Bruner 1989; de Certeau

1984). Some U.S. anthropologists, Kenyan intellectuals, and foreign tourists might experience Bomas as being superficial and inauthentic—but that would be to miss the point. At Bomas, traditional dances are placed in such a high-tech setting and the production is so professional that the dances become detraditionalized. The modern auditorium, the bar, the signs, and the commercialism are not necessarily experienced by Kenyan visitors as an intrusion, for they serve to remind the Kenyans that they are not in a tribal village but in a national folklore museum.

Although the issue for some Kenyan intellectuals is authenticity, the issue for many Kenyan tourists, based on my interviews, is doubt about the validity of the nationalistic message of Bomas. The message of the producers is not necessarily the one received by their tourist audience. Kenyan people from all segments of society are very well aware of the reality of ethnic conflict in Kenyan society, and hence those Kenyans who visit Bomas have their doubts about the ethnic harmony portrayed there. The understanding of Kenyans in this respect is similar to the Americans who celebrate the Abraham Lincoln rags-to-riches narrative that everyone can be president, yet they know that no American of African, Native, Asian, or Hispanic descent, and no woman or Jew, has been elected president of the United States.

In this sense, Bomas is like Lévi-Strauss's (1967:202–228) definition of a myth, in that it tries to resolve a contradiction between a vision of Kenyan national integration and the reality of ethnic conflict and separatism, just as in the United States the Lincoln myth tries to resolve a contradiction between an ideology of equality and an actuality of discrimination. The function and the promise of national myths is to resolve contradictions, if not in life, then in narrative and performance. Nor is it a false consciousness, as the Marxists would have it, for most Kenyans and Americans are aware of these discrepancies.

At Mayers Ranch, many tourists had their own doubts, which they expressed to me, for the performance was too picture perfect, too neat and well scheduled, and the back stage of the performance as well as the actualities of Maasai life were too well hidden. Tourists vary, for to be a tourist is not a fixed slot to be occupied but is a role to be fashioned and performed (Jules-Rosette and Bruner 1994). Some tourists willingly surrendered themselves to the experience of the Mayers performance. One tourist told me that he was on vacation in Africa to relax, and he simply accepted whatever was offered to him. For him, there was no questioning gaze, or at least it was suppressed. Others behave as if they are in a graduate anthropology seminar. They are obsessed with issues of authenticity and question the truth value of everything. They ask, "Are these Maasai for real?"

One American student at Mayers Ranch during my visit kept muttering to herself and to anyone else who would listen that the Maasai were being exploited, which may have been the case. The African-American tourists who complained about Mayers to the Kenyan government did not see the performance as the producers intended, as a story about the English and the

Maasai, but focused on skin color, as an example of whites producing blacks. This is interesting as it exports an American political sensibility to an African context (Bruner 1996a). Tourists, however, like the rest of us, have the ability simultaneously to suspend disbelief and to harbor inner doubts, and sometimes to oscillate between one stance and the other. The questioning gaze may be pushed aside, so that tourists may delight in the excitement and danger of being with the Maasai and play, in their imagination (even temporarily and tentatively) with the colonial slot into which they are being positioned. For them, Mayers was good theater, and many made a conscious effort to engage the Mayers fantasy and to identify with the plot and the characters, at least during performance time, despite inner doubts.

The Intrav tour agency that took the group to the Sundowner was skilled and sophisticated in catering to upscale tourists. It was an "Out of Africa" tour not just in the sense of the Isak Dinesen book, but in the sense of being literally "out" of Africa, above Africa, so as to protect the tourists from hassles, waits, and crowds, and to shield them from experiencing the darker side of Africa—the poverty, starvation, brutality, disease, dirt, corruption, and civil wars. The Sundowner itself went smoothly but there was an earlier instance, a memorable occasion in Tanzania, when Africa broke through the bubble. The tourists I spoke with were very disturbed about it. On a trip from Lake Manyara to Ngorogoro Crater, over a two-hour ride, the cars carrying the tourists passed a number of painfully poor Tanzanian villages. As each village came into view, emaciated children dressed in rags ran after the cars with outstretched hands, hoping for a handout, and they continued running even after the cars had passed far beyond them. The drivers did not stop, but I saw many of the tourists continuing to look back along the dusty road at the desperate children. Afterward, with pained expression, one woman tourist commented on the shocking disparity of wealth between the members of the tour group and the Tanzanian villagers, noting the contrast between our luxury and their poverty. Another said she felt ashamed to have spent so much money on a vacation while these villagers had nothing. It was a fleeting but significant moment. The tourists talked about it for days and were obviously distraught. Its significance extended beyond that one specific incident to the entire tourist itinerary, raising the larger question in the tourist consciousness, what else was being concealed on their tour of Africa? The incident materialized an inner doubt. By carefully orchestrating the "Out of Africa" tour, the agency had tried to suppress and silence parts of Africa, but they did not entirely succeed.

The tourists' identification with Africans in this instance is reminiscent of the position of the character Dennis Finch-Hatton in Isak Dinesen's *Out of Africa* (1938). In that book, Finch-Hatton, a white colonialist, casts a critical eye on the institution of colonialism, identifies with the independent pastoral Maasai, and is ultimately buried in a Maasai grave. In structural terms, he was a bridge between the civilized and the wild, flying freely over the African landscape, with the ability to move back and forth between the two

domains of the binary. The tourists on the "Out of Africa" tour who participated in the Sundowner may want to be accepted, even blessed, by the primitive Maasai, if only temporarily, as a kind of absolution for the privileged
position that haunts the edges of their dreams. They may relish the gifts,
smiles, and dancing on the Sundowner as evidence that they are liked, or at
least welcomed, by the Maasai. The African-American woman on a walking
tour with the Maasai who encountered the lions may retell that story, not only
as a tale of unexpected adventure (always a source of good stories for tourists) but as a way of identifying herself with the Maasai.[17]

At Mayers, Bomas, and the Sundowner, there are always doubts among
the tourists about what they are "seeing," doubts that differ from tourist to tourist, but that move beyond what has so artfully been constructed for them. The
questioning gaze is a penetration of the constructedness devised by the producers, but it is also more, in a number of respects. First, there is always an unpre-
dictability of meaning about any performance, for individuals attribute their
own understandings to the event, which may not be predicted in advance, and
these understandings may change over time. Second, some tourists apply a
frame to the activity of sightseeing and to everything else that occurs within the
tour. A well-traveled tourist, for example, once whispered to me as we were
about to watch a performance, "Here comes the tourist dance." It made no difference to her what particular ethnic dance was on display, except that it was
presented within a touristic frame. It was a tourist dance, period. For other tourists, more inclined to surrender, an immersion in the physicality of the dance
activity itself was more important than any explanation or attribution of meaning. This verges on what Kirshenblatt-Gimblett (1998:203–248) describes as
an avant-garde sensibility, where the experience itself is more important than
the hermeneutics. Further, in many cases tourists simply do not understand
what they are seeing and make no effort to interpret Maasai dance and culture.
Even to those tourists most willing to open up to the experience and to accept
the producers' fantasy, there is still, in MacCannell's terms, "an ineluctable
absence of meaning to an incomplete subject" (2001:34). It is what Kirshenblatt-Gimblett (1998:72) has called the irreducibility of strangeness. Urry's
(1990, 1992) tourist gaze is too empiricist, too monolithic, too lacking in
agency, and too visual to encompass these varied tourist reactions. The tourist
gaze does not have the power of Foucault's (1979) panopticon, for it is not all-
seeing and enveloping. It is variable, and there are seepages and doubts.

In this article, I have described how the Maasai of Kenya are displayed
in three tourist sites originating in different historical eras and in disparate
social milieus. I emphasize that touristic representations of a single ethnic
group are multiple and even contradictory. I also discuss the parallels between
tourism and ethnography especially evident in the concept of the questioning
gaze. I demonstrate how ethnicity, culture, and authenticity gain and lose
meanings in diverse touristic and world contexts. My approach has been to
study local tourist performances by the methods of ethnography, to take

account of tourist agency, and then to compare systematically the various sites with attention to the national and global frames within which they are located. Constructionism, my main theoretical thrust, is not an escape from history or ethnography. Such an approach enables the ethnographer to explore similarities and differences, to embrace complexity, and to open up new possibilities.

Source: Reproduced by permission of the American Anthropological Association from *American Ethnologist*, Volume 28, Issue 4, Pages 881–908, November 2001. Not for sale or further reproduction.

Acknowledgments

Early versions of this article were presented at a conference on tourism in September 1999 at the Department of Anthropology, Yunnan University, Kunming, People's Republic of China, and in January 2000 at the University of Illinois workshop on sociocultural anthropology. I am indebted to the participants for helpful comments, to Alma Gottlieb, Arlene Torres, Nicole Tami, Richard Freeman, Bruno Nettl, the anonymous reviewers of *American Ethnologist*, and the University of Illinois Foundation and Ann and Paul Krouse for financial support enabling my wife and me to participate in the 1999 African trip. In all of my fieldwork, my wife, Elaine C. Bruner, has been an insightful and helpful partner.

Notes

[1] Recent works on tourism include Abram et al. 1997; Boissevain 1996; Castaneda 1996; Chambers 2000; Cohen 1996; Crick 1994; Dann 1996; Desmond 1999; Handler and Gable 1997; Kirshenblatt-Gimblett 1998; Lanfant et al. 1995; Lavie and Swedenburg 1994; Löfgren 1999; Nash 1996; Oakes 1998; Picard 1996; Rojek and Urry 1997; Schein 2000; and Selwyn 1996.

[2] Adams 1998 and Cheung 1999 are exceptions.

[3] My "questioning gaze" was inspired by MacCannell's (2001) concept of the "second gaze," which he developed in opposition to Urry's (1990) "tourist gaze." I agree with most of MacCannell's critique of Urry. See also Kasfir 1999.

[4] When referring to the Maasai people, current scholarly practice is to use a double *aa*, derived from the language group Maa. The game reserve Masai Mara, a proper name, is spelled with a single *a*.

[5] In 1984, Barbara Kirshenblatt-Gimblett and I did fieldwork together at Mayers Ranch, which we published, and at Bomas, which we did not publish. I returned to Kenya in 1995 and 1999, revisited old sites, gathered new data, and initiated fieldwork on Maasai tourism on the Mara, including the Sundowner. For the past 15 years, Kirshenblatt-Gimblett has influenced my work on the Maasai and on tourism.

[6] Members of the tour group had to obtain visas, but their passports were collected by the Intrav tour guides who handled all the immigration and customs arrangements.

[7] Bomas of Kenya was initiated by the government in 1971 and opened in 1973 under the Kenya Tourist Development Corporation, a part of the Ministry of Tourism and Wildlife.

[8] As there are 42 ethnic groups in Kenya, but only 11 traditional villages in Bomas, many groups are left out, although some are represented in performance. There is no representation of minorities such as the resident Indian population.

[9] It will be helpful to examine the charges for admission to the Bomas performance. At the time of my visit, a Kenyan citizen paid about one-third the amount charged to a foreign tour-

ist, and a resident child paid only about one-third of the amount paid by a Kenyan adult, making it financially feasible for many Kenyans to come to Bomas for a family outing with their children.

[10] The African Classic Tours (1986) brochure states:

> Here in East Africa, we can still view the world as our primitive ancestors saw it, in its natural state, without the influences of modern civilization. . . . Here are the living remains of prehistoric human cultures, people who still live by hunting and gathering: nomadic peoples living in small family groups. Here we can view the daily struggle for survival . . . and see people and wildlife living, for the most part, unaffected by our rapidly changing society.

[11] All quotes are from the brochure for the Intrav "On Safari in Africa" trip February 2 to 25, 1999.

[12] At this point, I must acknowledge the ambiguity of my subject position especially at the Sundowner, for I oscillated between being a tourist and being an ethnographer, on the one hand enjoying the scene, talking with the tourists, avidly taking photographs, and on the other hand studying the event, making ethnographic observations, and writing field notes (see Bruner 1996b). All ethnographers occasionally experience a similar oscillation, between being there as a participant in another culture (merging into the ongoing activity) and the demands of being a scholar, striving for the distance and objectivity necessary to write for an anthropological audience. I have felt this tension the most in my work on tourism rather than in other ethnographic endeavors (cf. Bruner 1999).

[13] I am indebted to Mulu Muia, Duncan Muriuki, and to Jean Kidula for helpful information on the musical scene in Kenya. I also note that data was gathered by modern electronic means, by e-mail, and the Internet. Bomas, Kichwa Tembo tented camp, and Them Mushrooms all have their own Web sites.

[14] I do not know the relationship between the use of Hakuna Matata in "Jambo Bwana" and in the Elton John–Tim Rice song. Neither the lyrics nor music are the same, but the phrase, Hakuna Matata, is equally prominent in both songs.

[15] Them Mushrooms also are known for reggae, and for fusions of reggae with local musical traditions. Them Mushrooms are credited with recording, in 1981, the first reggae song in East Africa, with CBS Kenya Records. Their inspiration was Bob Marley, the Jamaican reggae musician (Them Mushrooms 2000). Reggae also has a political meaning, connected to the Rastafarians.

[16] Wood (1999) reports that funds flow inequitably to the Maasai chiefs and politicians, and there have been many accusations of corruption. Berger (1996) discusses these inequities, offers solutions, and shows how the Maasai are being integrated into the tourism industry in Kenya. Kiros Lekaris, Stanley Ole Mpakany, Meegesh Nadallah, and Gerald Ole Selembo have helped me better to understand how the Maasai on the Mara do profit economically from safari tourism.

[17] I thank an anonymous reviewer for the *American Ethnologist* for many of the ideas in this paragraph.

References

Abram, Simone, Jacqueline Waldren, and Donald V. L. Macleod, eds. 1997. *Tourists and Tourism: Identifying with People and Places*. Oxford: Berg.

Adams, Kathleen M. 1998. "Domestic Tourism and Nation-Building in South Sulawesi." *Indonesia and the Malay World* 26(75): 77–96.

Anagnost, Ann. 1993. "The Nationscape: Movement in the Field of Vision." *Positions* 1(3): 585–606.

Appadurai, Arjun. 1988. "Putting Hierarchy in Its Place." *Cultural Anthropology* 3(1): 36–49.

———. 1991. "Global Ethnoscapes: Notes and Queries for a Transnational Anthropology," in *Recapturing Anthropology: Working in the Present*, ed. Richard G. Fox, pp. 191–210. Santa Fe, NM: School of American Research Press.

Asad, Talal, ed. 1973. *Anthropology and the Colonial Encounter*. London: Ithaca Press.

Babcock, Barbara. 1990. "A New Mexican Rebecca: Imaging Pueblo Women," in *Inventing the Southwest*, [Special Issue] *Journal of the Southwest* 32(4): 383–437.

———. 1999. "Subject to Writing: The Victor Turner Prize and the Anthropological Text." [Special Issue] *Anthropology and Humanism* 24(2): 91–73.

Benedict, Burton. 1983. *The Anthropology of World's Fairs: San Francisco's Panama Pacific International Exposition of 1915*. London: Scolar Press.

Berger, Dhyani J. 1996. "The Challenge of Integrating Maasai Tradition with Tourism," in *People and Tourism in Fragile Environments*, ed. Martin F. Price, pp. 175–197. Chichester, UK: John Wiley and Sons.

Boissevain, Jeremy, ed. 1996. *Coping with Tourists: European Reaction to Mass Tourism*. Providence, RI: Berghahn.

Bomas of Kenya. 2000. Bomas of Kenya Limited. Electronic document available at http://www.africaonline.co.ke/bomaskenya/profile.html [accessed July 2, 2001].

Boorstin, Daniel J. 1961. *The Image: A Guide to Pseudo-Events in America*. New York: Harper and Row.

Bruner, Edward M. 1986. "Ethnography as Narrative," in *The Anthropology of Experience*, ed. Victor Turner and Edward M. Bruner, pp. 139–155. Urbana: University of Illinois Press.

———. 1988 [1984]. *Text, Play and Story: The Construction and Reconstruction of Self and Society*. Proceedings, American Ethnological Society. Long Grove, IL: Waveland Press.

———. 1989. "On Cannibals, Tourists, and Ethnographers." *Cultural Anthropology* 4(4): 438–445.

———. 1994. "Abraham Lincoln as Authentic Reproduction: A Critique of Postmodernism." *American Anthropologist* 96(2): 397–415.

———. 1996a. "Tourism in Ghana: The Representation of Slavery and the Return of the Black Diaspora." *American Anthropologist* 98(2): 290–304.

———. 1996b. "Tourism in the Balinese Borderzone," in *Displacement, Diaspora, and Geographies of Identity*, ed. Smadar Lavie and Ted Swedenburg, pp. 157–179. Durham, NC: Duke University Press.

———. 1999. "Return to Sumatra: 1957, 1997." *American Ethnologist* 26(2): 461–477.

———. 2000. *Ethnic Theme Parks: Conflicting Interpretations*. Paper presented at the annual meeting of the American Anthropological Association, San Francisco, November 16.

Bruner, Edward M., and Barbara Kirshenblatt-Gimblett. 1994. "Maasai on the Lawn: Tourist Realism in East Africa." *Cultural Anthropology* 9(2): 435–470.

Castaneda, Quetzil E. 1996. *In the Museum of Maya Culture: Touring Chichén Itzá*. Minneapolis: University of Minnesota Press.

Chambers, Erve. 2000. *Native Tours: The Anthropology of Travel and Tourism*. Long Grove, IL: Waveland.

Cheung, Sidney C. H. 1999. "The Meanings of a Heritage Trail in Hong Kong." *Annals of Tourism Research* 26(3): 570–588.

Chilungu, Simeon W. 1985. "Kenya: Recent Developments and Challenges." *Cultural Survival Quarterly* 9(3): 15–17.

Cohen, Erik. 1979. "A Phenomenology of Tourist Experiences." *Sociology* 13(2): 179–201.

———. 1996. *Thai Tourism*. Bangkok: White Lotus.

Crick, Malcolm. 1994. *Resplendent Sites, Discordant Voices: Sri Lankans and International Tourism*. Switzerland: Harwood Academic Publishers.

Dann, Graham M. S. 1996. *The Language of Tourism: A Sociolinguistic Perspective*. Wallingford: CAB International.

de Certeau, Michel. 1984. *The Practice of Everyday Life*, trans. Steven Rendall. Berkeley: University of California Press.

Desmond, Jane C. 1999. *Staging Tourism: Bodies on Display from Waikiki to Sea World.* Chicago: University of Chicago Press.

Dinesen, Isak. 1938. *Out of Africa.* New York: Random House.

Eggan, Fred. 1954. "Social Anthropology and the Method of Controlled Comparison." *American Anthropologist* 56(5): 743–763.

Errington, Shelly. 1998. *The Death of Authentic Primitive Art and Other Tales of Progress.* Berkeley: University of California Press.

Evans-Pritchard, E. E. 1940. *The Nuer.* Oxford: Oxford University Press.

Feifer, Maxine. 1985. *Going Places.* London: Macmillan.

Foucault, Michel. 1979. *Discipline and Punishment: The Birth of the Prison*, trans. Alan Sheridan. New York: Vintage.

Geertz, Clifford. 1983. *Local Knowledge: Further Essays in Interpretive Anthropology.* New York: Basic Books.

Geschiere, Peter. 1997. *The Modernity of Witchcraft: Politics and the Occult in Postcolonial Africa.* Charlottesville: University Press of Virginia.

Gilroy, Paul. 1993. *The Black Atlantic: Modernity and Double Consciousness.* Cambridge, MA: Harvard University Press.

Graburn, Nelson. 1989. "Tourism: The Sacred Journey," in *Hosts and Guests: The Anthropology of Tourism*, 2nd edition, ed. Valene L. Smith, pp. 21–36. Philadelphia: University of Pennsylvania Press.

Handler, Richard, and Eric Gable. 1996. *The New History in an Old Museum: Creating the Past at Colonial Williamsburg.* Durham, NC: Duke University Press.

Horne, Donald. 1992. *The Intelligent Tourist.* McMahons Point, New South Wales, Australia: Margaret Gee.

Hymes, Dell, ed. 1972. *Reinventing Anthropology.* New York: Vintage Books.

Jules-Rosette, Bennetta, and Edward M. Bruner. 1994. "Tourism as Process." *Annals of Tourism Research* 21(2): 404–406.

Kahn, Miriam. 2000. "Tahiti Intertwined: Ancestral Land, Tourist Postcard, and Nuclear Test Site." *American Anthropologist* 102(1): 7–26.

Kasfir, Sidney Littlefield. 1999. "Samburu Souvenirs: Representations of a Land in Amber," in *Unpacking Culture: Art and Commodity in Colonial and Postcolonial Worlds*, ed. Ruth B. Phillips and Christopher B. Steiner, pp. 66–82. Berkeley: University of California Press.

Kichwa Tembo. 2000. Kichwa Tembo Tented Camp. Electronic document available at http://www.ccafrica.com/destinations/Kenya/Kichwa/default.htm [accessed June 20, 2001].

Kirshenblatt-Gimblett, Barbara. 1998. *Destination Culture: Tourism, Museums, and Heritage.* Berkeley: University of California Press.

Knowles, Joan N., and D. P. Collett. 1989. "Nature as Myth, Symbol and Action: Notes Towards a Historical Understanding of Development and Conservation in Kenyan Maasailand." *Africa* 59(4): 433–460.

Lanfant, Marie-Françoise, John Allcock, and Edward M. Bruner, eds. 1995. *International Tourism: Identity and Change.* London: Sage.

Lavie, Smadar, and Ted Swedenburg, eds. 1994. *Displacement, Diaspora, and Geographies of Identity.* Durham, NC: Duke University Press.

Lévi-Strauss, Claude. 1967. *Structural Anthropology*, trans. Claire Jacobson and Brooke Grundfest Schoepf. New York: Anchor Books.

Leys, Colin. 1975. *Underdevelopment in Kenya: The Political Economy of Neo-Colonialism.* London: Heinemann.

The Lion King. 1994. Directed by Roger Allersand and Rob Minkoff. Walt Disney Pictures.

Löfgren, Orvar. 1999. *On Holiday: A History of Vacationing*. Berkeley: University of California Press.

MacCannell, Dean. 1976. *The Tourist: A New Theory of the Leisure Class*. New York: Schocken.

———. 1992. *Empty Meeting Grounds: The Tourist Papers*. London: Routledge.

———. 2001. "Tourist Agency." *Tourist Studies* 1(1): 23–37.

Marcus, George, and Michael M. J. Fischer. 1986. *Anthropology as Cultural Critique: An Experimental Moment in the Human Sciences*. Chicago: University of Chicago Press.

Mullaney, Steven. 1983. "Strange Things, Gross Terms, Curious Customs: The Rehearsal of Cultures in the Late Renaissance." *Representations* 3:45–48.

Nash, Dennison. 1989. "Tourism as a Form of Imperialism," in *Hosts and Guests: The Anthropology of Tourism*, 2nd edition, ed. Valene L. Smith, pp. 37–52. Philadelphia: University of Pennsylvania Press.

———. 1996. *The Anthropology of Tourism*. Oxford: Pergamon.

Oakes, Tim. 1998. *Tourism and Modernity in China*. London: Routledge.

Okumu, John J. 1975. "The Problem of Tribalism in Kenya," in *Race and Ethnicity in Africa*, ed. Pierre L. van den Berghe, pp. 181–202. Nairobi: East African Publishing Company.

Out of Africa. 1985. Directed by Sydney Pollack. Mirage Enterprises Production.

Pearce, Philip L. 1982. *The Sociology of Tourist Behavior*. Oxford: Pergamon.

Pemberton, John. 1993. "Recollections from Beautiful Indonesia (Somewhere beyond the Postmodern)." *Public Culture* 6(2): 241—262.

Picard, Michel. 1996. *Bali: Cultural Tourism and Touristic Culture*. Singapore: Archipelago Press.

Rojek, Chris, and John Urry, eds. 1997. *Touring Cultures: Transformations of Travel and Theory*. London: Routledge.

Rosaldo, Renato. 1989. *Culture and Truth: The Remaking of Social Analysis*. Boston: Beacon Press.

Sahlins, Marshall. 1981. *Historical Metaphors and Mythical Realities: Structure in the Early History of the Sandwich Islands Kingdom*. Ann Arbor: University of Michigan Press.

Schein, Louisa. 2000. *Minority Rules: The Miao and the Feminine in China's Cultural Politics*. Durham, NC: Duke University Press.

Selwyn, Tom, ed. 1996. *The Tourist Image: Myths and Myth Making in Tourism*. Chichester, UK: John Wiley and Sons.

Smith, Valene L., ed. 1989. *Hosts and Guests: The Anthropology of Tourism*, 2nd edition. Philadelphia: University of Pennsylvania Press.

Spear, Thomas, and Richard Waller. 1993. *Being Maasai: Ethnicity and Identity in East Africa*. London: James Currey.

Stanley, Nick. 1998. *Being Ourselves for You: The Global Display of Cultures*. London: Middlesex University Press.

Tedlock, Barbara. 2000. "Ethnography and Ethnographic Representation," in *Handbook of Qualitative Research*, 2nd edition, ed. Norman K. Denzin and Yvonna S. Lincoln, pp. 455–486. Thousand Oaks, CA: Sage.

Them Mushrooms. 2000. Electronic document available at:
http://www.musikmuseet.se/mmm/africa/mushrooms.html [accessed June 15, 2001].
http://stockholm.music.museum/mmm/africa/mushroom.html [accessed June 27, 2003].

Urry, John. 1990. *The Tourist Gaze*. London: Sage.

———. 1992. "The Tourist Gaze Revisited." *American Behavioral Scientist* 36(2): 172–186.

Vickers, Adrian. 1989. *Bali: A Paradise Created*. Berkeley: Periplus Editions.

Wood, Megan Epler. 1999. Ecotourism in the Masai Mara: An Interview with Meitamei Ole Dapash. *Cultural Survival* 23(2): 51–54.

10

Performing Tourism, Staging Tourism: (Re)producing Tourist Space and Practice

Tim Edensor

In this chapter, I draw on a series of associations, examples, and theoretical perspectives to explore the possibilities opened up by considering tourism as a form of performance. I suggest ways in which tourist studies might escape from the theoretical straitjacket that has bounded it for so long and further propose that tourism should be understood by its imbrication in the everyday rather than as a special, separate field of activity and enquiry.

By using the metaphor of performance, we can explore why we carry out particular habits and practices and consequently reproduce and challenge the social world. I will highlight the multiple, ever-changing structures of the tourist industry and the dynamic agency of tourists, which continually (re)produce diverse forms of tourism and space. Typologies (Smith 1989; Cohen 1979) can identify regularities but should be conceived as describing different tourist practices, rather than types of people, and as roles adopted, rather than social categories made manifest. The theoretical fixings that such delineations perpetrate deny the subjective reconstitution of tourism by tourists. Tourism is a process that involves the ongoing (re)construction of praxis and space in shared contexts. But this (re)production is never assured, for despite the prevalence of codes and norms, tourist conventions can be destabilized by rebellious performances or by multiple, simultaneous enactments on the same stage. I will explore the production of tourism as a series of staged events and spaces and as an array of performative techniques and dispositions.

Staging Tourism, Producing Dramas

Tourism takes place within meaningful spatial contexts. Different tourist ventures are carried out upon particular stages—on beaches and mountains, in cities, heritage sites, museums, and theme parks. These settings are distinguished by boundedness, whether physical or symbolic, and are often organized—or stage-managed—to provide and sustain common-sense understandings about what activities should take place. Indeed, the coherence of most tourist performances depends on their being performed in specific "theaters."

While such stagings cannot determine the kinds of performance that occur, the processes of commodification, regulation, and representation that reproduce performative conventions ensure that distinctive performances can be identified at most sites. Nevertheless, competing ideas about what particular sites symbolize may generate contrasting performances.

Tourist performance is socially and spatially regulated to varying extents. The nature of the tourist stage contextualizes performance: whether it is carefully managed, facilitates transit, and contains discretely situated objects (props) around which performance is organized or whether its boundaries are blurred, it is cluttered with other actors playing different roles, is full of shifting scenes and random events or juxtapositions, and can be crossed from a range of angles. Put another way, the organization, materiality, and aesthetic and sensual qualities of tourist space influences—but does not determine—the kinds of performances that tourists undertake. To explore these stagings, I have written elsewhere of the distinction between "enclavic" and "heterogeneous" space (Edensor 1998a, 2000).

Enclavic tourist space is akin to Sibley's "purified" spaces, which are strongly circumscribed and framed, wherein conformity to rules and adherence to centralized regulation hold sway (1988:412), or may be typified as "single-purpose spaces." Carefully planned and managed to provide specific standards of cleanliness, service, décor, and "ambience," the continual upkeep of enclavic spaces is crucial to minimize underlying ambiguity and contradiction. Tourists are subject to a "soft control" (Ritzer and Liska 1997:106)—guards, guides, and CCTV cameras that monitor tourists' behavior—whereas in order to maintain a clear spatial boundary, local workers are excluded. Shielded from potentially offensive sights, sounds, and smells, these "environmental bubbles" provide in-house recreational facilities, including displays of local culture.

Heterogeneous tourist space, by contrast, is "weakly classified," with blurred boundaries, and is a multipurpose space in which a wide range of activities and people coexist. Tourist facilities coincide with businesses, public and private institutions, and domestic housing, and tourists mingle with locals, including touts. Generally, tourism has often emerged in an unplanned and contingent process, and an unplanned bricolage of structures and designs provides a contrasting aesthetic context. In some ways, heterogeneous tourist spaces provide stages where transitional identities may be performed along-side the everyday enactments of residents, passers-by, and workers.

This schematic division is designed to draw attention to the material and symbolic context in which tourism is performed, yet equally, the nature of the stage is dependent on the kinds of performance enacted upon it. Care-fully stage-managed spaces may be transformed by the presence of tourists who adhere to different norms. Thus, stages can continually change, can expand and contract. Most stages are ambiguous; they are sites for different performances. A paradox of the production of tourist space concerns the intensification of attempts to design a themed space and the increasingly pro-miscuous nature of tourism, whereby tourist stages proliferate.

I now focus on the diverse ways in which tourism is staged by hum-drum and spectacular rituals, by the production of themed and designed spaces, through the nexus between tourism and film, in the commodification of cultures, and through the work of diverse workers.

Rituals and Dramas Staged for Tourists

Incorporating Rituals.   Grand traditional rituals such as the Trooping of the Colour and the Edinburgh Military Tattoo and various Independence Day celebrations, religious rituals, and historical commemorations often articulate a "meta-social commentary" (Geertz 1993) that celebrates and reproduces social ideals and conventions. In these "invented" ceremonies (Hobsbawm and Ranger 1983), the transmission of state ideologies is typi-cally achieved through grandiloquent pageantry and solemn, precise move-ments. These nationalist ceremonial dramas have the effect of inculcating specifiable forms of conduct and comportment, akin to what Paul Connerton (1989) describes as "incorporating rituals" (contrasted to "inscriptive" rituals such as photography and writing) through which groups transmit ideals and reproduce memory by mapping them onto symbolic and familiar spaces. Organized to minimize ambiguity, such dramas demand stylized and repeti-tive performances that conform to temporal and bodily conventions, forming part of "social habit memory." The organization of the stage and the frame-work for performance is designed to minimize improvisation, questioning, contestation, and mockery, although such subversions must be continually held at bay.

Pleasurable Carnivals.   Connerton (1989) argues that such rituals are most efficacious in their attempts to fix the meaning of sites and inscribe identity into the habit-body of the actors. His account usefully draws atten-tion to the somatic involvement in disciplined performances, but such

Members of the Evzones, a ceremonial unit of the Hellenic Army, guard the monument of the Unknown Soldier in front of the Greek Parliament and Presidential Mansion in Athens. (Photo by S. Gmelch)

embodied action is also apparent in more carnivalesque ceremonies, for more convivial, sensual, improvisational, and playful ceremonies can be equally powerful as memorable and significant events. Fixing performance does not always preserve it against staleness and irrelevance. Flexible and contingent performances, which promote affective and expressive performances, are equally successful in proving memorable tourist experiences

Dramas Bringing Workers and Tourists Together.   Besides these established festivals, many tourist attractions now use the site as a theatrical setting. Employing actors to take on both situated and roving roles, these small dramas frequently coerce visitors into performing with the paid actors. They range from the sophisticated dramas staged at Universal Studios in Los Angeles to the short historical playlets staged on Stirling's medieval streets.

At Granada Studios in Manchester, UK, visitors are encouraged to enter a simulacrum of the interior of the House of Commons. They are channeled into opposition and government benches whereupon a humorous parliamentary debate is staged by professional actors, who undertake antagonistic stances with regard to a preselected topical issue. The orotund enunciations of these actors are supplemented by visitors who are cajoled into taking on roles in support of particular political positions. Indeed, the success of the occasion partly depends on the degree to which the tourist participants are able to immerse themselves in their roles.

An eighteenth-century cotton mill, Quarry Bank Mill, is a popular heritage attraction in Cheshire. Besides the displays of social conditions and the working looms that visitors inspect, several costumed actors wander around the site, approach visitors, and entangle them in dramas and role-play. One such character is the recruitment officer of the mill, dressed in tweeds and with authoritative demeanor, who demands of parents that they encourage their children to work in the factory. The actors imaginatively dramatize the historical prevalence of child labor by encouraging parents to take up a playful make-believe role toward their child. By imploring that they take up the offer of work, or encouraging their hostility toward the labor hirer, parents in turn embroil the child in the drama. Likewise, at The Apprentice House,

> a team of museum interpreters bring the house the life. Dressed in costume, they engage visitors in conversation . . . often in-role as one of the real characters who lived at the house. . . . Visitors are encouraged to touch all

A costumed blacksmith demonstrates his craft at Quarry Bank Mill. (Photo by Inc/ Shutterstock.com)

> the objects; test the straw filled beds, stir the porridge in the kitchen, and
> pump water from the well in the yard. (http://www.quarrybankmill.org.uk)

Of course, provoking tourists to perform in these ways may backfire: they may feel uncomfortable and embarrassed at such intrusions.

These examples show the range of staged dramas provided in tourist contexts, from large rituals, to festive, playful engagements. They are distinguished by the kind of performative participation expected of tourists, by the level of stage-management, and whether they encourage or restrict improvisation and play.

Sceneography and Stage-Design

Besides these actual performances in distinct tourist settings, there is an ongoing proliferation of what Gottdiener (1997) calls "themed" spaces. Perhaps Chaney exaggerates in claiming that as tourists "we are above all else performers in our own dramas on stages the industry has provided" (1993:64), but there is nevertheless a profusion of such stages in specialized tourist enclaves and in more quotidian spaces. Highly encoded shopping malls, festival marketplaces, heritage sites, cultural quarters, and waterfront attractions comprise an expanding sector of tourist space. The extension of these themed spaces into shopping centers and high streets include themed pubs and cafés. The Rainforest Café, it is claimed,

> is unlike any other dining experience you'll encounter. Your adventure
> begins as soon as you check in at the elephant. Enter the dining area and
> it's like stepping into the jungle with a canopy of lush foliage overhead,
> wildlife along the way, and even a thunderstorm in the distance. (http://
> www.rainforest café.com)

The Celtic Dragon Pub Company offers three "Irish" themed design packages, namely, an "Irish country look," the "city pub," and the upscale "castle and manor house" theme where "all guests will feel like lords and ladies" (http://www/celtic dragonpubco.com).

Sugar Beach in Mauritius, an exclusive tourist enclave, reconstructs elements of an imaginary luxurious colonial past: "built in the style of a Creole plantation, complete with manor house" (http://www.tropical.co.uk/mauritus/sugarbe.html). Incorporating extensively landscaped lawns and hundreds of palm trees, the performances of "native" cultures can be sampled in staged shows.

In tourist enclaves like Sugar Beach, stage managers attempt to "create and control a cultural as well as a physical environment" (Freitag 1994:541), where strict environmental and aesthetic monitoring produces a landscape encoded with clear visual cues and codes. Through the use of such "sceneography" (Gottdiener 1997:73), the tourist gaze is directed to particular attractions and commodities and away from "extraneous chaotic elements," reducing "visual and functional forms to a few key images" (Rojek 1995:62). A limited range of mediatized motifs or a few key exoticisms are featured that, like many commodity-landscapes, promise infinite variety and difference while delivering a controlled, stereotyped "Otherness" (Mitchell 1995:119). Here, carnival imagery and ambience—the different, erotic and chaotic—is co-opted by designers.

These new technologies of entertainment penetrate mundane settings as well as touristic "honeypots," as selling culture becomes part of growth strategies. The sheer intertextuality of these themed spaces—the innumerable links with commodities, media, and other spaces—consolidate their effect with a string of associations. As always, however, we must be aware of over-determining the effect of such powerful commercial strategies on tourists.

Mediated Spaces

Another way in which sites can be dramatically contextualized, produced as theatrical spaces, is through capitalizing on a nexus between media and place. The production of film and television dramas in identifiable geographical settings has given rise to a proliferation of tourist sites.

After the Hollywood film *Braveheart*, which depicts William Wallace's fourteenth-century struggle against the English for Scottish independence, the Loch Lomond, Trossachs and Stirling Tourist Board produced an advertisement that read, "Where the Highlands met the Lowlands, step into the

A re-created "flake" on which cod were dried. Part of the Random Passage television miniseries set, now a popular tourist site, located in New Bonaventure, Newfoundland. (Photo by S. Gmelch)

echoes of Rob Roy, Robert the Bruce and William Wallace—Braveheart Country." In addition, they designed an advertisement for international transmission in cinemas before the showing of *Braveheart*. Combining scenes from the film with aerial views of the local Wallace Monument and surrounding scenery, the ad ends with the exhortation to "experience the very heart of Scotland: Stirling is Braveheart Country." This explicit dramatic representation of Stirling was responsible for a massive increase in tourist numbers in the years following the film. Subsequently, new guided tours visited key sites of the conflict, and theatrical presentations and exhibitions were promoted to consolidate interest in the story. Nevertheless, as I have argued elsewhere (Edensor, 1998b), this Hollywood portrayal did not act to empty out all meaning from the Wallace myth. On the contrary, the film and the ensuing expansion of tourism led to a more intense, contested, and reflexive search for the contemporary political and cultural significance of Wallace.

Key Workers

Phil Crang (1997) has examined how the tourist product is performed by tourist workers, who are trained to enact roles that fit in with their institutional setting and express attributes such as deference, eagerness to please, and friendliness. These "cast members"—as they are appositely termed at the various Disney theme parks—are often required to wear outfits and expressions that harmonize with themed environments. Crucially, these environments are "meaningful settings that tourists consume and tourism employees help produce" (Crang 1997:143). Here I want to discuss three kinds of workers who produce staged tourism in different ways.

Directors and Stage Managers. The stage management of tourist space, the directing of tourists, and the choreographing of their movement can reveal the spatial and social controls that assist and regulate performance. For instance, at the Taj Mahal, stage management is the work of a host of workers from cleaning teams, stonemasons and other artisans, gatekeepers, police, gardeners, and guides who maintain its upkeep. To retain its allure of perfection, the stage needs to be kept uncluttered and pristine. Directors are most evident in guided tours where guides direct tourists to look at particular features, suggest places for photographic performances, and provide scripted commentary. For instance, large parties are directed to the seat where Princess Diana sat and are invited to emulate the Royal photograph. These tour personnel also choreograph tourists' movements, chaperoning them along prescribed paths and restraining those who stray. Such tourist choreographies—sequential, linear, and purposive—have been compared to the patterns of migratory birds as "they trace and retrace the same restricted set of options" (MacDonald 1997:153). Thus, "appropriate" behavior and performative procedures are regulated by these key personnel who, by synthesizing meaning and action, reinforce a commonsense praxis and re-encode enactive norms.

Performing Cultures, Performing "Otherness." In collecting signs of local or national distinctiveness, tourists feast on indigenous "folkloric" customs. Tour companies and hotels often organize displays of "native" dancing and music, selecting which cultural aspects are accessible and which should be edited out, charting a course between "exoticism" and comprehensibility. Performances are typically devised to titillate tourists without alienating them by sticking too closely to complicated cultural meanings. Where non-Western dramas are produced for Western tourists, the colonial origins of much tourism becomes acutely highlighted as, for instance, when smiling dancing girls posture for the camera. This cultural staging inevitably raises controversies about the reproduction of stereotypes associated with primitivism, exoticism, and eroticism. Paradoxically though, it may also replenish moribund local traditions (Wood 1998).

The Roles of Cultural Intermediaries. Finally, I want to suggest that not all the roles of tourist workers are as rigid as they may seem. For example, they may act as cultural intermediaries who oil the wheels of tourist–local interaction and exchange. The work of these people raises the complex negotiation of roles between themselves and tourists and the cultural power expressed by each in contexts of interaction: whether there is scope for independent action or whether their actions are institutionalized by the need to conform to tourist expectations and managerial decisions about delivering the tourist product.

Tourists as Performers

Besides the increasingly staged nature of tourism, tourist space is also (re)produced by tourists, who perform diverse meanings about symbolic places, dramatizing their allegiance to places and kinds of action. Tourist performance maps out individual and group identities and alludes to imagined geographies of which the stage may be part.

Below, I provide diverse examples to highlight distinct forms of tourist enactment and the conventions that contextualize and inform them. I explore directed and identity-oriented performances and then look at some enactments that contest these norms. Tourist epistemologies are shaped by an orientation toward the kinds of experiences that are available, how they can be achieved, and what is appropriate in their execution. When tourists enter particular stages, they are usually informed by preexisting discursive, practical, embodied norms that help to guide their performative orientations and achieve a working consensus about what to do. Here performance is a "discrete concretization of cultural assumptions" (Carlson 1996:16) that mingle everyday and tourist codes of action.

Performance is an interactive and contingent process that succeeds according to the skill of the actors, the context within which it is performed, and the way in which it is interpreted by an audience. Even the most delineated social performance must be reenacted in different conditions, and its reception may be unpredictable. Each performance can never be exactly reproduced, and fixity of meaning must be continually strived for (Schieffelin 1998:196–199).

Directed Performances

I have discussed above how tourist stages are replete with cues and directors. Props, stagehands, stage managers, and directors constitute a support network that facilitates, guides, and organizes tourist performances according to normative conventions and industry imperatives. Tourist spectacles are contextualized for visitors by the professional interpreters of "customized" travel. Besides these key workers, Mark Neumann points out:

> Tourists are rarely left to draw their own conclusions about objects or places before them. Instead, they more often confront a body of public discourse—signs, maps, guides and guide books—that repeatedly mark the boundaries of significance and value at tourist sites. (1988:24)

This may be an exaggeration, but at information-saturated and carefully themed tourist sites, it can be difficult to avoid being drawn to information boards, staged spectacles, and evident pathways. In addition to these signs, guidebooks are also replete with cues about what to look at, what information to consider. As condensed suggestions to familiarize tourists with cultures and spaces—shorthand cues for performance—such directions inevitably omit infinite other ways of looking at and understanding sites. In this sense, guidebooks are a kind of master script for tourists, which reduces disorientation and guides action (see Bhattacharyya 1997). Every one of the numerous accounts about and guidebooks to the Taj Mahal recommends when the site should be viewed—at which time of day the light is most beneficial. Although each time has its champions—"moonlighters," "mid-dayers," and so on—the discourse acts to engage tourist consideration about the how and when of gazing (Edensor 1998a). However, rather than impugning the outlook of tourists who conform to such expectations, it is worth remembering that the desire for comfort, familiarity, and predictability assists relaxation. By not resisting the apparatus of meaning and action, tourists may be choosing to avoid the usual work and domestic imperatives. There is pleasure in opting out of responsibility.

Identity-Oriented Performances

Certain tourist performances are intended to draw attention to the Self. Tourism becomes a vehicle for transmitting identity by undertaking a particular form of travel in a particular style. For instance, backpackers are often concerned with distinguishing themselves from others—from package tourists, who they often regard as not individualistic. They like to wander off the "beaten track" and may seek apparently unorthodox mystical, drug-enhanced, and other countercultural experiences. Yet they often rely on *Lonely Planet* and *Rough Guides* to mediate their experience of unfamiliar places and customs. Moreover, part of being a backpacker entails sharing and disputing practical, aesthetic, and ethical aspects of "backpacker lore."

In this shared milieu of space, action. and meaning, status and distinction is acquired and transmitted. Thus, performance centers upon how far off the beaten track they have gone, the quality of their encounters with "locals," and their commitment to backpacking—variously identified by the length of the trip, degree of hardship, and disdain for material comforts, goods, and experiences regarded as "touristic (Edensor, 1998a; Desforges 1998; Munt 1994). In addition, there are a number of signs that are wielded in the performance of this status-oriented identity. Clothing is often "rough and ready," and apparently signifies scorn for fashion, or is local apparel to signify "going native." Books are used among backpackers to signify a shared disposition towards exploration, a form of cultural capital that signifies a sophisticated facility to attune oneself to cultural "Otherness" (favorites on "The List" include *The Beach, Out of Africa, 100 Years of Solitude, Zen and the Art of Motorcycle Maintenance, Catch 22*).[1]

Nonconformist Tourist Performances

Above I have considered the normative performance of tourism, the tight adherence to scripts, roles, and direction. Now I explore kinds of tourist performance that "escape" from normative enactment. As Judith Butler has pointed out, knowing the codes of performance via "forced reiteration of norms" (1993:94), besides fixing meaning, also provides a template from which to deviate and offers an opportunity to mark subjectivity by rebelling against these conventions.

Ironic, Cynical, "Post-Tourist" Performances. As Feifer (1985) has contended, "post-tourists" revel in the artificiality and staging of much tourism. This seems akin to what Goffman (1959) calls "role-distance," here expressed as a reflexive awareness of the constructed nature of a role but an unwillingness to challenge it. Nevertheless, post-tourists enact a mildly subversive performance, revealing tourist conventions. This is exemplified by the ironic performance of American tourists at the Taj Mahal. Standing before the monument as a member of their party wielded a video camera, framing them from the most conventional angle, the tourists engaged in horseplay and pulled grotesque faces and looks of mock astonishment. The following exchange took place:

TOURIST 1: OK guys, line up and look astonished.

TOURIST 2: Yeah, but . . . it's great, I suppose—but what does it do?

TOURIST 3: Bob had the best line—"The Taj is amazing, but boring."

TOURIST 1: Come on, let's do the photo so we can get outta here.

The tourists are cynically questioning the significance of the Taj and undermining orthodox notions about how the attraction should be gazed upon romantically and beheld with intense seriousness. Through their comments and their performance before the camera, they also critique the conventions of tourist framing and the centrality of performing dutiful acts of photographic recording (Edensor 1998a:133).

Resistant Performances.   The regulation to which many tourist performances are subject might appear to mitigate against transgressive behavior, but tourists are never compelled to enact specific conformist performances. Tourists may acknowledge and accept direction and control and yet be prepared to trade self-expression for the benefits of consistency, reliability, and comfort. However, acceptance of control can generate a frustration that engenders tactical revolt and an unwillingness to play particular roles.

Before a 40-strong tour-bus party of English tourists disembarked and made their way to the Taj Mahal, they were told by their tour guide that after 30 minutes, they were to gather at the exit to the monument so that they could fulfill the day's schedule. This short stop produced consternation among many in the party, who felt that this was insufficient time to visit what was, after all, the highlight of their week-long trip to India. This anxiety was even more pronounced inside the grounds of the Taj, where sensing precious time slipping away, they tried to photograph the mausoleum from many angles and attempted to indulge in romantic gazing. Their exertions were swiftly curtailed by the guide who ordered them to return to the bus so that they might squeeze in a visit to a marble craft emporium—where he might reap commission from any purchases the tourists might make. The complaints were loud and many. They had not had enough time, they were being rushed around and bossed about, and they would not stand for it. Thus, the tourists won a small concession from the tour organizers by negotiating an extra half-hour at the site.

Resistance against the directors and choreographers of performance can be reactive to the overzealous prescription of roles. However, where performances are more amorphous and open-ended, and scripts and actions are not tightly managed, "there is scope for lying, creative ambiguity, deliberate misdirection . . . improvised codings of subversive messages" (Palmer and Jankowiak 1996:236). Tourists may deviate from organized tours in ways akin to how, according to Michel de Certeau (1984), pedestrians (temporarily) transform public space and transmit alternative meanings by using "tactics" to reappropriate space.

Improvisational Performances.   Normative performance and its direction obfuscate the actual contingency of performance and the innumerable performative possibilities available. As Schutz declares, "Social performances may bypass or negotiate with normative rituals, by organizing a patchwork or bricolage of meanings and actions to generate new dramatic configurations"

(1964:72–73). In fact, the confrontation with difference that is part of tourism can facilitate improvisational performances, and where this is allied to a desire to force oneself to challenge habitual behavior or an experimental disposition to try on unfamiliar roles, such improvisation is engendered.

A particularly apposite example of this is in the performance of barter, into which many tourists to non-Western settings are initiated. The performance of barter, which, as Buie describes, is a sensual as well as economic activity, an "art," a "ritual," and a "dance of exchange" (1996:227), is a dramatic encounter that is characterized by improvisatory response including wit, melodramatic appeals to fairness, and stoicism.

Involuntary Performances. Although performances may be exclusive affairs, designed only to reinforce communal solidarity among participants, it may be the case that onlookers, especially if they enact different forms of performance at the same site, either fail to understand the resonance of Others' performance or disparage their competence or the meanings they impart. We can never predict how a performance is likely to be read. Occasionally, the involuntary effects, at variance to the intended meaning, can produce disorientation among performers and audience, perhaps producing a state of acute self-awareness brought on by the response of locals who perhaps regard the performance as involuntarily comedic. For instance, watching a boatload of tourists disembark from a ferry at the port of Tangiers in Morocco was a crowd of young locals who watched with hilarity as passengers and their heavy suitcases came tumbling down a particularly slippery gangplank, creating a free slapstick show. One elderly American female tourist stood at the top of the gangplank, shrieking, "There's no order! There's no order!" to the merriment of the audience. Tourists were either profoundly disorientated and outraged by the lack of organization or played their roles as fall guys with good humor.

Conclusion

The world is increasingly full of cultural encounters in tourist space. I have argued that there may be competing enactments on tourist stages that purvey notions about what actions are "appropriate," "competent," and "normal." Normative performances—conforming to the instructions of stage managers and directors—reveal how social and cultural power can inscribe meaning and action on bodies. Where these conventions clash, performative negotiations may be set in motion and a reflexive awareness of habitual performance may occur. Alternatively, as with the way in which backpackers mock the rituals of package tourists, other performers can be ridiculed.

A range of tourist roles can be enacted, from the disciplined to the improvised. I have emphasized the imbrication of the everyday and tourism, where the everyday is both routine and full of disruption. Accordingly, tourist performance also includes unreflexive assumptions and habits but contains moments where norms may be transcended. By tracing those settings and practices that enable greater scope for improvisation, we are able to see how the material and sensual qualities of particular spaces interrupt the equanimity of disciplined and regulated embodied dispositions.

It may seem that the kinds of postmodern stagings I have identified proffer a dystopian future for tourism where every potential space becomes intensively stage managed and regulated as part of the commodification of everything. While there is no doubting the power to define the normative that inheres in these modes of promoting space and culture, such strategies can never eclipse the potential for innovative performance. However, at the same time as this homogenizing process, this closing in, is occurring, there is an unceasing proliferation of tourist spaces and practices that open up the world, invade the everyday, and expand the repertoire of performative options and the range of stages upon which tourists may perform.

Source: For a more detailed discussion, see "Staging Tourism: Tourists as Performers," *Annals of Tourism Research* 27(2):322–344, 2000.

Note

[1] I am grateful to Lindsey Coffee for this insight

References Cited

Bhattacharyya, D. 1997. "Mediating India: An Analysis of a Guidebook." *Annals of Tourism Research* 24:371–389.

Buie, S. 1996. "Market as Mandala: The Erotic Space of Commerce." *Organisation* 3:225–232.

Butler, J. 1993. *Bodies That Matter: The Discursive Limits of Sex*. London: Routledge.

Carlson, M. 1996. *Performance: A Critical Introduction*. London: Routledge.

Chaney, D. 1993. *Fictions of Collective Life*. London: Routledge.

Cohen, E. 1979. "A Phenomenology of Tourist Experiences." *Sociology* 13:179–202.

Connerton, P. 1989. *How Societies Remember*. London: Cambridge University Press.

Crang, P. 1997. "Performing the Tourist Product," in *Touring Cultures: Transformations of Travel and Theory*, eds. C. Rojek and J. Urry. London: Routledge.

de Certeau, M. 1984. *The Practice of Everyday Life*. Berkeley: University of California Press.

Desforges, L. 1998. "'Checking Out the Planet': Global Representations/Local Identities and Youth Travel," in *Cool Places: Geographies of Youth Cultures*, eds. T. Skelton and G. Valentine. London: Routledge.

Edensor, T. 1998a. *Tourists at the Taj*. London: Routledge.

———. 1998b. "Reading Braveheart: Representing and Contesting Scottish Identity." *Scottish Affairs* 21(1): 135–158.

———. "Staging Tourism: Tourists as Performers." *Annals of Tourism Research* 27:322–344.

Feifer, W. 1985. *Going Places*. London: MacMillan.

Freitag, T. 1994. "Enclave Tourist Development: For Whom the Benefits Roll?" *Annals of Tourism Research* 21:538–554.

Geertz, C. 1993. *The Interpretation of Cultures*. London: Fontana.

Goffman, E. 1959. *The Presentation of Self in Everyday Life*. New York: Doubleday.

Gottdiener, M. 1997. *The Theming of America*. Oxford: Westview Press.

Hobsbawm, E., and T. Ranger, eds. 1983. *The Invention of Tradition*. Oxford: Blackwell.

MacDonald, A. 1997. "The New Beauty of a Sum of Possibilities." *Law and Critique* 8(2): 141–159.

Munt, I. 1994. "The 'Other' Postmodern Tourism: Culture, Travel and the New Middle Classes." *Theory Culture and Society* 11:101–123

Neumann, M. 1988. "Wandering through the Museum: Experience and Identity in a Spectator Culture." *Border/Lines* Summer:19–27.

Palmer, G., and W. Jankowiak. 1996. "Performance and Imagination: Toward an Anthropology of the Spectacular and the Mundane." *Cultural Anthropology* 11(2): 225–258.

Ritzer, G., and A. Liska. 1997. "'McDisneyization' and 'Post-Tourism': Complementary Perspectives on Contemporary Tourism," in *Touring Cultures: Transformations of Travel and Theory*, eds. C. Rojek and J. Urry. London: Routledge.

Rojek, C. 1995. *Decentring Leisure*. London: Sage.

Schutz, A. 1964. *Collected Papers: Vol 2*. Den Haag: Martinus Nijhoff.

Schieffelin, E. 1998. "Problematising Performance," in *Ritual, Performance, Media*, ed. F. Hughes-Freeland. London: Routledge.

Sibley, D. 1988. "Survey 13: Purification of Space." *Environment and Planning D: Society and Space* 6:409–421.

Smith, V. (ed). 1989. *Hosts and Guests: The Anthropology of Tourism*. Philadelphia: University of Pennsylvania Press.

Wood, R. 1998. "Tourist Ethnicity: A Brief Itinerary." *Ethnic and Racial Studies* 21:218–241.

11

Deceivingly Difficult: Asian Guides with Asian Tourists in an Asian Destination

Noel B. Salazar

Asia's market share in global tourism has increased dramatically over the last few decades (UNWTO 2016). In countries like China, India, and South Korea, the emergence of a rising Asian middle class that can afford to travel is quickly turning the region into one of the most attractive tourist markets. As a result, Asian tourism hot spots, like destinations elsewhere in the world, are competing to obtain their piece of the lucrative Asian tourist pie (Pearce and Wu 2016; Winter, Teo, and Chang 2008). Singapore, Hong Kong, and Thailand are already strongly positioned; China is the fastest rising star; and competition is high in Malaysia, Indochina (Vietnam, Cambodia, and Laos), South Korea, the Philippines, and Indonesia. Here, by way of an ethnographic case study, I examine how tourism in Yogyakarta (commonly referred to as Jogja), Indonesia, has been opening up to Asian tourists and how local tour guides have adapted their practices, originally oriented toward Western tourists, to fit what they perceive to be the interests and expectations of Asian clients. The research described here was part of a larger multisited study of guiding discourses and practices (Salazar 2005, 2006, 2007, 2010, 2012a).

Jogja, Never Ending Asia

Yogyakarta is the name of one of Indonesia's 34 provinces and its capital city, situated in central Java. At the beginning of the new millennium, the neologism "Jogja" was introduced as a brand name to market the region, since the letter *Y* was believed to be a more difficult alphabetical start for international audiences. It also appears in the catchphrase "Jogja, never ending Asia" used by both the provincial government and the private sector to lure investors, traders, and tourists to the area. Although processes of globalization are evident in many domains of daily life in Jogja, the current tourism discourse, as uttered by the local government, by travel agencies, and by tour guides alike, focuses on cultural heritage sites and traditional arts and crafts performed or produced in the city or in its vicinity (Salazar 2010).

Jogja has been receiving sizeable numbers of international tourists for almost four decades. It became a mass destination in the 1980s and is the third most visited destination in Indonesia, after Bali and Jakarta. Apart from the historical city center around the Sultan's Palace, the most important attractions are the eighth-century Buddhist monument of Borobudur and the ninth-century Hindu temple complex in Prambanan, both recognized as UNESCO World Heritage Sites (Salazar 2016). Foreign visitors used to come mainly from Europe (Germany, the Netherlands, and France) and Japan. However, potential Asian markets are developing in Singapore, Malaysia, South Korea, China, and India.

It is important to note that these visitor trends reflect not only the changing numbers of Asian and Western tourists but also larger geopolitical developments, which have made shorter haul trips to less expensive intraregional destinations within Asia easier (Winter, Teo, and Chang 2008). One of the reasons tourism in Bali recovered faster than expected after the 2002 bombings, for instance, was the relaxed reaction by visitors from Japan and Taiwan who greedily accepted the heavily discounted flights and hotel room rates. These developments, together with the fact that there is a growing population of middle-class Asians who can afford to travel abroad (Pearce and Wu 2016), prompted the Indonesian authorities to consider boosting tourism promotion within Asia.

The focus on this definitely makes sense for Jogja, because the region has long-standing cultural and religious ties with many parts of Asia. While the eyes of many local entrepreneurs remain turned to "the West," others are increasingly turning toward Asia. However, the growing presence of Asian tourists poses many challenges for Jogja's tourism service providers. Interestingly, this is not because tourism of Asian origin is a new phenomenon. Actually, Asian tourists (especially Japanese) began arriving in Jogja as early as Western visitors did. In the past, however, tourism consultants from Western-dominated international organizations such as the World Bank, ICOMOS, and UNESCO focused exclusively on the development of Western markets, and local tourism personnel were originally trained to serve Western clients (Salazar 2016). The analysis below is limited to a case study of the interaction between local tour guides and nondomestic Asian tourists in Jogja. Situating this encounter in this broader context helps to understand why Jogja's guides tend to valuate Asian tourists rather negatively. Since Japanese tourists are by far the largest group of Asian origin, the focus is on their encounters with local guides.

"They Left as Quickly as They Came": Jogja à la Japanese

It is around 5:30 A.M. when I meet Pak Suhardi in front of a local tour operator's office in the center of Jogja. I had interviewed this freelance Japanese language guide a couple of weeks earlier and he had kindly agreed to let me observe one of his tours. As soon as the driver of the company's minivan arrives (wearing the same batik uniform as Suhardi), we set off for the city's airport to pick up the clients. Indonesia attracts Japanese visitors for a number of reasons (Yamashita 2003). While waiting at the airport, Suhardi tells me that Jogja started receiving significant numbers of Japanese tourists in the 1980s. The Borobudur exhibition held in Japan in 1981 made Jogja popular as a possible cultural tourism destination. Since 1985, the Province of Yogyakarta also has had a sister city partnership with Kyoto Prefecture.

Except for a small number of independent travelers, most Japanese tourists come as one-day transit visitors from Bali. It is just after 6:30 A.M. when the clients walk through the airport's customs gate. Suhardi is lucky because today's group is not accompanied by a Balinese tour leader (as is often the case), meaning that he will be able to serve them himself. Because the plane has been delayed by a half hour, there is no time to waste. Suhardi greets the group by bowing in a typically Japanese way (with the back straight, the hands at the sides, and the eyes down), and we immediately leave for Borobudur. In the minivan, he briefs the tourists in detail about the program of the day.

The Japanese visitors, seven in total, had all attended a conference on fine arts in Bali, which included a day trip around Bali. The island reminded them of past landscapes and cultural roots that no longer exist in present-day urbanized Japan. Their experience corresponds to Matsuda's (1989:43–45) observations about Japanese tourism to Bali. In her study, she stressed the perspective not only of exoticism but also of nostalgia. The Balinese barong dance is reminiscent of the Japanese lion dance, the Hindu temples remind Japanese visitors of those in Kyoto and Nara, and rice terraces are quite normal in Japanese rural areas. Matsuda's analysis applies remarkably well to Jogja, too. Unfortunately, Japanese day-trippers from Bali are on a tight schedule and only catch a glimpse of traditional Javanese village life. Experi-

A group of Japanese tourists and their on-site guide entering the main temple complex at Prambanan, Central Java, Indonesia. (Photo by author)

ential tourism activities such as learning how to cultivate rice, for instance, would be extremely popular, but there is simply no time for them. Besides, the tourists are tired upon their arrival in Jogja, having left their Balinese hotel in the middle of the night. While Suhardi has dozens of interesting stories and jokes ready to entertain them, his clients prefer to rest a little instead and hardly touch their nicely packaged breakfasts.

Upon arrival in Borobudur, Suhardi gently wakes his clients and gives them a brief historical introduction to the site. According to the tour operator's schedule, Suhardi has about one hour and a half to walk from the parking lot to the entry gate, queue to pay the entrance fees, walk almost half a mile to reach the monument, climb the seven levels, and descend the monument to walk all the way back to the parking lot. Because it is impossible to cover the entire site in such a short time, Suhardi carefully selects some popular highlights: (1) the few uncovered bas reliefs of Borobudur's hidden foot depicting desires and worldly temptations, (2) some of the panels on the first and second galleries telling the story of Prince Siddhartha, and (3) the upper platform with its 72 small stupas (with statues of the Buddha sitting inside the pierced enclosures) surrounding one large central stupa.

I notice that the tourists politely listen to his narratives but, in contrast to most Western groups, ask no questions. Once we have reached the top, Suhardi invites the male tourists to touch the hand and the female tourists to touch the foot of one particular Buddha statue. According to local lore, this brings good luck (and it creates good photo opportunities too). The Japanese tourists are happily surprised that the backpack Suhardi carried all the way up contains a small water bottle for each. They immediately show their gratitude by bowing. After drinking, the group is given ten minutes to walk around and take pictures of the magnificent platform and the surrounding lush landscape. This gives Suhardi a chance to rest a little and chat with some of his colleagues.

Being a devout Muslim, Suhardi has had to acquire in-depth knowledge about Buddhism, and, being a guide for Japanese tourists, he does not fail to make the necessary links between Buddhism in Indonesia and in Japan. (In both countries the form of Buddhism that established itself was Mahayana Buddhism, or the Great Vehicle.) Before descending, Suhardi points to the luxurious Amanjiwo Hotel, which can be seen from where they stand, and remarks: "For the Presidential Suite, 2000 dollars per night. Have you ever been there? I have only been there once: in my dreams! . . . OK, let's return to reality now." He can only dream about staying at an expensive place like the Amanjiwo Hotel. Yet, this is a hotel his affluent clients can afford. In other words, for the Japanese it is reality, while it might be harder for them to imagine the socioeconomic conditions in which Suhardi lives (a small compound with shared bathroom and kitchen for his family and that of his younger brother). At the foot of the monument, Suhardi takes some pictures of the group. Our last stop before heading back to the minivan is the plaque commemorating the large restoration project of Borobudur (1975–1982). Of course, Suhardi points out that Japan was one of the 27 countries who generously contributed to the fundraising campaign.

On our way back to Jogja, we stop at a silverware workshop. The group receives a brief explanation of the production process and is then invited to look around in the huge shop. However, the clients seem more interested in its toilet than in its wares. Suhardi tells me that when Japanese tourism boomed, from the mid-1980s until the mid-1990s, guides received extra commissions by bringing Japanese to souvenir shops. This largely compensated for the fact that Japanese tourists do not customarily tip. Nowadays, there is often not enough time for them to shop and, when there is, the tourists are not interested in buying (partly because they can find the same souvenirs in Bali).

Since the clients have not had a decent breakfast, we have an early lunch at a typical tourist buffet restaurant located on Jogja's ring road. While eating, I ask Suhardi how he learned about Japan and Japanese culture. Since he cannot afford to travel to Japan, although he would love to, he reads Japanese books and magazines at a local university library and uses the Internet to obtain extra information about specific topics. Some of his senior colleagues have cable television, and they occasionally get together to watch the *Nippon*

Hoso Kyokai (Japanese Broadcasting Corporation) station. Suhardi also tries to attend cultural activities organized by the Japan Foundation. In his personal library, he has a copy of a locally produced manual that specifically addresses the characteristics and needs of Japanese tourists (Desky 1999). Suhardi stresses that this is not so difficult because Japanese and Javanese "culture" are similar. He gives the examples of politeness, social etiquette, and the importance of purchasing souvenirs for family and friends who stayed at home. Punctuality remains a difficult point for many Javanese who, as Suhardi jokingly remarks, live in a "culture of *jam karet*" (flexible time, or the continuous uncertainty of scheduled time arrangements).

Speaking of which, the driver comes by to tell us that the clients have finished eating and we have to hurry up because the last guided tours of the Sultan's Palace start before 1:00 P.M. Suhardi instructs the Japanese-speaking palace guide to bring his clients back to the entrance in 45 minutes. While we are waiting, he tells me how he became a guide. Suhardi used to work as a clerk at a local travel agency. He decided to enroll in a two-year intensive Japanese language course because at the time there were still many tourists from Japan and not enough guides. In order to obtain his license, he took part in a short three-month course organized by the provincial tourism authority. He immediately became a member of the local tour guide association. In fact, the Japanese language guides are the largest subgroup within the association, although the number of Japanese clients has declined drastically. According to Suhardi, this decrease is mainly due to the exaggerated fear in Japan of infectious and other diseases. He recalls how an outbreak of cholera among returning Japanese tourists in 1994 and 1996 led to a pronounced decline in tourists thereafter. In 2003, there was the outbreak of SARS and in 2005 there was a bird flu pandemic.

The tourists arrive ten minutes too late and, since we are already behind schedule, Suhardi decides to skip the souvenir shopping around Malioboro Street, the city's major commercial area. Instead, we drive straight to the last attraction of the day, the Prambanan temple complex. On the way, I notice the once celebrated Ambarrukmo Palace Hotel, built in 1966 with funds provided by war reparations from Japan. Suhardi fails to mention it. "Don't mention the war," or, in this case, the Japanese occupation of Java (1942–45), seems to be a guiding motto throughout the tour. This oppressively dark period before Indonesia's national liberation heavily affected life in Jogja, both economically and socially, and Javanese prefer to forget it. It is much easier to talk about their politically neutral heritage, such as Prambanan. Because it is in the middle of the afternoon, the heat is oppressive, and the Japanese tourists are suffering and markedly tired, Suhardi slowly strolls around the three main temples and keeps his explanations to an absolute minimum. Providing drinking water and shade are more important priorities.

After an hour and a half, we rush to the airport and the driver gets nervous because there is too much traffic. Arriving at the airport we learn that the plane back to Bali is delayed by an hour, which gives Suhardi the first

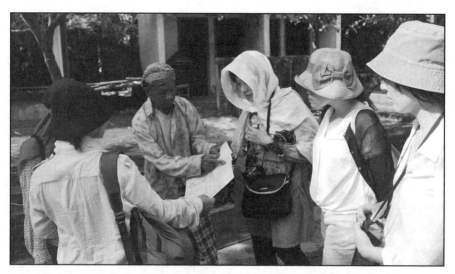

Local Javanese guide showing Japanese tourists a map with the distribution of graves at the Imogiri Royal Graveyard Complex, Yogyakarta, Indonesia. (Photo by author)

(and last) opportunity of the day to really get to know his clients. Remembering their interest in art, he tells the group how important Jogja is for the Indonesian art scene. The Japanese had no clue that the city is home to the Indonesian Institute of Fine Arts and one of the most active contemporary art scenes in the country. A missed opportunity, according to Suhardi, and they will miss the beautiful Ramayana Ballet, too, performed every night in an open-air theatre that uses the Prambanan temples as a fairytale background. In addition, there are the shadow puppet plays, the gamelan concerts, the Javanese court dances, and the Affandi Museum (exhibiting over 250 paintings by this renowned Indonesian artist). Is all of this not reason enough to return to Jogja for a longer visit? The Japanese kindly nod.

On the way back to the city center while stuck in the evening traffic, I ask Suhardi to evaluate the tour. Although he is certainly experienced enough to know the intricacies of Japanese culture, he still finds it difficult to please Japanese guests (cf. Sugiantoro 2000:69–72). Suhardi tells me that he prefers older Japanese clients, like the ones today, because they are usually fascinated by stories about the rural life around Jogja—the nostalgic element Matsuda (1989) refers to in her discussion of Bali. Unfortunately, as I witnessed myself, there is virtually no time to show them any of the province's village life (and many Japanese have already taken a similar tour on Bali). It clearly frustrates Suhardi that he has so little time that he cannot even tell them much about Jogja. He recalls how, a couple of years ago, an irritated Japanese tourist had almost shouted at him "enough stories!" (The man wanted to get some sleep in between the group's sightseeing walks.)

Seeing and Selling Jogja through "Asian Eyes"

The ethnographic description above of a typical Japanese tour of Jogja challenges Cohen's (1985) assertion that guiding is evolving and shifting from managing logistics to facilitating experience, from playing a pathfinder role to that of a mentor, moving from leadership toward mediating and away from the outer- toward the inner-directed sphere, with the communicative component becoming the center of the professional guide's role. Clearly, Suhardi's narratives and explanations were of minor importance to his clients throughout the trip. Rather, it was imperative for him to demonstrate that he was taking good care of them. In contrast to guided tours for Western tourists (which I also observed while I was in Jogja), the stress seemed to be on the service component of the guiding job (Salazar 2010). Why these differences?

Despite the homogenizing trends of global tourism, the needs and interests of international tourists are multiple and often culturally influenced. Some academics argue, rather bluntly, that the biggest cultural differences are to be found between Asian and Western societies (e.g., Samovar et al. 2015). Others have tried to empirically show that the needs and tastes of Western tourists are, indeed, very different from those of Asian clients (Reisinger and Turner 1999, 2002a and b). Throughout my own travels around the globe, I have noticed that many Asians are interested in visiting internationally renowned landmarks and modern and sophisticated attractions such as theme parks and shopping centers. They love to evaluate the development levels of other places and search for iconic representations of modernity. Many Westerners, on the other hand, like to experience the exotic beauty of (well-conserved) natural and cultural heritage sites. One should critically wonder, however, whether these stereotypical differences are really "cultural" or whether they might simply refer to various stages of tourism development. This would assume that all tourism develops in the way it has developed in the West. Most anthropologists would argue that artificially opposing "the West" and "Asia" does injustice to the multiple fault lines that crosscut this cultural binary: nationality, ethnicity, race, class, gender, et cetera.

Regardless of the conflicting explanations given, there are differences between tourists from different cultural backgrounds, and these have real implications for tourism. How to market Jogja as a destination for tourists of Asian origin? Should it be promoted as the old cultural center of Java (as is done for Western markets) or is it wiser to advertise the city as a hotbed of youthfulness and innovation? Although there are an increasing number of exclusive shopping malls, Jogja lacks high-tech theme parks and soaring skyscrapers. Moreover, most malls largely cater to locals; they do not sell the arts and crafts for which the region is famous, making them less interesting for tourists. If the only sights left for Asians to visit are Borobudur and Prambanan, the two World Heritage Sites, they can easily do that on a day trip or as transit visitors, hereby seriously limiting the impact they have on the local economy.

Independent of how Jogja and other destinations are being marketed, Asian tourists currently come to Indonesia for a relatively short time. Because they travel mostly in organized tour groups, they have limited contact with local people. They develop their perceptions of Indonesians mainly through their direct face-to-face contact with service providers, who are often their only contact points. Local tour guides, who spend a considerable amount of time with tourists, know that client satisfaction is best achieved when understanding their cultural background, including their values and perceptions of the world (Pond 1993). One would expect Indonesian guides to have little difficulty dealing with Asian visitors because of their cultural proximity (although the existence of shared "Asian values" is debatable). Moreover, what is gained by guiding people from similar cultural backgrounds can be lost due to communication problems. To serve Asian clients, guides have to learn difficult new languages, and local language schools do not possess the best human resources and learning materials. Besides, many guides have been professionally trained to work with Westerners, studying Western-produced guiding methods and techniques (Salazar 2010). What they have learned through such formal training is not readily transposable to a work context with Asians. Finally, cultural proximity does not mean that there are no cultural or other differences at all.

Tour guides' perceptions of foreign tourists, no matter whether they are Asian or not, are often trapped in cultural stereotyping. Many guides in Jogja, including Pak Suhardi, talk about Japanese tourists in ways that reinforce the common stereotype that Japanese are not that interested in heritage narratives and always seem in a hurry, only having time to take snapshots. Even if this were true, it does not mean less work for the tour guides. While Asian clients might need less interpretative information, they do expect constant attention and entertainment. Guides still provide explanatory narratives that are skillfully adapted to shared Asian frames of reference, but they sensibly invite disinterested tourists to roam around the visited sites and take pictures instead. Assuming that Asians are less willing to engage in physical efforts than Western tourists are (as the cultural stereotypes go), guides adapt their tour itineraries accordingly. For instance, there is less on-site walking. Local tour guides clearly seem to ascribe these perceived behavioral differences to cultural factors.

However, it is an easy way out to explain the different roles guides play when dealing with Western and Asian tourists as culturally determined. Alternative interpretations can be offered, including structural characteristics of tourism, such as the length of annual holidays and the history of traveling abroad, and are at least as salient. In many Western industrialized countries, for example, there has been a marked tendency for the minimum annual vacation period to be increased. Westerners visiting Indonesia have at least two weeks of vacation and do not need to rush from one sight to the other. Many of them have extensively traveled abroad and seen many of the world's landmarks. They are therefore increasingly looking for experiential types of tourism, in which the mentor or mediator-style of guiding gains importance. Popular examples in Indonesia include batik-making, rice planting, and cooking. Asian tourists generally have much less time at their disposal, and for many, the tradition of traveling abroad for leisure is newer. Since they have less travel experience and usually speak neither English (the most widespread language in global tourism) nor the local language, Asians are dependent on local guides as pathfinders to lead them around safely. In a sense, guiding tourists of Asian origin resembles much more the work of a tour manager, escort, or leader than that of a culture broker. In other words, structural factors are as important, if not more important, than cultural elements in understanding perceived Western–Asian differences.

Many Asians traveling to Jogja belong to the rapidly growing class of *nouveau riches*. This new Asian middle class is the result of the burgeoning economies of various Asian countries and characterized by conspicuous consumption (Robison and Goodman 1996). These people are salaried, live in rapidly urbanizing or already urban settings, are comparatively young, and seek to spend their surplus money on entertainment and leisure. Already in the 1990s, the international media was filled with stories about Asia's new rich and their "sexy" and often rampant consumption patterns. Although they have been depicted as "superficially Western, essentially Oriental, and representing the majority of the population" (Pinches 1999:1), in reality this cultural construction of the new rich in Asia totally neglects the wide cultural variance between and within Asian countries. Nevertheless, these culturalist accounts seem very influential and have a wide rhetorical power, even in tourism. It is believed that when traveling, the mere fact of visiting a famous site, and taking pictures or shooting video as proof for those who stayed at home, is deemed more important for these new rich than is learning about the history of the place.

This larger socioeconomic context enables us to link local observations to broader forces and power dynamics. It helps us to understand why it is, for example, that the guides in Jogja often devalue their Asian clients. Partly as a legacy of the Dutch colonial era, having close contact with a "white" person is considered as status enhancing. In the personal imagination of many guides, Westerners act as their gateway into a better world, a Promised Land they know from television programs, advertisements, and movies (cf. Salazar and Graburn 2014). The privileged interaction with Westerners nourishes their dreams of escape from their harsh life. Asian tourists are perceived as sociocultural (and racial) proxies, people who have (materially) "made it" in their lives and are able to travel abroad. Many Asians devotedly embrace their role of *nouveau riche* by being much more demanding toward service personnel. The Indonesian guides, as providers of paid-for services, often have to work harder for these clients, usually without receiving tips. They have little choice but to faithfully play this guiding role.

Conclusion

Tour guides have to engage in a complex negotiation of roles between themselves and tourists, other service providers, tour operators, and local people and the sociocultural power expressed by each of these stakeholders during interaction. This case study of Asian tourists in Jogja, and Japanese visitors in particular, illustrates that there are various ways to facilitate a quality experience for the client. For Asian tourists, guides are there to help fulfill the dream of a perfect vacation (Salazar 2012b), but their expectations and imaginaries are different from those of Western clients. Whereas Western tourists usually judge the quality of tour guides by evaluating the quality of their explanatory commentaries, what matters most to Asian tourists is how they are personally treated as guests. The guide is expected to be a good organizer (instrumental) and a good entertainer (social) of the group, more than an information-giver (communicative) or culture broker (interactional) for the individual tourists. As illustrated and explained above, Indonesian guides working with Asian tourists have to pay more attention to tour management than to the management of the tourists' experience. This emphasizes their leadership roles (both instrumental and social) over their (interactional and communicative) mediator roles. This is a small piece of evidence that, given the historical and current socioeconomic context, instead of representing a traditional or former stage of tourism development, Asian tourists are fostering a different, new "culture of tourism." As such, this ethnographic study inscribes itself in a growing field of research on tourism of Asian origin that problematizes the universality of existing theoretical frameworks explaining particular aspects of tourism.

Source: For a more detailed discussion, see "'Enough Stories!' Asian Tourism Redefining the Roles of Asian Tour Guides." *Civilisations* 57(1/2):207–222, 2008.

References cited

Cohen, Erik. 1985. "The Tourist Guide: The Origins, Structure and Dynamics of a Role." *Annals of Tourism Research* 12(1): 5–29.

Desky, Mahidin A. 1999. *Melayani wisatawan Jepang*. Yogyakarta: AdiCita.

Matsuda, Misa. 1989. "Japanese Tourists and Indonesia: Images of Self and Other in the Age of Kokusaika (Internationalization)." MA thesis, Faculty of Asian Studies, Australian National University.

Pearce, Philip L., and Mao-Ying Wu, eds. 2016. *The World Meets Asian Tourists*. Bingley: Emerald.

Pinches, Michael. 1999. *Culture and Privilege in Capitalist Asia, New Rich in Asia Series*. London: Routledge.

Pond, Kathleen L. 1993. *The Professional Guide: Dynamics of Tour Guiding*. New York: Van Nostrand Reinhold.

Reisinger, Yvette, and Lindsay W. Turner. 1999. "A Cultural Analysis of Japanese Tourists: Challenges for Tourism Marketers." *European Journal of Marketing* 33 (11/12): 1203–1227.

————. 2002a. "Cultural Differences between Asian Tourist Markets and Australian Hosts, Part 1." *Journal of Travel Research* 40 (February): 295–315.

————. 2002b. "Cultural Differences between Asian Tourist Markets and Australian Hosts, Part 2." *Journal of Travel Research* 40 (May): 374–384.

Robison, Richard, and David S. G. Goodman, eds. 1996. *The New Rich in Asia: Mobile Phones, McDonald's and Middle-Class Revolution.* London: Routledge.

Salazar, Noel B. 2005. "Tourism and Globalization: 'Local' Tour Guiding." *Annals of Tourism Research* 32(3): 628–646. doi: 10.1016/j.annals.2004.10.012

————. 2006. "Touristifying Tanzania: Global Discourse, Local Guides." *Annals of Tourism Research* 33(3):833–852. doi: 10.1016/j.annals.2006.03.017

————. 2007. "Towards a Global Culture of Heritage Interpretation? Evidence from Indonesia and Tanzania." *Tourism Recreation Research* 32(3):23–30.

————. 2010. *Envisioning Eden: Mobilizing imaginaries in tourism and beyond.* Oxford: Berghahn.

————. 2012a. "Shifting Values and Meanings of Heritage: From Cultural Appropriation to Tourism Interpretation and Back," in *Global Tourism: Cultural Heritage and Economic Encounters*, eds. Sarah M. Lyon and Christian E. Wells, pp. 21–41. Lanham: Altamira.

————. 2012b. "Tourism Imaginaries: A Conceptual Approach." *Annals of Tourism Research* 39(2): 863–882.

————. 2016. "One List, a World of Difference? The Dynamics of Global Heritage at Two Neighbouring Properties," in *World Heritage on the Ground: Ethnographic Perspectives*, eds. Christoph Brumann and David Berliner, pp. 147–170. Oxford: Berghahn.

Salazar, Noel B., and Nelson H. H. Graburn, eds. 2014. *Tourism Imaginaries: Anthropological Approaches.* Oxford: Berghahn.

Samovar, Larry A., Richard E. Porter, Edwin R. McDaniel, and Carolyn S. Roy. 2015. *Intercultural Communication: A Reader.* 14th Edition and 40th Anniversary Edition. Boston: Cengage Learning.

Sugiantoro, Ronny. 2000. *Pariwisata: Antara obsesi dan realita.* Yogyakarta: AdiCita.

UNWTO. 2016. *UNWTO Tourism Highlights.* Madrid: United Nations World Tourism Organization.

Winter, Tim, Peggy Teo, and T. C. Chang, eds. 2008. *Asia on Tour: Exploring the Rise of Asian Tourism.* London: Routledge.

Yamashita, Shinji. 2003. *Bali and Beyond: Explorations in the Anthropology of Tourism.* Trans. Jerry S. Eades. New York: Berghahn.

12

Producing and Consuming Heritage Tourism: Recent Trends

Dallen J. Timothy

Heritage-based tourism is one of the most pervasive forms of tourism today as it was even in ancient times. Heritage is what humankind inherits from the past and utilizes in the present, cherished by society for its educative, scientific, economic, political, and identity value (Graham, Ashworth, and Tunbridge 2016). Because of its immense socioeconomic importance, heritage has become one of the most pervasive and salient resources for tourism in many parts of the world. Tourists' interest in and consumption of the past help bolster the identity of destination communities and empower them by deeming their patrimony important and worthwhile (Timothy 2015). Tourism's use of the past also provides jobs, regional income, and tax revenue. In some places, cultural heritage is the only reason tourism exists.

Heritage tourism, which some estimates suggest comprises between 50 and 80 percent of all travel, takes many forms. This chapter briefly discusses these and establishes the basic tenets of heritage tourism. It then examines several emerging trends and considerations/developments influencing heritage tourism.

Heritage Supply and Demand

Scholars and marketing specialists frequently categorize tourism into types, such as ecotourism, sports tourism, medical tourism, and heritage tourism. Heritage tourism itself can be divided into subtypes based on the locales visited, products consumed, or the experiences tourists seek, which differ from place to place and person to person. Almost anything inherited from the past can become a cultural heritage commodity.

Heritage as a tourism product is often defined as being either tangible or intangible. Examples of tangible heritage include military attractions (e.g., battlefields, war memorials), literary heritage (e.g., locales highlighted in books or movies, birthplaces of famous authors), dark attractions (e.g., cemeteries, concentration camps), historic buildings (e.g., castles, forts), archaeological sites (e.g., ancient ruins), human settlements (e.g., rural villages, historic cities), industrial relics (e.g., mines, factories), and religious attractions (e.g., temples, churches). Intangible heritage products include arts (e.g., handicrafts, artwork), language (e.g., spoken languages, calligraphy), folkways (e.g., folklore, games), gastronomy (e.g., recipes, flavors), music and performing arts (e.g., dance, songs), sports (e.g., competitive traditions, rules), festivals (e.g., food festivals, religious pageants), and religion (e.g., rituals, beliefs) (Timothy 2011). In most cases, tangible and intangible patrimony are inseparable, as is exemplified by the growing number of folk life museums and "ethnic parks" throughout the world that demonstrate how life might have been at some given period of time among certain cultures. Many of the services utilized by tourists, such as restaurants, accommodations, and transportation, can become an important part of the heritage experience as when a restaurant serves local specialties, a hotel has particular historical importance, or a mode of transportation is also marked/featured as a heritage attraction (e.g., historic railways). As should be evident, cultural heritage is broad and encompasses a wide range of resources that are tapped for tourism or that could become tourism products.

Consumers of cultural heritage come in many forms. At one end of the spectrum are history buffs or staunch heritage enthusiasts, who travel specifically to participate in cultural heritage-based activities or to visit particular historic locales. Train aficionados systematically visiting railway museums or riding famous historic railway lines, sports enthusiasts "collecting" stadium visits, or fans of classical literature traveling the Mediterranean seeking sites associated with the Greek Empire are examples of "serious" heritage tourists (Stebbins 1996). On the other end of the spectrum are "casual" heritage tourists—people who have little intrinsic interest in heritage but who visit historic sites as part of a wider itinerary or who happen upon a historic building that strikes them as worthy of a quick photo or stopover (Timothy 2011). Examples of casual visitors include cruise passengers participating in a portside tour of a tea plantation or papaya farm, or shopping tourists who stop to take selfies at a famous farmers' market. The majority of heritage consumers lie somewhere between these two extremes.

Research suggests that most devoted heritage visitors are between the ages of 30 and 60 years, have higher than average incomes, are well educated, and prefer to visit historic sites with family members (Adie and Hall 2017; Herbert, Prentice, and Thomas 1989). They also tend to stay longer in a destination, spend more money, and immerse themselves deeper into a local community than other types of tourists.

Contemporary Trends and Issues

The rest of this chapter focuses on three factors that directly affect the supply and demand for heritage tourism: technology and social media, the recent recognition of nontraditional forms of heritage, and issues or considerations related to scale.

Social Media and Technology

Social media and technology are extremely important in heritage tourism, and not just for the tourists themselves. Social media–based, user-generated knowledge now plays an important role in travel decision making (Hudson and Thal 2013). The number of people sharing their travel experiences, writing online reviews, and posting holiday photographs and videos on social media is growing exponentially each year (Munar and Jacobsen 2014).

Tourist photograph of Angkor Wat, Cambodia, will soon become a post on social media. (Photo by S. Gmelch)

Travel-specific ratings platforms such as TripAdvisor provide information about visitors' experiences as well as recommendations and rankings of the most desirable attractions, activities, hotels, and restaurants at a destination (Banerjee and Chua 2016). These social media platforms are directly relevant to heritage tourism, especially from a marketing and management perspective since they shape people's decisions to participate in certain cultural events, dine in restaurants that serve traditional cuisine, stay in heritage hotels, or visit particular museums.

Social media is also being used in a very intentional manner by cultural attractions and destinations to promote themselves (Pepe and Bournique 2016; Yoo and Lee 2015). This has serious implications for marketing costs, truth in advertising, and other management considerations. For example, social media is a less expensive means of disseminating information to a wider consumer audience and can help increase a destination's competitiveness (Leung, Law, Van Hoof, and Buhalis 2013).

Internet- or GPS-based technology also plays a role in heritage tourism. There is a growing interest among destination planners and managers, academic researchers, and tourism marketers in the spatial behaviors and flows of tourists in historic cities and museums and at archaeological sites (Shoval and Ahas 2016; Toha and Ismail 2015). With visitors' volunteer participation, many studies have been conducted utilizing this technology (Grinberger, Shoval, and McKercher 2014). GPS-based tracking devices provide an understanding about visitors' favorite locales within a historic urban center or at which scenic areas they spend most of their time. They may also help in understanding differing visitation patterns between first-time and repeat visitors, modeling tourist routes and itineraries, and monitoring visitor impacts in parks and heritage areas. As a research tool, tracking devices deliver more accurate accounts of people's spatial behaviors than self-reported answers on surveys can provide (Shoval and Isaacson 2009).

The same digital technology may enhance the heritage experience for visitors. This is particularly true among younger attendees who rely heavily on mobile phone–based technology for their information and entertainment. For instance, the number of "smart destinations" is growing. These are places that increasingly rely on information and communication technology to promote themselves and provide information and services to residents and tourists. Masses of data are available through smartphone apps and other devices that enable people to order food, call an Uber or taxi, locate a hotel or museum, purchase tickets, or acquire historical and geographic data about a place. With this realization, more individual cultural sites are beginning to provide volumes of data and digital guides through innovations such as QR codes and smartphone apps (Bohlin and Brandt 2014; Solima and Izzo in press).

Recognizing Nontraditional Heritage Tourisms

Several types of tourism that are not normally regarded as having much to do with heritage do indeed reflect traditions inherited/passed down from the past. These include, among others, pilgrimage, agritourism, sport tourism, dark tourism, volunteer tourism, food tourism, and some elements of touristic visits to friends and relatives (VFR). This section briefly examines only dark, volunteer, and pilgrimage tourism as salient forms of heritage tourism from a supply-and-demand perspective. While other authors in this volume provide detailed case studies on dark tourism (Isaac) and volunteer tourism (Garland), here I provide a more general overview.

While sites of death and human suffering, such as concentration camps, battlefields, cemeteries, and prisons, have exuded some degree of appeal to people for centuries, only recently has visiting them been recognized by scholars and destination managers as a legitimate subsector of tourism. This so-called "dark tourism" involves visits to places where human-caused and natural disasters, suffering, and death occurred, or sites indirectly associated with these (Hartmann 2014; Lennon and Foley 2000). This is an important form of heritage tourism and can be found in nearly all parts of the world.

Mass grave marker at Choeung Ek, the location of one of Cambodia's former "killing fields" where at least two million civilians were executed by the Khmer Rouge regime of communist Pol Pot. Today, it is a Buddhist Memorial Park visited by domestic and international tourists. (Photo by S. Gmelch)

Although the range of dark destinations and attractions is nearly interminable, some of the most prominent attractions today include slavery sites, battlefields and war memorials, cemeteries, natural disaster locations, concentration camps, locations of famous crimes, criminal museums, dungeons, prisons, sites of nuclear catastrophes, and as Isaac describes in this volume, active conflict zones. These places and events are among the most important heritage narratives of countries and regions.

Not every dark attraction exists at the same level of darkness or has the same impact on every audience. Some dark sites radiate deeper feelings and more negative sentiments than others, and the experience is not the same for each locale or for each visitor. Visitors' own interests, whether or not a site was built intentionally as a tourist attraction or developed organically owing to the infamy of the events that occurred there, the type of event or suffering that occurred, and the degree to which a site is emphasized in political ideology and discourse, all shape the tourist experience (Sharpley 2009; Stone 2006). Owing to the sensitive nature of what these attractions demarcate or commemorate, unique management approaches are required to ensure that the site's interpretation, presentation, and marketing are done tastefully and cautiously, bearing in mind sensitive audiences, including victims and victims' family members (Kerr and Price 2016; Kidron 2013).

Volunteer tourism also has salient heritage connections. This refers to people traveling for the purpose of doing something good for the Earth or for humankind. It is an ostensibly altruistic experience that involves people traveling, typically on their own expense, to serve the needs of others (Butcher and Smith 2015; Wearing 2001; Garland this volume). This may entail helping build houses or dig wells, teaching illiterate populations to read, planting trees in a nature preserve, or fixing trails in a national park. Several aspects of volunteer tourism overlap specifically with cultural heritage. Volunteers play a crucial part in staffing museums and other heritage places (Holmes 2003). In the Western world, most heritage sites are nonprofit or public organizations and are therefore especially reliant upon volunteer staff members, even temporary ones including tourists who have come to volunteer and spend their holiday in the locale (Jago and Deery 2001). Heritage volunteers are inspired by a wide range of motives, including altruism, self-fulfillment, socialization, skills development, social status enhancement, the ability to pursue a hobby or interest, or simply to use up spare time (Jago and Deery 2001; Timothy and Boyd 2003; Garland this volume).

Other "volunteer vacations" further scientific knowledge through active heritage conservation and exploration. It is becoming more common for people to undertake educational, altruistic, and active holidays. One manifestation of this is to participate in an archaeological dig or conservation effort. Dozens of archaeology tour companies have been established specifically to offer package deals for the archaeologically curious, who volunteer on a dig or at a museum (Timothy 2011). They work with governments and scientific teams to assess the labor needs of various digs and conservation efforts and provide some degree of training and exercises to familiarize volunteers with the history and geographical context of the site they will visit. In addition, participants are minimally trained in the art and science of digging, sifting, cleaning, and cataloging and may be involved in one or all of these activities. Many historical discoveries have been made through the efforts of volunteer travelers.

Many projects depend on volunteer labor to ensure that deadlines are met and to help stretch budgets. Volunteers are key to the success of many archaeological sites, museums, and national monuments, especially in the contemporary climate of austere government budget cutbacks. Museums, national parks, national monuments, interpretive centers, archives, and historic homes are becoming increasingly reliant upon volunteers, many of whom travel from home to spend their holidays helping clean, catalog, repair, maintain, and interpret.

Religious tourism or pilgrimage is one of the oldest forerunners to modern tourism. It involves people traveling to sites primarily for religious or spiritual purposes—to commune with a deity, to seek forgiveness for sins, or to fulfill religious obligations. Some pilgrims' sole desire is to travel in piety without worldly distractions, their sole aim being to seek spiritual enlightenment. Others combine pilgrimage with other activities, such as sightseeing, recreational pursuits, or staying in luxury hotels along the way. Still others are hardly pilgrims at all. Instead, they visit sacred sites out of curiosity or as part of a larger cultural itinerary. Regardless of motive, activities undertaken, or length of stay, pilgrimage is one of the most pervasive forms of heritage tourism today. The rituals, prayers, hymns, communions, sacred spaces, poetics, and historic buildings are all important elements of human heritage that contribute to the spiritual experiences of pilgrims and cultural undertakings of others in religious contexts (Timothy and Olsen 2006).

Issues of Scale

Scale is an important concept in understanding, planning, and promoting heritage tourism. One manifestation of scale is the extent of market reach. The most visited heritage sites are either global (e.g., the Great Wall) or national (e.g., a Civil War battlefield). Much less attention is paid by destination managers and tourism promoters to the lower-order scales of the local and personal, yet these also play an important role in tourists' destination choices (Timothy 1997). Local heritage—a museum or monument devoted to an area's cultural past—is likely to appeal primarily to domestic tourists or residents of a given region. Personal heritage, which is perhaps the smallest scale of heritage, actually prompts people to range more widely in search of their personal history. Genealogy and family history are important leisure pursuits today, and for many enthusiasts, visiting ancestral lands becomes part of who they are, solidifying the connection between their personal identity, familial legacy, and a tangible place (Timothy 2008).

Genealogy travel and personal heritage tourism manifest in many ways but are characterized primarily by visits to filial homelands; visiting historic clan areas and ancestral farms; spending time in archives, churches, and cemeteries; meeting local people who may or may not be distant relatives; and dining on locally produced foods that might represent what one's ancestors ate. Genealogy centers and family history libraries have emerged throughout the world to assist people in identifying their roots and locating the places of their forebears. Genealogy tours are becoming increasingly common, and many destinations that have experienced large-scale emigration have begun to realize the potential profitability of catering to the travel needs of their diasporic populations abroad (Basu 2007; Higginbotham 2012; Timothy 2008).

The second scale-related issue is the size and deemed importance of a particular heritage place. The tourism industry has long focused on the most elaborate, grand, and ostentatious heritage sites in the world such as the Great Wall of China, Machu Picchu in Peru, the Statue of Liberty in New York, the Coliseum in Rome, or Red Square in Moscow. These tend to be major symbolic locales, tangible forms of heritage, and heritage that is very old. In fact, the lavish heritage sites that tourism focuses on actually represent the heritage of a very small portion of humankind. What percentage of the world's past and present inhabitants were kings, queens, generals, and presidents? Not many, but the tendency is for tourism to promote and utilize this aspect of heritage overwhelmingly to brand places and sell products. The United Nations Educational, Scientific and Cultural Organization (UNESCO) has contributed to this unbalanced view of the past with its overwhelming emphasis on the grandiose and universal heritage, while simultaneously ignoring the vernacular heritage of the world. Indeed, the majority of the world's cultural heritage is rather ordinary, intangible, and not so old. Nonetheless, there appears to be a growing interest among serious heritage tourists to recognize the importance of smaller-scale heritage (Timothy 2014a and b).

Heritage branding is the third notion related to scale. Destination "brands" may develop organically through time as places that become famous and well established. Destinations may also be branded as part of an intentional promotional effort to distinguish them from their competitors. There is a common, albeit erroneous, perception that places branded with the heritage label will spontaneously receive greater numbers of visitors than unbranded localities.

National heritage brands have existed for decades throughout the world. For example, in the United States, the National Park Service (NPS) maintains a list of more than 2,500 National Historic Landmarks, which includes objects, structures, sites, and historic districts that demonstrate exceptional historical significance for the nation (National Park Service 2017a). The related designation, the National Register of Historic Places (NRHP), which is also overseen by the NPS, focuses more broadly on the identification, evaluation, and protection of heritage resources at the national, regional, and local levels. There are more than 90,000 properties and 1.4 million individual objects listed on the NRHP (National Park Service 2017b).

On the global scale, the most popular heritage brand is by far the UNESCO World Heritage List (WHL). As of mid-2017 there were 1,062 World Heritage Sites (WHSs) in 167 countries, with many more on the Tentative List (UNESCO 2017). Several countries actively vie for WHS designations, applying for the UNESCO brand for their own sites and locales each year. Italy and China have the most WHSs with 52 each, followed by Spain (46), France (42), and Germany (41). Many countries view the WHL as a marketable brand that will automatically increase visitation, but research shows that this is not necessarily the case and that the WHL brand does not always result in positive outcomes for host communities (Buckley 2004; Jimura 2011; Smith 2002). Instead, other factors such as existing popularity of the site before its inscription, physical access to the site, and market access in terms of the cost and time it takes to get there are more influential (Timothy 2011).

The final issue related to scale is the popular trend in cultural trails. These are linear routes of varying lengths that tourists may follow and are found in both urban and rural areas. Generally, they derive from one of two sources: organic development or purposive planning (Timothy and Boyd 2015). Organic trails form over time as linear corridors once plodded by hunters, traders, pilgrims, or migrants continue to be used today as transportation passageways, recreation paths, or long-distance tourist routes. Purposive trails are intentionally planned routes that aim to generate income through tourism as well as protect natural and cultural resources, provide recreational opportunities, and educate the public. They may be short- or long-distance trails that connect nodes, or specific sites and attractions, so that they emphasize a specific theme. Purposive trails have been adopted by many countries and regions as a tool for connecting small sites that would not attract much visitor attention on their own but by becoming part of a larger circuit do. Thus, trails can be a means of increasing the visibility of a local or regional attraction, extending its interscalar market reach through route-based collaboration. Many themed trails exist in all parts of the world and frequently focus on the lives of famous individuals, certain industries, architectural styles, farm products, and industrial innovations. Some prominent examples include the European Route of Jewish Heritage, the Oregon Cheese Trail, the European Route of Industrial Heritage, the Stellenbosch Wine Route, and the Shakespeare's Way walking trail.

Conclusion

Every place has heritage, although not all heritage is saleable as a tourist commodity. When understood in its totality, heritage is quite comprehensive and includes world famous and iconic attractions, as well as national and local monuments of lesser repute. Nevertheless, they are all important elements of humankind's heritage. Scale is a critical part of understanding the consumption and production of heritage tourism. It influences heritage in many ways, such as how personally connected heritage consumers might be to a specific historic place, politically driven decisions on which elements of the past should be protected and promoted, the branding efforts of heritage destinations, and the development of cultural trails to connect individual heritage nodes into large-scale linear resources that can be used to promote heritage themes within a destination.

Cultural heritage in one form or another is the basis of a majority of global tourism. It influences how people in heritage destinations see themselves and how tourists perceive them. Like all forms of tourism, heritage tourism can be a blessing or a curse. As long as the past remains a saleable commodity, tourists will continue to visit, bringing with them the potential to benefit local communities through increased employment, regional income, and tax revenue, as well as the potential to harm communities through overcrowding, cultural appropriation, and social change. To maximize the benefits of tourism and minimize its negative aspects, it is incumbent upon countries, regions, and localities to identify their heritage potential by understanding the heritage market, the relationships between heritage and other forms of tourism, the issue of scale, and the role technology plays in providing memorable experiences.

Source: For a more detailed discussion, see "Contemporary Cultural Heritage and Tourism: Development Issues and Emerging Trends," *Public Archaeology* 13:1–3, 30–47, 2014.

References Cited

Adie, B. A., and C. M. Hall. 2017. "Who Visits World Heritage? A Comparative Analysis of Three Cultural Sites." *Journal of Heritage Tourism* 12(1): 67–80.

Banerjee, S., and A. Y. Chua. 2016. "In Search of Patterns among Travellers' Hotel Ratings in TripAdvisor." *Tourism Management* 53:125–131.

Basu, P. 2007. *Highland Homecomings: Genealogy and Heritage Tourism in the Scottish Diaspora*. London: Routledge.

Bohlin, M., and D. Brandt. 2014. "Creating Tourist Experiences by Interpreting Places Using Digital Guides." *Journal of Heritage Tourism* 9(1): 1–17.

Buckley, R. 2004. "The Effects of World Heritage Listing on Tourism to Australian National Parks." *Journal of Sustainable Tourism* 12(1): 70–84.

Butcher, J., and P. Smith. 2015. *Volunteer Tourism: The Lifestyle Politics of International Development*. London: Routledge.

Graham, B., G. Ashworth, and J. Tunbridge. 2016. *A Geography of Heritage: Power, Culture & Economy*. London: Routledge.

Grinberger, A. Y., N. Shoval, and B. McKercher. 2014. "Typologies of Tourists' Time–Space Consumption: A New Approach Using GPS Data and GIS Tools." *Tourism Geographies* 16(1): 105–123.

Hartmann, R. 2014. "Dark Tourism, Thanatourism, and Dissonance in Heritage Tourism Management: New Directions in Contemporary Tourism Research." *Journal of Heritage Tourism* 9(2): 166–182.

Herbert, D. T., R. C. Prentice, and C. Thomas, eds. 1989. *Heritage Sites: Strategies for Marketing and Development*. Aldershot: Avebury.

Higginbotham, G. 2012. "Seeking Roots and Tracing Lineages: Constructing a Framework of Reference for Roots and Genealogical Tourism." *Journal of Heritage Tourism* 7(3): 189–203.

Holmes, K. 2003. "Volunteers in the Heritage Sector: A Neglected Audience?" *International Journal of Heritage Studies* 9(4): 341–355.

Hudson, S., and K. Thal. 2013. "The Impact of Social Media on the Consumer Decision Process: Implications for Tourism Marketing." *Journal of Travel & Tourism Marketing* 30(1-2): 156–160.

Jago, L. K., and M. A. Deery. 2001. "Managing Volunteers," in *Quality Issues in Heritage Visitor Attractions*, eds. S. Drummond and I. Yeoman, pp. 194–216. Oxford: Butterworth-Heinemann.

Jimura, T. 2011. "The Impact of World Heritage Site Designation on Local Communities—A Case Study of Ogimachi, Shirakawa-mura, Japan." *Tourism Management* 32(2): 288–296.

Kerr, M. M., and R. H. Price. 2016. "Overlooked Encounters: Young Tourists' Experiences at Dark Sites." *Journal of Heritage Tourism* 11(2): 177–185.

Kidron, C. A. 2013. "Being There Together: Dark Family Tourism and the Emotive Experience of Co-Presence in the Holocaust Past." *Annals of Tourism Research* 41:175–194.

Lennon, J., and M. Foley. 2000. *Dark Tourism: The Attraction of Death and Disaster*. London: Thomson.

Leung, D., R. Law, H. Van Hoof, and D. Buhalis. 2013. "Social Media in Tourism and Hospitality: A Literature Review." *Journal of Travel & Tourism Marketing* 30(1-2): 3–22.

Munar, A. M., and J. K. S. Jacobsen. 2014. "Motivations for Sharing Tourism Experiences through Social Media." *Tourism Management* 43:46–54.

National Park Service. 2017a. *National Historic Landmarks Program*. Available at: https://www.nps.gov/nhl/ (accessed June 29, 2017).

National Park Service. 2017b. *National Register of Historic Places*. Available at: https://www.nps.gov/nr/ (accessed June 29, 2017).

Pepe, M. S., and R. Bournique. 2016. "Using Social Media as Historical Marketing Tool for Heritage Sites in Eastern New York State." *Journal of Applied Business Research* 33(1): 123–134.

Sharpley, R. 2009. "Shedding Light on Dark Tourism: An Introduction," in *The Darker Side of Travel: The Theory and Practice of Dark Tourism*, eds. R. Sharpley and P. Stone, pp. 3–22. Bristol: Channel View Publications.

Shoval, N., and R. Ahas. 2016. "The Use of Tracking Technologies in Tourism Research: The First Decade." *Tourism Geographies* 18(5): 587–606.

Shoval, N., and M. Isaacson. 2009. *Tourist Mobility and Advanced Tracking Technologies*. London: Routledge.

Smith, M. 2002. "A Critical Evaluation of the Global Accolade: The Significance of World Heritage Site Status for Maritime Greenwich." *International Journal of Heritage Studies* 8(2): 137–151.

Solima, L., and F. Izzo. in press. "QR Codes in Cultural Heritage Tourism: The New Communications Technologies and Future Prospects in Naples and Warsaw." *Journal of Heritage Tourism*.

Stebbins, R. A. 1996. "Cultural Tourism as Serious Leisure." *Annals of Tourism Research* 23:945–48.

Stone, P. 2006. "A Dark Tourism Spectrum: Towards a Typology of Death and Macabre Related Tourist Sites, Attractions and Exhibitions." *Tourism* 54(2): 145–160.

Timothy, D. J. 1997. "Tourism and the Personal Heritage Experience. *Annals of Tourism Research* 34(3):751–754.

———. 2008. "Genealogical Mobility: Tourism and the Search for a Personal Past," in *Geography and Genealogy: Locating Personal Pasts*, eds. D. J. Timothy and J. Kay Guelke, pp. 115–135. Aldershot: Ashgate.

———. 2011. *Cultural Heritage and Tourism: An Introduction*. Bristol: Channel View.

———. 2014a. "Contemporary Cultural Heritage and Tourism: Development Issues and Emerging Trends." *Public Archaeology* 13(3): 30–47.

———. 2014b. "Views of the Vernacular: Tourism and Heritage of the Ordinary," in *Contemporary Issues in Cultural Heritage Tourism*, eds. J. Kaminski, A. Benson, and D. Arnold, pp. 32–44. London: Routledge.

———. 2015. "Cultural Heritage, Tourism and Socio-Economic Development," in *Tourism and Development: Concepts and Issues*, 2nd ed., eds. R. Sharpley and D. J. Telfer, pp. 237–249. Bristol: Channel View Publications.

Timothy, D. J., and S. W. Boyd. 2003. *Heritage Tourism*. London: Pearson.

———. 2015 *Tourism and Trails: Cultural, Ecological and Management Issues*. Bristol: Channel View Publications.

Timothy, D. J., and D. H. Olsen, eds. 2006. *Tourism, Religion and Spiritual Journeys*. London: Routledge.

Toha, M. A. M., and H. N. Ismail. 2015. "A Heritage Tourism and Tourist Flow Pattern: A Perspective on Traditional versus Modern Technologies in Tracking the Tourists." *International Journal of Built Environment and Sustainability* 2(2): 85–92.

UNESCO. 2017. *World Heritage List*. Available: http://whc.unesco.org/en/list/ (accessed June 30, 2017).

Wearing, S. 2001. *Volunteer Tourism: Experiences that make a difference*. Wallingford, UK: CABI.

Yoo, K-H., and W. Lee. 2015. "Use of Facebook in the US Heritage Accommodations Sector: An Exploratory Study." *Journal of Heritage Tourism* 10(2): 191–201.

13

From Pilgrimage to Dark Tourism? A New Kind of Tourism in Palestine

Rami K. Isaac

Tourism has long been important to Palestine. Many of the Holy Land's historical and religious sites are located in Palestinian areas—in Bethlehem, Jericho, Nablus, Hebron, and East Jerusalem. Tourism currently contributes 14 percent of Palestine's gross domestic product (GDP). About half this revenue comes from domestic tourists, mainly Palestinians living in Israel; most of the rest comes from international tourists who arrive on pilgrimages to Christian religious sites. Which sites they visit depends upon the religious denomination they belong to, since different churches have their own "sacred" sites. Christian pilgrimage is not a unified phenomenon, and there are noticeable differences between Catholic and Protestant pilgrims (Fleischer 2003). A typical pilgrimage to the Holy Land (Palestine and Israel) lasts nine or ten days. The average itinerary includes four or five days in Jerusalem with visits to Bethlehem, Jericho, and the Dead Sea and about the same time in northern Israel where the focus is on Nazareth, the Sea of Galilee, and other sites.

After the establishment of the Palestinian National Authority in 1993, several essential steps were taken to market and encourage tourism development in Palestine. The first step was an economic agreement signed between Palestine and Israel in May 1994 (*Alternative Tourism Journal* 2004). This agreement allowed the Palestinian Authority to regulate state finances, levy taxes, and standardize import policies between Israel and Palestine. It also established the Israeli Shekel as the official legal tender and helped to export Palestinian products such as olive oil and wine to the global market, which formerly had been prohibited. Most importantly for this discussion, it focused on the free movement of tourists in and within the West bank and the Gaza Strip.

The second step taken was the establishment of the Palestinian Ministry of Tourism and Antiquities, which took responsibility for recognizing and supporting the tourism industry in the West Bank and the Gaza Strip. The ministry accomplished a lot, reorganizing internal transportation, developing tourism agencies and restaurants, and rehabilitating religious and cultural events. Palestine's tourism industry, however, is fundamentally controlled by Israel, which has a stranglehold on the flow of international tourists, from issuing visas to controlling flights, lodging, and the provision of Israeli guides and tours within the country (Isaac and Ashworth 2012). All major Palestinian towns and cities also have Israeli checkpoints (more will be said about this later) that control who enters and exists these cities, including tourists. Pilgrims on an organized tour travel freely, whereas individual tourists are required to go through checkpoints. For example, in Bethlehem, all individual travelers need to go through the so-called terminal border control, a huge system. When incidents occur in Israel, such as a suicide bombing, the whole border is closed and tourists are not allowed to enter Bethlehem. So "free travel" really depends on the political situation and importantly on the mood of checkpoint soldiers. What led to this situation? And might the Occupation, ironically, provide a new tourism outlet?

The Palestinian Situation

Since the beginning of the twentieth century, Palestine has witnessed complicated changes in its political circumstances, most notably the creation of Israel in 1948 and the 1967 war during which Israel occupied the West Bank of the Jordan River (including the old city of East Jerusalem), the Gaza Strip, and the Golan Heights obtained from its Arab neighbors. These events created catastrophic political, economic, and social circumstances that have deeply affected the lives of the Palestinian people. With their homes demolished and land confiscated, most Palestinians became refugees in 1948, forced to live in camps in neighboring Jordan, Lebanon, and Syria (Morris 2004). In many ways, Palestine was wiped off the map. Historic Palestine is now known as Israel. Those Palestinians who remain within Israel's borders reside in three fragmented areas: Gaza, the West Bank, and Jerusalem. Communities in each area are further fragmented and their boundaries confined by the network of roads that connects the 190 illegal and armed Israeli settlements that have been built on former Palestinian land. In spite of many peace negotiations and agreements made with Israel over the years, much of Palestinian life remains tightly controlled by Israel. It controls all movements of people and goods to, from, and within Palestine (Alternative Tourism Group 2008), as well as most Palestinian water resources (Isaac 2017). In the West Bank, Palestinians are locked into 70 tiny enclaves that comprise just 42 percent of its territory and are encircled by 500 checkpoints and additional temporary inspections—the so-called flying checkpoints—(Moïsi 2009) and by the Segregation Wall (B'tselem 2002; Halper 2005).

Israel began building the Segregation Wall in June 2002 to separate Israel from Palestine. The wall is five times as long and twice as high as the Berlin Wall that once separated communist East Germany from West Germany. The Segregation Wall now extends more than 450 miles—the distance from London to Zurich and greater than that between Boston and Washington DC. A 65-yard-wide strip of no-man's land runs the length of the wall, erasing the agricultural fields and houses once located within it. The residents of thirty-eight Palestinian villages can no longer farm or access major services such as hospitals and clinics; students are unable to reach their universities (see Harker 2009). Even those portions of the Wall that are constructed of see-through fencing are protected by sensors, trenches, security roads, minefields, checkpoints, watchtowers, and military patrols. More than 50,000 Palestinians are now trapped between the border (Israeli checkpoints at the entrance of all Palestinian cities) and the Wall, facing impoverishment and ultimate transfer (United Nations 2005).

A section of the Segregation Wall that separates Palestinians from Israel's Jewish citizens. (Photo by VanderWolf Images/Shutterstock.com)

The old city of East Jerusalem, the heart of pilgrimage tourism in the region, was occupied by Israel in 1967 and is now surrounded by checkpoints, encircled by the Wall, and isolated from its social and geographical surroundings (Isaac 2009, 2010b; Isaac and Ashworth 2012). Palestinian residents of East Jerusalem are isolated from the wider West Bank society; 55,000 people are confined in neighborhoods completely encircled by walls and forced to pass through slow and humiliating "terminals" (security checkpoint buildings) before being able to go to school, to work, to shop, or simply to visit relatives or friends outside. On the other side of the Wall, more than two million Palestinians are confined within the West Bank (Harper 2008).

In 2004 the International Court of Justice in The Hague, the Netherlands, ruled that the Segregation Wall was illegal and ordered Israel to dismantle it. Israel refuses to comply. Many other forms of international pressure have been placed on Israel to stop building settlements, end its military occupation, and work with the Palestinians to find a viable and peaceful two-state or one-state solution. It is far beyond the scope or intent of this chapter to explore these options, but the international community is in agreement that a human rights–based solution must be found—one that guarantees justice, equality, and liberty for all people living between the Jordan River and the Mediterranean Sea. Until that happens, Palestinians will continue to suffer and the entire area will continue to be characterized by tension, instability, violence, and death—the exact situation more tourists are interested in seeing and experiencing.

Palestinians prepare to pass through the Bethlehem checkpoint in the Segregation Wall. (Photo by Ryan Rodrick Beiler/Shutterstock.com)

Dark Tourism

Researchers have documented a growing fascination among tourists with visiting sites associated with suffering, tragedy, death, conflict, and atrocities (Cohen 2011; Logan and Reeves 2009; Stone and Sharpley 2008). These include places as diverse as the battlefields of Gettysburg or Culloden, Nazi concentration camps, Cambodia's killing fields, and the Fukushima exclusion zone in Japan. Various terms have been suggested to characterize this practice including "black spot" tourism (Rojek 1993), "thanatourism" (Seaton 1996), "morbid tourism" (Blom 2000), and "dark tourism," first coined by Foley and Lennon in 1996. Given the bleak and unnatural state of affairs existing in Palestine, as described above, the Occupied Territories would seem to be a natural dark tourism site, and some steps have been taken in this direction.

The Alternative Tourism Group (ATG) in Bethlehem, a Palestinian NGO established in 1995, specializes in tours that critically examine the politics as well as the history and culture of the Holy Land. Its goal—in keeping with responsible tourism operators elsewhere—is to promote tourism that creates economic opportunities for local people and educates tourists. The hope is also that personal exposure to the real situation in Palestine and cross-cultural interaction between tourists and local Palestinians will ultimately contribute to the peace process.

Tourists on ATG tours witness the daily incursions of the Israeli military into Palestinian towns and cities. They learn about the quarter million internally displaced Palestinians who live in their homeland yet are defined by Israeli law as "absentees" and deprived of legal rights to their land, homes, and property (Carter 2006; Halper 2005, 2008; Isaac and Platenkamp 2010). They see the destruction and disorganization of spaces and cities caused by Israeli regulations, systematic military control, and physical structures like the Segregation Wall. These acts of "spaciocide" and "urbicide" (Hanafi 2009) have also robbed Palestinians of places imbued with memories and social meanings.

Tourists on ATG tours get to meet with Palestinian families and listen to their stories. They visit Palestinian refugee camps in Nablus, Bethlehem, and Jenin where they are introduced to the existing conditions of refugees and learn about the Al-Nakba ("disaster" or "catastrophe")—the mass destruction and depopulation of Palestine in 1948 during which about 750,000 Palestinians were forced to leave their homes and some 500 Palestinian localities were demolished. (Palestinian refugees and their offspring now form the largest refugee population in the world according to the United Nations.) All these stories and "facts on the ground" or "see it for yourself" experiences have an impact whatever tourists' initial motivation may have been for making their trip to the Holy Land.

According to Lennon and Foley (2000) dark tourism is a chronologically modern (twentieth century onward) and primarily Western phenomenon. Initially it was nonpurposeful. Tourists ended up visiting such sites due to "serendipity, the itinerary of tour companies or the merely curious who happened to be in the vicinity" (Lennon and Foley 2000:32). Today, it is much more deliberate with more tourists seeking such places and experiences out, and more tour operators making it possible. Seaton calls dark tourism "thanatourism," the travel dimension of "thanatopsis" (Greek for "meditation on" or "contemplation of death") and defines it as "travel to a location wholly, or partially, motivated by the desire for actual or symbolic encounters with death, particularly, but not exclusively, violent death" (1996:240). Another motivation for engaging in dark tourism is to learn—to better understand the scope of and reasons behind the tragic sites visited, whether historic battlefields, natural disaster areas, or active war or occupation zones. Richter (1980) claims that tourists' journeys can be viewed as representing their ideological values and beliefs. When tourists choose to go on a holiday to a country that is experiencing war and political instability, they are likely to be politically oriented. They might support one side or another in the conflict or they are simply intrigued by it and want to know more about its origins, presence in everyday life, and likely consequences. Tourists in this case are witnessing history in the making where danger is an additional attraction, providing an emotional edge to their experience.

Until the Israeli occupation ends and Palestinian human rights are restored, Palestinians should think about actively promoting dark tourism. The Segregation Wall alone is a sight to behold. Some tourists are already visiting the area not only *despite* war and conflict but *because* of it (Isaac and Ashworth 2012). The tours offered by the Alternative Tourism Group, described earlier, show that some tourists are interested in learning about the politics behind the Occupation and seeing for themselves the reality of Palestinian life today. Obviously Palestine has the potential to attract more tourists than those who come for spiritual uplift or to see sacred sites, and there is an economic motive to do so. This tourism sector is not as profitable as might be expected since these pilgrimage visitors generally seek low-budget, low-margin travel programs and it is subject to high seasonal fluctuations, peaking around religious holidays. Pilgrimage tourists are also less susceptible to tourism marketing since their motivation is a spiritual one. The work of the Palestinian Ministry of Tourism and Antiquities has already broadened its tourism capacity, although its capacity to draw tourists is severely hampered by the closures and military checkpoints that restrict the free flow and movement of residents *and* tourists between Israel and Palestine and between cities within the West Bank (Al-Rimmawi 2013). But even this restriction would be part of the appeal of a dark tourism experience. The Palestinian Ministry of Tourism and Antiquities and independent tour operators, including the Alternative Tourism Group, should think seriously about *explicitly* marketing Palestine as a site for dark tourism—a pilgrimage of a very different sort.

Source: For a more detailed discussion, see Rami Isaac and Gregory Ashworth, "Moving from Pilgrimage to 'Dark' Tourism: Leveraging Tourism in Palestine," *Tourism, Culture and Communication* 11:149–164, 2012.

References Cited

Al-Rimmawi, Hussein. 2013. "2003 Palestinian Tourism: A Period of Transition." *International Journal of Contemporary Hospitality Management* 15(2): 76–85.

Alternative Tourism Group. 2008. *Palestine and Palestinians*. Beit Sahour, Palestine: ATG.

Alternative Tourism Journal. 2014. "A Conflict between Two Narratives." Beit Sahour, Palestine: ATG.

Blom, Tom. 2000. "Morbid Tourism—a Postmodern Market Niche with an Example from Althorp." *Norsk Geografisk Tidsskrift—Norwegian Journal of Geograph* 54(1): 29–36.

B'tselem. 2002. *Land Grab: Israel's Settlements Policy in the West Bank*. Jerusalem: B'tselem.

Carter, J. 2002. *Palestine: Peace Not Apartheid*. New York: Simon and Schuster.

Cohen, Erik. 2011. "Educational Dark Tourism at an 'in Populo' Site: The Holocaust Museum in Jerusalem." *Annals of Tourism Research* 38:193–209.

Fleischer, Aliza. 2003. "The Tourist behind the Pilgrim in the Holy Land." *Hospitality Management* 19:311–326.

Foley, Malcom, and John Lennon. 1996. "JFK and Dark Tourism: A Fascination with Assassination." *International Journal of Heritage Studies* 2:198–211.

Halper, Jeff. 2005. "Israel in a Middle East Union. A Two Stage Approach to the Conflict." *Tikkun* 21(1): 17–21.

———. 2008. *An Israeli in Palestine: Resisting Dispossession, Redeeming Israel*. New York: Pluto Press.

Hanafi, Sari. 2009. "Spacio-cide: Colonial Politics, Invisibility and Rezoning in Palestinian Territory." *Contemporary Arab Affairs* 2:106–122.

Harker, Christopher. 2009. "Student Im/Mobility in Birzeit, Palestine." *Mobilities* 4(1): 11–35.

Isaac, K. Rami. 2009. "Can the Segregation Wall in Bethlehem Be a Tourist Attraction?" *Tourism, Hospitality, Planning and Development* 6:221–228.

———. 2010a. "Alternative Tourism: New Forms of Tourism in Bethlehem for the Palestinian Tourism Industry." *Current Issues in Tourism* 13:21–36.

———. 2010b. "Moving from Pilgrimage to Responsible Tourism: The Case of Palestine" *Current Issues in Tourism* 13:579–590.

———. 2017. "Transformational Host Communities: Justice Tourism and the Water Regime in Palestine" *Tourism, Culture and Communication* 17:139–158.

Isaac, K. Rami, and Gregory Ashworth. 2012. "Moving from Pilgrimage to Dark Tourism: Leveraging Tourism in Palestine." *Tourism, Culture and Communication* 11:149–164.

Isaac, K. Rami, and Vincent Platenkamp. 2010. "Volunteer Tourism: A Moral Perspective," in *Tourism, Progress and Peace*, eds. Ian Kelly and Omar Mouffakir. London: CABI International.

Lennon, John, and Malcom Foley. 2000. *Dark Tourism*. London: Continuum.

Logan, William, and Keir Reeves. 2009. "Introduction: Remembering Places of Pain and Shame," in *Places of Pain and Shame: Dealing with Difficult Past*, eds. William Logan and Keir Reeves. London: Routledge.

Moïsi, Dominique. 2009. *The Geopolitics of Emotion: How Cultures of Fear, Humiliation and Hope Are Reshaping the World*. New York: Doubleday.

Morris, Benny. 2004. *The Birth of the Palestinian Refugee Problem Revisited*. Cambridge, UK: Cambridge University Press.

Rojek, Chris. 1993. *Ways of Escape: Modern Transformations in Leisure and Travel.* London: Palgrave MacMillian.

Seaton, Tony. 1996. "From Thanatopsis to Thanatourism: Guided by the Dark." *International Journal of Heritage Studies* 2:234–244.

Stone, Philip, and Richard Sharpley. 2008. "Consuming Dark Tourism: A Thanatological Perspective." *Annals of Tourism Research* 35:574–595.

United Nations Office for the Coordination of Humanitarian Affairs. 2005. *The Humanitarian Impact of the West Bank Barrier on Palestinian Communities.* Jerusalem: OCHA.

14

Music on the Edge: The Commodification of an Irish Musical Landscape

Adam Kaul

The Cliffs of Moher is a stunningly beautiful, elemental landscape of sea, stone, and sky. Located in County Clare on Ireland's west coast, they extend 5 miles (8 km) between the villages of Doolin and Liscannor, rising from sea level to a height of 700 feet (214 m). It is probably no wonder that people have been traveling there for centuries, long before there was anything we might call a "tourist industry." As early as 1835, the regional landlord, Cornellius O'Brien, built a tower at the Cliffs' highest point to accommodate visitors. As tourism expanded and democratized in the latter half of the twentieth century, the site became a prominent stop on tourist routes. By the 1980s and 1990s when "mass tourism" really took off, throngs of visitors flocked to the Cliffs, crystallizing its reputation as one Ireland's premier tourist destinations. Today, close to a million tourists visit the Cliffs annually.

Musicians have been busking for tourist tips at the Cliffs of Moher for generations. Some have been playing at the site regularly for 20 years or more. But in late 2006, just over a month before the grand opening of a lavish new interpretive center there, it was announced that the local circuit court ordered that unlicensed busking and commercial trading cease. Instead, a new licensing scheme would be implemented allowing a smaller number of buskers to play at the site under strict regulations. As reported in the national newspaper, *The Irish Times* (2006), at one point, the County Council suggested that they would hold auditions to vet musicians. Although this did not end up taking place, it was never made clear how the county bureaucrats were going to assess the quality of the musicians' playing. While it was within the County Council's legal right to regulate the site, the musicians and the public strongly objected. At best, musicians' activities would be severely restricted under the new rules; at worst, they might be barred from the site altogether. Several musicians who regularly played at the site were handed trespass notices and told to vacate the premises. Some complied, but others called the Council's bluff and simply played on. One local resident told me, "The buskers—to their credit—I mean, I'm so pleased they did this—it was only maybe three or four of them, they just said, 'No, we're not moving. We're going to carry on.' They were treated appallingly."

The conflict between buskers and the developers of the new center quickly spun out of control, and the public outcry on behalf of the musicians was widespread. Meanwhile, a letter signed by dozens of famous Irish musicians was sent to the Clare County Council pleading with them to open a dialogue with the buskers. A highly charged narrative quickly took hold that placed local musicians in stark opposition to the economic interests of the tourism industry. Accusations and counteraccusations were made, privately and through the press. Local and national media outlets fanned the flames with dramatic headlines like "No Moher Buskers" and "Busk Off if You're Rubbish!"

A number of questions emerge about this situation, some specific to this case and some general. What exactly led to the conflict in the first place, and how did it so quickly become part of the national conversation? What is the proper balance between music making and money making? And more broadly, what can this case tell us about the ways in which tourism enterprises have come to increasingly manage the activities of people who work at tourist sites? While very real disagreements exist between buskers and the managers who run the interpretive center, I suggest in this chapter that an underlying identity crisis fueled the public discourse. Both traditional Irish music and the Cliffs of Moher have emerged as symbolic markers of Irish identity, and in an atmosphere of tighter regulations, overdevelopment of tourism ventures, and a severe economic recession in Ireland at the time, the conflict between music and tourism at the Cliffs of Moher touched a raw nerve.

In what follows, I use several intersecting frames of analysis to explain the multifaceted tensions that emerged at the nexus between tourism and music at the Cliffs. First, a political economy approach to the neoliberal commodification of the site and various actors' activities there is warranted. Second, the site's importance as a national symbol and the similarly heady significance of music's place as a marker of Irish identity naturally lends itself to an analysis of changing notions of Irishness in a post–Celtic Tiger, postcrash era. At the core of this case study is an analysis of the inherent tension between commerce and culture.

Commodifying an Irish landscape

The ownership of the property where the new interpretive center is situated is complicated. Originally, 35 separate farming families owned various sections of the Cliffs, but significantly, there has always been a public right-of-way along the cliff edge. In the 1970s, as tourism began to intensify, a regional tourism body called Shannon Development secured a "compulsory purchase order" of one section near the highest portion of the Cliffs where a car park, toilets, and tearooms were built. As it developed the site, independent local vendors began to set up souvenir shops. Buskers began to play there regularly, too. Discussions to further develop the site began as early as the 1980s. This followed a larger pattern across Ireland as the government began to actively promote tourism development to stimulate a flagging economy. As annual tourist numbers increased into the hundreds of thousands, legitimate concerns specific to the Cliffs were raised. These included an increase in litter, rapid erosion of the natural landscape, severe pressure on the modest public facilities, and a serious threat to public safety. Signage and fencing were obviously not effective deterrents for the public who felt compelled to cross (and even destroy) barriers so that they could approach the cliff edge.

Tourists at the Cliffs of Moher clamber over the wall meant to restrain and protect them. (Photo by author)

During the initial planning stages, disagreements between the Clare County Council and Shannon Development led the County Council to pursue the project on its own. The final result of the planning process was an extravagant interpretive center called *The Cliffs of Moher Experience* that cost just under €32 million and was opened by the Irish prime minister in 2007 with a great deal of fanfare. In many ways, the project has been a fantastic success. Unfortunately, though, the national economy began to falter and then buckle completely almost immediately thereafter, leaving the Council with a massive bill to pay in a crippled economy.

The new structure is an example *par excellence* of what Professor of Film Studies at the University College Dublin Diane Negra has labeled the "new Irishness." The impetus for the new center emerged out of the Celtic Tiger era of the 1990s and early 2000s when the economy grew at an astounding pace. Ireland was often celebrated—too soon it now seems given the sharp economic crash that began in 2008—as "an economic miracle." Going beyond the obvious economic transformation of Ireland during this time period, Negra argues that this era also ushered in a new set of cultural and personal values that displaced "sentimentality, pathos, nostalgia, volatility and vitality" (2010: 839). "The New Irishness," she writes, "is more austere, more profit-minded, and more efficient than pre-Celtic Tiger models of selfhood. It centralizes makeover strategies in which both the self and the landscape are to be relentlessly improved upon and developed for maximum efficiency" (2010:850). She also notes that part of this transformation was to replace the "traditional" representative symbols of Irishness (shamrocks, rainbows, and rural "folk") with modern architectural aesthetics that symbolized Ireland's new identity as cosmopolitan and globalized.

The main building at *The Cliffs of Moher Experience* exhibits exactly the kind of austere, hypermodern, fluid architectural design that she describes. It is set completely into the hillside with expanded trails and viewing platforms along the Cliffs' edge. Inside, there is a large gift shop, two restaurants, and a cavernous exhibit hall. It is a truly impressive facility that has won several design awards, and the developers proudly advertise its low impact on the environment. The facility may be the perfect symbol of this successful, wealthy "New Irishness," but the planning process for the new development and its subsequent management sparked numerous and ongoing controversies. Only 2 years before its official opening, the project leaders had to revise their cost estimates upward eightfold from the original projections.

Much of the local population in the area also resent the fact that they are now actively discouraged from entering the site without paying newly implemented parking fees. Cultural geographer Noel Healy and his colleagues (2012) report that several coach-tour operators temporarily boycotted the site when they were told that they would be charged eight times as much in parking fees. And then, there was the very public dispute between the developers and buskers. One local told me, "On a weekly basis, I'm not kidding, almost week-by-week, it was a guaranteed [newspaper] story. People were fed up with reading about it. It got to the point if you talk to local people—if you just say 'The Cliffs'—a lot of people will say, 'Oh, don't talk to me about the Cliffs'!" To some extent, it could be argued that these points of conflict are the natural result of a major new development in the region; however, it is also clear that the developers' aggressive moves to rapidly take managerial and economic control of the site initiated an adversarial posture that demanded a total ownership and appropriation of the Cliffs of Moher.

While "ownership" is commonly understood to be a fairly simple legal matter, it is actually often complicated. "Ownership," write anthropologists Mark Busse and Veronica Strang, can be perceived "as a set of processes through which people assert and contest rights rather than a static bundle or structure of rights" (2011:4). Despite the fact that the County Council legally owns the interpretive center at the Cliffs of Moher, in Ireland there is a long-standing tradition that the public has access to the coastline protected by the 1993 Roads Act. Having a right-of-way through the County Council's property does not automatically allow people to engage in commercial trading there though, whether it takes the form of selling souvenirs or playing music for tips. In practice, the protection of this right-of-way by the tourism authorities has been mixed. On the one hand, the authorities secured permission from the local landowners to develop a more secure walking path along the whole 8-km length of the Cliffs' edge from Doolin in the north to Liscannor in the south, complete with permanent fencing and pavements. This effectively instantiated the tradition of open access. On the other hand, the developers of the new center have made active attempts to limit access as well. Parking along the road leading to the Cliffs has been banned, so visitors are no longer able to use their right-of-way unless they hike uphill many miles to the main site. Instead, they are now funneled into the center's car park, which currently charges a fee for every adult passenger. Even though the charge is modest, it is often cited by locals as an indicator that the site has been "taken over" and "ruined" by the County Council and its subsidiary corporation, The Cliffs of Moher Ltd.

Why should this be so? More is at work here than an arguably modest increase in parking fees. At least part of the public's unease in this case is the seemingly porous relationship between the government and private enterprise, and the complicated (and often confused) understanding of "ownership" of the site. There is a widespread perception that the subsidiary corporation of the Clare County Council is appropriating the bulk of the tourist trade, such that the corporation reaps most of the profits, and also discouraging locals from visiting the site. If ownership is a process of asserting ones rights, then it is clear that the County Council and its subsidiary corporation "own" the Cliffs of Moher significantly more now than they used to. I would suggest that the issue with the increased charges at the car park along with other actions taken by the developers have become emblematic of the larger concern with the neoliberal privatization of public resources in general, and an important part of what motivates people is of course cultural rather than simply political or economic. A simplified public discourse contends that what was once a national resource is now a commodified tourist product. People are understandably uncomfortable when a landscape so pregnant with cultural and national meaning is developed and privatized by macro-scale institutions that have garnered so much distrust due to the economic crash in Ireland.

The Cliffs of Moher is more than just a destination for international tourists or a point of economic and political contention for locals. It is a *quintessential* Irish landscape, used in many instances as a national cultural symbol, and in that sense it is a highly charged space. Indeed, it is not overstating the case to claim that the Cliffs have become one of a collection of metonyms for Irishness at home, and they are promoted as a visual representation of Irishness for international tourists abroad. Nationalized rural landscapes like the Cliffs are also commonly imbricated with nationalized cultural practices, in this case with traditional Irish music. Tourist expectations contribute to this conflation of the landscape with Irish music. One busker at the site, a harpist, told me, "I sing a lot of folk music, so lots of Irish ballads, you know, because that's what tourists like to hear. . . . People come here—they love the music. They love the atmosphere it creates. . . . I think the music makes it more Irish."

For many, there is a romantic and evocative union of land, music, and identity at the Cliffs. In an interview with another local musician in which I asked about the basic features of the "west County Clare style" of fiddle playing, she described aspects of the local landscape that influence her playing including the Cliffs, but did not mention a single musicological technique. This synthesis of Irishness, Irish music, and the landscape is nothing new, and it goes well beyond this one locale. There has been a long-standing fetishization of the land in Ireland, which has led to a romantic notion that Irish cul-

Musician and tourists on the path leading to the Cliffs of Moher. (Photo by author)

ture, traditions, and even kinship are derived directly from the land itself. As far back as the 1930s, anthropologist Conrad Arensberg, who conducted ethnography for a short time near the Cliffs of Moher, wrote, "A particular ancestral line is inseparable from a particular plot of earth. All others are 'strangers to the land'" (1959:83). So, describing the Cliffs of Moher not just as an Irish landscape but also as a "musical landscape" has real resonance.

Making Money, Making Music

Just as the relationship between commerce and culture has created tension at the Cliffs of Moher, a similarly awkward relationship occurs at the nexus between money making and music making. As tourism developed into a major part of the economy in the 1980s and 1990s in the West of Ireland, pub owners on the more heavily trafficked tourist routes began to pay musicians a set amount at the end of the evening if they agreed to play sessions to draw tourists in. It was a system that evolved slowly, institutionalizing an older set of values in which musicians' contributions were rewarded with gifts of food, drink, and occasional monetary payments. On the surface, it appears that musicians are spontaneously playing music for the fun of it, although behind the scenes things are more complex. Money generated from the tourists passes through the pub, which is then turned into a kind of "gift" given to the musicians at the end of the night. The point I want to make here is that in the pub session context musicians have largely been able to strike a balance between making money and maintaining a significant level of control over the production of their music.

At the Cliffs, like in the session context in pubs, a system evolved slowly over time between the musicians who played there. Buskers necessarily spread out over the site so that the music would not overlap sonically. An informal number of regular spots, called "pitches," were established, and a hierarchy developed based on seniority and how regularly one played there. Musicians who depended on busking at the Cliffs, and/or had been playing there for many years, garnered higher status among the buskers and were therefore paid due deference because of their achieved status. Buskers new to the site had to learn these informal rules. The new licensing scheme rather rigidly formalized what was an organic egalitarian system. Following the implementation of the new regulations, there were five official pitches, all marked with a numbered sign, and only 10 musicians were able to obtain a license at any given time. Seniority still plays a role.

A newer busker at the site described how the informal system of seniority calcified into a more formal arrangement: "When I came along in 2006, we all got the licenses together, but obviously recognized the fact that these people were already there, and that's fine . . . three of the pitches were pretty much claimed, if you like, from day one." Many buskers only play for a morning or an afternoon, so some pitches are shared among several musicians. All of these arrangements about who gets what pitch are worked out among the musicians themselves.

Interestingly, unlike the session context in which the commercial exchanges are hidden from view, busking collapses the act of music making and money making. In fact, the act of tipping by a passerby is a central characteristic of the collective performance. Buskers put out a hat, a basket, or a music case into which tourists deposit Euros. The commercial relationship is there for anyone to see, but it is seen as an exchange of gifts since no fee or payment is required and because it seems that musicians are in control of the arrangement. Nevertheless, the fact that buskers depend on gift giving rather than a set fee can create dramatic variability in a day's earnings. According to one busker, "The smallest [amount I made] was probably €3 [a little over US$3] after two hours. . . . And [another] day, I made 70 quid [over US$90]. . . . I opened my bag, took out the basket, took off my flute case and my whistles and all, and I've already got money falling in the basket!"

According to buskers, tourists often drastically overestimate how much they make in a day. Tourists are also increasingly confused about buskers' relationship to the corporation that runs the site, wrongly assuming that the musicians are paid employees. "We're not employed," one of the buskers emphatically pointed out to me. "You know, a lot of people think we are, but we're not." As a result of this confusion, the tips that buskers receive have declined dramatically since the opening of the new center. "It's not easy to make money up here," one of them told me, "and it's not as easy to make money as it was [before the new licensing system]." The contract that musicians are now required to sign limits what they can do. They are no longer allowed to sell their own CDs directly to the public. Instead, they must sell them in the official gift shop, but since tourists typically purchase a CD impulsively on the spot, musicians report a drastic decline in sales. What's more, management takes a significant cut of all CD sales to pay for the value added tax (VAT) and something they characterize as a "handling charge." The contract does not make musicians employees of the center, and it certainly offers them no remuneration for their services. So, not only has the management attempted to take near-total control over the activities of musicians at the Cliffs, they have also negatively impacted their income. To say the least, many musicians are not happy, and several simply left permanently. Given this rather severe loss of control, this is a classic case of touristic commodification in my view.

"Busk Off if You're Rubbish"

One interesting aspect of the conflict between musicians at the Cliffs of Moher and tourist developers is the partial disconnect between the dramatic public discourse about it and the actual grievances of the musicians at the site. The shrillness of the debate in the press seemed symptomatic of a larger identity crisis caused by a rapid culture change wrought by the Celtic Tiger era and the subsequent economic crash. Some of the claims made on both sides of the debate at the Cliffs were hyperbolic, misleading, and personal. For example, one of the project leaders at the Clare County Council in charge of developing the new center claimed in *The Irish Times* that "one [busker] had a dog that attacked passing tourists," and in another news article in England's tabloid *The Sun* (2007), the same official disparaged the buskers' musicianship: "It had become an easy way to make money—you go up there with a tin whistle and whether you can play or not, probably some people will throw you some money in hopes you might stop playing." Likewise, an administrator at the site told me, "There are certain noise restrictions because it's a protected area for sea birds. . . . Now, all of the, sort of—you know— the Celtic harp, the banjo, the tin whistle, the concert flute, the fiddle, the guitar, most of them are played unamplified. But you'd see guys setting up there with their bass guitar and blasting out AC/DC." No one I have spoken to over the years has ever seen anyone playing AC/DC covers at the Cliffs, and given the natural noise created by the wind and surf, the claim about music interfering with puffins' reproduction seems rather far-fetched. Hyperbole became the name of the game, and the conflict made for good headlines like these that reduced the complexities of the story down into an easily digested narrative: "Buskers Banned," "Battle for the Buskers," "Buskers Face the Music," "No Moher Buskers," and "Busk Off if You're Rubbish."

On the other side of the debate, conspiratorial rumors circulated that the county officials were submitting the musicians' names to the Irish Tax & Customs Department because they assumed musicians were dodging their taxes. And as mentioned earlier, a now-famous open letter expressing concern about the future of the buskers at the Cliffs was signed by 43 famous Irish musicians. Despite all of this public attention, even the musicians who busk at the Cliffs felt that the whole issue was spun out of control. In fact, several of them told me that the press missed some very real problems that were more mundane. Many musicians at the Cliffs did not even mind the fact that *some* new regulations were put into place or that they needed to obtain a license because it reduced the informal competition that took place before. For buskers who are trying to make a living by playing music, their concern is at least in part about how to *intensify* the commercialization of the music for *individual* profits, while for the public, it seems to me that there is a broader concern with commercializing and regulating the site and musicians' activities there *at all*.

Conclusion

So how does one begin to disentangle this conflict, and the balance between commerce and culture? There seem to be at least two significant but slightly different understandings at work about the appropriate relationship between music making and money making in this situation. While some of the more hostile actions taken against musicians at the Cliffs of Moher were clearly adversarial, more was going on here for the general public than the livelihoods of a small handful of musicians. For buskers at the Cliffs, very practical concerns about their contractual relationship with the Interpretive Center are at the heart of the matter. They are trying to make a living by playing music, so their concern is at least in part about how to *intensify* the commercialization of the music for *individual* profits, while for the public, it seems to me, there is a broader concern with commercializing and regulating the site and musicians' activities there *at all*. Elsewhere I have made the distinction between commercialization (simply put, a general increase in commerce) and commodification (commercialization that results in a loss of control of the means of production), and the difference is key in an instance such as this. Buskers at the Cliffs of Moher are very interested in commercializing their activities further, precisely because it makes up part, or all, of their livelihood. What is worrisome is that the new relationship between the tourism authorities and the musicians has nothing to do with commercialization itself but instead the appropriation of the production of the music and a reduction in the benefits of the commercial exchange for the musicians. To put a finer point on it, the internal debate at the Cliffs is not about *whether* to commercialize the music but instead how to do so and who benefits.

All of this occurred in a postcrash era when anxieties about what it means to be Irish in the modern world seem even more pressing. I would suggest that what is at work for the public in the demonization of the tourism authorities and the valorization of the musicians is at least in part the new Celtic Tiger version of Irishness colliding headlong into older narratives of Irishness. It should come as no surprise that this kind of confusion resulting from rapid social and economic change caused a crisis of identity as well.

Symbolic sites of national identity, as Tim Edensor writes (2002:46), are "usually claimed by competing groups, who invest them with meanings which are attuned to their political project or identity." Furthermore, nationalized cultural *spaces* and nationalized cultural *practices* are difficult to disentangle, as the developers of the new interpretive center at the Cliffs of Moher discovered. The Cliffs have come to be conceptualized as a musical landscape, and the attempt to separate the music from the place was probably always doomed to fail. Although perhaps unintentional, I find it striking that by banning nontraditional Irish music from the site, one result has been to "purify" a sense of Irishness at the Cliffs of Moher, consolidating the notion that the *Irish* musical tradition is part and parcel of this *Irish* landscape.

Regardless of the genre, the tourism authorities have appropriated the processes of musical production and consumption for their own purposes, dramatically reducing the amount of control musicians have over their art form. As a result, instead of an egalitarian, multivocal, sonically cacophonous musical landscape, the tourism authorities have made every effort to create a site that speaks with their singular voice. "The Irish countryside," writes Adrian Peace (2005:496), "has become in effect a perennial site of struggle," one that is not simply economic or political but also cultural. In the wake of a massive economic collapse in 2008 that was largely caused by overdevelopment, overemphasis on privatization, and general greed, the heavy-handed actions of the Clare County Council against a small group of traditional musicians set off a firestorm because there is a sense that commonly held identity markers like the Cliffs of Moher and traditional music have been transformed into profitable tourism products. If Diane Negra is correct that the Celtic Tiger reconfigured not only the Irish economy but also Irish identity, then a more fundamental question remains about what it means to be Irish in the *post*–Celtic Tiger era.

Source: Adapted from "Music on the Edge: Busking at the Cliffs of Moher and the Commodification of a Musical Landscape." *Tourist Studies* 14(1):30–47, 2014.

References Cited

Arensberg, C. 1959. *The Irish Countryman: An Anthropological Study.* Cambridge, MA: Harvard University Press. Reissued Long Grove, IL: Waveland Press, 1988.

Busse, M., and V. Strang. 2011. "Introduction: Ownership and Appropriation," in *Ownership and Appropriation*, eds. V. Strang and M. Busse, pp. 1–19. Oxford: Berg.

Edensor, T. 2002. *National Identity, Popular Culture and Everyday Life.* Oxford: Berg.

Healy, N., H. Rau, and J. McDonagh. 2012. "Collaborative Tourism Planning in Ireland: Tokenistic Consultation and the Politics of Participation." *Journal of Environmental Policy and Planning* 14(4): 1–22.

Negra, D. 2010. "Urban Space, Luxury Retailing, and the New Irishness." *Cultural Studies* 24(6): 836–53.

Peace, A. 2005 "A Sense of Place, a Place of Senses: Land and Landscape in the West of Ireland." *Journal of Anthropological Research* 61(4): 495–512.

The Irish Times. 2006. "Cliff Buskers May Face Audition," 1 September, 2.

The Sun (England). 2007. "Busk Off If You're Rubbish," 5 February.

15

Tasting: Wine Tourism in the Napa Valley

Sharon Bohn Gmelch

MILES: *Let me show you how this is done. First thing, hold the glass up and examine the wine against the light. You're looking for color and clarity. Just, get a sense of it. OK? Uhh, thick? Thin? Watery? Syrupy? OK? Alright. Now, tip it. What you're doing here is checking for color density as it thins out towards the rim. Uhh, that's gonna tell you how old it is, among other things. It's usually more important with reds. OK? Now, stick your nose in it. Don't be shy, really get your nose in there. Mmm . . . a little citrus . . . maybe some strawberry . . . [smacks lips] . . . passion fruit . . . [puts hand up to ear] . . . and, oh, there's just like the faintest soupçon of like asparagus and just a flutter of a, like a, nutty Edam cheese . . .*

JACK: *Wow. Strawberries, yeah! Strawberries. Not the cheese . . .*

— Sideways, 2004

As the popularity of the film *Sideways* suggests, wine is now a central component of a sophisticated lifestyle for many Americans. It is intertwined with the way they dine and entertain and how they enjoy a quiet evening at home. Wine consumption in the U.S. reached a tipping point in 2007 when, for the first time, "core" wine drinkers (those who drink wine more than once a week) outnumbered "marginal" drinkers (those who drink wine infre-

199

quently). New wine regions are developing all the time, both in the U.S. and abroad. And with them, so is wine tourism.

Tourism to wine-producing regions is not an entirely new phenomenon. In the seventeenth and eighteenth centuries, visiting well-known vineyards was part of the European "Grand Tour" undertaken by young British elites to absorb high culture and finish their education. Individual connoisseurs also traveled to their favorite wine regions; British philosopher John Locke toured France's vineyards in the 1670s, as did Thomas Jefferson in the 1780s. Wine did not become an organized and specific travel interest, however, until 1855, when the wines of Bordeaux were classified and a guide was published for visitors to the Paris Exhibition. Bordeaux then acquired an identity as a tourist destination, and specific chateaus began attracting visitors. By the 1920s, Germany also had well-established tourist wine routes. Today, some form of wine tourism can be found in virtually every wine-growing region of the world.

No place is more associated with wine in the United States than California's Napa Valley. Wines were first made there in the 1850s, mainly by European immigrants from countries with wine-making traditions. A decade later, Napa had fifty recognized vintners. The industry's development came to a halt, however, in 1919 with passage of the Volstead Act, which prohibited the manufacture, transport, and sale of all alcoholic beverages.[1] After Prohibition ended in 1933, it took decades for California's wine industry to revive. Only in the 1960s did the situation begin to turn around. As America's middle class expanded and more Americans traveled abroad, they were exposed to cultures where wine was consumed regularly, boosting the demand for wine. This, combined with the leadership and marketing skill of Napa vintner Robert Mondavi and the triumph of two Napa wines at a special blind tasting in Paris in 1976—the so-called Judgment of Paris—turned the Napa Valley into America's premier wine producing region and wine tourism destination.[2]

This discussion explores the wine tourism experience in Napa, from the settings in which it takes place to the activities that visitors engage in. It examines the rewards of wine tourism for individuals. Wine is not just a drink; it is also a social commodity. "Taste" is not only one of our senses, it is also a form of cultural capital. The economic benefits of tourism for the wine industry are also explored. The discussion is based on archival research and on fieldwork conducted in the Napa Valley between 2006 and 2010, with follow-up fact-checking in 2017. Fieldwork included participant observation at Napa wineries; interviews with tourists, wine educators, and others involved in the tourism-wine nexus; and a survey of 161 wine tourists.

Napa's Wine Tourists

Most wine tourists to Napa are well-off and well-educated. According to a large-scale survey by Purdue University's Tourism and Hospitality

Research Center, nearly three-quarters are college graduates; one-third hold master's degrees or doctorates. Most are domestic tourists, with Californians—many from the San Francisco Bay area—making up over half. They typically visit the valley with a partner or a few friends or family members. Very few bring children since, as one limousine driver explained, "Wine country is an adult playground." In other respects, Napa's wine tourists are a diverse group with widely different levels of wine knowledge—like Miles and Jack in *Sideways*.[3]

When tasting room servers, tour guides, and wine educators are asked to classify Napa's wine tourists on the basis of their wine knowledge, three groupings emerge. "Aficionados" or "collectors" are knowledgeable connoisseurs who usually keep well-stocked home wine cellars. They typically visit Napa several times a year, sometimes by private plane, specifically to buy wine, often spending thousands of dollars. They tend to do only special or "reserve" tastings of expensive, limited-production wines and enjoy engaging in "wine talk" and receiving "VIP treatment" while at the wineries they frequent. "Hobbyists" or "middle-of-the-road wine drinkers" are less knowledgeable but enjoy wine and the wine tourism experience. They tend to be younger and want to learn more about wine in order to enhance their enjoyment of it. They frequently describe themselves to tasting room staff by varietal, as in "I'm a cab [Cabernet Sauvignon] person." They are likely to belong to a wine-tasting group at home and to one or more wine clubs in the valley. "Novices" or "neophytes" constitute the third category. They know relatively little about wine but are sufficiently curious to want to learn more and to see what the Napa Valley is all about. They tend to visit wineries whose brands, like Mondavi and Sutter Home, they are familiar with from their local liquor or grocery store. Most are value conscious and usually have a price point above which they will not spend.

Although most wine tourists do come to Napa for the wine, whether to buy or simply to taste and learn, they also come because it is a desirable destination. It is beautiful and, for northern Californians especially, a convenient place to unwind or to celebrate a birthday, anniversary, promotion, or honeymoon or to hold a bachelorette party. It offers an adult sensory experience comprised of fine wine, fine food, and other indulgences like spas, massage, thermal baths, and hot air ballooning. For international visitors, Napa has become a must-see California destination; it has name recognition and cachet, like Tuscany and Provence, to which it is often compared.[4]

Napa's Tourism Landscape

Cradled by mountains, the Napa Valley is just over thirty miles long and a few miles wide, giving it an intimate feel. It is perfect for touring, with more wineries within easy reach than in any wine region of the world. What tourists see is a true winescape with row upon row of trellised grapevines advancing across the narrow valley floor and up the lower slopes of the Vaca and Mayacamas ranges. From January to March, wild mustard blooms between the dormant vines, turning the valley floor an iridescent yellow. By April the wildflowers have bloomed and the vines have experienced "bud break" when new shoots emerge. Tourists begin to arrive in numbers in May as the vines leaf out and set fruit. In summer the valley is a carpet of green. By late July the berries begin ripening and in August most grapes change color from green to yellow or purplish-red, a developmental change called veraison. "Crush" or harvest usually occurs in September and October; the exact timing depends upon the variety of grape, a particular vineyard's location, and that year's weather. A second wave of tourists arrives now, adding to the heightened activity of the grape harvest when the fields are filled with the sight and sound of farmworkers handpicking the ripened clusters, the roadways are busy with tractors ferrying grape-filled gondolas to the wineries for processing, and the smell of grapes wafts through the air. By November, as winter dormancy sets in, the vines' foliage transmutes into autumnal golds, red, and orange before dropping. This also signals the end of prime tourist season.

Winery architecture contributes to Napa's natural appeal. Wineries come in all styles, from historic buildings (including original stone wineries from the 1800s) to neo-rustic barns or ranch-like structures, from architect-designed showpieces to replicas from other places. The latter include a castle built from stones imported from an Italian monastery, a replica Monticello, a Persian temple, a Venetian estate, and a Cape Dutch farmhouse. Long-term locals typically regard these as inappropriate to the history of the valley and contributing to its "Disneyfication."

Most wineries are pleasantly landscaped in a style that befits their architecture and their "story"—the narrative they have created to distinguish themselves from other wineries in the valley. Some are planted with California natives like poppies and valley oaks. Others evoke the Mediterranean with grasses, olive trees, and fountains. Still others suggest wine's Old World heritage with European-style formal gardens of roses and boxwood hedges. Wineries can also function as showcases for their wealthy owners' interests evident in sculpture gardens and art displays. A few wineries eschew all decorative trappings and highlight this fact in their advertising: "the inspiration for Rutherford Ranch comes from the hardworking early settlers of this region. Instead of image and spin, the success of our efforts relies exclusively on tangible results—wine quality so good it speaks for itself. Rutherford Ranch favors substance over pretense. We don't waste our resources on fancy wine centers or fanciful stories."

Today, five million tourists visit Napa each year. The valley now has nearly 500 wineries, most of which have tasting rooms that are open to the public. Tourists drive up and down the valley in their personal cars or tour in hired limousines, vans, or small buses. Most head north on Highway 29, stopping at three to five preselected wineries along the way; others take the quieter Silverado Trail. There is no shortage of information on where to stop. Unless their driver or tour guide has made the decision for them, most people have searched the Internet, consulting wine blogs and websites, to decide which wineries to visit. The Napa Valley Vintners' searchable site lists every winery in the valley and each one's unique features including gardens, caves, and art displays. Word-of-mouth is also important, especially for small "boutique wineries" with limited production. Sometimes tourists are lured off the road by the look of the winery or its name recognition. Most stay a night or two in one of the valley's upscale resorts or hotels, dining out at their restaurants or those run by a famous chef. Other tourists make a day trip to the valley, usually as part of a visit to San Francisco.

In some wine regions—in Italy, Australia, as well as other parts of California, for example—wineries are considered to be as much in the hospitality business as they are in wine making. Many have restaurants, extensive gift shops, and even inns and wedding chapels and derive much of their revenue from corporate dinners, parties, wedding receptions, and other non-wine retail sales.[5] Resident Napans' fears about what similar developments would do to their valley led to passage of the Winery Definition Ordinance (WDO) in 1990 that prohibits Napa's wineries from engaging in ancillary activities, including having restaurants.[6] It also explains a phenomenon that some tourists find confusing and mildly annoying, namely the signs they encounter at many winery entrances, which state that tastings are "by appointment only." This restriction does not reflect snobbery but rather was mandated by the WDO, which limits the number of tourists a winery can receive each day.

While architecture and landscaping suggest what lies inside, the tasting room is the real public face of wineries and the site of wine tourism. Most are handsomely appointed, featuring a lot of wood, stone, and other natural materials. They impart an air of sophisticated yet casual elegance—a fitting environment for imbibing wine, the ultimate artisanal agricultural product. Napa's tasting rooms vary in size from intimate to spacious. At Hall Winery in Rutherford, for example, tourists may sample the winery's "exclusive" wines at a long table in a 14,000-square-foot cave under a massive chandelier depicting a vine's root system adorned with Swarovski crystals. In contrast, Saddleback Cellars in Oakville has wedged a tiny bar and wine-barrel table into a storage area with western memorabilia hung on the wall. Most of its visitors choose to sample its wines at the picnic tables outside.

Tasting and the Tasting Room Experience

"Next to wine quality," says tasting room consultant Craig Root, "the most critical part of a successful tasting room is staff, staff, staff." Good tasting room associates, or servers, through their words of welcome, friendly smiles, and attentive but not overly solicitous service, create the special experience wine tourists seek. "We wrap them up in a genuine welcome," summarized one.

When visitors approach a tasting counter, they are invited to look at the list of wines being poured and briefly told about the types of tastings available. Once they reach a decision, the server begins pouring a flight of wines—typically one-ounce servings of four to six wines. Most tastings begin with some of the winery's whites, move to the reds, and often end with a dessert wine or port. As the server pours each wine, s/he announces the vintage and varietal: "This is a 2014 Cabernet Sauvignon." Most will then describe the wine's characteristics. A Cabernet Sauvignon, the valley's dominant wine, may be described as having the "distinctive flavors of chocolate, berry, and mineral" or as "a lush, fruit-forward wine with balance from beginning to end." If the wine is a blend, the server will usually describe the varietals used to create it: "This 2012 Arcturus is a blend of 62 percent Cabernet Sauvignon, 21 percent Merlot, 15 percent Cabernet Franc, and 2 percent Petit Verdot."

Good servers gear their conversation and the amount of wine talk they engage in to tourists' interest and knowledge level. They often mention foods that the wine complements. "This is our salad and sushi wine," a server at Raymond Winery told one tasting group. "It's one of the few we make that doesn't see the inside of an oak barrel." The best are adept at making wine tasting enjoyable and the process of wine making understandable, using analogies and metaphors such as "a winemaker selecting barrels is like a chef selecting herbs" and "an oak barrel adds flavor to the wine, like a cinnamon stick adds flavor to your hot chocolate." They can also answer questions like "How many bottles of wine does a grapevine produce?" (four to six) or "How many grapes are in a glass of wine?" (about a half pound per five-ounce glass).

Servers often mention where a wine's grapes were grown: on the winery's property, from a single vineyard block, and so forth. If prompted, they may go on to discuss what distinguishes its *terroir* from other places in the valley.[7] *Terroir*—a term most Americans struggle to pronounce—refers to the physical features of soil, slope, and microclimate that interact to give the grape varietals grown there unique characteristics. Conversations between wine servers and tourists may cover many facets of the wine-making process as well as interesting facts about the winery. This is when terms like "Brix" (a measure of sugar content and grape ripeness) may be introduced. At Newton Vineyard, tasting groups are informed that their wines are "unfiltered" and "unfined" (that nothing has been done to remove suspended solids) in order to avoid stripping them of their distinct aromas and flavors. At Frog's Leap Winery, one of the valley's certified "green" wineries, servers inform tourists about its sustainable farming philosophy and environmental measures such as solar panels.

Most servers, wine educators, and tour guides will also impart a little of the winery's history and lesser facts they deem interesting. If a winery is family owned and operated, this will be highlighted. (It also will be a featured part of the winery's story on promotional materials.) Family ownership contributes to the image the wine industry wishes to project, namely, that wine is an artisanal product lovingly produced by people whose lives are devoted to it. Common expressions like "a great wine springs from love and humility" and "it takes a great poet to make a great wine" convey this romantic view of wine making. Words like "passion," "quality," and "handcrafted" recur on winery websites, as does language that stresses a winery's lengthy wine-making tradition: "6th generation Napan," "California roots," "French heritage," or "Italian heritage." Finally, if a winery's winemaker is well-known—has produced an award-winning or highly rated wine—this will be mentioned.

Wine tastings are intended to proceed at a leisurely pace. Only the most popular brand-name wineries during the height of tourist season discourage visitors from lingering at the tasting counter since having people crowded together, sometimes three deep, is antithetical to their individual enjoyment as well as to wine sales. As Miles attempted to instruct Jack, wine is meant to be relished—swirled in the glass and held up, its color admired; swirled some more, and then smelled, its "nose" or aromas inhaled; sipped and held in the mouth, its "mouth feel" appreciated; moved about the tongue, its tastes discerned and savored; and then swallowed or spit into the provided container.

The flavor and enjoyment of wine emerges out of a complete sensory experience that melds sight, smell, and taste. Everyone responds to wine differently. Genetic factors a play a role, but learned and associative factors are equally, if not more, important. These include the social environment in which a person consumes wine—such as the company they are with and the ambiance of the setting—as well as their prior experiences and cultural or ethnic backgrounds. Flavors and smells that are familiar to one person, for example, may not be to another. The more a person

A couple "tastes" at the Robert Sinskey Vineyards in the Napa Valley. (Photo by author)

learns about wine, the more his or her responses to a particular wine are conditioned by that knowledge (even overriding a genetically programmed aversive reaction to a taste). The best servers, if they have enough time, attempt to understand each individual's palate by asking questions about their likes and dislikes.[8]

In addition to tasting rooms, many wineries offer vineyard tours. Here tourists learn about the planting of rootstock, grafting, and the training and pruning of the vines as well as the life cycle of grapes. Most wineries also offer tours of their production facilities, during which guides explain how their wines are made. Those that have aging caves are especially popular with tourists.

The Rewards of Wine Tourism

For most tourists, wine tasting is enjoyable. It is a relaxing activity done in a pleasant setting. The alcohol in wine—unless a tourist has been scrupulous about not swallowing in order to keep his or her palate sharp—also promotes relaxation. All tourism is a form of consumption. In this case, not only the literal consumption of wine but also the acquisition of intangibles, like experience and status. In his 1899 classic, *The Theory of the Leisure*

Tourists learn about the wine-making process at Grgich Winery. (Photo by Trenton McManus; courtesy of Wine Train)

Class, economist Thorstein Veblen coined the terms "conspicuous consumption" and "conspicuous leisure" to describe two ways people gain and signal status. Wine tourism combines both. Being knowledgeable and discerning about wine is a sign of sophistication and a form of cultural capital. "It is knowledge a person seeking upper-middle-class status should have," explained cultural anthropologist Kenji Tierney in an interview:

> Because social class in America is less based on heredity than in Europe, we rely more on displays of "taste" and acts of consumption. My students [at an East Coast liberal arts college] all say, "Oh, you have to know about wine." What they mean is they need to know about wine so they can talk intelligently about what they're drinking and create the right impression with future clients and in-laws. This may not be the conscious motivation people have for going to the Napa Valley, but it lurks in the background for many and helps explain why so many wine tourists are college educated and affluent. For the working class, knowing about wine is less socially "useful"; it doesn't bring the same social rewards and fewer are motivated to go wine tasting.

Being able to discern and name the subtle aromas and flavors within a wine—to recognize dried currants, sage, raspberry jam, black tea, vanilla, soy sauce, cedar, and the like—is not a natural skill, yet many people are sufficiently curious about wine and motivated to work at it. Visiting Napa is one way of acquiring such skill.

As French sociologist Pierre Bourdieu argued, our "dispositions" to value certain things and to behave and think in certain ways are based on our family, class background, education, and the social arenas we operate in during our adult lives. Different classes value different things, including types of food and drink, entertainment, and art, yet the cultural standard of what "good taste" is at a given point in time is always defined by a society's elites. People who didn't acquire the "tastes" appropriate to their aspirational social class at home or in school often experience "class anxiety." "One reason people go to art museums is to see what taste has been culturally approved," continued Tierney, "what artwork is appropriate or 'the good stuff.' It's very similar with wine tourism." In the film *Sideways,* Jack seems to be free of class anxiety, while Miles may well be afflicted: "Jack: *Man! That's tasty!* Miles: *That's 100% Pinot Noir. Single vineyard. They don't even make it any more.* Jack: *Pinot Noir?* Miles: *Mmm-hmm.* Jack: *Then how come it's white?* Miles: *Oh, Jesus. Don't ask questions like that up in wine country. They'll think you're some kind of dumbshit, OK?*"

Knowledge, experiences, and products that signify status can be used by people in two ways: exclusion and inclusion. Drinking fine wine and traveling to the Napa Valley, which is difficult to do cheaply, can be used by individuals in an exclusive sense to differentiate themselves from others who have not done so. Many forms of tourism are used in this way. ("I've been to

Angkor Wat." Left unsaid is, "You haven't."). Wine tourism can also be used inclusively as a form of self-classification by which individuals ally themselves with others whose interests and lifestyle they share or wish to share. Having been to Napa and knowing about wine enhances one's claims to being a sophisticated person.

Wine tourism is also important to the wine industry. Tasting rooms allow tourists to learn about and sample wines in beautiful and congenial settings, creating positive memories and associations that transfer into future sales. According to winemaker Pam Starr:

> When tourists come here [to Crocker & Starr] and see the rocks in our soil, see the topography, smell the environment, see that we are located in open ag land and are part of a historic district, they leave with a sense of being part of our winery, our vineyard, and the Napa Valley. When they go home and open a bottle of our wine, they relive the experience and re-create other moments from their vacation and the feelings they had in Napa being away from their crazy work schedule.

Tasting rooms are also valuable profit centers. For many small and medium-sized wineries, they are their largest source of revenue. Tasting room profitability becomes clear when compared to what a winery makes from the normal three-tier distribution system in which a hypothetical case of wine retailing for $240 (or $20 per bottle) is first sold to a distributor for about $130, then sold at "wholesale" to a retailer for about $180, who, in turn, sells it to the public for $240. Tasting rooms bypass both the distributor and the retailer, selling wines directly to the public at the retail price. A few Napa wineries only sell from the tasting room.

Most tastings in the Napa Valley were free until the late 1970s when, as the number of tourists grew, fees were introduced to offset the costs of the wine being dispensed and of tasting room labor. Entry-level tastings now cost an average of $25 for four wines, but twice that if "Reserve" or "Special Selection" wines or wine and food pairings are involved. Some tastings are quite lavish and even more expensive. At Swanson Vineyard's "salon" eight people sit around a table beautifully set with flowers and Riedel stemware and enjoy wine, small portions of food, and conversation guided by a knowledgeable and witty host. Unlike the nineteenth-century Paris salons after which it is styled, however, the conversation typically revolves around wine rather than the literature, art, and politics of the day; the winery advertises the experience as "decadence with a wink."

Wine clubs are another by-product of tourism. They first appeared on the Napa scene in the mid-1980s as a marketing tool to build wineries' relationships with their customers. Today, however, wine clubs are an important and profitable adjunct to the tasting room. Tourists who become members pay for three or four yearly shipments of two to four bottles of well-priced wine as well as invitations to special events and other perks. Having a tasting room but not a wine club—which ensures guaranteed purchases and consumer loyalty—was likened by one industry professional to "building a car without a fuel injector." Tasting rooms normally operate at a 30 percent profit margin and, as mentioned, are the largest source of income for many small and medium-sized wineries in the valley. If a winery also has a wine club, this profit margin can increase to 50 percent. Tourists who become club members also become ambassadors for Napa's wineries, serving their wines in homes across America and beyond.

Belonging to a wine club allows tourists to stay connected to their favorite wineries and to memories of their Napa experience. Back home, they enjoy the luxury of having a wine shipment arrive at their door, the pleasure of drinking it, and the social cachet of serving it to guests. They can also continue their wine education by consulting the accompanying tasting notes and information (e.g., winemaker notes, wine–food pairings, and recipes) contained in the club's newsletter. On future visits to the valley, they will enjoy membership perks such as complimentary tastings, members-only lounges, special dinners, and "release parties" that celebrate the winery's release of a new vintage with wine, food, and entertainment. Wine club names—which typically include words like "ambassador," "select," "connoisseur," "premier," "preferred," "signature," and "classic"—suggest exclusivity; the word "club" itself suggests privileged membership.

Final Thoughts

Visits to wine regions like the Napa Valley have become increasingly popular. One reason is the growth in wine consumption globally. But more people today are also interested in more actively engaging with the places they visit and in supplementing the "tourist gaze" (passively looking at historic sites, art, or natural wonders) with other sensory or bodily experiences. Wine tourism satisfies these desires. It offers the sounds and rhythms of nature and the visual beauty of a rural landscape—enhanced by vineyards, winery architecture, and landscaping—with the opportunity to concentrate on other senses, particularly smell and taste, by sampling wine and dining on fine wine and food. In Napa, tourists can also indulge their sense of touch—beyond the "mouth feel" or textural experience of wine and fine food—through spa treatments, body massage, and thermal baths.

Visiting wine regions also satisfies other tourist quests. For those just developing an interest in wine, it offers the opportunity to learn about this artisanal product and how it is made and to acquire cultural capital. For regular wine drinkers and connoisseurs it offers the opportunity to expand their knowledge and appreciation of wine through "tasting," the quintessential wine tourism activity. Wine regions are also appealing because they contrast with most tourists' familiar surroundings, which are typically urban, thus providing one of tourism's central experiences—difference of place. Because wine is branded on the basis of its geographical origin, visiting the Napa Valley means traveling to the source—the real and only place where a particular wine or wines could be made. Thus, wine tourism appeals to many tourists' unconscious quest for authenticity, which is enhanced by the nostalgia that rural, agricultural environments evoke.

Source: Adapted from *Tasting the Good Life: Wine Tourism in the Napa Valley* (with G. Gmelch). Bloomington: Indiana University Press, 2011.

Notes

[1] Some Napa wineries survived by producing wine for medicinal or sacramental purposes; others marketed their grapes in the eastern United States for the legal home production of wine. A few continued to illegally produce wine and sell it out the back door.

[2] In 1968, Napa County's board of supervisors created the Agricultural Preserve Zone. It replaced one-acre zoning with a minimum lot size of twenty acres, and soon doubled to forty. It was a radical idea at the time, designed to preserve open space, prevent overdevelopment, and protect agriculture. It has allowed the Napa Valley to retain its agricultural and rural atmosphere—the bedrock of both its wine and wine tourism industries.

[3] In 1976 Steven Spurrier, British-born wine expert and Paris wine shop owner, came up with the idea of organizing a blind tasting of California and French wines to celebrate the bicentennial of the American Revolution. Two of Napa's wines won the top prizes: a 1973 Stag's Leap Cabernet Sauvignon and a 1973 Chateau Montelena Chardonnay.

[4] In the survey that anthropologist George Gmelch and I conducted of 161 Napa Valley wine tourists, only 7 percent considered themselves to be "very knowledgeable" about wine, 59 percent thought they were "moderately knowledgeable," and 34 percent reported that they were "not at all knowledgeable." Studies of wine tourists in New Zealand and Victoria, Australia, have found similar self-reported levels of prior wine knowledge.

[5] China has a growing wine industry at home and abroad. In 2017, a Chinese investor began a major wine project in Riverside County in southern California, which would include a wine resort and residential community of multimillion-dollar homes surrounded by private vineyards.

[6] In practice, the ordinance sometimes is loosely applied and in 2010 it was modified to allow wineries to serve food with wine as long as the charge to customers for such "tastings" did not exceed their cost. It also allows wineries to hold business meetings and retreats as long as at least half the content focuses on wine making or wine education.

[7] The Napa Valley comprises a single American Viticultural Area (AVA), or appellation, which is divided into sixteen subappellations meant to reflect physical differences in terroir. While a few of Napa's sub-appellations relate closely to soil type and microclimate, marketing concerns and past land usage have shaped where the boundaries have been drawn. Most of Napa's sub-appellations are too big and diverse to offer a truly unified terroir.

[8] Our genes dictate the number of taste buds we possess (most of us have about ten thousand), the amount of protein in our saliva and the rate at which it is produced, and our sensitivity to hot and cold. All this affects our experience of wine.

16

Souvenirs, Animals, and Enchantment: Encountering Texas Cowboy Boots

Chris Gibson

I disembarked the plane and followed the signs to the baggage carousel, passing glass display cabinets filled with cowboy boots. There were all sorts—brown, black, multicolored, snakeskin, lizard skin—with Cuban heels and ornate, ostentatious designs: inlaid sewn butterflies, chilies, and scorpions. At any other airport, waiting for a suitcase, one might linger in front of a TV screen showing a loop of local news and weather updates. Here in Texas, there is a cabinet filled with locally crafted cowboy boots. Welcome to El Paso—the cowboy boot capital of the world.

The cowboy boot is the quintessential souvenir of Texas and a product of an artisanal trade with deep regional historical roots. It is also an enchanted object—a fashion-souvenir whose constituent materials and the animals from which they come evoke unsettling combinations of feelings and sensory responses among tourists. Through this seemingly parochial item we can reflect on how humans make and enchant material things via geographical and popular cultural mythologies and entangle ourselves in increasingly complex flows of people, animals, and place (Ramsay 2009)—connecting tourists with circuits of craft, commodification, and collecting across cultural difference (Hitchcock and Teague 2000; Ateljevic and Doorne 2003). Seemingly trivial, cowboy boots are an entry point into questions of morality and

211

materiality, mobility, and the value of local cultural production within processes of tourism commodification.

In this chapter I follow the Texas cowboy boot in time and place, from Western-wear shops in the tourist districts of Texan cities to small boot-making workshops on the Mexican–American border, as well as back in time to an earlier phase of colonial popular culture, when myths of frontier cowboy masculinity and tourism had already begun to fuse. This chapter draws on archival work in El Paso and at the Smithsonian and Library of Congress in Washington DC (where histories of boot making, tourism, and cowboy marketing were traced) and from fieldwork undertaken across Texas in 2010 and again in 2012 (when interviews were conducted with boot retailers and boot makers in twenty participating workshops, and with tourists engaged in informal conversations about boots).

Boot making survives in Texas as a niche cultural industry, linked to histories of Spanish colonialism, ranching, popular culture, and tourism (DeLano and Rieff 1981). Texas became the hub for the mass manufacturing of cowboy boots in the mid-twentieth century, with demand fed by Western movies and TV shows and the booming tourist market opened up by interstate highways. Factories such as Tony Lama, at its height, employed 1,200 workers producing as many as 3,500 boots per day (Gibson 2016a). Mass manufacturing has since then largely moved offshore, in search of cheap labor and materials. Yet cowboy boots are still made by hand in small workshops with reputations for craftsmanship—serving a market dependent on Texan corporate executives, dedicated collectors, and bootscootin' tourists. I focus here on the encounters with cowboy boots experienced by tourists, for whom boots are an exotic souvenir rather than a regular item of dress. For them, the cowboy boot's regional cultural distinctiveness and animal origins evoke mixed visceral and emotional responses—of delight and disgust—that open up opportunities to question the exploitative character of capitalist commodity production and tourist commodification, as well as human relationships with nonhuman others.

The iconic Texas cowboy boot is a very material object of mobility—made by hand, by (mostly) Mexican migrant artisans who use slowly accrued haptic skills with a variety of leathers to assemble an artifact of fashion, fable, and travel. Behind the remarkable longevity of cowboy style—epitomized in boots—is the allure and continuing marketability of cowboy imagery in a global cultural economy (Hobsbawm 2013). The cowboy myth is one of the most enduring American pop culture fabrications (Gibson 2016b), and it underpins formal tourism marketing in Texas, providing a palette of regional cultural signifiers, encompassing imagery of rodeos, Western fashion, Tex-Mex food, and music.

Making sense of tourist encounters with cowboy boots requires exploring visuality, sensuality, and materiality: the myths of the lonesome rider and the frontier landscape, the promise of mobility enshrined in the boot designs themselves, the tactility and animality of the skins with which the boots are made. In rural work, in film, on stage, or in the rodeo ring, and at festivals, in America and beyond, an assortment of clothes, boots, holsters, horses, saddles, and spurs visualize and hyperbolize cowboy identities. The cowboy boot is an especially multivalent object: a malleable signifier, the wearing of which enables macho, camp, and conservative masculine bodily identities to be performed, as well as country femininities, tourist fantasies, and brazen sexualities (Gibson 2013). The cowboy boot links nineteenth-century cowboys as a specific type of agricultural worker with contemporary urban tourists, popular culture, and the global leather trade.

The approach I take here follows what Coles, Hall, and Duval (2005) describe as postdisciplinary critique: viewing tourism less as a coherent "production system" or even a distinct phenomenon and more as an outcome of jostling and overlapping assemblages, a hybrid phenomenon blending different industries, the state, "nature," the informal sector, the capitalist and noncapitalist economies, and all manner of technologies, materials, substances, and infrastructures (Gibson 2009:329). In this case it is a souvenir—the cowboy boot—that provides the starting point for analysis.

This chapter speaks to an emerging research agenda in tourism studies focused on materiality, and especially around souvenirs and their entanglements in cultural economies of craft production, host–tourist interactions, and material affordances (Ateljevic and Doorne 2003). Beyond research on souvenir markets and tourist purchasing preferences (e.g. Asplet and Cooper 2000) are such questions as the meaning of souvenirs and for whom does it bear that meaning (Hitchcock and Teague 2000); the agency and inherent qualities of souvenirs in relational networks of cross-cultural translation (Jóhannesson 2005); souvenir objects as repositories of memory and recognition (Franklin 2010); souvenir giving within wider familial and cultural contexts (Kael 2012); and the extent to which souvenirs facilitate the performance of "polysensual tourism experiences" among tourists who are self-aware of their status as tourists (Morgan and Pritchard 2005:29). As discussed below, such polysensual performances enroll not just the visual but also touch and smell.

And in the case of boots, we can both recognize the souvenir as an affective object and consider its very fabrication, following not just the whole commodity "thing" but its constitutive materials into darker regions of animal slaughter and leather trading. Exactly what kind of moral economy results hinges on both the means and manner of production, and on the modes and spaces of consumption. These are enchanted objects, whose leather materials and animal origins are vital to marketability—key selling points that mark the boots as "cowboy," and as "Texan." But those same materials and animal origins evoke a "strange combination of delight and disturbance" as Jane Bennett (2010:xi) puts it. In what follows, I accordingly discuss the cowboy boot at the intersection of three threads: colonial legacies (including emergent frontier tourism); popular culture, tourism, and souvenir production and consumption; and subsequent animal encounters unleashed in moments of tourist–souvenir interaction.

Colonial Legacies

The generally accepted wisdom is that cowboys emerged as a specific form of frontier rural worker in the American South and West, a variant on the already-present *Mexican vaqueros* who worked under poor conditions on colonial cattle ranches from the 1500s onwards (Dary 1989). They were far from a romanticized figure: rounding up, moving, and branding cattle were considered some of the lowest forms of work, and vaqueros were effectively indentured labor. The vaqueros' form of pastoral work moved northward in the 1700s and 1800s as cattle ranching spread into modern California, New Mexico, Arizona, and Texas, where Americans "adopted and modified many of the vaqueros' tools, techniques, and customs and thereby created their own cowboy culture" (Dary 1989:xi). The 1860s to the 1880s was a period characterized by gigantic transcontinental cattle drives from Mexico and Texas toward railheads in Kansas, across California and the West, and up into the high plateau Rocky Mountain states. The archetypal cowboy is said to have emerged within this relatively short, confined time period—before the advent of fences, stock feed, and railways.

The accouterments of cowboy style mostly stem from this period. Belying the contemporary (false) association between cowboy culture and white American nationalism, cowboy practices, equipment, and apparel translated European, Middle Eastern, and Spanish–Mexican antecedents: cowboy saddles and lariats retained vaquero style; their riding style reflected origins in Andalusia (which in turn absorbed Moorish influences), and horses and bulls retained Mediterranean genetic code (Dary 1989:7–8). The practice of branding cattle with unique identifying markers was Mexican, as was the use of the rope *lazo* (later *lasso*) to trap cattle, the practice of wearing spurs on ankles as a disciplining technology for horse riding (cf. Hurn 2011), and *rodear* (to "go around" or to encircle), the act of rounding up cattle to prevent them from becoming too "wild" (which became *rodeo*). The iconic "look" of cowboys, so central to later pop culture and tourism marketing, also reflected vaquero origins: protective *chaparreras* (chaps) and bandanas were Mexican; while the Spanish sombrero evolved into the cowboy hat (George-Warren and Freedman 2006). The cowboy "look" has a distinctive material cultural history, and that history is entwined with Spanish colonialism.

The exception to this was boots. Originally desperately poor and barefoot, vaqueros could not afford riding boots. The iconic cowboy boot emerged rather later, as a hybrid blend of Civil War–era military and English "Wellington" boots with vernacular boot-making adaptations, notably in Kansas and

Texas (Beard and Arndt 1992). Such adaptations included a sharp toepiece, high heels and reinforced steel arches (for finding and locking into stirrups securely), and high vertical tops for protection from scrub, with stitching patterns to reinforce the tops and prevent slouching. Early boots from the 1880s and 1890s had the silhouette of the classic cowboy boot, though they were plain in design. Ostentatious embellishments would come later.

Notwithstanding the agricultural origins of Texas boot making, the promulgation of the cowboy myth was a decidedly urban affair, fueled by popular culture and tourism. Diffusion of frontier myth through popular culture was already rampant by the time of the great cattle drives, and tourists had themselves "gone West" in search of the authentic cowboy, at precisely the time that American society became more industrialized and urbanized (Gibson 2013). Indeed, by the 1850s, and preceding the golden age of the cowboy on the cattle trail, American readers were already devouring "the tall tales in which . . . the mythic hero of the Tennessee wilderness, battled nature, killed Indians with his bare hands, and subdued wild animals" (Rupp 1999:54). By the 1860s and 1870s working cowboys were "aware that their occupation had attracted the popular imagination, and some tried to cash in by writing their stories or giving exhibitions. . . . By the late 19th century most . . . probably knew that their occupations exemplified heroic masculinity" (Wilk 2007:23).

Cowboy mythology spread rapidly in the late nineteenth century. The cowboy figure globalized early, through Remington and Russell paintings, dime novels, postcards, children's toys and stories, sheet music, and fashion. Later it spread through silent and singing cowboy movies, country music radio shows, and television Westerns and films (Hobsbawm 2013). The cowboy "look" completely relied on the fantasies of urban audiences for its endurance. Buffalo Bill Cody's touring Wild West Show started an urban craze for all things cowboy—"children's toys, chocolates, candies, cigar boxes, cabaret songs, operettas, books, comic books, postcards, anything that could be printed or designed" (Rainger 2000:170). To attract attention and dazzle crowds, traveling cowboy showmen and rodeo tricksters wore larger and more exaggerated cowboy hats, increasingly decorative embroidered shirts and chaps, and high-heeled boots with evermore intricate inlay, tooling, and silverware embellishments (Bull 2000; Weil and DeWeese 2004).

As early as the 1850s tourists could be found at places such as St. Louis (at that point on the perceived western edge of Anglo-American civilization), seeking glimpses of Western frontier life and Indian culture, decked out in leather shirts and riding boots in preparation for an "authentic" Western experience (Nottage 2006). City dwellers purchased Western costumes as tourists, visiting "dude ranches" across the West from the 1870s onwards (Manns and Flood 1997). Newly minted states such as Montana and Wyoming marketed themselves to migrants and tourists as "Western" through the cowboy figure. The cowboy costume, itself a hybrid of agricultural work needs and pop culture hyperbole, became *de rigueur* ranchwear for an entirely new form of tourism—enabling tourists to "go native" by adopting what was perceived as local dress and participating in such activities as horse riding and cattle roundups.

Popular Culture, Tourism, and Souvenir Production and Consumption

Cowboy clothing as we have now come to know it—Western snap shirts, chaps, blue jeans, boots, hats—settled into a mass-production formula in the 1930s and 1940s with the rise of rodeo, Wild West shows, and visual media, especially film (Bull 2000). Wild West performers, rodeo riders, and Western silent film stars such as Tom Mix and Buck Jones sewed their costumes themselves or had extravagant outfits made by expert tailors such as Nathan Turk, Rodeo Ben, and Nudie Cohn, conveniently concentrated in Hollywood (Nudie and Cabrall 2004). Another phase of cowboy mobility ensued with screen idols such as Hopalong Cassidy following the earlier trails of Buffalo Bill Cody's Wild West Shows to Australia and beyond (Elder 2013). Rather than buying stock clothes from dry goods stores (as might working cowboys), rodeo, film, and recording stars had tailors and boot makers produce evermore stylized and exaggerated designs that amplified their masculinity and sex appeal for cinema audiences and live crowds at rodeos or concerts.

In consequence, nationwide demand grew for decorative boots, a seemingly authentic yet always invented, form of American apparel. Television magnified this demand in the 1950s and 1960s with serial Western dramas and the intense marketing of childhood heroes. A proper pair of cowboy boots was essential for dressing up and playing "cowboys and Indians." Boots also became the defining tourist souvenir of a visit to the Western states, especially Texas; compulsory attire on dude ranches and ideal wearable objects to bring back from road trips across the West was made possible by the newly opened interstate system.

To meet this demand, the Western-wear and boot-making industries aggregated and expanded in key urban centers in the West. Cowboy shirts, jackets, and jeans grew as domestic apparel industries in Denver (Rockmount, Miller), Los Angeles (H-bar-C, Nudie), and San Francisco (Levis), while boot making concentrated in both El Paso, with its cheap labor and access to skilled Mexican boot makers, and Fort Worth, a major cowtown with access to investment capital (in neighboring Dallas) and growing tourist numbers. In addition, El Paso was (and still is) a major leather trade import/export city, with major railroads, highways, and both formal and informal routes of leather importation concentrated there. Lines of hats, shirts, and boots emerged from specialist postwar cultural/fashion companies such as Justin, Tony Lama, ACME, and Nocona—a handful of once-tiny boot-making workshops that scaled up production to become quasi-Fordist factories churning out standard line boots. They supplied metropolitan department stores, Western-wear retail chains in Western and Midwest cities (servicing both the ranch and costume cowboy markets) and sold boots via widely popular mail-order catalogues that enabled East Coast Americans to buy "genuine" Western boots from afar. The boots themselves were marketed as pop culture objects and as a higher cost, regionally distinctive souvenir. The models carried suitably macho, adventurous frontier names: "The Idaho," "The Ranger," "The Laredo," "The Thunderbird," "The Stallion," "The Sharpshooter."

Boot-making workshops interviewed for this research described tourists as a consistent and important component of their market. Big factories such as Tony Lama and Lucchese, both still operating in El Paso, sell boots to tourists in factory outlets on interstate junctions on the outskirts of the city. Meanwhile, niche custom makers such as Tres Outlaws and Rocketbuster in El Paso and M. L. Leddy's in Fort Worth aim to sell vintage designed boots to discerning tourists. In hip tourist districts of Austin and Dallas there are specialist antique boot dealers. Cowboy boots feature in tourism advertisements, on the cover of American editions of Lonely Planet guidebooks, and in airport arrivals terminals. Boot barns sell them by the thousand. There is also a consistent high-end trade, attracting wealthy collectors to Texas who visit principally to be fitted for boots. As one boot maker in Fort Worth described: "we have a lot of people that literally fly into town in their private plane, come here, get measured, get back on the plane and go home. We go pick them up if that's what we have to do. That happens way often."

In Fort Worth, thousands of tourists buy boots to wear to rodeos or to clubs such as Billy Bob's (the world's largest honky-tonk). At one level, this is dressing up and playing cowboy/cowgirl as part of a holiday. At another, such tourist consumption is a loose link to the dude ranch tradition, revisiting, reconstructing, and reclaiming the Western myth. A countermodern turn of sorts focuses on "consuming, reviving, reusing and reappraising older objects" (cf. Franklin 2011:161). In this case it is crucial that the boots are vintage styled. This form of souvenir consumption "hold[s] still in an aestheticized manner, the look, the feel, the technology, the actual materiality and culture of times past *through its objects*" (Franklin 2011:165, emphasis in original). For collectors, boots are seen as living remnants of a rural, pre-modern, pre-Fordist manufacturing technique, things made well by human hands—and in the case of custom workshops, often by the very person who measures one's feet. Workshops marketing high-end boots to tourists purposely hold on to archaic production techniques such as pegging soles by hand and carving personalized lasts (shoe molds) that are kept on file for future reference. The names of boot makers and places of production are proudly displayed inside the boots—provenance assured.

Custom boots are expensive and are usually a one-off purchase for tourists—except for the most ardent, and wealthy, collectors. They are made to last lifetimes, marketed via the cultural association between leather and connotations of "classic timelessness" (Leslie and Reimer 2003) and the allure of hand-crafted skill (cf. Sennett 2009). Boot collectors fly into El Paso or Fort Worth to be measured after spending weeks or months planning a pair of boots. Boots made with skins crafted with care and creativity last much longer than those produced in a factory; the former ages and matures, molding to accommodate the quirks of one's feet. Collectors care and treasure them—in the case of custom-made boots, these are expensive objects costing from US$500 to $10,000—and many owners have theirs resoled and wear them for life. They are put on mantelpieces, brought out for special occasions, and become family heirlooms.

Mass tourists might rarely indulge to this extent, but they evidently do spend hours in boot shops in a quandary over which pair to buy. Visiting a boot-making workshop or even a cheaper boot barn is a time-consuming, and expected, part of a holiday in Texan cities. Boots are not disposable things—a far cry from many other souvenirs, but rather are highly aestheticized objects that, like tattoos, are worn on the body as overtly symbolic markers of personal style and taste. The same kind of thinking goes into buying them: which designs, and skins, are the most accurate statement of one's personal identity and style?

There remains a massive diversity of styles, boot heights, and subcultural inflections (punk boots, rock 'n' roll boots, linedancing boots, "sexy" boots, "tough" masculine boots bordering on motorcycle gang style, elegant

Some of the styles available at Rocketbuster boots in El Paso, Texas. (Photo by author)

boots, novelty boots). Unmoored from a claim to agricultural "authenticity," the cowboy's fantasy and stereotypical elements eventually became visual tools for predominantly urban tourists to dress up, play, and perform a raft of subject identities.

Materialities of Tourist–Animal Encounters

A third thread is the manner in which boots bring tourists into contact with nonhuman others, through the trade in animal skins. Where tourism research has considered the place of nonhuman animals, it has tended to be through themes such as tourists gazing at animals deemed wild or scenic (cf. Franklin 1997; Curtin 2005) or through assessing the ethics of animal welfare in tourism (Hughes 2001). Meanwhile a growing theme in research on souvenirs and materiality is to disrupt "the assumption that objects simply await enlivening by human subjects" (Ramsay 2009:198). In the case of cowboy boots, tourists come into grizzly contact with an assortment of nonhuman animals, feeling their dead skins, smelling them, and *wearing* them.

There is a deep paradox between the making and selling of boots, which requires the absolute power of humans over animals skinned for their leather and the inherent agency, and indeed the resonant animality, of the very skins from which they are produced. The tendency of skins, as leather, to retain animal traces is in Texas responsible for the textural, sensual responses elicited both among boot makers who manipulate skins into boots and amongst tourists by touching, feeling, and smelling hides.

Boot making requires an absolute rendering of animals as inanimate, the reduction of diverse beings to a selection of available leathers. But those animal skins continue to have affective power after death; indeed boots are only marketable because of their feel, smell, color, and texture. The expected performance of tourists is to discuss with boot retail assistants which animal skins they want on their boots, on their special souvenir. Custom boot makers especially discuss with customers which batches of leathers smell and feel great, and often where they were sourced. Meanwhile, part of the skill of boot making is the ability of craftspeople to know the feel, strength, malleability, and application of various skins (from various parts of animals) in the construction of the object. Master boot makers know how to best position and how far to stretch a skin over a last, which parts to use on hard-wearing heels and vamps, which skins to line the uppers against which human skin rub, and which kinds of snake or lizard skin to use as inlay for decorative purposes. All of this is premised on the human mastery of animal deaths for industrial processing, while the preconfigured animal qualities of skins resonate as a constraint to and an enabler of possibilities.

Souvenirs thus link tourists to global geographies of trade—in this case of leather—and accompanying questions about the lives lived by the animals being worn: those culled (such as kangaroo, one of the most commonly used skins because of its strength and softness), domesticated animals farmed for skins (especially alligators, crocodiles, and ostriches), and those still hunted "wild." The tourist browsing boots in a Western-wear shop or flipping through samples of leathers in a custom workshop is not spared from acknowledging the animal origins of the material. Tourists unaccustomed to recognizing the animal origins of their footwear can be overheard asking whether the animals were raised in farm-like conditions (appealing to a sense of what Lubinski (2002) called "benevolent dominion") or hunted (for many Americans, seen as a "fairer" playing field for the animal). Shop assistants in boot barns are rarely able to answer tourists' questions accurately about where the leathers come from and the conditions under which the animals lived. Retail assistants will not reveal (or even know) that leather from alligators and snakes is often obtained by skinning them alive (Plous 1993). In boot barns selling cheap mass-produced boots, the complex global production chains that, for instance, link high-quality cowhide from tanneries in Italy to deforestation in the Amazon, basin are hidden (Siegle 2013). The boot as souvenir object therefore also invites consideration of both the animal rights debate and a postwilderness environmental critique.

Unlike shop assistants in boot barns, custom boot makers can usually point quite precisely to the provenance of skins: kangaroos, for instance, are culled "wild" in Australia, where they now roam throughout pastureland in larger numbers than before colonization, without widespread hunting from Aboriginal people. Their skins are shipped to Italy for tanning (because of tight pollution laws in Australia) and then imported into the United States. Ostrich, meanwhile, is farmed and tanned in South Africa. Whereas once alligator skins came from Florida where alligators were hunted "wild," they are now farmed and tanned in Southeast Asia and Brazil. Elephant, hippo, giraffe, and wildebeest skins made their way onto mid-twentieth-century boots via poaching in Africa. When I toured workshops in Texas in both 2010 and 2012, custom boot makers showed remnant stocks of those leathers, which they had inherited from previous generations of boot makers. Such skins have been progressively banned from the leather trade since the 1980s and did largely disappear from commercial boot production—only for some of them, notably elephant, to reappear in the last few years as "legitimate" supplies have been found from culling programs and sanctioned hunts in Africa.

Some boot makers insist on using only commercially raised leathers and steer clear of imported skins with likely dubious provenance (implying a moral preference for domesticated over "wild" nature); others limit designs to kangaroo and calf skins and specialize instead in delicate inlay work on retro boots, avoiding "exotics" altogether. Others buy the whole range of possible animal skins from leather traders in El Paso and are reticent to discuss where they come from. One El Paso boot maker even spends considerable periods of time traveling the world himself in order to source skins—to alligator farms in Brazil and to tanneries in France, Italy, and Japan—so he can feel with his hands the highest-quality, most expensive skins in the world before buying them.

The comparison with other forms of footwear and leather products is worth making, too. Just as certain animals are culturally encoded as acceptable to eat (and others as taboo), it has become mundane to wear cattle on our feet via sneakers or business shoes, to use leather handbags or furniture—and to be desensitized to the animal origins of such materials.[1] Beyond vegans, people purchasing sneakers, ballet slippers, or leather bi-

Leather samples at custom boot-making workshop in Fort Worth, Texas. (Photo by author)

cycle seats rarely consider the animals contained therein. In Texas, some tourists are clearly revolted upon seeing an array of animal skins on cowboy boots. But such encounters also confront the reality of death and the utilitarian purposes to which humans put animals. Unlike animal meat, which is rendered inanimate and impersonal through euphemisms such as "pork," "beef," and "veal" (Plous 1993), in boot shops the animals are labeled—indeed, they are a central part of the attraction. And unlike cow leathers used on sneakers and many handbags, which are colored and cut to belie animal origins ("temporal and spatial distancing . . . to insulate the public" [Plous 1993:20; see also Purcell 2011]), on cowboy boots the texture, imperfections, and smell— the animality of the skin—are up front and even celebrated. Although premised on the slaughter of animals for human utility, this form of boot making inserts animal materiality in the immediate lives of humans, on their walking feet—where peculiar forms of animate agency persist.

Conclusion

Cowboy boots are the product of an especially vivid form of regional cultural production, and a souvenir object filled with paradox: they evoke an idealized past of American frontier masculinity and hand-crafted production, as well as a quintessential symbol of American whiteness, even though colonial origins were a hybrid of Mediterranean, English, and Moorish influences. Wearing cowboy boots enables self-conscious performance of "Western" and "country" tourist identities. They are objects of nostalgia, linked to 1950s' and 1960s' popular culture motifs. But they also reaffirm human violence— bounded by the necessity of breeding, raising, hunting, killing, and wearing animals (Buller and Morris 2003:217). And yet, the curious case of cowboy boots also opens up space for debate about acknowledging animality and the agency of nonhuman others, even after death (cf. Jones 2003). Meanwhile, the increasingly mass-produced boot market maintains the visibility of the skin and its animal origin but draws the boots, and the tourists, into different kinds of exploitative relations and geographies of material things. Certain objects are thus, as Ramsay (2009:200) argues, "enchanting and enchanted," objects of attachment *and* estrangement. Cowboy boots aestheticize death but push consuming tourists to consider—even if temporarily—their own moral positioning vis-à-vis wearing hides. A shopping trip for boots in Texas is one fleeting moment where modernity's denial of animal subjectivity is overcome, however problematically, and a new and ethically fraught form of tourist–animal encounter is enabled.

Source: For a more detailed discussion, see "Souvenirs, Materialities, and Animal Encounters: Following Texas Cowboy Boots," *Tourist Studies* 14(3):286–301, 2014.

Note

[1] Plous (1993) cites a study of children that, for instance, showed that only a fifth could correctly identify leather as an animal product.

References Cited

Asplet, M., and M. Cooper. 2000. "Cultural Designs in New Zealand Souvenir Clothing: The Question of Authenticity." *Tourism Management* 21:307–312.

Ateljevic, I., and S. Doorne. 2003. "Culture, Economy and Tourism Commodities: Social Relations of Production and Consumption." *Tourist Studies* 3:123–141.

Beard, T., and J. Arndt. 1992. *The Cowboy Boot Book*. Salt Lake City: Gibbs Smith.

Bennett, J. 2010. *Vibrant Matter: A Political Ecology of Things*. Durham: Duke University Press.

Bull, D. 2000. *Hillbilly Hollywood: The Origins of Country & Western Style*. New York: St. Martins Press.

Buller, H., and C. Morris. 2003. "Farm Animal Welfare: A New Repertoire of Nature-Society Relations or Modernism Re-embedded?" *Sociologia Ruralis* 43:216–237.

Coles, T., C. M. Hall, and D. T. Duval. 2005. "Mobilizing Tourism: A Post-Disciplinary Critique." *Tourism Recreation Research* 30:31–41.

Curtin, S. 2005. "Nature, Wild Animals and Tourism: An Experiential View." *Journal of Ecotourism* 4:1–15.

Dary, D. 1989. *Cowboy Culture: A Saga of Five Centuries*. Lawrence, KS: University Press of Kansas.

DeLano, S., and D. Rieff. 1981. *Texas Boots*. New York: Penguin.

Elder, J. 2013. "How Hopalong Rode in and Lassoed Melbourne." *The Sunday Age*, 7 July. www.theage.com.au/victoria/how-hopalong-rode-in-and-lassoed-melbourne-20130706-2piyj.html

Franklin, A. 1997. *Animals and Modern Cultures: A Sociology of Human-Animal Relations in Modernity*. London: Sage.

———. 2010. "Aboriginalia: Souvenir Wares and the 'Aboriginalization' of Australian Identity." *Tourist Studies* 10:195–208.

———. 2011. "The Ethics of Second-Hand Consumption," *Ethical Consumption: a Critical Introduction*, eds. T. Lewis and E. Potter, pp. 156–168. London and New York: Routledge.

George-Warren, H., and M. Freedman. 2006. *How the West Was Worn: A History of Western Wear*. New York: Abrams.

Gibson, C. 2009. "Geographies of Tourism: Critical Research on Capitalism and Local Livelihoods." *Progress in Human Geography* 33:527–534.

Gibson, C. 2013. "The Global Cowboy: Rural Masculinities and Sexualities," in *Sexuality, Rurality and Geography*, eds. A. Gorman-Murray, B. Pini, and L. Bryant, pp. 199–218. Lanham MD: Lexington.

———. 2016a. "Material Inheritances: How Place, Materiality and Labor Process Underpin the Path-Dependent Evolution of Contemporary Craft Production." *Economic Geography* 92(1):61–86.

———. 2016b. "How Clothing Design and Cultural Industries Refashioned Frontier Masculinities: A Historical Geography of Western Wear." *Gender, Place & Culture* 23(5):733–752.

Hitchcock, M., and K. Teague. 2000. *Souvenirs: The Material Culture of Tourism*. Oxon, UK: CABI.

Hobsbawm, E. 2013. *Fractured Times: Culture and Society in the 20th Century*. London; Little, Brown.

Hughes, P. 2001. "Animals, Values and Tourism—Structure Shifts in UK Dolphin Tourism Provision." *Tourism Management* 22:321–329.

Hurn, S. 2011. "Dressing Down? Clothing Animals, Disguising Animality?" *Civilisations* 59:109–124.

Jóhannesson, G. T. 2005. "Tourism Translations: Actor-Network Theory and Tourism Research." *Tourist Studies* 5:133–150.

Jones, O. (2003) "'The restraint of beasts": rurality, animality, Actor Network Theory and dwelling', in Cloke, P. (ed), *Country Visions*, Pearson, Harlow UK, pp. 283-307.

Kael, H. 2012. "Of Gifts and Grandchildren: American Holy Land Souvenirs." *Journal of Material Culture* 19:133–151.

Leslie, D., and S. Reimer. 2003. "Fashioning Furniture: Restructuring the Furniture Commodity Chain." *Area* 35:427–437.

Lubinski, J. 2002. *Introduction to Animal Rights*. Detroit: Michigan State University.

Manns, W., and E. C. Flood. 1997. *Cowboys and the Trappings of the Old West*. Santa Fe, NM: Zon International.

Morgan, N., and A. Pritchard. 2005. "On Souvenirs and Metonymy: Narratives of Memory, Metaphor and Materiality." *Tourist Studies* 5:29–53.

Nottage, J. H. 2006. "Fashioning the West: The Pre-twentieth century Origins of Western Wear," in *How the West Was Worn: A History of Western Wear*, eds. H. George-Warren and M. Freedman, pp. 10–35. New York: Abrams.

Nudie, J. L., and M. L. Cabrall. 2004. *Nudie the Rodeo Tailor*. Salt Lake City: Gibbs Smith.

Plous, S. 1993 "Psychological Mechanisms in the Human Use of Animals." *Journal of Social Issues* 49:11–52.

Purcell, N. 2011. "Cruel Intimacies and Risky Relationships: Accounting for Suffering in Industrial Livestock Production." *Society & Animals* 19:59–81.

Rainger, J. G. 2000. "French Cowboys: The Guardians of the Camargue and Buffalo Bill," in *The Cowboy Way: An Exploration of History and Culture*, ed. P. H. Carlson, pp. 167–178. Lubbock TX: Texas Tech University Press.

Ramsay, N. 2009. "Taking-place: Refracted Enchantment and the Habitual Spaces of the Tourist Souvenir." *Social & Cultural Geography* 10:197–217.

Rupp, L. J. 1999. *A Desired Past: A Short History of Same-sex Love in America*. Chicago: University of Chicago Press.

Sennett, R. 2009. *The Craftsman*. New Haven: Yale University Press.

Siegle, L. 2013. "Luxury Leather and the Amazon." *The Guardian*, 3 March. http://www.guardian.co.uk/environment/2013/mar/03/luxury-leather-and-amazon-deforestation (accessed 21 March 2013).

Weil, S., and G. D. DeWeese. 2004. *Western Shirts: A Classic American Fashion*. Salt Lake City: Gibbs Smith.

Wilk, R. 2007. "Loggers, Miners, Cowboys, and Crab Fishermen: Masculine Work Cultures and Binge Consumption." Paper presented to the Yale Agrarian Studies Program, November 30, http://www.yale.edu/agrarianstudies/colloqpapers/12wilk.pdf

Part III: Tourism's Many Implications and Dilemmas

Locals attempt to control tourist behavior on the Greek island of Santorini. (Photo by Sharon Gmelch)

17

Community-Based Ecotourism in Costa Rica: Who Benefits?

Lynn Horton

In the late 1980s, the Osa Peninsula of southwestern Costa Rica was still a remote, "off the beaten track" travel destination with very limited tourist services and a way of life centered on traditional activities of agriculture, cattle ranching, and gold panning. A decade later, small planes transporting ecotourists buzzed overhead and backpackers filled dozens of new small hotels (*cabinas*). Local taxis and expatriate SUVs clogged the main streets of the peninsula's new ecotourism hub, Puerto Jiménez.[1] The number of annual peninsula visitors exploded from several thousand in 1990 to over 20,000 a decade later (Van den Hombergh 1999). These transformations on the Osa peninsula reflect Costa Rica's emergence as Latin America's leading ecotourism destination. By the 2000s, the tourism sector employed 12 percent of Costa Rica's labor force and had become the country's second leading source of foreign exchange (Zamora and Obando 2017; Inman 2002). Nature was a big draw, as over half of Costa Rica's one million tourists visited at least one protected area (Zamora and Obando 2017).

Ecotourism has been a catalyst for economic, social, and environmental transformations in rural Costa Rica, even as the nature and normative desirability of such change is under debate. Support for ecotourism now forms part of state policy. Government officials and many NGOs have lauded ecotourism as a qualitatively distinct market-based process that improves quality of life and empowers local communities with minimal negative environmen-

Ecotourists explore the coast of Osa Peninsula, Costa Rica. (Photo by Rob Crandall/ Shutterstock.com)

tal impacts. Critics contend, however, that as Costa Rica's latest transnational activity, ecotourism perpetuates historical patterns of inequality, social exclusion, and environmental degradation associated with past patterns of dependent, agro export-led growth in Central America.

To address these issues, this case study focuses on the Osa peninsula, where relative geographic isolation inhibited the presence of transnational capital and international chain hotels, making it a "best-case" scenario for examining the potentials of community-based ecotourism. It approaches ecotourism as an inherently political process that incorporates power struggles over access to land, natural resources, economic benefits, as well as representations of the environment and quality of life (Cheong and Miller 2000; Mowforth and Munt 2016). This chapter explores the winners and losers in ecotourism; its economic, environmental, and sociocultural impacts, and the ways in which relationships of nationality, class, and gender and forms of collective mobilization are reshaped through ecotourism processes.

Defining Ecotourism

Ceballos-Lascuráin first defined ecotourism as "traveling to relatively undisturbed or uncontaminated natural areas with the specific objective of studying, admiring, and enjoying the scenery and its wild plants and animals, as well as any existing cultural manifestations" (qtd. in Fennell 1999:30). In contrast to mass tourism, associated with packaged trips by large groups and a preponderant role for transnational corporations, ecotourism is characterized as flexible, small-scale, responsible activities in natural environments carried out by individuals or small groups (Mowforth and Munt 2016). In practice, however, the lines may blur, as roughly half of visitors to Costa Rica fall under the definition of "soft" ecotourists, traditional "sun and sand" mass tourists who also make excursions to natural destinations (Honey 2008; Zamora and Obando 2017).

Similar to other regions, Costa Rica draws North American and European ecotourists who are relatively well educated and affluent—one survey found 68 percent hold a college degree and 36 percent have an income over $100,000 (*Tico Times* 2002). They seek to temporarily escape mundane and stressful lifestyles in industrial societies and experience novelty and authenticity through consumption of third-world tourist destinations like Costa Rica. Ecotourists, with their commitment to the environment and social justice, should be minimal-impact visitors. In the best-case scenario, ecotourism provides income and control for local communities, builds environmental awareness, generates direct and indirect support for conservation, revitalizes local cultures, and strengthens human rights and democratic movements (Fennell 1999).

Critics are skeptical, however, that ecotourism represents a qualitatively different or preferable form of development (Duffy 2002; Honey 2008). Despite its more laudable environmental and social intentions, ecotourism, like mass tourism, does not necessarily challenge in any profound way systems of power and unequal accumulation. Likewise, although ecotourism is conceptualized as small-scale and locally controlled, economic concentration and corporate influence within the ecotourism sector are common. In sociocultural terms, status-seeking Northern "egotourists" may be particularly intrusive and disruptive of local cultures precisely because they seek out more remote and "untouched" travel destinations (Mowforth and Munt 2016).

Costa Rican Park Creation and Ecotourism

One critical precondition for Costa Rica's ecotourism boom was the government's rapid expansion of protected areas in the 1970s and 1980s to eventually incorporate one quarter of national territory (Zamora and Obando 2017). On the Osa peninsula, a U.S. corporation, Osa Forest Products (OFP), controlled some 47,000 hectares of land but invested little in this property, leaving some 80 percent of the peninsula covered in rain forest in the late 1960s (Rosero-Bixby et al. 2002; Van den Hombergh 1999). Over the next decade, the presence of gold drew hundreds of peasant migrants to the Osa peninsula. These squatters claimed some 10,000 hectares of OFP land and clashed, at times violently, with OFP personnel until President Daniel Oduber took the land from OFP in 1975 to create the 41,789-hectare Corcovado National Park.

The Costa Rican government's early park creation and its more general "environmental exceptionalism" reflected in large part the bipartisan influence of a small group of Costa Rican scientists/conservationists with transnational contacts and close personal relationships with high-level politicians (Evans 1999; Wallace 1992). For their part, the local Osa squatters, who struggled for the expropriation and distribution of OFP land to peasants, generally opposed the creation of the national park.

Such "top-down" environmentalism fails to address underlying inequalities that propel deforestation and rests on a deepening of state and elite control over land and natural resources that traditionally served as a local commons and subsistence safety net. In the case of Osa, the Costa Rican state hastened the end of the agricultural frontier model of subsistence and upward mobility subsidized by the exploitation of the peninsula's natural resources. "Global" environmental claims were privileged over localized claims to land and natural resources. After a series of protests in the mid-1980s, the artisan gold miners eventually received land and monetary compensation from the government. These gold miner protests helped hasten a shift in government policy from an exclusionary, "policing" environmental model toward sustainable, income-generating activities such as ecotourism designed to address community needs.

Ecotourism on Osa

While state environmental policies laid the groundwork, in practice, Costa Rica's rapid expansion of both mass and ecotourism was largely the result of private-sector initiatives (Cordero and van Duynen Montijn 2002). In contrast to Costa Rica's northern Pacific beaches where transnational hotel chains dominated, on the Osa peninsula individual North American and European investors led the initiative to purchase land with ecotourism potential in the late 1980s (Minca and Linda 1999). Hotel chains did not invest in the peninsula, likely because of the zone's geographical remoteness and lack of infrastructure, as well as the deterrent effects of its relatively high level of social organization (*Tico Times* 2002; *Tico Times* 2003).

The individual foreign investors who began to buy up property on the peninsula in the early 1990s possessed key economic and cultural advantages. First, they had access to capital to purchase land and invest in ecotourism infrastructure. In contrast, under neoliberal economic reforms, local Costa Ricans had more difficulty accessing bank loans. Foreign investors also participated in fluid, transnational social networks, which enabled them to recognize the peninsula's ecotourism potential much sooner than Costa Ricans, who were still embedded in more localized social and cultural networks.

Through these initial investment patterns and de facto patterns of economic exclusion, a three-tiered model of ecotourism participation evolved on Osa. On the top tier were small to medium-sized, largely foreign-owned, ecolodges with up to several dozen salaried employees. These ecolodges, located on private reserves with rain forest and beach access, on the edges of Corcovado National Park, and in Drake Bay, offered a dozen or more rooms ranging from $50 to several hundred dollars a night. They attracted the more well-off ecotourists, and while local informants estimated that as many as one quarter of such ecolodges would run into financial difficulties, they also offered the greatest opportunities for profit. The peninsula's second tier of ecotourism enterprises consisted of some 35 *cabinas*, modest lodging with an average of three to eight rooms, located in the town of Puerto Jiménez, which catered largely to budget travelers and backpackers (COBRUDES 1997). The cabina owners, generally more well-off residents of the town before ecotourism, charged from $10 to $20 a night for lodging and employed family labor, along with one or two salaried, usually part-time, workers. In addition to cabinas, local Costa Ricans operated taxi, fishing, aquatic, and horseback riding services for ecotourists. The third tier of participation in ecotourism was that of less well-off Costa Ricans who were employed in service roles—as cooks, maids, handymen, caretakers, guides, and so on—generally by the foreign-owned enterprises.

Economic Impacts of Ecotourism

Informants from community organizations and government agencies in Puerto Jiménez estimated that 20 percent of the population worked directly in ecotourism, while another 60 percent received indirect economic benefits. Similar to other ecotourism zones of Costa Rica, Osa residents identified the generation of new employment opportunities as the most important economic benefit of ecotourism. In Puerto Jiménez in particular, ecotourism overtook gold mining, farming, and ranching—the latter two already in decline due to neoliberal reforms—as a central economic activity. Ecotourism on Osa did not so much disrupt more traditional local or nationally oriented economic activities, as much as it offered new income-generating opportunities, within the limitations of foreign ownership described above.

Labor conditions in the traditional mass tourism sector—low pay, long hours, and the unstable, seasonal nature of the work—are often disadvantageous to or even exploitative of local workers (Stronza 2001). On the Osa peninsula, however, ecotourism wages, approximately 2,400 colones ($8) per day in 2000, were generally on a par with or higher than other sectors, such as agriculture, which paid 1,500 colones ($5) per day. Ecotourism positions that required specific skills and training generally paid higher wages. Nature guides, for example, earned an average of $50 per day. On the negative side, during the high season, work hours were often long, with cooks, for example, reporting shifts of twelve hours or more; during the rainy, low season, a number of the ecolodges temporarily laid off employees.

Proponents stress that, in comparison to other globalized economic activities, small-scale ecotourism offers greater opportunities for local power and control (Scheyvens 1999). On Osa peninsula, however, an important degree of economic control shifted toward North Americans and Europeans who, in a pattern that extends across Costa Rica, took control of substantial portions of the peninsula's coastal, ocean-view and forested land to create private reserves that averaged 440 hectares (COBRUDES 1997). Loss of local control of land and natural resources was also accelerated by ecotourism's land speculation on the peninsula. According to Puerto Jiménez real estate agents, during the 1990s the value of coastal, ocean-view, and forested land on the peninsula doubled every year. As the ecotourism boom took hold, peninsula ocean-front property sold for as much as much as $25,000 per hectare, and land purchase became prohibitively expensive for many Costa Ricans.

Even prior to ecotourism, however, the peninsula had been characterized by stratified landholding patterns. Ecotourism was an intensification of this trend, rather than a rupture of egalitarian society. In the 1980s, exclusion was physical, as gold miners were removed by force from the newly created national park. In later decades, less visible but powerful market processes excluded key groups—poorer Costa Ricans without access to capital and communities without beachfronts, ocean views, rain forest, or infrastructure—from profitable ecotourism opportunities.

Despite a discourse of support for small-scale ecotourism dating from the 1990s, the Costa Rican state in practice tacitly reinforced inequality. The Costa Rican government only weakly enforced regulations to limit foreign control of coastal land, and tourism tax incentives and subsidies were disproportionately captured by large-scale and international tourism enterprises (Honey 2008). Small-scale ecotourism operators in Puerto Jiménez received little support from the Costa Rican Institute of Tourism. Such government policies that aligned toward large-scale tourism investors reflected the increasingly transnational nature of the Costa Rican state, the deepening hegemony of neoliberalism in the region, and, in some instances, the personal economic interests of government officials (*Tico Times* 2003).

Environmental Impacts of Ecotourism

Local residents widely credited the park creation with bringing deforestation on the peninsula almost to a halt. Likewise, studies of the Osa peninsula did not identify serious negative environmental impacts in the first phase of the ecotourism boom (COBRUDES 1997; Rosero-Bixby et al. 2002). The key environmental problems identified on the peninsula—logging in the Golfo Dulce Forest Reserve, poaching in the national park, agrochemical runoff into the gulf, and solid waste disposal in the towns—were generally linked to more traditional extraction and agricultural activities (COBRUDES 1997; MIDEPLAN 2003; Van den Hombergh 1999). Indirectly, ecotourism helped shift local participation away from such environmentally damaging activities and also provided a material underpinning for collective mobilization on environmental issues discussed below.

Local informants reported that most ecolodges left as much rain forest intact as possible on their properties, built structures in styles that blend into the natural environment, and employed technologies such as solar panel heating and environmentally friendly waste control measures (Lapa Rios 2002). It was not clear, however, if such sustainable practices would continue. Other zones of Costa Rica, in a more advanced stage of ecotourism development, have experienced serious environmental deterioration. The small, but very popular, national park of Manuel Antonio, for example, has received over 250,000 visitors a year and has suffered overcrowding; a proliferation of hotels, bars, tourist concessions; damage to plants and animals; and pollution (Honey 2008; *Tico Times* 1999a).

Sociocultural Impacts of Ecotourism

Ecotourism visitors to Costa Rica generally possess a series of advantages over local residents—higher levels of wealth, education, and status, and participation in broader, transnational institutional and social networks—which potentially allow them to advance social and cultural power at the local level (*Tico Times* 2002). Critics contend that, however it is packaged, ecotourism can, at most, be considered "green" capitalism (Duffy 2002; Mowforth and Munt 2016). As such, it is inextricably linked to unequal distributional impacts and practices and beliefs of competition, individualism, material accumulation, and consumption. Such processes may disempower local peoples, fragmenting communities, limiting collective action, and restraining imaginings of qualitatively different forms of development.

On the Osa peninsula, ecotourism appears to have intensified a more long-term dynamic of capitalist modernization—a movement away from a rural Costa Rican culture of frugality and commitment to family and community relations toward greater commodification and efficiency. These implicit and explicit cultural requisites, embedded in ecotourism as a market-based activity, signified for certain local groups the transformation of a valued way of life and even a cultural loss. Gold miners, for example, exchanged a more autonomous lifestyle for the capitalist disciplines of supervision, hierarchy, and externally defined work schedules. Likewise, during high season, the long hours required by ecotourism disrupted family and social life in a way that more traditional economic activities on the peninsula did not.

Ecotourism also may shift class, gender, and interethnic relations in the very heart of communities. Women on Osa peninsula in particular experienced ecotourism differently from men. Traditional gender norms in rural Costa Rica limited women's income earning opportunities. With the arrival of ecotourism, however, women began to take an active role in opening cabinas, restaurants, and other small businesses. Ecotourism did not necessarily challenge or subvert traditional gender roles but rather was viewed as a "natural" extension of women's household roles of cleaning, cooking, and serving others (Apostolopoulos et al. 2001).

In interviews, women credited their participation in ecotourism with providing them income they could more directly control and positive opportunities to interact with foreigners. Yet within the ecotourism sector, gender stratification persists. Typically, the well-paying jobs that require higher levels of skill and extended periods of time outdoors—nature guides, fishing and scuba diving expedition leaders, for example—were still filled largely by men. Young women in particular also sought out romantic and/or sexual encounters with ecotourists and expatriates. Multiple informants in the town of Puerto Jiménez identified such relationships, as well as an increase in prostitution, as important negative social impacts of ecotourism. Such relationships in theory could offer women temporary escape from the constraints of local patriarchal gender norms. Observers suggested, however, that given the often wide differences in age, power, and wealth between local women and male ecotourists, in practice such relationships tended to be more exploitative than opportunities for local women.

The power differentials between local residents and foreign ecotourist entrepreneurs, however, should not be overstated, as ecotourism in some instances facilitated more sustained and egalitarian interactions. Long-term Costa Rican residents identified some expatriates and ecotourists as contributors to positive social change through medical services, environmental education seminars, programs for single mothers, and other community projects on the peninsula.

Conflicting Environmentalisms

Prior to the ecotourism boom, many Osa residents viewed the natural world from an instrumentalist perspective, as a space of hardship and danger to be overcome, whose primary function is to serve the material subsistence needs of the human population. While instrumentalist representations of the environment persisted on the peninsula, new, localized socioenvironmental discourses and forms of collective mobilization, relating to ecotourism in the

Puerto Jiménez zone in particular, took shape. Local support for rain forest conservation increased, as it was seen as critical to sustaining ecotourism income on the peninsula in the long-term. Likewise, ecotourism formed the basis of a self-selection process through which environmentally conscious Costa Ricans relocated to the peninsula from other zones and utilized ecotourism to support a lifestyle of close contact with the natural world and environmental activism.

On an ideological level, expatriates and ecotourists brought to the peninsula a conceptualization of nature as a space of adventure, risk, aesthetic enjoyment, and leisure activity, while representing local practices and ways life as environmentally destructive. Local residents, however, have not been passive receptors of these external environmental discourses. Rather, longer-term peninsula residents expounded counternarratives that emphasized the history of local resistance to the logging activities of Osa Forest Products and the international mining companies that dredged the peninsula's rivers in earlier decades. This emergent socioenvironmental discourse of Costa Rican activists was grounded in nationalism and social justice concerns and embedded in long-term experiences of place, networks of family and friends, and local ways of life. A Costa Rican environmental activist highlighted these tensions as she described a debate with a European colleague:

> The difference between the two of us is that I live inside of this country and I can't stop thinking about the people who live here. It is not enough just to put up demonstration parcels and buy up land . . . the impact of the conservation measures on the local population has been very hard. They are told you can't use certain nets at the mouths of the rivers to fish and don't touch the animals. People are here with their arms crossed [doing nothing].

This localized environmental perspective questioned many of the precepts of market ideologies and the global advance of materialism and commodification. In contrast to utilitarian views of nature, this discourse held that human beings share a fundamental ethical and spiritual relationship with the natural world. As one Costa Rican community activist argued:

> People have an innate appreciation of beauty. They appreciate the ocean, seeing the dolphins leap. As human beings, we cannot deny the connection between ourselves and nature. Those who first came and cut down the forests, it hurt them. The *campesino* says, "I was destructive." We have to recognize the power of natural resources over human beings. The majority love nature that gives them life.

In this perspective, "quality of life" was framed as daily contact with the natural environments of beaches and rain forests, time for leisure, and relative material simplicity—in other words, the opposite of stressful capitalist routines in "cement prisons" of artificial urban environments.

New Forms of Collective Mobilization

Ecotourism also provided a material and ideological base for new forms of local mobilization against the plans of a transnational wood product company, Stone Container Corporation, to build a wood chip plant on the peninsula (see Van den Hombergh 1999). Costa Rican activists, drawn largely from the ecotourism sector, opposed the wood chip plant on both nationalist and environmental grounds. The project was seen to threaten local control and environmental conditions needed to maintain ecotourism. Costa Rican activists also launched a campaign to denounce illegal logging in the Golfo Dulce Forest Reserve by Costa Rican companies, allegedly with the complicity of corrupt local officials (*Tico Times* 1997). While foreign ecotourism operators had gained substantial economic power on the peninsula, in interviews activists noted that expatriates tended to take a more limited and backstage role in this environmental activism, in part not to undermine the nationalist credibility and political effectiveness of the campaigns.

These environmental campaigns were opposed by local Costa Ricans who were concentrated in the agricultural, ranching, and logging zones and held an instrumentalist environmental perspective. The Osa environmental activists in turn sought political support from Costa Rica's national conservationist sector and national and international environmental NGOs. They launched media and political lobbying campaigns and employed direct action techniques, such as demonstrations and highway blockages, to successfully pressure policy makers. Eventually they prevailed in winning state support to halt the establishment of a wood chip plant on the gulf and placing a moratorium on logging (*Tico Times* 1999b).

Conclusion

The Osa case study highlights a series of preconditions—an absence of powerful transnational economic actors, a generous natural resource endowment, a democratic government, and a local population with a history of collective action and resistance—which should facilitate genuine community-controlled ecotourism. On Osa, ecotourism has not so much disrupted such traditional activities as it has economically revitalized zones like Puerto Jiménez and expanded opportunities for salaried and self-employment. Similarly, the initial phases of ecotourism on Osa did not bring the type of negative environmental impacts seen in smaller, more intensely visited Costa Rican national parks.

On the negative side, Osa's ecotourism boom, built upon policies of top-down environmentalism, has further eroded local control of and access to land and natural resources on the peninsula and has advanced state and foreign influence on the peninsula. Even in zones like Osa, where transnational corporations have not yet penetrated, smaller-scale patterns of stratification and exclusion are still likely to emerge. On Osa, such hierarchies of nationality, social class, and gender were reproduced through unequal initial access to land, capital, and cultural knowledge; unequal insertion in social and institutional networks; restrictive gender norms; and the absence of redistributive, leveling state policies.

Osa peninsula can be conceptualized as a space of both resistance to and engagement with the external ideologies and cultural practices that have arrived with ecotourism. Ecotourism has also been a catalyst in the emergence of an empowered group of local activists who have successfully challenged the presence of transnational corporations and struggled for local control over natural resources, ecotourism, and the future of the peninsula. The coupling of Osa to global flows and processes of ecotourism has in part stimulated a resurgence of a more localized and place-centered way of life for some residents, even as other groups are drawn more deeply into "modern" and transnational ways of being. Although the class and cultural tensions that underlie these interactions should not be underestimated, ecotourism also offers at least the potential to forge more complex, cross-national and cross-class advocacy networks centered upon common values and discourses of social justice and localized environmentalisms.

Source: For a more detailed discussion, see "Buying Up Nature: Economic and Social Impacts of Costa Rica's Ecotourism Boom," *Latin American Perspectives* 36:107, 2009.

Note

[1] This case study incorporates data from 32 interviews and observation carried out in the ecotourism center of Puerto Jiménez and La Palma, a nearby agricultural community largely excluded from ecotourism. I interviewed key figures active in ecotourism and community issues, as well as local NGO and government officials.

References Cited

Apostolopoulos, Yorghus, Sevil Sonmez, and Dallen J. Timothy (eds.). 2001. *Women as Producers and Consumers of Tourism in Developing Regions*. Westport, CT: Praeger.

Cheong, So-Min, and Marc L. Miller. 2000. "Power and Tourism: A Foucauldian Observation." *Annals of Tourism Research* 27(2): 371–390.

Consejo Bruqueño Para el Desarrollo Sostenible (COBRUDES). 1997. *Diagnóstico socioeconómico de la región Brunca*, COBRUDES.

Cordero, Allen, and Luisa van Duynen Montijn. 2002. "¿Turismo sostenible en Costa Rica?" *Imaginarios sociales y turismo sostenible*, eds. Daniel Hiernaux-Nicolas, Allen Cordero, and Luisa van Duynen Montijn, pp. 37–129. FLACSO Costa Rica.

Duffy, Rosaleen. 2002. *A Trip Too Far: Ecotourism, Politics and Exploitation*. London: Earthscan Publications Ltd.

Evans, Sterling. 1999. *The Green Republic: A Conservation History of Costa Rica*. Austin: University of Texas Press.

Fennell, David A. 1999. *Ecotourism: An Introduction*. New York: Routledge.

Honey, Martha. 2008. *Ecotourism and Sustainable Development: Who Owns Paradise?*, 2nd ed. Washington, DC: Island Press.

Inman, Críst. 2002. *Tourism in Costa Rica: The Challenge of Competitiveness*, INCAE. www.incae.ac.cr/ES/clacds/investigacion/pdf/cen653.pdf (accessed 29 March 2017).

Lapa Rios. 2002. *Eco-Tourism and Lapa Rios: Goals and Action*. www.laparios.com.

Minca, Claudio, and Marco Linda. 1999. "Ecotourism on the Edge: The Case of Corcovado National Park, Costa Rica," in *Forest Tourism and Recreation: Case Studies in Environmental Management*, eds. Xavier Font and John Tribe, pp. 103–126. Oxon, UK: CABI.

Ministerio de Planificación Nacional y Política Económica (MIDEPLAN). 2003. *Plan Regional de Desarrollo 2003–2006 Región Brunca.* MIDEPLAN.

Mowforth, Martin, and Ian Munt. 2016. *Tourism and Sustainability: Development and New Tourism in the Third World*, 4th ed. New York: Routledge.

Rosero-Bixby, Luis, Tirso Maldonado-Ulloa, and Roger Bonilla-Carrión. 2002. "Bosque y población en la Península de Osa, Costa Rica." *Revista de Biología Trópica* 50(2): 585–598.

Scheyvens, Regina. 1999. "Ecotourism and the Empowerment of Local Communities." *Tourism Management* 20(2): 245–249.

Stronza, Amanda. 2001. "Anthropology of Tourism: Forging New Ground for Ecotourism and Other Alternatives." *Annual Review of Anthropology* 30:261–283.

Tico Times. 1997. "Critics: Logging Probe in Reserve a 'Whitewash.'" *Tico Times*, 1 August.

———. 1999a. "Beach Park Imperiled by Overdevelopment." *Tico Times*, 26 November.

———. 1999b. "Passions Boil Over in Osa: Environmentalists Clash with Police over Logging." *Tico Times*, 26 February.

———. 2002. "Ambitious Tourism Plan Unveiled." *Tico Times*, 5 April.

———. 2003. "Fiesta Premiere Resort Opens in Papagayo," *Tico Times*, 7 November.

Van den Hombergh, Helena. 1999. *Guerreros del Golfo Dulce: industria forestal y conflicto en la Península de Osa, Costa Rica*. Departamento Ecuménico de Investigaciones.

Wallace, David Rains. 1992. *The Quetzal and the Macaw: The Story of Costa Rica's National Parks*. San Francisco: Sierra Club Books.

Zamora, Natalia, and Vilma Obando. 2017. *Biodiversity and Tourism in Costa Rica, 2001*, www.cbd.int/doc/nbsap/tourism/CostaRica(Tourism).pdf (accessed 29 May).

18

In Search of the Narwhal: Ethical Dilemmas in Ecotourism

Ralf Buckley

Can one be an unethical ecotourist? Here I set out to show that this question is neither trivial nor straightforward.

Most definitions of ecotourism, even the more restrictive ones (Buckley 1994), focus on observable criteria such as tourism products and settings, management of environmental impacts, guided interpretation for clients, and perhaps some contribution to conservation (Buckley 1994, 2003; Fennell 2003; Weaver 2001). Certainly, there are complexities in interpreting and implementing any of these (Buckley 2003), but these are second-order.

Demanding that ecotourism be defined by ethical rather than behavioral considerations is very different. Definitions of ethics, whether philosophical, professional, or general, are based on morals and require individuals to make moral judgements. This is not the same as requiring people to follow rules of behavior, even if these rules are labeled as codes of ethics rather than codes of conduct or legal regulations.

The ethical theme has been quite pervasive in the ecotourism literature, raised especially by authors such as Honey (1999) and Malloy and Fennell (1998). Most recently Fennell (2004) has argued that a responsible ecotourism industry necessarily involves moral underpinnings, in the form of theoretical and practical reverence for nature. More generally, Malloy and Fennell (1998) and Fennell (2004) argue that while most businesses "feel that ethics are only useful if they are good for business," ecotourism should be "based on principled values and ethics." I do not disagree with this philosophy. But as outlined below, I do not think that an ethical test can easily be incorporated into operational criteria for any practical application of ecotourism. Therefore, I would argue that it is not in fact realistic to define ecotourism in ethical terms.

If my argument is accepted, then unethical ecotourists are perfectly possible. This position may be repugnant to many readers. So this is not a trivial issue. Indeed, it is a very complex one. To illustrate the difficulties, let us consider a real-life case study, outlined below.

Case Study: High Arctic Sea Kayak Tour

There are relatively few commercial sea kayak tours in the High Arctic. The season is short, access is costly, and conditions can be difficult, so tours are expensive and appeal only to experienced sea kayakers. One such tour is operated by Blackfeather Inc., based in Ontario, Canada (Blackfeather 2005). This company operates a two-week self-supported sea kayak trip out of Pond Inlet near the northern tip of Baffin Island. The tour features a search for narwhal in a number of steep-sided narrow sounds, and is advertised as "In search of the narwhal" (Blackfeather 2005).

The trip uses collapsible kayaks, and these, together with all camping equipment, food, and other supplies, are brought in by plane specifically for the trip, carried as excess baggage by the guides and clients. The tour starts with a speedboat shuttle to the furthermost point, taking about five hours. The kayaks are then assembled and loaded, and the group paddles back to Pond Inlet over a period of 10 days or so. When I took part in this trip we saw narwhal near the drop-off point, but not subsequently. Sea kayaking in this area is safe only during the relatively brief summer breakup of the ice, and this takes place after nesting seabirds have already migrated south. The landscape is spectacular but rather bleak, and the weather is variable.

Local Communities and Narwhal Hunting

There is only a short period of the year when these sounds are accessible by boat, and many of the Inuit families in Pond Inlet and other settlements take advantage of the weather and the open water to establish fishing and hunting camps on the shores of the sounds. While such camps no doubt have a long traditional history, technologies have changed greatly. A number of locals now have large, fast and seaworthy boats, often purchased with Canadian Government assistance, and they also have high-powered, high caliber modern rifles, which they use to shoot at surfacing narwhal and other whales. Narwhal are hunted partly for the tusks, and partly for the blubber, which is known locally as muktuk and considered a great delicacy. International trade in narwhal tusks and other body parts is prohibited under the Convention on International Trade in Endangered Species (CITES 2005). According to local

Narwhal. (Photo by Linda Bucklin/Shutterstock.com)

Inuit, however, several cruise ships visit Pond Inlet each year, and their passengers are always keen to buy narwhal tusks. The majority of purchasers, reportedly, are from Asian nations, which are not signatory to CITES.

Evidence of Hunting

How did we know that narwhal were being killed? We saw numerous boats and heard a number of rifle shots. Indeed, when we looked at these boats through our binoculars we often saw their occupants looking back at us through their telescopic sights, a somewhat unnerving experience. We saw the flensed carcass of a young narwhal drifting near a beach. And most importantly, we met Inuit hunters who showed us narwhal tusks, with the root portions still blood-covered, wrapped in blankets inside their fishing boats. The Inuit were friendly and likeable people, clearly proud of their prowess, but also clearly aware that taking tusks is frowned upon by Canadian Government officials. They showed us their boats, their rifles, and the tusks, and told us who buys them, but they did so surreptitiously and spoke to us individually, without witnesses.

Community-Centered Perspectives

From the perspective of the individual Inuit hunters, this arrangement may seem quite satisfactory. As with Indigenous peoples in other developed nations (such as Australia), they receive taxpayer-funded subsidies, which on a per capita basis may be quite substantial relative to average income in the country concerned. On the other hand, the aggregate value of these subsidies is miniscule in comparison with the value of natural resources extracted from traditional lands by colonial industries. Hence it may seem quite reasonable to the Inuit in Pond Inlet that some members of their community have high-speed and seaworthy fishing vessels provided by the Canadian Government. Such vessels, however, need maintenance and fuel, and if sea kayaking tourists will pay for the all-day trip out to where the narwhal congregate, that is a remarkably convenient way for the local guides to earn cash income. And once there, it would clearly be very inefficient for the locals to return to Pond Inlet and then set out on a separate hunting trip to the same place. It makes far more sense to drop the tourists off and then go directly to hunt narwhal. And the profit from the charter and from the later sales of narwhal tusks provides the cash income to buy fuel for the boats, and goods from the trading co-op in Pond Inlet.

Narwhal were hunted traditionally, albeit in much smaller numbers and with very different technologies. Perhaps narwhal numbers are decreasing. But there are many hunters, and even if one hunter stops hunting narwhal, the others will continue. Besides, Europeans hunted many of their species into extinction, so why should they tell Inuit peoples how to manage narwhal?

Conservation-Centered Perspectives

In the eyes of the conservation biologist the situation is rather different. Narwhal are endangered. Inuit are not. Inuit used to hunt narwhal for subsistence, whereas now they hunt them for cash. Traditionally the hunt was carried out using handmade kayaks and harpoons; modern technologies are very different. Yes, distant ancestors of modern Canadians took resources from many traditional Inuit lands, and modern international corporations continue to do so. But this is nothing to do with the narwhal. Traditionally, Inuit villages may not have set limits on narwhal hunts, but the Canadian Inuit are now part of Canada, and the Canadian nation provides them with much of their current lifestyle and material goods, including both boats and firearms. Inuit, therefore, have an obligation to observe Canadian law, including that relating to the hunting of narwhal and trade in narwhal tusks.

Tourist Perspectives

Perspectives of fee-paying tour clients may depend on the attitudes and experience of the client concerned. For some tourists, a 10-day High Arctic sea kayaking holiday represents extreme adventure, where the major goal is simply to complete the trip. On our trip, for example, there was an older couple who were particularly concerned to paddle not just to the normal take-out point near Pond Inlet but right back to Pond Inlet itself. When we did see narwhal, this couple watched from onshore rather than paddling out. For our two guides, in contrast, a trip such as this is an easy and routine exercise, unless an unexpected and extended period of bad weather sets in. We may have been traveling in collapsible kayaks above the Arctic Circle, but we were generally close to shore, protected from open ocean swell, and by no means alone. We saw a number of Inuit camps and fishing boats that could have rescued us if need be, and the guides did have radio contact, though they kept this concealed from the clients. Another of the tour clients had previous sea kayaking experience in Greenland, of which he seemed rather proud. He was interested in narwhal but also seemed somewhat frightened of them. He was concerned about narwhal hunting, but perhaps he may have been ambivalent because he wanted to identify with the Greenlanders and hence perhaps indirectly with the Canadian Inuit.

Personal Impressions

For myself, I knew that Canadian First Nations peoples now hunt whales with rifles and outboard-powered fishing boats. I was not surprised to find that some members of the Pond Inlet Inuit community hunt narwhal, whereas others make money from narwhal tourism. I was familiar with issues relating to the use of modern technologies by Indigenous peoples to hunt species that, in the past, were hunted only by traditional means; and to hunt for cash, whereas traditionally they hunted for subsistence or cultural reasons. Other examples include dugong hunted by Aborigines in Australia; birds of paradise in Papua New Guinea; and an enormous range of terrestrial mammals throughout Africa, Asia, and South America.

Naively, however, I had not expected that there would be so close a link between tourism and hunting, with the former effectively providing fuel for the latter. Not surprisingly, the few narwhal we saw dived as soon as they became aware of our boats, presumably since they have come to associate boats with hunting. Naturally, this greatly reduces the enjoyment of watching narwhal, which after all was the main lure of the trip. Similar issues apply in areas of Africa where hunting concessions are immediately adjacent to national parks or photo safari concessions (Buckley 2003).

Ethical Issues

From a cultural perspective, selling narwhal tusks to international cruise ship passengers rather than local carvers represents a cultural change, but not a very large one relative to other cultural changes that the Pond Inlet Inuit have experienced. From an ethical or animal-rights perspective, a narwhal shot with a bullet is unlikely to die immediately, but neither is a narwhal speared with a traditional harpoon, so once again the change is minor.

From a conservation perspective, the changes are much more significant. In ecological terms, the critical issue is neither why the narwhal are killed nor how, but how many. Where individual animal parts can be sold for large cash prices, people will typically kill many more animals than if they are hunted solely for subsistence. This applies equally to narwhal tusks in the High Arctic, elephant ivory in Africa, tiger penises in Asia, or grizzly bear gall bladders in Russia. And with modern weapons, hunters can generally kill many more animals in a much shorter time than they could have done by traditional means.

It is argued by some that trophy hunting for sport can contribute to conservation (see, e.g., Buckley 2003:208–212). Perhaps so, where the numbers, ages, and sexes of animals taken are predetermined by knowledgeable wildlife biologists, and the hunt is controlled by well-policed regulations.

That does not, however, seem to be the case for the Pond Inlet narwhal hunt. The narwhal populations are indeed studied by Canadian marine biologists, and narwhal hunting is regulated by Canadian Government agencies, which specify maximum annual harvests and do indeed fly aerial patrols. This harvest, however, is intended for traditional cultural reasons, namely the supply of narwhal muktuk as a cultural food delicacy, and a limited supply of narwhal tusks for traditional art. It is not intended to supply narwhal tusks for cash sales to international buyers, since this is strictly prohibited under CITES. Effectively, therefore, from a Canadian Government perspective, the narwhal hunting we observed is illegal poaching for cash, under the guise of a legal hunt for traditional cultural reasons.

Ethical Options

Under such circumstances, how should an ethical ecotourist behave? Should we have been more concerned about the narwhal we came to watch, or the Inuit community our money was helping to support? Should we, as short-term visitors from far away, have attempted to remonstrate with local hunters and fishermen who have spent their entire lives in the area, winter as well as summer? What could we possibly say in a brief encounter on a windswept beach that would lead them to trust our opinion rather than their own experience, particularly since we were neither narwhal biologists nor familiar with narwhal population dynamics, narwhal hunt regulations, or permissible annual narwhal harvests? We knew only that narwhal are endangered, that they are listed under CITES, and that during our brief period in the sounds around Pond Inlet, the number of narwhal tusks we saw was more than 10 percent of the total number of live narwhal we saw.

Should we, perhaps, have reported what we saw to Canadian Government fisheries officers? And if so, what could they do? Should we, as tour clients, have relied on our guides to report to the tour company's head office, for them in turn to make an official report? Should we, perhaps, have drawn the company's attention to these issues, so that as a long-term commercial charter client of the fishing boat operators they could raise the issue in a tactful, culturally appropriate and unhurried way during future negotiations? We did, in fact, do some of these things but not others. I will lead readers to consider what they themselves think would have been appropriate and useful in the circumstances.

Narwhal are endangered and Inuit are not. In my own view, the survival of narwhal is more important than the cultural traditions of Inuit. It is certainly more important than the opportunity for particular individual Inuit to profit from the illegal sale of narwhal tusks to rich Asian cruise boat passengers. But others may view the issues differently. In addition, it is easy for me to express these opinions while sitting comfortably in a subtropical city in Australia. It would be considerably more contentious to do so while traveling in a fishing boat in the High Arctic—particularly, for example, if that fishing boat had recently rescued a group of inexperienced tourists from a set of swamped sea kayaks. Not, I should add, that any of us capsized. But we might have. So, did I and my fellow ecotour clients act ethically, or not? Does the tour company act ethically in running these tours, or not? If not, why not? And if not, are we still ecotourists?

Conclusions

It seems to me that no matter how concerned we may be, as Fennell (2004) encourages, to take an ethical approach to ecotourism, it is in fact quite difficult to establish "a common pool of core values which allow us to articulate what it is that ecotourism must be" (Fennell 2004:119). As I have tried to show in the example above, ecotourism may involve ethical issues that are not necessarily straightforward, particularly where ethical concerns relating to endangered species conflict with ethical concerns relating to Indigenous or impoverished peoples, as is quite often the case.

Perhaps there is a possible resolution. We expect doctors and other professionals to act ethically, but we do not define medicine in terms of ethics. Perhaps we can define ecotourism without reference to ethical criteria, but still expect ecotourists to act ethically. Sounds good? OK, then what should we have done, as ethical ecotourists? And what, if anything, should the tour company do?

Source: From *Journal of Ecotourism* 4(2): 129–134, 2005. Reprinted with permission of the author and Taylor & Francis.

References Cited

Blackfeather Inc. 2004. "In Search of the Narwhal." http://www.blackfeather.com/kayak/kayak_pondinlet.htm (accessed January 1, 2005).

Buckley, R. C. 1994. Ecotourism: A framework. Annals of Tourism Research 21, 661–669.

———. 2003. *Case Studies in Ecotourism*. Oxford: CAB International.

CITES. 2005. "Convention on International Trade in Endangered Species of Wild Fauna and Flora." http://www.cites.org (accessed January 6, 2005).

Fennell, D. A. 2003. *Ecotourism: An Introduction*, 2nd ed. New York: Routledge.

———. 2004. "Deep Ecotourism: Seeking Theoretical and Practical Reverence," in *New Horizons in Tourism: Strange Experiences and Stranger Practices*, ed. T. V. Singh. Wallingford: CABI Publishing.

Honey, M. 1999. *Ecotourism and Sustainable Development: Who Owns Paradise?* Washington, DC: Island Press.

Malloy, D. C., and Fennell, D. A. 1998. "Ecotourism and Ethics: Moral Development and Organizational Cultures." *Journal of Travel Research* 26:47–56.

Weaver, D. B. 2001. *The Encyclopedia of Ecotourism*. Wallingford: CABI Publishing.

19

Dreams and Realities: A Critical Look at the Cruise Ship Industry

Ross A. Klein

Sitting on the deck of a luxury cruise ship, enjoying the warmth of the sun and a gentle ocean breeze gazing at the deep blue sea or picturesque coastline—are these images a dream or are they real? According to the cruise industry and individual cruise lines, the "dream" is the "reality." For many cruise passengers it is also true or nearly so. Even if their cruise experience does not correspond exactly to the images contained on cruise line websites or the expectations created by brochures, the overwhelming majority of passengers is satisfied with their cruise experience, and many say they want to cruise again. Cruises are a popular vacation choice; by some measures, they are the fastest growing segment of the tourism industry.

Changes in Cruising Over Time

The current cruise industry began in the 1960s. As transoceanic travel was taken over by airplanes, many "cruise ships" were left underutilized or idle, giving rise to new companies that stepped in to take advantage of the situation. Many major cruise lines began at this time: Princess Cruises (1965); Norwegian Caribbean Line (1966—later to become Norwegian Cruise Line); Royal Caribbean Cruise Line (1970); and Carnival Cruise Lines (1972). Only Royal Caribbean relied on new purpose-built cruise ships. Many companies came and went over the ensuing years, and others merged into the three major cruise corporations in North America today (as shown in table 1). There are other "large" players in the industry such as MSC Cruises and Disney Cruise Line, but the "big three" dominate, and each has expanded operations to China and Southeast Asia.

Other significant changes have also occurred over time. Ships operating in the 1970s generally accommodated 600 to 1,000 passengers. New ships have gotten increasingly larger. In 1985, Carnival Cruise Lines (CCL) unveiled the 46,000-ton *Holiday* and touted it as the largest ship ever built for vacation cruises. The ship could carry 1,500 passengers. Eleven years later the 101,000-ton *Carnival Destiny* entered service as the largest ship with a maximum passenger capacity of 3,400. In 1999 Royal Caribbean International (RCI) followed with *Voyager of the Seas* (142,000 tons and capacity for 3,840 passengers), which was eclipsed ten years later by the first of the Oasis-class ships, the 225,000 ton *Oasis of the Seas*, with accommodation for 5,400 passengers double occupancy (two persons per cabin) but space for 6,300 passengers. The most recent Oasis-class vessel, *Harmony of the Seas*, can accommodate 6,780 passengers.

As ships grew in size, they changed. Classic ocean liners (the pre-1960s era) had considerable open deck space from which tourists could view the ocean. Passengers could sit and relax, away from other people and enjoy being at sea. New cruise ships have converted much of this open space into

Table 1: Three Major Cruise Corporations in North America

Cruise Corporation	Cruise Lines in 2017	Year Merged
Carnival Corporation	Carnival Cruise Lines	—
	Holland America Line	1989
	Seabourn Cruises	1992
	Costa Cruises	1997
	Cunard Line	1998
	Princess Cruises	2003
	P&O Cruises	2003
	AIDA Cruises	2003
	P&O Australia	2003
Royal Caribbean Cruises Limited	Royal Caribbean International	—
	Celebrity Cruises	1997
	Pullmantur Cruises	2006
	Azamara Club Cruises	2007
	TUI Cruises	2009
	SkySea Cruise Line	2015
Star Cruises	Star Cruises	—
	Norwegian Cruise Line	2000
	Crystal Cruises	2016
with Apollo Management:	Norwegian Cruise Line	2007
	Oceania	2008
	Regent Seven Seas Cruises	2008

The lido deck on Royal Caribbean's *Explorer of the Seas*. Note how most deck chairs face inward, away from the sea. (Photo by Robert Wood)

revenue-producing ocean view and balcony cabins. The "outdoors" is now confined to a central area, often two or three decks in height, around the pools and other activity centres. Many large cruise ships have installed giant screens above the main pool area, for showing movies and recorded rock concerts and for other forms of entertainment day and night.

Larger ships have also changed the nature of cruising. It is now common to find ten or more restaurants on board, many which charge a fee. Former traditional elements of cruising such as formal dinner nights and midnight buffets have been discarded or severely curtailed. The sheer number of people also affects the general dynamic among passengers and the nature of their experience. When new larger ships were being first introduced, a cruise line executive observed, "Cruising on a mega ship compared to a small ship is like going to a cocktail party with 2,000 people compared to going to a party at someone's house. In the first instance, chances are that you will only remember the meatballs, in the second instance, you will remember the people you meet" (CINQ 1998:104). It is difficult to imagine what he would say about ships three times larger.

With size, the cruise ship has increasingly become more like a land-based resort or amusement park and less like the traditional image and experience of cruising. This is not necessarily bad; it is just different. The cruise ship industry increasingly relies on generating onboard revenue to maintain profitability.

Some activities are still provided without cost, but many now have fees that quickly add up for both the passenger and the cruise ship's bottom line. A new ship may have a rock climbing wall, ice skating rink, golf simulator, virtual reality and video games, range of enrichment classes, casino, art auctions, and a full agenda of entertainment. It will also have shopping—lots of shopping. Royal Caribbean's Voyager-class ships have a four-story-tall shopping mall—the "Royal Promenade"—deep in their bowels that run much of the length of the ship. According to one writer, "The idea is to grab a larger slice of the vacation market by offering so many things to do and places to explore on board—so that even people who do not particularly care for sea cruises may want to go because the experience may not seem like they're on a ship" (Blake 2003:6).

Although ships have gotten larger and have changed architecturally, they have not changed appreciably in terms of space ratio—a measure used to compare the relative space per passenger on a cruise ship. It is computed by dividing the gross registered tonnage of a ship by the number of passengers it holds double occupancy. Most "old" ships had a space ratio in the low-to-mid-30s. Most mass market cruise ships today have a similar space ratio. The per passenger space increases with the "class" of the cruise line—from mass market cruise lines such as CCL and RCI to premium lines like Celebrity and Holland America Line and ultra-luxury lines such as Silversea and Seabourn.

Changing Economics of Cruise Tourism

After two years of losing money, upstart Carnival Cruise Lines slashed prices, opening casinos and discos on board, and devising other ways to generate onboard revenue. It finally turned a profit in 1975. According to Micky Arison, current Chairman of the Board of Carnival Corporation, this was the beginning of the "Fun Ship" concept, which was not initially so much a grand plan as an immediate strategy to generate enough income to meet weekly payroll (Dickinson and Vladimir 1987). But it began a trend whereby cruise lines generate increasing proportions of their net income from passengers' onboard spending. By the 1990s, most cruise lines had a manager of onboard revenue whose job was to oversee the generation of income on board and to seek new venues for generating revenue. Modern cruise ships were on their way to becoming "little more than floating bed factories with shops and restaurants attached. Time spent at sea is simply a matter of getting from A to B with an emphasis on cajoling those trapped inside into spending their money on shopping, drinks, and other extras" (Ashworth 2001).

Although the price of cruises in the 2000s remained somewhat stable, corporate profits continued to increase significantly. Carnival Corporation was earning more than $2 billion a year in net profit and paid virtually no income taxes in the U.S. Onboard revenue had become a key element in the new economic reality of cruise tourism. Income previously made from ticket sales was now generated after passengers are on board. Cruise columnist Mary Lu Abbot warned in November 2004 that "extras can cost more than the cruise." Since then onboard revenue has continued to grow. In 2006, the Big Three cruise operators had a combined net revenue of $3.5 billion earned from passenger spending on board. That translated into a profit of $43 per passenger per day (more profit than generated from ticket sales) and constituted 24 percent of the total net revenue for all cruise companies combined; the percentage is significantly higher for many of the U.S.-based mass market cruise lines (Cramer 2006). The $43 per passenger per day is as much as 50 percent higher in 2017.

The top sources of onboard revenue vary from ship to ship and between cruise lines, but the top five are normally bars and lounges, casinos, shops, extra tariff restaurants, and (on some ships) art auctions. Additional income is derived from shore excursions sold on board (50 percent or more of what a passenger pays goes to the cruise line), spa services, communications services, enrichment programs, various entertainment and/or activity venues, and many other services that passengers want and need. The bottom line is that a cruise ship has become expert at separating tourists from their money in return for a positive experience.

Changing Relationships with Ports

The relationship between cruise ships and ports has also changed over the years. The biggest shift is attributable to numbers. Arriving at a Caribbean port in the 1970s or 1980s with 500 other cruise passengers is very different than arriving with 5,000 passengers—plus another 10,000 or 15,000 or so from other ships in port at the same time. This not only influences the cruise passengers' experience, it also has a profound impact on the local community. Many locals suffer "cruise passenger fatigue" early in the season.

There is also an economic challenge for ports. Many countries/ports agonize over how to improve spending by cruise passengers, but they rarely look at the ways their plans are undermined by the context. The most obvious question is whether passengers have any money left to spend onshore given the range of onboard spending options. This is particularly salient given that cruises in the 2010s attracted a wider range of people, including those economically minded passengers who chose a cruise over a land-based vacation because it appeared to be a better bargain based on its advertised price. These passengers may save for years for their "cruise of a lifetime" and have limited funds after paying for the cruise itself. Their spending on board most certainly influences their ability to spend onshore.

An even larger problem for many ports is their uncritical acceptance of the assumption that cruise passengers on average spend 100 USD in each and every port of call. It is on this basis that ports and national governments extrapolate the cruise industry's economic impact. Few undertake indepen-

A cruise ship dwarfs Venice. (Photo by Jaro68/Shutterstock.com)

dent empirical research to determine actual passenger spending. As a result, they have unrealistic expectations and are quickly disappointed. Many ports blame themselves for not generating the kind of income promised.

Unfortunately, as passenger numbers have increased, onshore spending per passenger has decreased. A 1994 study commissioned by the Florida-Caribbean Cruise Association (FCCA) found passengers, on average, spent 372 USD on the island of St. Thomas. The average for the Caribbean region was 154 USD per passenger per port. Another study done for the FCCA six years later found that spending on St. Thomas had fallen by over half to 173 USD per passenger; the overall average in the region decreased by nearly half to 90 USD per passenger per port (PWC 2001). Excluding Cozumel and St. Thomas, spending per port ranged from 54 USD to 87 USD with an average per port of 73 USD. Despite significant decreases in spending during the 1990s and 2000s, and levels of spending well below most countries' 100 USD expectation, Caribbean ports still act as though each cruise passenger is going to spend this amount.

Since the early 1990s cruise lines have increasingly developed a shopping program, a program whereby passengers are given maps and encouraged to shop at certain "preferred" stores where, they are told, the prices are better. In fact, the cruise line receives a significant payment for advertising these stores. Most cruise lines in the Caribbean now also use private islands in order to capture an even larger portion of passengers' discretionary spending; this replaces at least one port of call with further loss of revenue for ports in the region. Cruise lines have also constructed, purchased, and/or leased cruise terminals (e.g., Cozumel, Mahogany Bay, Roatan, Turks and Caicos), which further complicates the economics of the port–cruise line relationship.

Explorer of the Seas taken from a beach at Labadee, Royal Caribbean's "private island," which is actually a peninsula of Haiti. (Photo by Robert Wood)

One way in which ports derive some income is through per-passenger fees paid by the cruise line. However, for most ports the income does not cover all the expenses associated with hosting the cruise ship, including maintenance of the wharf and facilities used by cruise ships. This is even more difficult given the pressure from cruise lines to keep port fees as low as possible, always with the threat that their ships can easily shift to another port (Klein 2005).

These economic features are largely invisible to passengers, as they should be. Tourists are on the ship for a vacation and in that regard, the cruise ship provides a good experience often at a fair price. Part the ability to deliver a good product at a reasonable price is that passengers are enticed, if not forced, to spend more onboard and the ship itself generates significant income from onshore.

Being a Conscientious Cruiser

While cruise lines offer a reasonably predictable positive vacation experience, cruise tourism is not without its issues. Four of the most important are: environmental concerns, labor issues, onboard crime, and health and liability. These need to be discussed to counterbalance the overwhelming positive image presented by brochures, websites, and the media.

Environmental Issues

The cruise industry has a checkered history with regard to environmental practices. While projecting an image of environmental sensitivity and responsibility a pattern of environmental violations exists. In the late-1990s and early-2000s, the "Big Three" paid 60 million USD in fines for environmental violations including discharging hazardous chemicals and oily bilge (Klein 2008). The issue re-emerged in 2017 when the Carnival Corporation agreed to pay a fine of 40 million USD after Princess Cruises was caught discharging oily bilge—at a time when Carnival Corporation was already on probation for earlier violations. In 2016, the Carnival Corporation and RCCL disclosed that it had paid a fine to Alaska for violating its air pollution standards. Most cruise lines have historically had difficulty meeting both air quality requirements and Alaska Water Quality Standards (see www.cruisejunkie.com/alaskafines.html).

A discussion of the waste streams from cruise ships can be found in *Getting a Grip on Cruise Ship Pollution* (www.cruisejunkie.com/FOE.pdf). Waste streams include black water (toilets and medical waste—about five gallons per person per day), grey water (sinks, showers, galley—about 90 gallons per person per day), solid waste (food waste, trash, packaging, glass, recyclables—about seven kilograms per day per person), oily bilge from ship operations (about 10,000 gallons per day), and exhaust from incinerators and from fuel use. Modern ships have what are known as Advanced Wastewater Treatment or Purification Systems for treating black water and grey water. These systems are a huge improvement over the Marine Sanitation Devices (MSD) they previously used and that are still found on older ships (pre-2000), but they are not without issues, as fines in Alaska (the only jurisdiction that monitors waste water streams from cruise ships) illustrate. Even advanced systems are challenged by heavy metals (copper, zinc, nickel), ammonia, fecal coliform, and biological oxygen demand, although they are a huge improvement over waste water discharged in the ocean in the 1980s and 1990s.

Cruise ships increasingly recycle that which can be recycled, as long as there is economic value in doing so. Other solid waste (including glass) and food waste is either ground and dumped at sea or is incinerated. Incineration poses concerns with regard to how close to shore incinerators are permitted to operate, that which is incinerated (particularly plastics, which can produce furans and dioxins), and how ash is treated—is it treated as hazardous waste and landed ashore or is it dumped at sea?

All ships have systems for dealing with hazardous waste (segregated and off-loaded ashore) and oily bilge. They use oily water separators so what they discharge into the sea has 15 parts-per-million (ppm) oil content or less. Ships are increasingly being regulated with regard to fuel they use. In 2015, the North American Emission Control Area required the use of low sulfur fuel (0.1 percent) when a ship is within 200 miles of the U.S. or Canadian coastline. This requirement is spreading globally and will soon be in place in many coastal waters. Many cruise ships request and receive waivers for compliance with these emission requirements by using smokestack scrubbers, which allows them to continue using dirtier fuel because what comes out of the smokestack has been "cleaned," although there is debate around the nature of the effluent released after scrubbing.

Labor Issues

One appeal of a cruise vacation is the price. A cruise can cost less than 100 USD a day per person, including food and entertainment. Another way prices are kept low, besides charging passengers for many onboard services, is by containing labor costs. The typical cruise ship worker has a minimum 77-hour work week (308 hours a month) and may work ten months or more continuously without a day off (officers work much less). The length of a worker's contract, and often the nature of the work, is related to skin color and/or national origin. A lighter-skinned worker is more likely to work "above deck" directly with passengers. Skin color or national origin may also influence a crew member's pay. Those on a "European contract" are paid more and work fewer months than those on a "Central American or Asian contract."

There are many issues related to labor on cruise ships—more than can be discussed in this short chapter. Besides most crew members' long hours and minimal time off, some—such as those who work in the engine room or galley—rarely see the light of day. The workplace is also hierarchical and quasi-military in the way it is run, with workers having limited recourse to any grievance procedures. Of critical importance is their low wages. The bulk of income for service workers on most mass market cruise lines is derived from centralized tips charged to passengers. A dining room waiter or room steward may earn in total (wages plus tips) 1200–1500 USD a month, and a bar waiter or bartender 700–1000 USD a month. Those below deck can earn as little as 500–600 USD a month. Workers are drawn from many countries with cruise lines paying little, but by the standards of their home country amounts that are attractive. Many employees pay a recruiting agent to secure their position and may incur costs getting to the ship.

Onboard Crime

Crime on cruise ships is seldom discussed, yet studies of mass market cruise lines have found rates of sexual assault that are 50 percent higher than those on land (see Klein and Poulston 2011); more alarming is that 34 percent of victims are under the age of 18 (Senate Commerce Committee 2013). The problem of sexual assault is not recent—the first media reports appeared in the 1980s—though the nature of the problem has shifted from one predominately of crew members against passengers to more incidents of passenger-on-passenger than crew member-on-passenger assault. And it would appear that the victims are increasingly minors.

Like a small city, a cruise ship also has its share of thefts and robbery and physical assault. Some of these crimes are publicly reported on a U.S. Department of Transportation website. These reports, however, are limited to those crimes listed in the Cruise Vessel Security and Safety Act (CVSSA) of 2010. Which incidents are reported is further limited because cruise ships' security determines what category a crime falls within. For example, a theft under 10,000 USD is not a reportable crime under the CVSSA, nor is unwanted sexual touching of a minor when labeled "groping." On a cruise ship all safety and security is provided by employees who report to the Master of the ship.

This is not to suggest that crime is a larger problem on a cruise ship than it is on land. But it is a problem. The website of International Cruise Victims Association (ICV) gives a more complete picture of the nature and range of the problem. The message to cruise tourists is, just because they are on vacation, does not mean it is safe to ignore the precautions they take on land.

Health and Liability

Several high-profile health incidents have occurred on cruise ships spawning media labels like "The Bug Ship," "The Barf Boat," and "The Poop Cruise." The first two incidents were related to a norovirus outbreak affecting more than 20 percent of passengers. Although most norovirus outbreaks are not newsworthy, the media takes interest when a large proportion of passengers are affected. Norovirus is an illness commonly found in institutional or social settings due to poor/lapses in hygiene. It has come to be known as "the cruise ship virus" because of the frequency of reports of illness on ships. While passengers may become overly concerned, the illness outbreaks are a reminder to practice good personal hygiene, including hand washing. Most cruise ships attempt to limit the spread of illness by quarantining actively ill passengers and crew members to their cabins. This has some success, except both passengers and crew resist reporting when they are ill, knowing the consequences will be quarantine.

A second issue is the quality of health care on a cruise ship. Most medical facilities offer little more than a neighborhood clinic; they are only equipped to handle regular maladies and to stabilize a patient with a serious medical condition. The ship's physician and other medical staff are not only available to passengers on a fee-for-service basis, they provide medical care to the shipboard crew and officers, which, with the large number of crew members, makes for an active medical practice without having to treat passengers.

Few tourists think about onboard medical care when they embark on a cruise and few end up needing serious care, but there have been issues. Multiple court cases in the U.S. over medical malpractice have upheld the view that ship physicians are independent concessionaires and that cruise lines are not liable for their practice. This changed in 2014, however, with a U.S. Court of Appeals for the Eleventh Circuit decision in *Franza v. Royal Caribbean Cruises*. After a passenger had been misdiagnosed and the provision of medical care inordinately delayed, both of which contributed to the passenger's death, the court ruled that cruise lines were liable for the care their shipboard physicians provided (Dickerson and Cohen 2015). It is too early to know what impact this ruling will have.

Passengers need to be aware of the limitations of medical care on a cruise ship. They should not expect the ship to be equipped with their prescription drugs or that emergency services comparable to a hospital are available. Air medical evacuations are not uncommon when a ship is close enough to land, but this is not always the case, and there is always the chance that a passenger will be transported to a foreign country. Cruise lines encourage passengers to have travel insurance for just this reason.

In Closing

The product delivered by the cruise industry and through cruise tourism continues to evolve. The nature of cruising changed as ships grew in size; it is also changing as the product is tailored to meet the cultural expectations of the clientele being served. For example, the cruise product offered to Chinese tourists is quite different than that traditionally provided to North Americans. There are even subtle differences between cruise lines catering mainly to a European clientele, and to people speaking different languages. It is interesting to look at how cruising is represented online and in brochures based on the country or clientele being targeted. Even more interesting may be a comparison between how cruising is depicted by the "class" of a cruise line—look at the nature of the cruise experience presented at the CCL or RCI website versus the website of Silversea or Seadream Yacht Club.

Part of the evolution of cruise tourism has included the growth of passenger onboard spending. Cruise passengers today often spend more on the ship than they do for the cruise fare itself. There are several websites serving cruise passengers with information, some of which include details about the various onboard charges by different cruise lines, including centralized gratuities, all-you-can-drink beverage packages, and extra tariff restaurants; the charge for shore excursions provided in each port of call can be found at the cruise line's website. It may be interesting to search this information and to figure out how much you are likely to spend on board a cruise. How does this jibe with the image of cruises as an all-inclusive vacation?

One of the challenges is to be conscientious cruise passenger. What this means on the one hand is to be aware of issues related to cruise tourism, particularly issues around labor, the environment, and onboard safety and security. We cannot change industry practices, but we can avoid individually contributing to what we may see as an unjust system. For example, how can awareness of the nature of crew members' work life influence how we treat those crew members (not just in terms of gratuities)? Does it make a difference that many working on a cruise ship earn as little as 1.50 USD an hour—would you accept employment for that pay, 11 hours a day every day? Similarly, we can deny that crime exists on a cruise ship, or we can use that knowledge to take the same precautions on a cruise ship that we do on land. How would the fact that 34 percent of sexual assault victims on cruise ships are under the age of 18 influence your supervision and oversight of a young cousin, niece, or nephew, or your own children, on a cruise?

In many ways a cruise vacation is an excellent choice, although the conditions are sometimes less excellent for those who serve the cruise passenger, especially cruise ship workers. Like any tourism product, knowledge provides a foundation for realistic expectations and a richer enjoyment of the experience, but also a better sense of the issues that might be a concern. The goal of this chapter was to provide information about cruise tourism that is not normally found in brochures in order to achieve a more balanced view of the dreams and realities of cruise tourism.

Source: Written expressly for *Tourists and Tourism*.

References Cited

Abbott, M. L. 2004. "Extras Can Cost More than the Cruise." *New Orleans Times-Picayune*, November 7. www.nola.com/base/living-0/109981480177200.xml (accessed November 7, 2004).

Ashworth, J. 2001. "A Ship that Thinks It's a Conference Centre." *The Times* (London), July 14. LexisNexis Academic (accessed June 30, 2017).

Blake, S. 2003. "'Megaship' Set to Sail. *Florida Today* (November 12), p. 6.

CINQ. 1998. "Who Said It?" *Cruise Industry News Quarterly* (Winter).

Cramer, K. 2006. "The Art of Piracy." *Broward-Palm Beach New Times*, November 9. www.browardpalmbeach.com/news/the-art-of-piracy-6333162 (accessed November 10, 2006).

Dickerson, T. A., and J. A. Cohen. 2015. "Medical Malpractice on the High Seas." *New York Law Journal* (3 March). www.newyorklawjournal.com/id=1202719354971?keywords=barbetta&publication=New+York+Law+Journal (accessed March 4, 2015).

Dickinson, R., and Vladimir, A. 1997. *Selling the Sea: An Inside Look at the Cruise Industry.* New York: Wiley & Sons.

Klein, R. A. 2005. *Cruise Ship Squeeze: The New Pirates of the Seven Seas.* Gabriola Island, BC: New Society.

———. 2008. *Paradise Lost at Sea: Rethinking Cruise Vacations.* Halifax, NS: Fernwood Books.

Klein, R. A., and J. Poulston, J. 2011. "Sex at Sea: Sexual Crimes Aboard Cruise Ships," *Tourism in Marine Environments* 7(2): 67–80.

PWC. 2001. *Economic Contributions of the F-CCA Members Lines to the Caribbean and Florida.* Price Waterhouse Coopers. July 27. f-cca.com/downloads/summary.pdf (accessed March 5, 2003).

Senate Commerce Committee. 2013. *Consumers Have Incomplete Access to Cruise Crime Data.* July 24. Washington, DC: U.S. Senate Committee on Commerce Science, and Technology.

20

Medical Tourism: Reverse Subsidy for the Elite

Amit Sengupta

Medical tourism is big business. In India, it was worth an estimated 3 billion in 2014 and is projected to reach $8 billion by 2020 when the global medical tourism market is projected to reach $40 billion (Srivastava 2017; Grant Thornton 2015; PTI 2015). Thus, by 2020 India would account for 20 percent of the global market in medical tourism. These figures are significant, when contrasted with India's overall health care expenditure of $20 billion in the public sector and $50 billion in the private sector (IMF 2016). The government of India has decided "to promote India as a quality Health care destination for persons across the globe, so as to gainfully utilize the health care expertise and infrastructure available in the country" (Ministry of Health and Family Welfare n.d.). In 2016 India's Prime Minister, Narendra Modi, inaugurated a government web portal (www.IndiaHealthCareTourism.com) to boost medical tourism by guiding potential patients in their search for treatment options. It lists 93 medical centers, 30 Ayurveda (traditional system of medicine in India) and wellness centers and one special category center.

Within Asia, three countries—India, Thailand and Singapore—accounted for about 60 percent of the total revenue from medical tourism in the region in 2012 (PTI 2014). Apart from the perceived allure of the "Orient," and the fact that Indian medical professionals are proficient in English and many foreign patients are familiar with Indian doctors who practice in large numbers in the West, the principal attraction of India's medical tourism industry lies in its cost-effectiveness. For example, hip replacement surgery, which normally costs around $57,000 in the United States, can be performed for $7,000 in India. Cardiac bypass surgery, which costs around $133,000 in the United States, costs $7,000 in India (Jose and Sachdeva 2010). But there are two other major contributing factors: the sustained growth of corporate hospitals and private hospital chains across India and the government's promotion of medical tourism as part of public policy.

Avenues for Growth of Medical Tourism

While the private sector has always been a prominent source of medical care in India, neoliberal economic policies have created the conditions for its rapid growth. Today, India's private expenditure as a percentage of total health expenditure is one of the highest in the world, accounting for around 70 percent of the country's total health expenditure and about 3 percent of its GDP (World Health Statistics 2015). India has experienced rapid economic growth over the last decade. This, coupled with stagnation in the amount of public funds allocated to health care, translates into an enormous increase in private expenditure on health. A large proportion of this private expenditure comes from elites who have disproportionately prospered as a result of these same neoliberal policies. Although they constitute less than 10 percent of India's population, in absolute numbers—given India's total population of over 1.3 billion—India's elite is much larger than the elite in most countries of the globalized North. Thus, while national policies have opened the way for the penetration of the corporate sector into medical care to maintain its growth and service to India's elite, the private health care sector needs additional revenue. The global health care industry—projected to rise to $8.7 trillion by 2020—makes for an obvious target (Deloitte 2017).

Diverse avenues have been opened up for the growth of medical tourism in India. Since 2006, the government has issued M (medical) visas to patients and MX visas to their accompanying spouses. In 2009, the Ministry of Tourism extended its market development assistance scheme to cover hospitals that have been certified by the Joint Commission International (an international organization that accredits health care facilities) and the National Accreditation Board for Hospitals (the country's premier health care accrediting institution). The Ministry of Tourism is also actively promoting medical tourism through overseas road shows where market development assistance is also provided to medical and wellness tourism service providers for this purpose (Deloitte 2017). This market development scheme offsets travel companies' costs for overseas marketing. Through this program, hospitals become eligible for financial assistance to cover the cost of medical tourism publicity, including printed material, travel and stay expenses for sales-cum-study tours taken by hospital staff, and participation fees for trade fairs and exhibitions.

Reproductive Tourism

Another major driver of medical tourism in India has been what can be loosely termed "reproductive tourism," that is, the provision of reproductive services and technologies such as in vitro fertilization (IVF) and surrogate parenthood.[1] Internationally, there is wide variety in the extent to which different countries regulate reproductive technologies. This has resulted in a flow of medical tourists into countries such as India, Thailand, and China, where reproductive technology regulations are lax. The attraction of India as a destination for reproductive tourism also lies in the low cost of infertility treatment and the availability of state-of-the-art facilities. An average IVF cycle in India costs $3,000 compared to $10,000 in the U.S. (Agarwal 2016a). India, until recently, did not have guidelines to prohibit foreigners from hiring Indian women to be surrogates and became known as the "surrogacy hub" of the world—the preferred destination for foreign tourists looking for surrogate mothers. Only in 2016 did the Indian government unveil a draft bill to ban commercial surrogacy (Agarwal 2016b). Meanwhile, the majority of people in India have poor access to health care, with women suffering the most. Thus, while women from across the world flock to India to take advantage of the booming market for assisted reproductive technologies, a very large number of Indian women lack basic health care.

Women are truly invisible in India's public health system; the latest available data indicate that just 17 percent of women have had any contact with a health worker. Even where some type of public health care facility exists, women's access is compromised. Only 18 percent of the primary health centers in the country offer the services of a female doctor. Only 17 percent of doctors practicing modern medicine are women, and this plummets to 6 percent in rural areas. The number of female doctors is only .5 per 10,000 population in rural areas (Agarwal 2007; Rao et al. 2011). This is especially important in large parts of rural India, where conservative norms prevent women from freely discussing their ailments with male doctors. The paucity of women doctors in rural settings is closely linked to the lack of basic facilities for them (and all health personnel), including those related to housing and safety.

The lack of health services for women is also reflected in the fact that only 21 percent of pregnant women report having received the full range of ante natal care; in rural areas the figure is under 17 percent (*thepharmaletter* 2017).

As a consequence of poor public facilities and their low health status, nearly 45,000 Indian mothers die due to causes related to childbirth every year, accounting for 17 percent of such deaths globally. The maternal mortality ratio in India, or the number of maternal deaths per 100,000 live births, was 174 in 2015, an unacceptably high figure (WHO 2015). Women's health is also inextricably linked to violence, which many face as a routine part of their lives. Among women aged 15–49, a third report having experienced physical violence, and 9 percent sexual violence. Nearly a third of married women have been victims of spousal violence (Sahoo and Pradhan 2007).

Indian women wait at a rural clinic in Bihar Province. (Photo by Travel Stock/ Shutterstock.com)

Virtual Collapse of Public Services

Neoliberal reforms initiated in the early 1990s led to severe and sustained cuts in budgetary support for various welfare measures. Between 1990 and 1994, there was a precipitous fall in social-sector spending in India, including on health care. While there has been some restoration in public expenditure since then, in GDP terms health expenditure (already one of the lowest in the world) declined from 1.3 percent in 1990 to 0.9 percent in 1999 and has languished at just over 1 percent of GDP to date. In contrast, the private health care industry has witnessed an unprecedented boom in the past decade, growing at an over 15 percent compound annual growth rate, more than twice the growth rate for all services (Sundararaman and Muraleedharan 2015).

In the aftermath of these reforms, the costs of both outpatient and inpatient care increased sharply as did the cost of hospitalization in both public and private facilities. The average cost of health care in India doubled between 1987 and 2005 and tripled between the 2005 and 2015 (Sundararaman and Muraleedharan 2015). At both public and private facilities the increase has been higher in rural than in urban areas. The 2017 National Health Policy reported that "over 63 million persons are pushed to poverty every year due to [rising] health care costs" (Ministry of Health and Family Welfare 2017).

As a consequence of neoliberal economic reforms, many public health facilities have been virtually dismantled. The National Health Policy of 2017 acknowledged that the government's flagship National Rural Health Mission (NRHM) received budgetary support that was "only about 40% of what was envisaged for a fully revitalized NRHM Framework" (Ministry of Health and Family Welfare 2017). All this has forced people to look for other options, boosting the private health care sector and increasing its legitimacy.

The virtual collapse of the public health system has led to the emergence of a rapidly growing disorganized and unregulated private sector, where profitability overrides rationality and equity. The health care balance has now been skewed towards urban tertiary-level health services while denying poorer sectors of society access. A large spectrum of providers exists within the private medical sector, ranging from individual practitioners to small dispensaries and nursing homes to large corporate-run hospital chains that thrive thanks to tax subsidies and the government's outsourcing of public-sector functions to private providers. To maximize their profitability, the top end of the private medical sector—promoted by corporate entities—has sought to diversify into more lucrative areas. The medical tourism market was an obvious choice.

Targeting the Elite

The private corporate-run medical sector clearly wishes to target the elite. In an interesting consolidation of industry interests, leading Indian private hospitals, health care providers, and travel and medical tourism industry officials have come together to form an association—the Indian Medical Travel Association—that aims to work "together to make India the leading global healthcare destination."[2] The industry is also promoting the National Accreditation Board for Hospitals, which had, by 2014, granted accreditation to 227 hospitals, with about 1,200 others in various stages of application (Kannan 2014). What is important to note is that such accreditation programs are limited to a small percentage of India's over 50,000 private hospitals. This development is leading to a differentiation within the private hospital sector, where high-quality care will be provided through a few high-priced hospitals that specifically target the Indian elite and foreign tourists. The private sector has consistently resisted efforts to regulate and set standards that would ensure quality care and minimum standards in the overwhelming majority of private hospitals.

As Oxfam International writes with respect to Africa,

> the private sector provides no escape route for the problems facing public health systems in poor countries. . . . Evidence available shows that making public health services work is the only proven route to achieving universal and equitable health care. . . . Public provision of health care is not doomed to fail as some suggest, but making it work requires determined political leadership, adequate investment, evidence-based policies and popular support. (2009:4)

Many of these elements are absent in the policy framework that promotes neoliberal reforms. As Oxfam International contends, "to look to the private sector for the substantial expansion needed to achieve universal access [to medical care] would be to ignore the significant and proven risks of this approach and the evidence of what has worked in successful developing countries" (2009:5).

In fact, evidence in India points to the increasing brunt of unequal access that is borne by the most marginalized sectors of Indian society. Neo-liberal policies have created a creamy layer of Indian elite whose consumption patterns parallel those of the global elite. They seek care today in world-class facilities built to cater to the elite—both Indian and foreign. In contrast, the poor are being denied basic health care. Data available indicate that "financial constraints" are increasingly cited as the reason for not accessing medical care. In rural areas, lack of adequate finances was cited by 15 percent of people as the reason for not accessing medical care in 1986–87. This rose to 28 percent in 2004. The corresponding figures are 10 and 20 percent, respectively, in urban areas (NSSO 2006).

India is one of the most preferred destinations for medical tourism with around 420,000 medical tourists in 2015 (Grant Thornton 2015). The Indian government sees this as a win-win situation. For example, the 2002 National Health Policy states: "To capitalize on the comparative cost advantage enjoyed by domestic health facilities in the secondary and tertiary sectors, [the policy] strongly encourages the providing of . . . services to patients from overseas" (Ministry of Health and Family Welfare 2002:34). Such services, the policy goes on to explain, will be "deemed exports" and will be made eligible for all fiscal incentives extended to export earnings.

Implied in the government's promotion of medical tourism is the premise that the revenues it earns will strengthen health care in the country. But evidence to date is to the contrary. Corporate hospitals have repeatedly dishonored the conditions for receiving government subsidies by refusing to treat poor patients free of cost—and they have got away without punishment (Sengupta 2008). Many top specialists in corporate hospitals are drawn from the public sector, thereby promoting a brain drain of health professionals into private corporate hospitals. Urban concentration of health care providers is widely documented: 59 percent of India's practitioners (and 73 percent of allopathic practitioners) are located in metropolitan centers. Medical tourism intensifies the trend of health professionals moving to large urban centers and, within them, to large, corporate-run specialty institutions.

Conclusions

Clearly there is a disjunction between the government's perceived need to support medical tourism and the state of public health services for ordinary

Indians. If services related to medical tourism were taxed sufficiently to support public health, the revenue that medical tourism generates could benefit health care throughout India. Instead, the medical tourism industry receives tax concessions. The government grants benefits to private facilities that treat foreign patients, such as lower import duties and increased depreciation rates (from 25 to 40 percent) for life-saving medical equipment, among other breaks. Valuable land is set aside for private hospitals, and at reduced rates. India's medical tourism industry also receives a significant subsidy that few acknowledge: a pool of medical professionals. Though there has been a recent spurt in the growth of private medical colleges since the 1990s, the best medical colleges are located in the public sector where medical education is almost wholly subsidized by the government. Most good physicians train in public hospitals and then go on to work in private facilities, representing an indirect support for the private sector at an estimated $90 to $110 million annually (Sengupta and Nundy 2005). Thus, the competitive edge that has enabled the medical tourism industry to move aggressively into the international market is actually paid for by Indian taxpayers, who receive nothing whatsoever in return.

Source: Updated and adapted from "Medical Tourism: Reverse Subsidy for the Elite." *Signs* 36(2): 312–319, 2011. Reprinted with permission of the University of Chicago Press.

Notes

[1] The market for assisted reproductive technologies in India was estimated at $230 million in 2015 and is projected to reach $760 million by 2020.

[2] See the Indian Medical Travel Association's website at http://www.indiantourismecatalog.com/india_medical/medical_travel_association.html

References Cited

Agarwal, N. 2007. "Bulletin on Rural Health Statistics in India." Government bulletin. Ministry of Health and Family Welfare, Government of India, New Delhi. http://mohfw.nic.in/Bulletin%20on%20RHS%20-%20March,%202007%20-%20PDF%20Version%5CTitle%20Page.htm

———. 2016a. IVF: High Potential Baby-Making Business in India, AURUM, November 14, 2016. http://www.aurumequity.com/ivf-india/

———. 2016b. India Unveils Plans to Ban Surrogacy, BBC News, 25 August 2016. http://www.bbc.com/news/world-asia-india-37182197

Deloitte. 2017. "Global Health Care Sector Outlook." https://www2.deloitte.com/global/en/pages/life-sciences-and-healthcare/articles/global-health-care-sector-outlook.html

Grant Thornton. 2015, October. *Transformative Evolution: From "Wellness" to "Medical Wellness" Tourism in Kerala.* New Delhi: Grant Thornton LLC.
http://www.grantthornton.in/globalassets/1.-member-firms/india/assets/pdfs/grant_thornton_report-transformative_evolution.pdf

IMF (International Monetary Fund). 2016, October. "World Economic Outlook Database." http://www.imf.org/external/pubs/ft/weo/2016/02/weodata/weorept.aspx?pr.x=45&pr.y=1&sy=2015&ey=2020&scsm=1&ssd=1&sort=country&ds=.&br=1&c=534&s=NGDPD%2CNGDPDPC%2CPPPGDP%2CPPPPPC&grp=0&a=

Jose, R., and S. Sachdeva. 2010. "Keeping an Eye on Future: Medical Tourism." *Indian Journal of Community Medicine* 35(3): 376–8. Available from: http://www.ijcm.org.in/text.asp?2010/35/3/376/69247

Kannan, R. 2014, May 28. "NABH Sets New Entry-Level Standards for Accreditation of Hospitals." *The Hindu*. http://www.thehindu.com/news/national/nabh-sets-new-entrylevel-standards-for-accreditation-of-hospitals/article6055157.ece

Ministry of Health and Family Welfare. 2002. *National Health Policy 2002*. https://www.nhp.gov.in/sites/default/files/pdf/NationaL_Health_Pollicy.pdf

———. 2017. *Situation Analyses, Backdrop to the National Health Policy—2017*. New Delhi: Ministry of Health and Family Welfare. https://mohfw.gov.in/sites/default/files/71275472221489753307.pdf

———. n.d. *Brief about Medical Tourism*. https://mohfw.gov.in/about-us/departments/departments-health-and-family-welfare/medical-tourism

NSSO (National Sample Survey Organisation). 2006. "Morbidity, Health Care, and the Condition of the Aged." Report from the 60th round of the National Sample Survey, carried out from January to June 2004. National Sample Survey, Organization, Ministry of Statistics and Programme Implementation, Government of India, New Delhi.

Oxfam International. 2009. "Blind Optimism: Challenging the Myths about Private Health Care in Poor Countries." Oxfam Briefing Paper 125, February. Oxford, UK: Oxfam International. http://www.oxfam.org/sites/www.oxfam.org/files/bp125-blind-optimism-0902.pdf

PTI. 2014. September 1. "India Ranks among Top 3 Medical Tourism Destinations in Asia," *The Times of India*. http://timesofindia.indiatimes.com/business/india-business/India-ranks-among-top-3-medical-tourism-destinations-in-Asia/articleshow/41447360.cms

———, 2015. "Indian Medical Tourism Industry to Touch $8 billion by 2020: Grant Thornton." *The Economic Times*, November 1. http://economictimes.indiatimes.com/industry/healthcare/biotech/healthcare/indian-medical-tourism-industry-to-touch-8-billion-by-2020-grant-thornton/articleshow/49615898.cms

Sengupta, Amit. 2008. "Medical Tourism in India: Winners and Losers." *Indian Journal of Medical Ethics* 5(1): 4–5.

Sengupta, Amit, and S. Nundy. 2005. "The Private Health Sector in India." *BMJ* 19(November): 1157–1158.

Srivastava, M. 2017, April 1. "India Medical Tourism Industry to Reach $6 billion by 2018: Report." *live mint* E-paper. http://www.livemint.com/Home-Page/NX5IF0yZtnkCFz4vzxtt5N/India-medical-tourism-industry-to-reach-6-billion-by-2018.html

Rao, M., K. D. Rao, A. K. Shiva Kumar, M. Chatterjee, and T. Sundararaman. 2011. "Human Resources for Health in India." *Lancet* 377: 587–598.

Sahoo, H, and M. R. Pradhan. 2007, February. "Domestic Violence in India: An Empirical Analysis." Paper presented in National Seminar on Gender Issue and Empowerment of Women, Indian Social Institute, Kolkata.

Sundararaman, T., and V. R. Muraleedharan. 2015. "Falling Sick, Paying the Price: NSS 71st Round on Morbidity and Costs of Healthcare," *Economic & Political Weekly* 1(33): 17–20. http://www.im4change.org/siteadmin/tinymce/uploaded/Falling_Sick_Paying_the_Price.pdf

thepharmaletter. 2017, February 21. "Medical Tourism Will Help Drive Indian Pharma Industry to Reach $55 Billion by 2020." http://www.thepharmaletter.com/article/medical-tourism-will-help-drive-indian-pharma-industry-to-reach-55-billion-by-2020

WHO (World Health Organization). 2015. *Trends in Maternal Mortality: 1990 to 2015*. http://apps.who.int/iris/bitstream/10665/193994/1/WHO_RHR_15.23_eng.pdf

21

When Sex Tourists and Sex Workers Meet: Encounters within Sosúa, the Dominican Republic

Denise Brennan

There is a new sex-tourist destination on the global sexual landscape: Sosúa, the Dominican Republic. A beach town on the north coast, Sosúa has emerged as a place of fantasy for white European male tourists willing to pay for sex with Afro-Caribbean women. But European men are not the only ones who seek to fulfill fantasies. Dominican sex workers also arrive in Sosúa with fantasies: fantasies of economic mobility, visas to Europe, and even romance. For them, Sosúa and its tourists represent an escape: women migrate from throughout the Dominican Republic with dreams of European men "rescuing" them from a lifetime of foreclosed opportunities and poverty. They hope to meet and marry European men who will sponsor their (and their children's) migration to Europe. Yet, even though more and more women and girls migrate to Sosúa everyday, most leave the sex trade with little more than they had when they arrived.

This article explores this paradoxical feature of sex tourism in Sosúa, and examines why women continue to flock to Sosúa and how they make the most of their time while there. Through the sex trade in this one tourist town, see how globalization affects sex workers and sex tourists differently. In this economy of desire, some dreams are realized, while others prove hollow. White, middle-class and lower-middle class European visitors and residents are much better positioned to secure what they want in Sosúa than poor, black Dominican sex workers. Globalization and the accompanying transnational processes such as tourism and sex tourism not only open up opportunities but also reproduce unequal, dependent relations along lines of gender, race, class, geography, and history.

Why the Sex Trade? Why Sosúa?

Dominican women who migrate to Sosúa and its sex trade are seduced by the opportunity to meet, and possibly marry, a foreign tourist. Even if sex workers do not marry their clients, Sosúa holds out the promise of maintaining a transnational relationship with them, using new transnational technologies such as fax machines and international money wires. Without these transnational connections, Sosúa's sex trade would be no different than sex work in any other Dominican town. By migrating to Sosúa, women are engaging in an economic strategy that is both very familiar and something altogether new. I argue that they try to use the sex trade as an *advancement* strategy, not just a *survival* strategy. In short, these marginalized female heads-of-household try to take advantage of the global linkages that exploit them.

Though only a handful of women regularly receive money wires from ex-clients in Europe—and even fewer actually move to Europe to live with their sweethearts—success stories circulate among the sex workers like Dominicanized versions of the movie *Pretty Woman*. Thus, Sosúa's myth of opportunity goes unchallenged and women, recruited through female social networks of family and close friends who have already migrated, keep on arriving, ready to find their "Richard Gere." Yet what the women find is a far cry from their fantasy images of fancy dinners, nightclubs, easy money, and visas off the island. One disappointed sex worker, Carmen,[1] insightfully sums up just how important fantasy is to constructing the image of Sosúa as a place of opportunity: "Women come to Sosúa because of a big lie. They hear they can make money, and meet a gringo, and they come. . . . They come with their dreams, but then they find out it is all a lie."

Work choices available to poor Dominican women are determined not only by local factors, but by the global economy. Internal migration for sex work is a consequence of both local economic and social transformations and larger, external forces, such as foreign investment in export-processing zones and tourism. Just as international investors see the Dominican Republic as a site of cheap labor, international tourists know it as a place to buy cheap sex. In sex tourism, First-World travelers/consumers seek exoticized, racialized "native" bodies in the developing world for cut-rate prices. These two components—race and its associated stereotypes and expectations, and the economic disparities between the developed and developing worlds—characterize sex tourist destinations throughout the world. What do white men "desire" when they decide to book a flight from Frankfurt, for example, to Puerto Plata (the nearest airport to Sosúa)? I turned to the Internet for answers. Any exploration of the relationship between globalization, women's work choices in the global economy, and women's migration for work must now investigate the role the Internet has in producing and disseminating racialized and sexualized stereotypes in the developing world. The Internet is quickly and radically transforming the sex trade in the developing world, since online travel services make it increasingly easy for potential sex tourists to research sex-tourist destinations and to plan trips. I looked at Web sites that post writings from alleged sex tourists who share information about their sex trips.[2] In the process, they advertise not only their services but also Dominican women as sexual commodities. One sex tourist was impressed by the availability of "dirt cheap colored girls," while another boasted, "When you enter the discos, you will feel like you're in heaven! A tremendous number of cute girls and something for everyone's taste (if you like colored girls like me)!"[3] There is little doubt that race is central to what these sex tourists desire in their travels.

International Tourism: Who Benefits?

International tourism has not benefited poor Dominicans as much as many had hoped. Although development and foreign investment have brought "First-World" hotels and services to Sosúa, the local population still lives in Third-World conditions. The most successful resorts in Sosúa are foreign owned, and even though they create employment opportunities for the local population, most of the new jobs are low-paying service jobs with little chance for mobility. What's more, the multinational resorts that have moved into Sosúa have pushed small hotel and restaurant owners out of business. One such restaurant owner, Luis, comments on the effects of these large "all-inclusive" hotels (tourists pay one fee in their home countries for airfare, lodging, food, and even drinks) on the Sosúa economy:

> These tourists hardly change even US$100 to spend outside the hotel. Before the all-inclusive hotels, people would change between US$1000– 2000 and it would get distributed throughout the town: some for lodging, for food and entertainment. Now, not only do any of the local merchants get any of the money, but it never even leaves the tourists' home countries—like Germany or Austria—where they pay for their vacation in advance.

Foreign ownership, repatriation of profits, and the monopolistic nature of these all-inclusive resorts, make it difficult for the local population to profit significantly. Tourism is one of the largest industries in the global economy (Sinclair 1997), and it is not unusual for foreign firms to handle all four components of a tourist's stay: airlines, hotels, services, and tour operators. I interviewed the general manager (an Italian citizen) of a German hotel, for example, whose parent company is a German airline company. Eighty percent of the hotel's guests are German, all of whom paid for their airfare, lodging, and food in Germany. Furthermore, this German company imported most of its management staff from Europe, as well as the furniture, fabrics, and other goods necessary to run the hotel. So much for opportunities for local Dominicans.

Marginalized individuals in the global economy frequently turn to migration and more recently to tourism as an exit from poverty. Both migration and transnational relationships with foreign tourists are perceived as ways to access a middle-class lifestyle and its accompanying commodities. A several decades-old history of migration between the Dominican Republic and New York (Georges 1990; Grasmuck and Pessar 1991) and the transnational cultural, political, and economic flows between these two spaces, have led many Dominicans to look *fuera* (outside) for solutions to their economic problems. A preoccupation with goods, capital, and opportunities that are "outside" helps explain how sex workers and other Dominican migrants can view Sosúa as a place of opportunity. These women would go to New York if they could, but they do not have the social networks (i.e., immediate family members in New York) to sponsor them for visas, nor the contacts to underwrite an illegal migration. Migrating internally to Sosúa is the closest they can get to the "outside." Without established contacts in New York, they have a greater chance to someday get overseas by marrying a tourist (no matter how slight a chance) than they do of obtaining a visa. In many ways, hanging out in the tourist bars in Sosúa is a better use of their time than waiting in line for a visa at the U.S. Embassy in Santo Domingo. Carla, a first-time sex worker, explains why Sosúa draws women from throughout the country: "We come here because we dream of a ticket" (airline ticket). But without a visa— which they could obtain through marriage—Dominican sex workers cannot use the airline ticket Carla describes. They must depend on their European clients-turned-boyfriends/husbands to sponsor them for visas off the island. They are at once independent and dependent, strategic and exploited.

A question I routinely posed to sex workers (and others have asked me, as an anthropologist working with women who sell sex) is why they decide to enter sex work rather than other forms of labor? The majority of these women are mothers with little formal education, few marketable skills, limited social networks, and minimal support from the fathers of their children. They are poor Dominican women who have few means to escape from poverty and the periodic crises they find themselves in. Within this context, sex work appears as a potentially profitable alternative to the low wages they could earn in export-processing zones or in domestic service—the two most common forms of formal employment available to poor women.[4] Many poor Dominican women must find work within the insecure and even lower-paying informal sector.

Felicia and Margarita, two friends who had migrated to Sosúa from the same town, found that the employment opportunities available to them at home (e.g., hairstylist, waitress, domestic) did not sufficiently provide for their families. They summed up their dilemma this way: "If you have a husband who pays for food and the house, then you can work in jobs like hairstyling. Otherwise it's not possible to work in jobs like this." Maintaining the view that women's earnings are "secondary" or "supplementary," these women nevertheless became the primary breadwinners once they separated from their "husbands."[5]

Women can choose to enter the sex trade in other Dominican towns, so by choosing Sosúa they are choosing to work with foreign rather than Dominican men. The selection not only of sex work over other work options but also of Sosúa, with its foreign tourist clientele, over other Dominican towns demonstrates that sex work for these women is not just a survival strategy but rather a strategy of advancement. This "choice" of the sex trade *in Sosúa* presents an important counter example to depictions of sex workers (who are not coerced or forced into prostitution) as powerless victims of male violence and exploitation. Yet, without protection under the law, sex workers are vulnerable to clients' actions once they are out of public spaces and in private hotel rooms. They risk battery, rape, and forced unprotected sex. Sex workers in Sosúa, however, often discount the risks of violence and AIDS given what they see as the potential payoffs of financial stability or a marriage proposal. Recently, however, so many women have migrated to Sosúa from throughout the Dominican Republic that sex workers outnumber clients in the bars. Thus, in order to understand why women place themselves in a context of uncertainty and potential violence, we need to explore fully Sosúa's opportunity myth. How reliable are the payoffs and how high are the risks? Why might or might not women achieve "success" through sex work in Sosúa? Can these poor, single mothers benefit from globalization?

Sex Work: Short- and Long-term Strategies

Working with foreign tourists can represent considerable long-term financial gains for a sex worker and her extended family—far more than she could gain from factory or domestic work. Yet, not all women who arrive in Sosúa to pursue sex work want to build long-term transnational ties. Some have different long-term strategies, such as saving enough money to start a *colmado* (small grocery store) in their yard in their home communities. Others use sex work simply as a way to make ends meet in the immediate future. Those who hope to pursue long-term relationships with foreign tourists are often disappointed. Relationships go sour and with them their extended family's only lifeline from poverty disintegrates. For every promise a tourist keeps, there are many more stories of disappointment. Even the success stories eventually cannot live up to the myths.

Sex work yields varying levels of reward. Some women open savings accounts and are able to build houses with their earnings, while others do not have enough money to pay the motorcycle taxi fare from their boarding houses to the tourist bars. Why are some sex workers able to save, despite the obstacles, while most continue to live from day to day? Success at sex work in Sosúa depends both on a planned strategy and a real commitment to saving money as well as luck. I cannot emphasize enough the role chance plays in sex workers' long-term ties with foreign clients. Whether or not clients stay in touch with the women is out of their control. One sex worker, Carmen, was thus skeptical that the Belgian client with whom she spent time during his three-week vacation in Sosúa actually would follow through on his promises to marry her and move her to Europe: "I don't absolutely believe that he is going to marry me. You know, sure, when he was here he seemed to love me. But you know people leave and they forget." In fact, months later, she still had not heard from him. I helped Carmen write him a letter, which I mailed when I got back to the United States. It was returned to my address, unopened. Had she gotten the address wrong or did he give her a false address along with his proclamations of love and commitment to their living together?

Adding to the uncertainty and fragility of transnational relationships are other logistical obstacles to "success." Women must find ways to save money despite the drain on their resources from paying police bribes and living in an expensive tourist town where prices for food and rent are among the highest in the country. All of this combined with increased competition among sex workers for clients increases the likelihood of having to leave Sosúa with little or no money saved. Furthermore, the majority of women who arrive in Sosúa do not know what they are getting into. They have heard of police roundups and know that they must vie with countless other women like themselves to catch the attention of potential clients, but like most migrants they are full of hopes and dreams and believe that "it will be different for them." In gold-rush fashion, they arrive in Sosúa because they have heard of Sosúa's tourists and money, and they plan, without a specific strategy in mind, to cash in on the tourist boom. It only takes a few days in Sosúa to realize that the only hope they have to quickly make big money is to establish a transnational relationship. New arrivals see veteran sex workers drop by the Codetel office (telephone and fax company) every day, vigilantly looking for faxes from clients in Europe or Canada. If they want to receive money wires or marriage proposals from tourists overseas, they learn that they must establish similar ongoing transnational relationships.

Sex Workers' Stories

In order to explore how sex workers' time in Sosúa measures up to their fantasy images, I turn to three sex workers' divergent experiences. Their stories call attention to the difficulties of establishing a transnational relationship, as well as to its fragility. Through sex workers' accounts of their relationships with foreign men, we get a sense of just how wildly unpredictable the course of these relationships can be.

Elena and Jürgen: Building and Breaking Transnational Ties through Sex Work

This story begins with Elena's release from jail. After being held for two days, twenty-two-year-old Elena went to the beach.[6] When I saw her, back at her one-room wooden house, she was ecstatic. At the beach she had run into Jürgen, who had just returned to Sosúa from his home in Germany to see her. They had been sending faxes to one another since he had left Sosúa after his last vacation, and he had mentioned in one of his faxes that he would be returning. He did not know where she lived, but figured he would find her that evening at the Anchor, Sosúa's largest tourist bar and a place tourists go to pick up sex workers. He brought her presents from Germany, including perfume and a matching gold chain necklace and bracelet. Elena was grinning ear to ear as she showed off her gifts, talking about Jürgen like a smitten schoolgirl: "I am canceling everything for the weekend and am going to spend the entire time with him. We will go to the beach and he will take me to nightclubs and to restaurants."

Elena began preparing for the weekend. Her two sisters who lived with her, ages fourteen and sixteen, would look after her six-year-old daughter, since Elena would stay with Jürgen in his hotel. She chose the evening's outfit carefully, with plenty of help from her sisters, daughter, and friend, a young sex worker who also lives with them since she has very little money. Elena provides for these four girls with her earnings from sex work. They all rotate between sharing the double bed and sleeping on the floor. Spending time with a tourist on his vacation means Elena would receive more gifts, maybe even some for her family, and would make good money. So they helped primp Elena, selecting billowy rayon pants that moved as she did and a black lycra stretch shirt with long sheer sleeves that was cropped to reveal her slim stomach. She was meeting Jürgen at the Anchor, where I saw her later on, and she stood out in the crowd.

As soon as Jürgen's vacation ended, he went back to Germany with a plan to return in a couple of months. Since he was self-employed in construction, he could live part of the year in the Dominican Republic. Elena was very upset when Jürgen left and could not stop crying. Maybe Jürgen represented more than just money, nice meals, and new clothes. I had often heard sex workers distinguish between relationships with tourists *por amor* (for love) or *por residencia* (for residence/visas) but Elena's tears broke down that distinction.

Unlike Carmen's relationship with her Belgian client, Jürgen kept his word to Elena and wired money and kept in touch through faxes. Even more surprisingly, he returned to Sosúa only two months later. Within days of his return, he rented a two-bedroom apartment that had running water and an electrical generator (for daily blackouts). He also bought beds, living room furniture, and a large color television. Elena was living out the fantasy of many sex workers in Sosúa: she was sharing a household with a European man who supported her and her dependents. Jürgen paid for food that Elena and her sisters prepared and had cable television installed. He also paid for Elena's six-year-old daughter to attend a private school and came home one day with school supplies for her. Occasionally, Jürgen took Elena, her daughter, and her sisters out to eat at one of the tourist restaurants that line the beach where the tourists sun themselves.

Elena had moved up in the world: eating in tourist restaurants, sending a daughter to private school, and living in a middle-class apartment were all symbols of her increased social and economic mobility. As a female head of household who had been taking care of her daughter and sisters with her earnings from sex work, Elena was now able to quit sex work and live off of the money Jürgen gave her. Sex work and the transnational relationships it had built altered Elena's life as well as the lives of those who depended on her. But for how long?

Jürgen turned out not to be Elena's or her family's salvation. Soon after they moved in together, Elena found out she was pregnant. Both she and Jürgen were very happy about having a baby. He had a teenage son living with his ex-wife in Germany and relished the idea of having another child. At first, he was helpful around the house and doted on Elena. But the novelty soon wore off and he returned to his routine of spending most days in the German-owned bar beneath their apartment. He also went out drinking at night with German friends, hopping from bar to bar. He was drunk, or on his way there, day and night. Elena saw him less and less frequently, and they began to fight often, usually over money.

Eventually he started staying out all night. On one occasion, a friend of Elena's (a sex worker) saw Jürgen at the Anchor talking with, and later on leaving the bar with, a Haitian sex worker. Elena knew he was cheating on her. But she did not want to raise this with Jürgen, explaining that men "do these things." Instead, she focused her anger on the fact that he was not giving her enough money to take care of the household. Ironically, Elena had more disposable income before she began to live with Jürgen. Back then, she could afford to go out dancing and drinking with her friends—not to look for clients, but just to have fun. Now, without an income of her own, she was dependent upon Jürgen not only for household expenses but also for her entertainment.

On more than one occasion I served as interpreter between the two during their attempts at "peace negotiations" after they had not spoken to one another for days. Since Elena does not speak any German or English, she asked me to help her understand why Jürgen was mad at her as well as to communicate her viewpoint to him. In preparation for one of these "negotiations," Elena briefed me on what she wanted me to explain to Jürgen:

I want to know why he is not talking to me? And why is he not giving me any money? He is my *esposo* [husband—in consensual union] and is supposed to give me money. I need to know if he is with me or with someone else. He pays for this house and paid for everything here. I need to know what is going on. You know I was fine living alone before, I'm able to do that. I took care of everything before, this is not a problem. But I need to know what is going to happen.

Since they were living together and Jürgen was paying the bills, Elena considered them to be married. To Elena and her friends, Jürgen, as an *esposo*, was financially responsible for the household. But Jürgen saw things differently. He felt Elena thought he was "made of money" and was always asking him for more. He asked me to translate to her:

I'm not a millionaire. I told Elena last week that I don't like her always asking for money. She did not listen. She asks me for money all day long. I don't want to be taken advantage of.

One day, without warning, Jürgen packed his bags and left for Germany for business. Elena knew this day would come, that Jürgen would have to return to Germany to work. But she did not expect their relationship would be in such disarray, and that he would depart without leaving her money (although he did leave some food money with her younger sisters who turned it over to Elena). In Jürgen's absence, Elena took her daughter out of the private school once the tuition became overdue and she started working part-time at a small Dominican-owned restaurant. When Jürgen returned to Sosúa from Germany a couple of months later, they split up for good. Elena moved out of their apartment back to the labyrinth of shanties on dirt paths off the main road. Her economic and social mobility was short-lived. She had not accumulated any savings or items she could pawn during her time with Jürgen. Jürgen never gave her enough money so that she could set some aside for savings. And all the things he bought for the apartment were his, not hers. When they vacated the apartment, he took all of the furniture and the television with him.

Elena's relationship with Jürgen dramatically changed her life; she was, after all, having his child. But her social and economic status remained as marginal as ever. Even though she was living out many sex workers' fantasies of "marrying" a foreign tourist, she still lived like many poor Dominicans, struggling day to day without access to resources to build long-term economic security. When she and Jürgen fought and he withheld money from her, she was less economically independent than she was as a sex worker, when she was certain to earn around 500 pesos a client. Although sex workers take on great risks—of AIDS, abuse, and arrest—and occupy a marginal and stigmatized status in Dominican society, Elena's status as the "housewife" of a German resident was fragile and constantly threatened.

Jürgen now lives, Elena has heard, somewhere in Asia. Elena is back living in the same conditions as before she met Jürgen. She has not returned to sex work and makes significantly less money working in a restaurant. Her older sisters now help take care of their younger sisters, and Elena sends what money she can, though less than in her sex work days, to help out her parents.

Luisa's Money Wires

Luisa is an example of a sex worker whose transnational connections were those other sex workers envied, but her "success," like Elena's, ended without warning. She, quite remarkably, received US$500 every two weeks from a client in Germany, who wanted her to leave sex work and start her own clothing store. She told him she had stopped working the tourist bars, and that she used the money to buy clothes for the store. Yet, when he found out that she was still working as a sex worker, had not opened a store, and was living with a Dominican boyfriend, he stopped wiring money.

At this juncture, Luisa was in over her head. She had not put any of the money in the bank, in anticipation of the day when the money wires might dry up. She was renting a two-bedroom apartment that was twice the size and rent of friends' apartments. And she sent money home to her mother in Santo Domingo, who was taking care of her twelve-year-old son. She also supported her Dominican boyfriend, who lived with her and did not have a steady job. Other sex workers called him a *chulo* (pimp) since he lived off of Luisa's earnings and money wires. They saw Luisa as foolish for bankrolling her boyfriend, especially since he was not the father of her son. She began hocking her chains and rings in one of Sosúa's half-dozen pawnshops.

As lucky as Luisa was to meet this German client at the Anchor, most of the women working the Anchor night after night never receive a single money wire transfer. Those who do generally receive smaller sums than Luisa did, on a much more infrequent and unpredictable basis. And as Luisa's story demonstrates, a sex worker's luck can change overnight. There is no guarantee that money wires will continue once they begin. Luisa had no way of knowing that she would lose her "meal ticket," nor can she be certain that she will ever find another tourist to replace him. Furthermore, women cannot count on earning money in sex work indefinitely. Luisa is in her early thirties and knows that over the next few years it will be increasingly difficult to compete with the young women in the bars (some are as young as sixteen and seventeen, most are between nineteen and twenty-five). Yet, once women make the decision to leave Sosúa and sex work, they face the same limited opportunities they confronted before they entered sex work. They are still hampered by limited education, a lack of marketable job skills, and not "knowing the right people." In fact, obstacles to economic and social mobility might have increased, especially if they are rumored to have AIDS. They might have to battle gossip in their home community and the stigma associated with sex work. After years of working in bars they might have a substance-abuse problem. And they return to children who have grown in their absence.

Carmen's Diversification Strategy

Carmen's story, compared to Elena's, is one of relative success, in which her relationship with Dominican clients figures prominently. In fact, supplementing uncertain income with foreign tourists by working with Dominican clients, as well as establishing long-term relationships with Dominican *amigos/clientes fijos* (friends/regular clients), supplies Carmen with a steady flow of income. Another sex worker, Ani, explains the function of *amigos*:

> You don't always have a client. You need *amigos* and *clientes fijos*. If you have a problem, like something breaks in your house, or your child is sick and you need money for the doctor or medicine, they can help.

For Carmen, working with Dominicans has proven much more reliable than establishing ties with foreign men. Carmen has saved enough money from four years in sex work to build a small house in Santo Domingo (the capital city five hours away where she will retire to take care of her mother and children). She has managed to save more money than most sex workers. I asked her why she thinks she was able to save money, while many of her friends don't have an extra centavo, and she answered,

> Because they give it to their men. Their husbands wait at home and drink while their women work. Not me. If I'm in the street with all the risks of disease and the police, I'm keeping the money or giving it to my kids. I'm not giving it to a man, no way. If women don't give the money to the men, they (the men) beat the women.

She is careful not to let the men in her life know how much money she has saved in the bank (unlike Luisa), or the sources of the money. She has a steady relationship in particular with Jorge, who is her economic safety net, especially in times of crises. She describes their relationship:

> He is very young [she scrunched her nose up in disapproval of this point]. He lives with his mother in Santiago and works in a *zona franca* [factory in an export-processing zone]. He gives me money, even though he does not make a lot. He bought me furniture for the new house.

At times, the money Jorge gives Carmen is the only money she has. By establishing a relationship with a Dominican man, she has been able to supplement her unpredictable income from sex work. Though the money he gives her is in smaller sums than transnational money wires other sex workers receive, like Luisa, it is money she can count on, on a regular basis.

Carmen not only has diversified her clients, focused on achieving one specific goal (building a house), but she also has clear personal limitations working in a dangerous trade. Since she has a serious fear of the police, she refuses to work when they are making arrests outside of the tourist bars where many of the sex workers congregate to talk, smoke, or greet customers entering the bars. At one point when the police seemed to be making more arrests than usual, Carmen quit going to the tourist bars altogether. Instead, she took a bus to a small Dominican town about thirty miles away to work in a bar that caters to Dominican clients. Thus, she developed an alternate plan to working in Sosúa when necessary.

By pursuing local Dominican clients as well as trying to establish transnational connections, sex work is paying off for Carmen in the long term. Carmen refused to be seduced by the promise of a tourist enclave and the sweet talk of foreign tourists. Instead, she treated Sosúa as any other Dominican town with "brothels" and set up a roster of local regular clients. Carmen's gains have been slow and modest. Nevertheless, she saved enough money to begin constructing a small house, though thus far it has taken her four years, and she still needs enough money for windows. But she will leave Sosúa with her future, and her family's, more secure than when she first arrived. Stories about modest successes like Carmen's are not as glamorous as those with transnational dimensions. Rather, stories of transnational relationships and quick, big money circulate among the sex workers, like those of Elena and Luisa. Their more immediate and visible ascension from poverty are regaled and fuel the illusion of Sosúa as a place to get rich quick.

Conclusion

Foreign sex tourists clearly benefit from their geographic position in the global economy, as they travel with ease (no visa is needed to enter the Dominican Republic) and buy sex for cheaper prices than in their home countries. Dominican sex workers, in contrast, face innumerable constraints due to their country's marginal position in the global economy. Sosúa's sex trade is but one more site where, broadly, we can observe globalization exacerbating inequality and, more specifically, we can situate tourism and sex tourism as both relying on and reproducing inequalities in the global economy.

Like most prospectors in search of quick money, few sex workers who rush into Sosúa looking for a foreign tourist to solve their problems find what they were hoping for. It is of little surprise, however, that women, despite the obstacles to fulfilling their "fantasies" continue to arrive everyday. Women from the poorest classes have no other work options that pay as well as the sex trade with tourists in the short term. Nor do most other work options offer the opportunity to establish long-term relationships with foreign men. Although most transnational relationships are unlikely to alter sex workers' long-term economic and social status, they make far more financial gains than most women in the sex trade or other accessible labor options (such as domestic service or factory work).

Sex workers also slowly can make gains without transnational connections. Though difficult to achieve, these gains might prove more durable than those resting on a transnational relationship. Carmen's transnational ties never paid off, and consequently she did not come into a lot of money all at once.

But she still managed to save what she could over time. Her house represents security, but it does not catapult her out of *los pobres* (the poor). Her "success" is not on the same level as women with ongoing relationships with European men. But while these ties could dissolve at any time, Carmen's house will still be there. She looks forward to the day she completes her house and leaves Sosúa and its sex trade: "When I leave here I want to sit on the front porch of my new house with my mother and my children and drink a cold glass of juice. I want a peaceful life. No Sosúa, no men giving you problems."

Source: Adapted from "Globalization, Women's Labor, and Men's Pleasure: Sex Tourism in Sosúa, the Dominican Republic," *Urban Life: Readings in the Anthropology of the City*, 4th ed. George Gmelch and Walter Zenner (eds.), 2002, Waveland Press.

Notes

[1] I have changed all names.

[2] I did not join any of these sites, however. But, rather, looked at "satisfied customer" testimonials the sites post to try to entice new paying members.

[3] For more on the Internet and the sex trade see Brennan, Denise (2001), "Tourism in Transnational Places: Dominican Sex Workers and German Sex Tourists Imagine One Another," *Identities: Global Studies in Culture and Power* 7, 4 (1/01):621–63.

[4] These jobs, on average, yield under 1000 pesos a month, whereas sex workers in Sosúa charge approximately 500 pesos from foreign clients.

[5] Poor Dominicans are more likely to enter consensual unions than legal marriage. In fact, unless I specifically mention otherwise, sex workers are not legally married to their husbands. Yet since the women I interviewed referred to the men in their lives as "husbands" *(esposos)*, I also use this term.

[6] She paid 500 pesos (US$41.00) for her release—the standard bribe to the police.

22

Children and Sex Tourism: The Case of Thailand

Heather Montgomery

The discovery in the 1990s that Western men were traveling overseas in order to have sex with children has had a major impact on the media, on NGOs (nongovernmental organizations), and on international legislators. As a consequence, the last thirty years have seen concerted international efforts made to tackle the problem, and there have been vocal campaigns against child sex tourism, resulting in changes in national legislation in many countries, statements and task forces from the World Tourism Organisation, the inauguration of World Congresses against the Commercial Sexual Exploitation of Children, and a determination to stamp out the practice of foreign men traveling to countries in Asia and Africa in order to pay for sex with children. Despite all these actions, however, knowledge of the problem is still limited and there is not enough information on why children are being exploited, by whom, where this abuse takes place, and how it is organized. This chapter will examine what is known about child prostitution and child sex tourism, especially as it relates to Thailand, as well as what still needs examination and research. It will also suggest reasons why men buy sex from children in Southeast Asia and ask questions about the enduring appeal of the child or childlike prostitute.

A History of Prostitution in Thailand

Historically the overwhelming majority of prostitutes in Thailand were Thai women and girls with local clients, but as early as the 1920s there were concerns about international involvement in the Thai sex industry—both the numbers of foreign women working in Thai brothels and the numbers of Thai women selling sex to foreigners. In 1933 the League of Nations reported on the organized brothels of Thailand, claiming that Thai, Chinese, Burmese, and even Russian women were selling sex in Thailand (League of Nations 1933). By the late 1940s, there was evidence of a small-scale tourism industry providing foreigners with introductions to indigenous sex workers in Thailand. In 1949 a pamphlet entitled *Dream Lover* was published, written by the pseudonymous author Black Shadow, which described to the foreigner where and how he could obtain the sexual services of Thai and Chinese women in Bangkok, including "the Chinese of today and tomorrow indeed, very fresh, young and gay" (Black Shadow 1949, 26). It is not known how many men availed themselves of Black Shadow's advice, what the print run was, or how popular the book became, but it clearly served a market, and while the number of children catering to foreign men was probably minuscule at this time, it was certainly not unknown. More broadly, studies in the 1950s found that 90 percent of prostitutes in Thailand were aged 15–20 and there was evidence of some as young as 13 (Fox 1960).

Prostitution was criminalized in Thailand in 1960 as part of a wider plan to rid the country of "undesirables," and it remains the case today that, despite Thailand's reputation as a sexual paradise where "anything" goes, all prostitution is illegal (ten Brummelhuis 1993; Boonchalaksi and Guest 1994; Montgomery 2001b). The laws against it have rarely been enforced, however, with police turning a blind eye and, according to a 2008 report by the U.S. State Department, sometimes actively involved (Bureau of Democracy, Human Rights, and Labor 2009). Criminalizing prostitution certainly did not end it, and successive governments have implicitly or explicitly tolerated, condoned, and even encouraged it. Indeed, just at the point prostitution was prohibited legally, the numbers of women and girls selling sex increased exponentially due to the large numbers of foreigners coming to Thailand for the first time.

During the Vietnam War, the Thai government allowed the United States to station troops in Thailand and allowed American servicemen to use Thailand as a base for "R & R" (Rest and Recreation—which quickly became known as "I & I"—Intercourse and Intoxication). The large numbers of young Western men with money to spend led rapidly to the creation of bars and brothels set up to cater explicitly to foreigners, and it was during this period that a recognizable, large-scale sex industry started. After 1975, the troops had gone but had left behind the sex industry's infrastructure, in the form of clubs and bars, as well as the stereotype of beautiful, pliant, and docile Thai women who would fulfill every sexual fantasy for a small price. This infrastructure was easily harnessed to the needs of the Thai state, which wished to develop and modernize the economy. With no more money coming in from the Americans and with a very limited manufacturing and industrial base, Thailand needed other sources of revenue and, like other developing countries in the 1970s, viewed tourism as the way forward. Thailand was different than other countries, however, in that it already had a reputation for easily available commercial sex, and tourism promotion began to rely heavily on this fact. In 1980 the Thai Deputy Prime Minister laid out the view that while prostitution might be illegal it was an integral part of the strategy to modernize and develop the country:

> I ask all governors to consider the natural scenery in your provinces, together with some forms of entertainment that some of you might consider disgusting and shameful because they are forms of sexual entertainment that attract tourists . . . we must do this because we have to consider the jobs that will be created for the people. (qtd. in Ennew 1986:99)

By the 1990s, however, this policy of condoning sex tourism was coming under threat. Women's groups and antitourism activists began to campaign against the use of sex tourism as a way of promoting the tourist industry and began a series of high-profile publicity stunts in which they attacked the image of "brothel" Thailand. They picketed the Bangkok airport and targeted flights from Taiwan and Japan, which were seen as the worst countries for sending sex tourists, with placards that read "Thailand not Sexland" and "Gonorrhoea Express" (Montgomery 2008:907). At the same time, the issue of child prostitution began to be a specific concern with NGOs objecting to the ways in which Thai children were depicted as sexually available and part of the adult sex industry. One of their first victories was over Austrian airline Lauda Air's "Baby Club" advertising campaign. In 1992 an edition of Lauda Air's in-flight magazine featured a series of fictitious postcards from a number of the airline's destinations. The one from Australia showed a kangaroo, while the postcard from Thailand showed a naked, pubescent girl, surrounded by a heart inscribed with the words "from Thailand with love." The text on the back was signed off by "Werner, Gunter, Fritzl, Morsel, and Joe," with the words, "Got to close now. The tarts in the Bangkok Baby Club are waiting for us." Lauda Air claimed that the cartoon was a joke that had been misinterpreted but did withdraw it from circulation after these protests (Montgomery 2008).

More than anything else, it was the issue of child prostitution that galvanized public opinion nationally and internationally against sex tourism. Adult prostitution was illegal and was, increasingly, viewed as a vector for the spread of disease, particularly HIV and AIDS (Fordham 2005), but there remained debates over its morality, its necessity to the wider economy, and whether sex work could ever be a legitimate occupation (Oppermann 1998;

Kempadoo et al. 2005; O'Connell-Davidson 2005; Sánchez Taylor 2005). In contrast, sex tourism that involved children was universally condemned and there was no room for discussion or nuance. Reports began to appear in national and international newspapers, which told heart-rending stories of Southeast Asian girls, cruelly duped or sold by their impoverished and greedy parents into a life of prostitution. They would be taken to a brothel, forced to have sex with up to twenty clients a night, usually foreigners, and then be rescued by a kind-hearted charity, or journalist, only to discover they were HIV positive and had a limited time left to live (for a discussion of the portrayal of child prostitution in the international media, see Bishop and Robinson 1998 or Montgomery 2001a). The stories were repetitive, even stereotyped, the narratives based on recurring patterns of betrayal, abuse, rescue, and death, and the foreigner was always portrayed as the ultimate cause of the misery. Not surprisingly, the stories were emotive, somewhat sensationalist, but highly effective.

Focusing on child sex tourism as something uniquely wicked allowed campaigning groups to find common ground with governments, who might tacitly support sex tourism but could not be seen to condone child prostitution. It also enabled alliances to be made with those who supported sex workers' rights and campaigned for better regulation of the sex industry and those who wanted complete abolition. Child sex tourism was presented as an uncontroversial issue, above politics, economics, or vested interests. It could be understood within a straightforward moral framework of evil perpetrators and innocent child victims and did not require anyone to ask awkward questions about tourism as an economic development strategy, the position of women more generally in Thailand, and the widespread use of young prostitutes by local men (Muecke 1992).

At the forefront of these campaigns were ECPAT (End Child Prostitution in Asian Tourism, which later became End Child Prostitution, Child Pornography, and Trafficking of Children for Sexual Purposes) and ECTWT (Ecumenical Council on Third World Tourism), both of which drew very explicit links between tourism, child prostitution, and child trafficking (ECTWT 1990; ECPAT 1993; Montgomery 2001a). Their hard-hitting operations were extremely effective, gaining a great deal of national and international media attention. The campaigns focused not only on the abuse of the children but also on stories of Westerners in Thailand being arrested for molesting children but jumping bail or being let off on technicalities and then returning to their home countries where they could not be prosecuted (Montgomery 2010). Given the apparent invulnerability of such men, the appalling nature of the crimes being committed, and the public outcry about them, in the mid-1990s pressure began to mount on tourist-sending countries to pass extraterritorial legislation that would enable men to be prosecuted in their home countries for offenses committed against children abroad. In 1994 Australia became the first country to introduce extraterritorial legislation that brought in penalties of up to seventeen years' imprisonment for those convicted of sexual crimes against children overseas. Many European countries and the U.S. followed suit, and between 2002 and 2010 there were 65 convictions in the U.S. (Montgomery 2010).

The Nature of the Problem

Despite the public concern and changes in legislation, however, child sex tourism continues and, in some ways, the moral indignation that the subject arouses obscures certain aspects of the situations in which children caught up in prostitution live and work. There is still a dearth of information about how children meet clients, what is expected of them, and their paths in and out of prostitution (Montgomery 2001a; Montgomery 2001b; Ennew 2008). Their clients are even more unknown, and there is very little research (as opposed to anecdotal) evidence that sheds light on their motivations, how they operate, or their choices about which countries they will visit and where they can find opportunities for sexual activity with children (although for an excellent overview of the sketchy available evidence see O'Connell-Davidson 2005). While there has been talk of pedophile rings ordering sex from children as part of a holiday package, no evidence for this has ever been found (O'Connell-Davidson 2005), so researchers have tried instead to understand the types of men who might buy sex from children. This has led them to identify the "preferential" user and the "situational" user of child prostitutes (Finkelhor and Araji 1996). Men described as preferential users are those who fit more closely with popular understandings of "the pedophile" and are those men who actively seek out sex with children of a particular age and gender. Situational users are those men who might have sex with a child if offered, especially if the term "child" includes anyone under the age of 18, but whose sexual preferences are not necessarily for children. While this certainly makes sense on a conceptual level, there remains almost no direct research on the differences in behavior between the preferential or situational user. There is also an increasing recognition that there is no single "type" of exploiter and that they differ in age, gender, sexual orientation, ethnicity, and wealth. They may also not come on a package tour or on holiday but be long-term residents, military personnel, or businessmen.

There is also very little documented evidence about the nature and extent of the problem and a large amount of supposition, speculation, and sensationalism, based on very few, often extreme, cases, where individual men have been caught and prosecuted. Rarely, however, do accounts of arrests and prosecutions discuss the mechanisms of how sexual abusers are apprehended and what support is available for children asked to testify against them. There are no definitive figures, or even good guesswork, on how many children sell sex to tourists, or to Westerners more generally. Figures such as 10 million children worldwide working in prostitution are used on popular information sources such as Wikipedia, but this statistic is very hard to verify, and how many of these children have foreign clients is unknown. There are also claims that the rise in the number of child prostitutes (if indeed there has been one) is fueled in part by men turning to younger women and girls because they believe them to be free of sexually transmitted diseases, including AIDS (Muntabhorn 1992). It is also claimed that some Asian men believe that sex with a virgin can cure AIDS and other venereal diseases and that tourists from China or Taiwan actively seek out young, virgin children, although there is no ethnographic evidence (as opposed to much repeated and back referenced statements on the subject) to suggest that this is true. Similar comments have also been said about black South African men, and indeed about the clients of child prostitutes in nineteenth-century London, which suggests that concerns about virginity are as much part of campaigners' mythologies as they are about the actual behavior of child sex tourists. It is a reasonable suspicion that fears of infection might increase the demand for children, and in some interviews clients have admitted to evaluating women on their cleanliness and vitality (Sittitrai and Brown 1994). It may therefore be the case that younger women are seen as less risky than older ones, but there is no confirmation of this.

Creating Innocence

While the scale and extent of the problem is unknown, there is more research on the links between sex, travel, and the eroticization of the "ethnic Other" (Oppermann 1998; Crick 1989; Nagel 2003), and it is through an examination of these issues that it is possible to suggest some reasons why sex tourism continues and why men continue to have sex with children. In Thailand, ideas about youth, childishness, beauty, and ethnicity have been intentionally collapsed into each other by the sex industry and then manipulated, commoditized, and mapped onto the borderline between adulthood and childhood. Bars and brothels catering to foreigners exploit these ambiguities and are called names like "The Classroom" or "Baby-A-Go-Go" and feature young women dressed as uniformed schoolgirls. Ads for such places make a point of emphasizing that the girls are "very young," and some bars advertise that they have virgins for sale; one researcher noted that a Bangkok bar had a sign outside reading, "5 fresh virgins, 4 down, one to go" (Gilkes 1993). Whether or not this is true is impossible to verify: there is always an element of macho bravado and a desire to shock at such places, but such advertisements deliberately promote the allure (and illusion) of the sexually available child.

Differences between adults and children are intentionally blurred, and Western men are sold the image of the childlike Thai woman, who is unsophisticated, subservient, undemanding, submissive, and pliable. Research with sex tourists visiting Thailand has shown that Western men praise the simplicity, loyalty, affection, and innocence of Thai women and are attracted to their smallness, large eyes, and lack of body hair—all qualities usually associated with children (O'Connell-Davidson 1995). One remark from a 50-year-old Australian sex tourist exemplifies this, "Dealing with Thai women is like dealing with 13-year-old school kids. You treat them just the same and they are quite happy" (qtd. in Montgomery 2001a:141). Other researchers have reported similar comments in which sex tourists eroticize the smallness and the childlike qualities of Thai women. Cleo Odzer (1990:180) interviewed a Thai bar owner who claimed he "sexually preferred Thai women because they didn't have body hair. . . . He also complained that *farang* [foreign] women were too big," while Julia O'Connell-Davidson (1995:55) was told that Thai women are "all like film stars or models, aren't they? It's the hair and the skin and they're almost always petite, you know, slim and small." What is striking about these comments is how similar the qualities these men are looking for in Thai women are to those that pedophiles find sexually attractive in children. Wilson and Cox's 1983 study of seventy-seven pedophiles found that the physical traits that they listed as attractive included good looks, smooth skin, hairlessness, and smallness, while the personality traits included innocence, openness, and curiosity. The very qualities that most appeal to men who buy sex, therefore, are Thai women's supposed childishness so that women who look like pubescent girls are admired and paid for, even by men who would not actively seek out sex with children.

Such an attitude creates a situation where men are willing to have sex with a child in a foreign context and see no difference between a child and an adult. Indeed, the clients themselves deny and obscure any boundary, or as O'Connell-Davidson points out (2000:62), in many cases, they simply do not care about the difference between a 14-year-old and a 24-year-old as long as "they 'fancy' the look of her." Others will claim an intrinsic difference between Western and Thai children, either physically or in terms of their sexual behavior. In doing so, they deny the child status to all children because they convince themselves that categories of child and adult are different in Thailand and do not see a Thai 16-year-old, or even possibly a 15-, 14-, or 13-year-old, as a child. The focus on childlike and youthful sexuality commands a price in which age, except to a small group of preferential abusers, is not the main issue. Women who appear very young may well be as sought after as much as those who really are young, but to a foreigner who is unable or does not want to guess ages, any distinction becomes meaningless.

Other sex tourists continually try to negotiate ideas of normality and naturalness. They are very hostile to Arab and nonwhite men, claiming that Thai women prefer, and are attracted to, their own white skin. Heterosexual men express disgust and distaste for gays (who they often describe, without irony, as pedophiles). As O'Connell-Davidson (1995:54) argues:

It is acceptable for them, as heterosexual men, to exploit the economic misfortunes of Thai women, but homosexual men who do the same thing to Thai men are "sick." It is acceptable for them to pay a bar fine and take a 16-year-old girl back to their hotel for the night, but they expressed a desire to do physical violence to men who pay pimps to take 14- or 15-year-old boys back to their rooms. Their own observations of paedophiles, "gays" and "perverts" form an endlessly diverting topic for conversation between themselves and serve as a platform from which to assert their own moral superiority.

Other men draw on racist understandings of "other" cultures, claiming that early or incestuous sexual behavior is the norm so that Western notions of childhood or sexuality have no meaning in these contexts. When I was undertaking research on child prostitution in Thailand in the 1990s, I was often told by men in the tourist bars that "girls are taught how to fuck by their mothers" and that "the first men they ever fuck are their fathers." These men would go on to tell me that I did not understand Thai culture and its uninhibited attitudes toward sexuality, that sex in Thailand was different, more natural, and so making comparisons with other places was untenable. Nor is this confined to Thailand, and similar comments were also made by sex tourists in the Dominican Republic where men said:

> "Everyone's at it, fathers do it with their daughters, brothers do it with their sisters, they don't care. They'll do it with anyone, they do it with everyone, they don't care who it is or how old they are. They're like animals. . . . By the time a girl is 10 years old, she's had more experience than . . . well, an American woman or an Irish woman won't never have that much experience in her whole life. Girls learn it's the way to keep a man happy. It's natural to them, it's a natural way to please men." (O'Connell-Davidson 1995:64)

The paradox is that the childlike innocence being sold is false, and it is a commodity for sale, much like any other. The vast majority of women working in Thailand's foreign red-light districts are over 18, and many already have children. The crackdown on child prostitution that occurred during the 1990s targeted these bars, and it became rare for any bar owner to risk having underage girls on the premises. However, the illusion of innocence and inexperience is still desired. Many bar girls, when telling their stories, emphasize that they are new recruits, forced into the professions by poverty and are not "really" prostitutes, knowing that this is what their clients want to hear (Walker and Ehrlich 1994). What many sex tourists fail to realize is that the artlessness, "freshness," and childlike innocence that they most admire in Thai prostitutes are entirely commercialized. These women are fulfilling a fantasy and doing what is expected of them, and it is for that, as much as for sex, for which they get paid.

Conclusion

With so many unknowns and so much more research needed, child sex tourism is a difficult subject to write about or understand. Perhaps the only conclusion that can be drawn is that there are still large gaps in our knowledge and there are areas that need greater research and reflection. First, it is still unclear which men go to Thailand and other countries to buy sex from children, why they do so, and what might change their behavior. Extraterritorial legislation is in place in many countries, but its impact, beyond a small number of prosecutions, has not been examined. Research is needed on whether this legislation has changed the behavior of actual or potential abusers and whether they are deterred from buying sex with children, or only deterred from doing so in certain countries. There are suggestions that the fear of prosecution has meant that the problem of men seeking to buy sex from children has shifted geographically and that they are now traveling to Cambodia or Vietnam, where law enforcement is more lax. Child prostitution still remains a concern within Thailand, however, and a brief look at Thailand's English-language newspapers shows that men are still arrested for buying sex from children with some frequency (Montgomery 2010). Yet, the fear of prosecution may not deter men who do not actively seek out sex with children and do not see themselves as child abusers. The majority of men who have sex with children are not "preferential pedophiles" but are men who are unconcerned about actual age and do not differentiate between those who look very young and those who actually are very young.

Second, child pornography and its links to sex tourism, while beyond the scope of this chapter, is also a serious problem that needs examination. There are suggestions that men are likely to film themselves having sex with children and that while, until recently, such images were more likely to be produced noncommercially, shared between sexual abusers, and shown to their child victims (O'Connell-Davidson 2005), in the last 10 years, there has been an increase in commercially available child abuse images, particularly involving teenagers who may or may not be over the age of 18. There has been very little work done on where this abuse is being filmed, sold, and shared, and who watches it and the impacts this might have on men's travel decisions.

There will always be men who are sexually attracted to young children and who will go to considerable lengths to fulfill their fantasies, but these might not be the most prolific users of child prostitution. It is important to acknowledge this and also to examine and understand that there are greater numbers of men who do have sex with children without necessarily being attracted to children. In this chapter I have explored why this might occur and argued that as long as the sex tourism industry eroticizes and commercializes the attractions of childlike women, and encourages men to value and pay for sex with women who present themselves as young, innocent, and childlike, the sexual abuse of children will continue and the sexual demand for both childlike and/or actual children will not go away.

Source: For a more detailed discussion, see "Buying Innocence/Child-Sex Tourism in Thailand," *Third World Quarterly* 29(5): 903–917, 2008.

References Cited

Bishop, Ryan, and Lillian Robinson. 1998. *Night Marker: Sexual Cultures and the Thai Economic Miracle*. New York: Routledge.

Black Shadow. 1949. *Dream Lover: The Book for Men Only*. Bangkok: Vitayakorn.

Boonchalaksi, Wathinee, and Philip Guest. 1994. *Prostitution in Thailand*. Bangkok: Mahidol University, Institute for Population and Social Research.

Bureau of Democracy, Human Rights, and Labor. 2009. "Human Rights Report: Thailand. Washington: 2008 Country Reports on Human Rights Practices." http://www.state.gov/g/drl/rls/hrrpt/2008/eap/119058.htm (accessed November 1 2016).

Crick, Malcolm. 1989. "Representations of International Tourism in the Social Sciences: Sun, Sex, Sights, Savings and Servility." *Annual Review of Anthropology* 18:307–344

ECPAT. 1993. *Report on International Consultation*. Bangkok: ECPAT.

ECTWT. 1990. *Caught in Modern Slavery: Tourism and Child Prostitution in Asia*. Bangkok: ECTWT.

Ennew, Judith. 1986. *The Sexual Exploitation of Children*. Cambridge: Polity Press.

———. 2008. "The Exploitation of Children in Prostitution. Thematic Paper for the World Congress III against the Sexual Exploitation of Children and Adolescents, Rio de Janeiro, Brazil, November 2008." http://www.ecpat.net/WorldCongressIII/PDF/Publications/Prostitution_of_Children/Thematic_Paper_Prostitution_ENG.pdf (accessed November 1, 2016).

Finkelhor, David, and Sharon Araji. 1986. *A Source Book on Child Sexual Abuse*. London: Sage.

Fordham, Graham. 2005. *A New Look at Thai AIDS: Perspectives from the Margin*. Oxford: Berghahn.

Fox, Maurice. 1960. *Problems of Prostitution in Thailand*. Bangkok: Department of Public Welfare.

Gilkes, Michelle. 1993. "Prostitution in Thailand," BA diss. Long Island University.

Kempadoo, Kamala, Jyoti Sanghera, and Bandana Pattanaik. 2005. *Trafficking and Prostitution Reconsidered: New Perspectives on Migration, Sex Work, and Human Rights*. Boulder: Paradigm.

League of Nations. 1933. *Report of the Council by the Commission into the Traffic in Women and Children in the East*. Geneva: League of Nations.

Montgomery, Heather. 2001a. *Modern Babylon? Prostituting Children in Thailand*. Berghahn: Oxford.

———. 2001b. "Child Sex Tourists: Myths and Realities," in *Tourism and the Less Developed World. Issues and Case Studies,* 2nd ed., ed. David Harrison, pp. 191–202. Wallingford: CABI.

———. 2008. "Buying Innocence: Child Sex Tourists in Thailand." *Third World Quarterly* 29:903–917.

———. 2010. "Child Sex Tourism: Is Extra-Territorial Legislation the Answer?" in *Tourism and Crime*, eds. David Botterill and Trevor Jones, pp. 69–84. Oxford: Goodfellow Publishing.

Muecke, Marjorie. 1992. "Mother Sold Food, Daughter Sells Her Body—The Cultural Continuity of Prostitution." *Social Science and Medicine* 35:891–901.

Muntabhorn, Vitit. 1992. *Sale of Children*. New York: United Nations.

Nagel, Joane. 2003. *Race, Ethnicity, and Sexuality: Intimate Intersections, Forbidden Frontiers*. Oxford: Oxford University Press.

O'Connell-Davidson, Julia. 1995. "British Sex Tourists in Thailand," in *(Hetero)sexual Politics*, eds. Mary Maynard and June Purvis, pp. 42–64. London: Taylor and Francis.

———. 2000. "Sex Tourism and Child Prostitution," in *Tourism and Sex: Culture, Commerce and Coercion*, eds. Stephen Clift and Simon Carter, pp. 54–73. London: Pinter.

———. 2005. *Children in the Global Sex Trade*. Cambridge: Polity Press.

Odzer, Cleo. 1990. "Patpong Prostitution: Its Relationship To, and Effect On, the Position of Women in Thai society," PhD diss. New School for Social Research.

Oppermann, Martin. 1998. "Who Exploits Whom and Who Benefits?" in *Sex Tourism and Prostitution: Aspects of Leisure, Recreation, and Work*, ed. Martin Oppermann, pp. 153–159. New York: Cognizant Communication.

Sánchez Taylor, Jacqueline, and Julia O'Connell-Davidson. 2005. "Travel and Taboo: Heterosexual Sex Tourism to the Caribbean," in *Regulating Sex: The Politics of Intimacy and Identity*, eds. Elizabeth Bernstein and Laura Schaffner, pp. 83–100. New York: Routledge.

Sittitrai, Werasit, and Tim Brown. 1994. *The Impact of HIV on Children in Thailand*. Bangkok: Thai Red Cross Society.

ten Brummelhuis, Hans. 1993. "Do We Need a Thai Theory of Prostitution?" Paper presented at the Fifth International Conference on Thai Studies, SOAS, London.

Wilson, Glenn, and Cox, David. 1983. *The Child Lovers: A Study of Paedophiles in Society*. London and Boston: Peter Owen.

Walker, Dave, and Richard Ehrlich. 1994. *Hello My Big, Big Honey: Love Letters to Bangkok Bar Girls and their Revealing Interviews*. Bangkok: White Lotus.

23

Rethinking Volunteer Tourism?

Elizabeth Garland

In the years when I was teaching at a liberal arts college, it seemed that my students were always about to head off to build a library in Ghana, had just returned from volunteering at an orphanage in South Africa, or were busy raising money for a water project in Ethiopia. As an anthropologist specializing in African environment and development issues, I was delighted to see young people interested in a part of the world that means so much to me, but I also became increasingly troubled by the sense that working firsthand on African poverty had become a kind of credential for these (mostly American, mostly privileged) students, a box to be checked off in their preparation for success within the global economy. My lack of generosity toward them perhaps derived from the fact that so few students involved with Africa turned up in my courses on African culture and history. Sometimes volunteering inspires students to go on to take courses in the area in which they will be working, but often it does not, and few seemed to regard the kind of broad-based, contextual knowledge that I consider crucial to my own understanding of poverty (and everything else) on the continent to be a prerequisite before they undertook work there.

In this chapter I explore the social and political implications of the phenomenon increasingly referred to as volunteer tourism—the practice in which students like the ones from my college travel in order to volunteer in places like Ghana and South Africa. I begin by describing the rise and scope of the global volunteer tourism industry, and then discuss some of its pros and cons. I conclude by asking how volunteer tourism might be done better and make some specific recommendations for those involved with developing volunteer tourism programs and for teachers charged with advising or selecting students who wish to volunteer abroad. In the course of doing so, I hope that students reading this will reflect on their own motivations and practice.

The Rise of the Volunteer Tourism Industry

Traveling to other, poorer societies in order to help people is hardly a new phenomenon. Today's "voluntourists" stand on the shoulders of generations of missionaries, colonial bureaucrats, and development workers. The idea that one might pay money to volunteer overseas, however, is a relatively recent development. The concept was pioneered in the 1970s by the Earthwatch Institute, but so-called voluntouring did not really catch on at a significant scale until the 1990s, when the institution of the British gap year exploded onto the scene. Geared to young, university-bound people in the gap between high school and college, the idea of a gap year is for students to take some time off, mature a bit, see the world, and do something useful that will both "give something back" and distinguish them from their peers in their eventual careers and lives. As early as the 1980s, the desires of Western young people to travel for a while before settling down into adulthood had already translated into a consolidated backpacker niche within the international tourism industry (Huxley 2003; Wheeler and Wheeler 2005). What happened in the 1990s was that tour companies began to harness the spirit of off-the-beaten-path adventure associated with backpacking and to package and market products that promised similar experiences, in terms that sounded safe and educational enough to appeal to parents. Today, most gap-year participants are middle- and upper-middle-class British and Australian 18–20-year-olds, whose trips are financed primarily by their parents (Simpson 2004; Heath 2007). Today's gap-year students are catered to by dozens of for-profit companies, offering a wide range of more or less chaperoned, structured international experiences. A typical mid-sized company is the UK-based Africa/Asia/Americas Venture (www.aventure.co.uk), which describes itself with the slogan "Total Adventure with a Purpose." Many gap year programs take place in developing countries, and very often include a service or volunteer component.

From the perspective of the countries playing host to such programs, the rapid expansion in the 1990s of Western young people interested in volunteering overseas dovetailed perfectly with their own changed political-economic circumstances due to global neoliberal reform. As states undergoing macroeconomic "adjustment" in the late 1980s and 1990s devalued their currencies and scaled back government support for health care, education, and infrastructure, absolute living standards across the developing world deteriorated precipitously for those at the lower ends of the socioeconomic spectrum. The poor objectively got poorer during this time, and their "neediness" became more apparent to the Western gaze. The neoliberal retreat of the state also enabled an explosion in nongovernmental organizations globally, providing a ready institutional framework for international volunteering that had not existed previously. The volunteers were eager to help, the NGOs happy for the infusion of free labor and resources, the tour operators happy to profit by connecting the two, and the volunteer tourism industry was born, quickly growing well beyond the gap year to carve out a robust chunk of the broader tourist market in places like Africa, India, Southeast Asia, and Latin America. Today, tourists of all ages pay to volunteer in poor countries, with parents sometimes bringing their children with them, as entire families spend their holidays working at orphanages, building latrines or schools, or working on environmental cleanup projects. According to a 2006 survey conducted by the Travel Industry Association of America, 24 percent of Americans surveyed reported interest in taking a volunteer or service-based vacation (eTN 2006).

The Potential and Drawbacks of Volunteer Tourism

The scholarly literature on volunteer tourism is broadly divided between authors who are hopeful about the phenomenon and those critical of the industry. Typical in the first camp is Stephen Wearing, whose book, *Vol-*

Volunteers help rebuild a school destroyed by an earthquake in Trishuli, Nepal. (Photo by Mihai Speteanu/Shutterstock.com)

unteer Tourism: Experiences That Make a Difference (2001), argues that volunteer tourism represents a more self-conscious, meaningful, and sustainable form of tourist practice, one in which the emphasis is on altruism and giving back, rather than on consumption and profit making. For sustainable and ethical tourism advocates, volunteer tourism appears to be an exciting new means of harnessing the resource flows that underpin the tourism industry more generally—flows of disposable time and money in particular—in order to benefit the earth and the world's disadvantaged people. Volunteer tourism, in this view, is a basically pain-free mechanism for redistributing global resources, one that betters the world, while simultaneously fulfilling the desires of tourists and generating revenue for tour operators. Advocates note that volunteer projects bring development benefits to peoples and regions that are unlikely to/would likely not receive them otherwise, and positive claims are often also made for the powerful effects the practice has on the tourists who participate in it. Both industry and scholarly advocates contend that voluntouring expands participants' cross-cultural awareness and sensitivity and promotes transnational connection and understanding in the global era (e.g., Wearing 2001; Palacios 2010).

In contrast, those coming from a more skeptical perspective have argued that volunteer tourism programs build upon and reinforce existing inequalities, preconceptions, and stereotypes (e.g., Huxley 2003; Simpson 2004; Heath 2007; Raymond and Hall 2008). The industry is, after all, premised on the idea that one person's impoverishment or environmental degradation is another's opportunity for adventure and personal growth, rendering the structural inequities that characterize many host/guest encounters a fundamental and necessary feature of this sort of tourism. Indeed, although volunteer tourism programs are ostensibly about addressing the problems of socioeconomically disadvantaged communities, publicity advertising them often emphasizes the benefits—including the economic benefits—the programs bring to the tourists, rather than to their hosts (Heath 2007). Volunteer in Africa's website asks, for example:

> Are you looking for ways to make a difference while gaining relevant work experience to add to your resume? Do you want to learn new skills? Do you want to explore potential career areas? You can accomplish all of this, and more, by becoming a volunteer in Africa! Doing volunteer work in Africa can be one of the most rewarding and best investments you can make with your time. (Volunteer in Africa 2012)

As rhetoric like this makes clear, while poor people may be helped by such programs, addressing the broader inequalities between them and the Western volunteers is not a primary objective of the industry. On the contrary, these programs offer volunteers a means to improve their own marketability and socioeconomic power, which potentially increases rather than diminishes the inequality between them and those they set out to aid.

The industry's contention that volunteer touring promotes meaningful cross-cultural understanding also largely fails to bear up to scrutiny. Rather than emphasizing the importance of learning about other cultures, its discourse downplays the challenges of navigating cultural differences, typically promising positive, unproblematic cross-cultural encounters. Advertising materials assure tourists that they will be welcomed with open arms by their hosts, who are depicted in simple, stereotypic terms as needy cultural others, generic poor people eager and grateful for the assistance of benevolent Westerners (Huxley 2003; Simpson 2004). Such rhetoric is particularly explicit in volunteer programs in Africa, where ubiquitous images of poverty, disease, and suffering children (particularly AIDS orphans, which became almost talismanic of the industry) have positioned the region as a global symbol of undifferentiated need. Programs rarely provide tourists with the background information about underlying causes and local complexities necessary to get beyond such stereotypes, and interviews with returned volunteers show that most return home with their preexisting beliefs confirmed rather than challenged (Huxley 2003; Simpson 2004). Simpson (2004) reports that, in the absence of information on the origins and nature of global inequalities, volunteers often employ a kind of "lotto logic" to explain the poverty they encounter on their travels, concluding that some people are poor, and others wealthy, by simple luck of the draw. Another theme frequently articulated by volunteers is the "dignity-in-poverty" of the poor people they have met while abroad: "They're so happy, in spite of having nothing!" As Mathers (2010) has argued, this sort of bland, humanist appreciation of people living in poverty obscures and depoliticizes the historical circumstances that produced their poverty. In lieu of engaging with the histories and complexities of local contexts, volunteers tend instead to focus on the lessons they have learned about themselves—their own identities and senses of self-worth shored up through their encounter with needy cultural others. The effect is particularly acute in Africa, where an abundance of well-worn colonial and missionary— and, of late, celebrity—narratives provide Western tourists with vivid scripts for their own fantasy roles in the continent's salvation (Mathers 2010).

The actual effects that volunteer tourism programs have had on the sites where they are run, in Africa and elsewhere, have not yet been seriously studied by tourism scholars. What limited research has been done suggests that the impacts are far less positive than often asserted. Since the vast majority of volunteers are effectively unskilled with respect to the tasks they end up performing—most often as manual construction laborers or child care providers—they risk competing with local unskilled workers for the jobs in question, driving down local wages and taking away work from people who are typically among the poorest members of their societies (Richter 2010). Many critics have also argued that volunteer-driven development projects foster dependency among beneficiary populations and undermine a sense of local ownership, since they are implemented by outsiders rather than by the local population itself (Huxley 2003; Burns and Barrie 2005; Raymond and Hall 2008; McGehee and Andereck 2009; Palacios 2010). To this I would add that the regular arrival of wealthy, Western volunteers in poor, non-Western communities seems likely to reinforce people's sense of relative poverty and marginality, heightening their consciousness of their place in an unequal world system in which some are able to give aid and others are resigned to roles as aid-recipients. Such inequities can only be made more glaring by the fact that many volunteer tourists are young, and often female, and yet possess the kind of global mobility to which many disaffected, underemployed youth throughout the developing world aspire.

Harms can arise from volunteer tourism, as well, as a result of the industry's insensitivity to the cultural norms and priorities—and even the emotional and medical needs—of the populations it targets. Projects that focus on youth education through school building or English language instruction may not reflect the priorities that older members of the society possess, such as land acquisition or livestock holding. Resources lavished on children and young adults can also undermine the influence of elders as valued leaders in the community (Burns and Barrie 2005). Similarly, programs emphasizing women's and girls' empowerment may run up against deeply engrained gender norms, and yet the short-term, shallow structure of the tourism experience seldom allows volunteers to gain any sort of nuanced sense of the cultural stakes of the social changes they are promoting. Western cultural norms are often assumed to be universal and are promoted as unproblematically desirable (Huxley 2003; Simpson 2004; Raymond and Hall 2008).

The temporary nature of most volunteer tourism programs poses particular problems in the context of the thriving AIDS orphan tourism industry. Research from South Africa has shown that the regular arrival and departure of short-term foreign volunteers in orphanages actively contributes to the attachment difficulties of these already vulnerable children. As one social worker notes, "children in orphanages tend to approach all adults with the same level of sociability and affection, often clinging to caregivers, even those encountered for the first time only moments before" (Richter 2010:para 16). Volunteer tourists are able to connect quickly with such children, and many describe being moved by the intensity and intimacy of the bonds they form with them. When they leave, a few weeks or months later, however, "the children they leave behind have experienced another abandonment to the detriment of their short- and long-term emotional and social development" (Richter 2010:para 18). An additional concern is that African children cared for by a succession of Western strangers may over time come to associate all good things with foreigners, rather than with members of their own societies, posing challenges for their social integration and self-esteem over the longer term.

Finally, volunteer tourism programs can also pose challenges for the governments of the countries in which they take place. While a steady stream of tourists willing to undertake basic development work reduces pressure on taxed government social welfare and development agencies, it also arguably undermines, if not the capacity of these agencies to provide such services, then at the least the public rationale mandating that they do so. In this way, volunteer tourism can be said to weaken the state institutions of poor countries, posing problems for sustainability and governance in the longer term. Further, because volunteer tourists often travel and reside outside the bounds of formal tourism industries, staying in villages rather than hotels, and eating in local homes or establishments rather than in tourist restaurants, states capture less revenue from them than they do from more typical international tourists and have few ways to plan and manage their impact within the national tourism sector. Citing concerns about both the economic costs and undesired social impacts associated with increased international volunteering, the Government of Tanzania established a special visa category for volunteers, charging them a very high fee and demanding resumes and other documentation before granting them work permits, in the hopes of reducing their numbers, dissuading unskilled volunteers from coming, and more effectively monitoring and capturing revenue from those that do.

Toward More Responsible Volunteer Tourism

What this brief review suggests is that, in spite of its positive potential and rapidly growing popularity, volunteer tourism is associated with significant negative consequences for both host populations and, at least in some regards, tourists themselves. There are, of course, powerful political-economic and ideological forces that have molded the industry into its current form, and given the profitability of the formula, its basic structure is not likely to be reformed easily. Still, there does seem to be clear room for improvement in the way volunteer tourism is currently being practiced and, hence, a role for anthropologists to play in pushing the industry in a better direction. By way of conclusion, I highlight below three of the core issues, and point to ways these might begin to be ameliorated.

I would suggest that the most fundamental problem with volunteer tourism is simply the nature of the tourist desire to volunteer in a poor country in the first place. Cross thoughts of building resumes and gaining preprofessional credentials through international slumming are clearly self-serving and, I would argue, morally suspect. But even if we accept that most international volunteers are primarily motivated less by self-interest than by a genuine desire to learn about other places and do something to atone for and address global inequalities, the structural inequities of the industry remain problematic. The basic assumption by volunteers that they are qualified to work on the problems of people they have never met and know little about, simply by virtue of their own national, racial, or class backgrounds, reflects an inherent presumption of superiority on the part of the tourists that forecloses meaningful equality between them and their "hosts" from the outset. Instead of fostering connections between equals, in which assistance and learning are anticipated to flow in both directions, most volunteer tourism encounters are premised on the expectation of a more or less one-way trans-action (build their school, dig their latrine, take care of their orphans) that distances volunteers from the people with whom they come into contact. That tourists accumulate colorful stories and imagery from these people along the way may create an illusion of cross-cultural intimacy but does little to close this structural gap.

For volunteer tourism to move closer to its ideal as a vehicle for truly meaningful cross-cultural learning and connection, volunteer tourists need to start from a position not of superiority but rather of humility and openness. A good first step in this direction would be for institutions sponsoring such pro-grams to frame volunteering less as an occasion to "give something back"—the current industry refrain—than an opportunity to get to know a new part of the world and to learn how people with different cultural perspectives and material resources live. Since systemic poverty and other intractable prob-lems are virtually never solved through the efforts of short-term volunteers, volunteer programs should be recast as a means for volunteers to learn how such problems came to be the way they are and how local people envision and hope for their eventual resolution. Armed with such knowledge, volun-teers would then be well-equipped to have a more far-reaching impact on the problems that concern them, should they desire to continue working on them once they return home.

Reframing volunteering primarily as an opportunity for learning, rather than development work, brings me to the second big problem with much cur-rent volunteer tourism, namely, that it is so frequently carried out by people with an almost total lack of prior knowledge about the places they wish to go or the lives of the people they seek to assist. Ignorance of such things dimin-ishes volunteers' understanding of what is happening around them while they are in the field, undermines their ability to appreciate and respect local cul-tural mores and institutions, and increases the likelihood that they will retreat into their own, preexisting belief systems about human behaviors and motiva-tions. To counter such tendencies, programs that sponsor volunteer tourism ventures, and the institutions and individuals that guide potential volunteers toward them, should emphasize the importance of preparation—including language training—prior to travel and should provide adequate orientation once in country. Colleges and professors should require relevant coursework of students seeking their endorsement to go on volunteer programs and should encourage returned student volunteers to combine the firsthand knowledge they have gained with further exploration of the contexts they have visited through coursework and independent reading and research.

Finally, to address concerns about the impact of volunteer tourism proj-ects on local communities and host countries, sponsoring organizations—

including colleges and NGOs, as well as for-profit tourism agencies—need to build an awareness of the importance of local ownership, cultural appropriateness, and sustainability into their programs from the outset. Efforts should be made to respect and, where possible, work through host country governments and civil society organizations, coordinating volunteer projects with local agencies in ways that support, rather than undermine, their capacities and missions. In general, volunteer programs should fit with local and national priorities, and if volunteers do not have skills that would make them directly beneficial to these objectives, their energies should be redirected elsewhere, for example toward fundraising within their own countries in support of an NGO in the country in question.

Source: Adapted from "How Should Anthropologists Be Thinking about Volunteer Tourism?" *Practicing Anthropology* 34(3): 5–9, 2012. Used with permission of the author and the Society for Applied Anthropology.

References Cited

Burns, Peter M., and Simone Barrie. 2005. "Race, Space and 'Our Own Piece of Africa': Doing Good in Luphisi Village?" *Journal of Sustainable Tourism* 13(5): 468–485.

eTN. 2006. "Voice of the Traveler Survey." http://www.travelindustrydeals.com/news/1334 (accessed February 12, 2012).

Heath, Sue. 2007. "Widening the Gap: Pre-university Gap Years and the 'Economy of Experience.'" *British Journal of Sociology of Education* 28(1): 89–103.

Huxley, L. 2003. "Western Backpackers and the Global Experience: An Exploration of Young People's Interaction with Local Cultures." *Tourism, Culture and Communication* 5(1): 37–44.

Mathers, Kathryn. 2010. *Travel, Humanitarianism, and Becoming American in Africa.* New York: Palgrave MacMillan.

McGehee, Nancy Gard, and Kathleen Andereck. 2009. "Volunteer Tourism and the 'Voluntoured': The Case of Tijuana, Mexico." *Journal of Sustainable Tourism* 17(1): 30–51.

Palacios, Carlos M. 2010. "Volunteer Tourism, Development and Education in a Postcolonial World: Conceiving Global Connections beyond Aid." *Journal of Sustainable Tourism* 18(7): 861–878.

Raymond, Eliza Marguerite, and C. Michael Hall. 2008. "The Development of Cross-Cultural (Mis)Understanding Through Volunteer Tourism." *Journal of Sustainable Tourism* 16(5): 530–543.

Richter, Linda. 2010. "Inside the Thriving Industry of AIDS Orphan Tourism." *HSRC Review* 8(2). http://www.hsrc.ac.za/HSRC_Review_Article-195.phtml (accessed February 13, 2012).

Simpson, Kate. 2004. "'Doing Development': The Gap Year, Volunteer Tourists and a Popular Practice of Development." *Journal of International Development* 16(5): 681–692.

Volunteer in Africa. 2012. "Benefits of Volunteer Work in Africa." http://www.volunteeringinafrica.org/workbenefits.htm (accessed January 30, 2012).

Wearing, Stephen. 2001. *Volunteer Tourism: Experiences that Make a Difference.* Sydney: CABI Publishing.

Wheeler, Tony, and Maureen Wheeler. 2005. *Once While Traveling: The Lonely Planet Story.* Clarendon, VT: Periplus Editions.

24

Go Global, Think Local: Ethical Issues in Student Travel

Adam Kaul, with Seung Hwan Kim

In this final section in this edition of *Tourists & Tourism*, we point out some ethical challenges that tourism presents the traveler and suggest a few potential solutions (although, given the complexity of tourism, we also recognize that often there are no clear-cut answers). Some forms of travel are obviously problematic and should be resoundingly condemned. Examples include the kind of sex tourism described in this volume, "slum tours," resorts and cruises that are harmful to the environment, or the ways in which some "dark tourists" can gawk voyeuristically at human suffering. But even seemingly benign forms of travel raise all sorts of ethical questions. The concerns and approaches we raise in this chapter are applicable to all forms of travel, but we are particularly interested in reaching out to students here. In doing so, we focus specifically on educational study-abroad tours and service-learning trips.

I was inspired to write this essay after several conversations with the Assistant Director for International Student Life at Augustana College, Seung Hwan (Danny) Kim. Danny and I share an interest in the critical study of tourism and service-learning, but for different reasons. I find tourism to be a fascinating and powerful globalizing process that leads to multitudes of partial, precarious, and confusing intercultural interactions. Tourist sites are also places of intense cultural production and creativity. New adaptations, traditions, norms, and behaviors are born as a result of these interactions. Since culture is the core subject matter of our discipline, these are exciting places to mine anthropologically. There are important power dynamics at play in tourist settings, too, that beg to be exposed and analyzed. To use Anna Tsing's analogy about globalization, tourism cuts new channels into the global landscape, making those who control the new flows wealthier and more powerful, while those who are cut off by them are rendered less powerful or even exploited. When we consider the fact that tourism is one of the world's largest industries, it becomes clear that these new channels cut into the global landscape are powerful indeed. For that reason, the study of tourists and tourism is not only fascinating on an intellectual level, it is vitally important if we hope to advocate for those who live and work in these places. As social scientists, we have a moral obligation to tell their stories.

When we began to discuss our mutual interest in tourism and travel, I quickly realized that Danny's understandings and critiques are far more personal because he grew up hosting groups of North American and Asian high school students who were on service-learning trips to Paraguay where his missionary parents ran a Christian school. As a child, Danny enjoyed these group visits. The students often carried out short projects like teaching local children a few English words and phrases for a week before going home. Sometimes they entertained the children with theater or dance routines, which was a lot of fun. But as he got older he began to understand things a little differently. He started seeing that the logistical work that his parents had to do to host the groups was very time-consuming. He also began to realize that instead of helping out the children at the school, the service-learning projects often distracted them from their regular coursework. Meanwhile, their new English words and phrases were soon forgotten. Worse, he realized, these "voluntourists" were spending huge amounts of money on airfare, lodging, and food. It dawned on him that if a single group simply pooled their travel money and sent it to the school instead, his parents would be able to hire an additional teacher for an entire year. Who was serving who? he began to wonder.

Danny and I, somewhat nervously, decided to give a presentation about all of this at Augustana College. In my experience having had *critical* conversations about tourism and travel with students, colleagues, and administrators for many years, I knew what kinds of reactions to expect: shock, anger, and frustration. Study abroad and service-learning have become important markers of the college experience, and are often valorized as inherently righteous practices that ought not to be questioned. However, it is problematic to assume that study-abroad and service-learning abroad either have no impact on local people and places or they are solely positive. Part of the problem stems from the assumption that this kind of educational travel is distinct from tourism. I have heard students, professors, and others forcefully claim that they are not engaging in "mere tourism," which is assumed to be a superficial practice compared to supposedly deeper experiences on an educational trip abroad. Other words like "traveler" are used liberally and actively taught in order to make the contrast as clear as possible. Proponents of this idea assume that tourists learn nothing meaningful about the places they travel to and are not interested in doing so. At the same time, it is assumed that students on an educational tour have more "purpose" and will be radically and positively transformed by their experience. But isn't it the case that holidays can be deeply meaningful and transformative for some, and conversely isn't it also true that some students studying abroad spend less time learning about the places they visit and more time at the nearest McDonald's, on social media, in clubs, and worried about the internal social dynamics of the tour group? Attempting to distinguish ourselves from "mere tourists" only masks the problems that travel can create. In fact, it has the potential to quickly lead to a specific kind of privilege—a willful blindness to tourism's environmental, economic, and social impacts. Of course, tourism can be positive, but we should always ask "for whom?" Should we assume that all travel naturally expands the traveler's worldview and increases his or her intercultural competency? Isn't it entirely possible that traveling abroad might even do the opposite and lead to *more* ethnocentrism rather than developing greater sensitivity for cultural differences? Should we assume that because tourists spend money that tourism naturally benefits local communities? Isn't it the case that money, thoughtlessly spent in a tourist destination, might never reach local people at all? These are uncomfortable questions for students, faculty, administrators, and vacationers to hear, but they must be asked if we wish to travel responsibly. Happily, Danny and I found that the message of our presentation to our colleagues and our students was well received. We have even noted a recent shift in the conversation about the ethics of student travel on our campus, driven as much by students themselves who sincerely want to do the right thing. This is encouraging, but there is much more work to be done.

What do we need to think about in order to increase the positive impacts of tourism and empower local people who live in tourist destinations, and how can we minimize the negative impacts? Following Sharon Gmelch's point in her chapter "Why Tourism Matters," we believe it is critical to begin any discussion of ethical travel by recognizing a simple and powerful truth: tourism has major impacts on local people and places. Some consequences of tourism development can be positive while many are negative. As we have seen in this volume though, it is not always obvious when tourism development is good or bad. While there are some larger patterns, every local circumstance is unique, which, importantly, requires us as travelers to *sharpen* our critical thinking and our sense of ethics when we travel. This requires us to fight the more common instinct to be *freer* from a sense of ethics while on holiday (to "let your hair down and go wild"). We argue here that you will be able to relax far more if you know that you are trying to minimize the negative impact of your own travel by taking some careful steps before, during, and afterwards.

Quick Tips for Planning Your Next Trip Abroad

1. First, stop thinking about labels like "tourist" versus "traveler." Pretending you are morally superior to "tourists" only masks your privilege.

2. Critically examine who is most transformed by service-learning abroad.

3. Never set aside your ethics, social justice, or environmental consciousness. ("Go global, think local!")

   • Beforehand: learn about your historical-cultural relationship with the destination.

   • When booking hotels, tours, etc., do your research in order to make positive impacts, not negative ones. Go through organizations like www.ResponsibleTourism.org or http://www.tourismconcern.org.uk to identify businesses that will not exploit local people or the environment.

   • Once you arrive, travel with respect. Always be aware of your privilege and your ethnocentrism. Err on the side of listening and learning from local people instead of judging them or thinking you have something to teach.

   • When you return: apply lessons from your international experience to your own community and to your own life. Be more open to difference. Get more involved in service projects in your own backyard.

1. Stop worrying about your status as a tourist, and start thinking about ethics.   The word "tourist" has become a disparaging term equated with superficiality, but this usually reflects the traveler's own concern. People who live in places that are partly or wholly dependent on tourism usually have far more complicated views of tourists and tourism. Often, it is a love–hate relationship in which "bad" tourists are despised but "good" tourists are well liked and encouraged to come back. How can we become the "good" tourists?

The first and most important step is to stop pretending there is some sort of difference between "tourism" and other types of travel (e.g., study abroad, international service trips, etc.). The denial of one's status as a "tourist" is actually a denial of various forms of privilege, especially economic privilege. You cannot act ethically in an unequal power relationship until you recognize and acknowledge the inequality in the first place. Instead of worrying about labels, have a serious discussion (internally and with others) about what constitutes *ethical* travel and *ethical* tourism. When we *pretend* we are somehow different from tourists and therefore think we are morally or intellectually superior, we are simply in denial. And denial allows us to think erroneously that educational tourism does not have potential negative impacts on local places. That is absurd and dangerous. The truth is that locals will very likely see you as a tourist, especially if you are traveling in a group. Think about how many students in study-abroad programs stay in hotels, travel by bus in large groups led by tour guides, and then descend upon stores or restaurants *en masse*. Functionally it is the same as any other coach tour. Your educational motives might not matter to the people with whom you interact. Your impacts (both positive and negative) will be the same no matter what you call yourself.

2. Get real about who is transformed by international "voluntourism" (i.e., service-learning abroad).   Recognize that in most instances voluntourism is a learning experience for you rather than a transformative event for the local population. The reality is that local hosts are often required to do a lot of work to help you carry out your service project. Simultaneously, you will have expended vast resources to personally travel there when you could have sent money to a local NGO instead and made a greater impact. Does this mean that you should avoid participating in international service projects? Of course not. But you, your classmates, and your faculty leaders must think critically about what is really happening and plan the experience carefully in order to do the most good and the least harm. Ask yourself honestly: who is being empowered and transformed? Who is learning the most from whom? Who is gaining or losing social and economic capital? Who is doing the work to make your experience happen?

An acquaintance in New Orleans once told me how after Hurricane Katrina destroyed parts of the city, church groups from around the country descended on the city to help clean up and rebuild. Commonly, the groups had brightly colored t-shirts made with their organization's name printed on them. She said locals called them "tropical fish" because they swarmed around New Orleans like brightly colored schools of fish. And, she said, they left not having transformed New Orleans in any significant way but were instead transformed themselves by their own exposure to the complexity of the problems there. In this sense, we should follow the advice of Daniela Papi in her TED Talk about volunteer travel (https://www.youtube.com/watch?v=oYWl6Wz2NB8): stop thinking of it as "service-learning" and instead think about it as "learning how to serve."

Traveling to witness the vast complexities of poverty firsthand can be a good and powerful thing, but only if it later leads to positive, productive, and long-term action when you return home. Start by acknowledging that your trip was a hands-on learning experience for you rather than a chance to teach something to local people. Again, denying that one's incredibly brief interaction during the travel experience was at best neutral and sometimes even burdensome for local people only reinscribes unequal power relationships. Worse, it sometimes convinces the idealistic volunteer-traveler that they somehow helped solve a complex international problem. This can lead to what has been described as "guilt-alleviation," which often results in a combination of entitlement and inaction "back home." Much worse than that, as Garland discusses in her chapter "How Should Anthropologists Be Thinking about Volunteer Tourism?" voluntourism can sometimes even smack of paternalistic neocolonialism and/or a racialized "white savior complex."

Apply your new knowledge to local issues of poverty, or find a way to create long-term support for an international cause that works in the place you visited. The latter often means sending money to NGOs and local workers abroad—not as exciting perhaps as going there yourself, but often far more effective.

3. Get informed about the impacts and ethics of travel in general. As always, with knowledge comes responsibility. Once you have realized the social, environmental, and economic impacts of tourism from reading a book like *Tourists and Tourism*, it is on you to travel more ethically. Do your research ahead of time just like you would for any college assignment and, as with any college assignment, make sure your sources are credible. Be skeptical of your favorite guidebook. They are sometimes filled with erroneous or outdated facts and descriptions and can repeat stereotypes about local people and places. Verify descriptions by consulting multiple books as well as locally produced resources (e.g., websites) whenever possible. Look up scholarly sources about the history and culture of the destination from the books and databases in your library. Learn about the historic relationship between the place you are traveling to and your own national origin, since it will very likely impact your relationship with local people. Learn about local culture(s) before you arrive, and in all intercultural interactions be aware of your ethnocentrism and assumptions. As much as possible, be open to learning about new customs, behaviors, and foods instead of judging them. *Listen* to other cultural perspectives rather than *telling* others about how things are done "back home." When you feel the urge to talk about home when traveling, just remember: tourism workers and residents in and around tourist destinations have very likely interacted with many of your predecessors. They might know more about you than you think! Instead of talking about yourself, spend your time trying to listen and learn as much about the local culture as possible while you are there.

Be a critical thinker about the impacts of tourism because sometimes they do not match initial assumptions. For example, in some scenarios locals might get far more benefit from "mass tourists" who briefly pass through a town on an organized coach tour because they contribute a lot to the local economy but require less efforts from local people to service than do "voluntourists," "backpackers," or "study-abroad students" who are there to get heavily involved with local lives and yet might inject far less money into the local economy. Sometimes sticking to the "tourist script" is the most ethical thing to do. At other times, you might discover that the mass tourism routes you are being funneled into are having terrible negative social, economic, or environmental impacts and should be avoided. It will depend on local contexts, and even after a long day of walking through a new city and feeling exhausted and overwhelmed, it is crucial that you remain alert and think critically. While it is often unclear what the "right" thing to do is in a given scenario, the key point is to constantly question what the responsible option might be.

When done properly, tourism and travel *can* be an opportunity to create jobs and whole new industries, invest in the environment, and help local cultural traditions thrive. In this consumer-driven global service industry, consumer demand often creates the market. For example, one thing you might consider doing is staying at family-run accommodations instead of a large hotel chain. When you arrive at your destination, eat at small locally owned restaurants and buy souvenirs from local vendors. Ironically, perhaps, buying a completely "inauthentic," even kitschy, souvenirs from a local family might be incredibly empowering for them. If we all choose to ensure that our money gets into local hands instead of huge multinational corporations (e.g., resort "enclaves") or exploitative governments with bad human rights records, then tourism could be positively transformative no matter your motives for traveling. You can be an ethical traveler and have a positive impact on your spring break beach vacation too.

Pay for experiences and tours that do not exploit the disenfranchised. Sometimes, it might be better to go to a more staged cultural performance that provides locals with jobs and educates you about their traditions than always insisting on seeing behind the scenes. Consider the fact that sometimes staged cultural performances, even if they feel less "authentic" to you, are created in order to give local people some privacy. An Irish friend of mine who lived in a beautifully restored stone cottage in a coastal village semiregularly had more adventurous tourists who were determined to get off the beaten track climb over his stone walls onto his property, and in one instance, a group of tourists simply walked right into his house to take pictures while he sat eating lunch. As you might imagine, he much preferred the packaged coach tourists who came in a group, did what their tour guide told them, spent some money in local establishments, and then happily went on their way. On the other hand, some organized tours are themselves exploitative. For example, as Ross Klein points out in this volume, packaged cruise holidays can have degrading effects on local environments and economies. Some forms of cultural tourism also seem designed for gawking at impoverished local people who are encouraged to occupy something akin to a "living history village" and become dependent on tourists' purchase of handicrafts. If you do not think critically though, it will be difficult to be sure if a staged cultural performance is exploiting local people or providing them with a social boundary that protects their privacy. To "go global and think local," you must behave a little bit like an anthropologist: observe carefully and ask a lot of questions.

Travel should never be a time to set aside one's ethics, a sense of social justice, or one's responsibility as a global citizen. Tourism is often conceptualized as a leisurely time out, and as a result tourist behavior is often far more outlandish than it would be "back home." But given the incredible economic, social, and environmental impacts that tourism has on local places, there is no *more* important time to think about social justice than when we travel. It begins when we plan an ethical holiday or trip. Once we do that, we can truly relax when we arrive, knowing that we are decreasing the negative impacts and maximizing the positive economic benefits.

Everyone lives in various complex social and cultural systems, and traveling to a new location will also bring you into that new system. Understand your social identities and the privileges that you bring with you, because how people perceive you due to your identities will help define your experience abroad. The amazing corollary benefit of "thinking local" is that you will very likely have a more authentic experience by eating local foods, talking to local people who actually appreciate you being there, and maybe even having a positive impact.

Source: Written expressly for *Tourists and Tourism*.

Appendix A

Teaching Tourism through Ethnographic Film

Michael A. Di Giovine

In 2012, the Anthropology of Tourism Interest Group (ATIG) was founded to provide a dedicated network for members in the American Anthropological Association (AAA) interested in researching and teaching topics related to tourism. It is a robust group that surged to nearly 1,000 scholars at its inception, who identify with each of the four traditional subfields of anthropology (sociocultural anthropology, biological/physical anthropology, archaeology, and linguistic anthropology) and many applied fields (e.g., consulting, museum curatorship, preservation, NGO work). ATIG's mission is to enable collaboration among anthropologists working on tourism-related issues, disseminate anthropological research on tourism, foster intellectual exchange on current issues related to tourism, and assist members in the development of curricula for teaching the anthropology of tourism. It does so through active programming at the annual meeting, facilitating interactions across social media, and making information available on its website, http://atig.americananthro.org.

One of ATIG's first initiatives was to compile and publish a list of ethnographic films on tourism for instructors online. The list was generated by the ATIG membership and compiled by Naomi Leite, the inaugural Co-Convenor (2013–2016). It is posted online at: http://atig.americananthro.org/films-for-teaching-the-anthropology-of-tourism/.

Why start off with ethnographic films? Particularly in this age of technological progress (and prowess among the current student generation), visual anthropological methods such as photography and film have developed into a robust genre, a means of communicating deep cultural analysis in an accessible format.

We are inundated with technological media; television, film, and digital photography are ubiquitous—they are live-streamed, shared across social networks, and, inasmuch as they are taken and saved on smartphones, literally carried in everyone's pockets. Younger generations are also sensitized to obtaining news and social information that way (Young 2015). In response, today's neoliberal universities push for using such visual communication technologies in the classroom; they appeal to students' preferred methods of information consumption as well as perhaps even their need for "edutainment" (Disney 1954), and they can be easily utilized in lucrative online formats. Ethnographic films complement traditional lectures by bringing to life the lived experiences of their subjects, and, maybe more so than traditional written ethnography, powerfully convey their subjects' ethos by emphasizing three particular domains (see Collier 1975): "kinesics," or the significance of bodily expressions (Birdwhistell 1970); "proxemics," or the meaning and cultural use of space in human behavior (Hall 1966); and "choreometrics," or the choreography, sonority, and performativity of culture (Lomax 1968). Particularly in this age of interconnectedness and digitalization, where such films can be produced and shared with relative ease across the world, the utopian sentiments uttered a half-century ago by the great ethnographic filmmaker Jean Rouch may ring true today: ethnographic film is a "new language which might allow us to cross the boundaries between all civilizations" (1975:90).

Like classic forms of ethnography—participant-observation, ethnographic interviews, kinship elicitation, spatial mapping, etc., which were traditionally recorded by hand (or scratched into the sand!)—visual ethnographic techniques such as photography and documentary filmmaking originated in the colonial period, developing along with the technological advances that enabled the imperial system and its concomitant "white man's burden" of salvaging indigenous lifeways that were perceived to be lost through modernization. Margaret Meade, decrying the "wretched picture of lost opportunities" of just using a pencil and paper, had urged anthropologists to embrace ethnographic films for their seemingly more authentic and exacting forms of visceral and multisensory representations; she saw them as "better ways of recording many aspects of culture . . . [and] culture change" (1975:5) than written descriptions, whose authority seemingly relied more on the audience's trust in the anthropologist's truthfulness. As multisensory media, they were also believed to furnish a more complete archival record. "All over the world, on every continent and island, in the hidden recesses of every industrial city as well as in the hidden valleys that can be reached only by helicopter, precious, totally irreplaceable, and forever irreproducible behaviors are disappearing, while departments of anthropology continue to send fieldworkers out with no equipment beyond a pencil and a notebook," a frustrated Meade lamented (4). Indeed, Félix-Louis Regnault, who is credited with making the first ethnographic film in 1895, believed that film "preserves forever all human behaviors for the needs of our studies" (1931:306; see de Brigard 1975:15).

Just as contemporary anthropologists know that culture is always changing, we are also acutely aware that film doesn't objectively preserve or salvage human behavior; it is just as socially mediated as written ethnography—perhaps even more so, if we think of the multiple levels of manipulation that an audio-visual image goes through as it is processed: from the choice and staging of the subject to the placement and framing of the camera lens, from the editorial work (selection of shots, choice of cuts, use of special effects) to the context of viewing. Yet it is in this mediation that ethnographic film becomes useful, lest it simply becomes a record of form over an analytical conveyance of meaning (cf. Hastrup 1992:10). Indeed, in many ways, the "writing culture" turn of the late twentieth century (see Clifford and Marcus 1986) and the subsequent crisis of representation in anthropology only added to the robust development of ethnographic filmmaking for this very reason: largely gone is the Positivistic domination of anthropology as a rational "science of words," to use Meade's critical term (1975:5); all ethnographic communication is creatively constructed and mediated, requiring acts of interpretation and reflexivity on the part of anthropologist and audience. Ethnographic filmmaking is, in the words of Anne Grimshaw (2001), one of many "ways of seeing in anthropology."

Yet there is some discrepancy of what qualifies as an "ethnographic film." In its broadest sense, ethnographic films are audio-visual representations that reveal social patterning (see de Brigard 1975:13). This definition is quite expansive, and, when considering either a film's form or function, or its real-life social impacts, nearly anything can be of ethnographic value as either data or analysis. (To wit, I introduce my Anthropology of Tourism class with a screening of Danny Boyle's turn-of-the-millennium Hollywood blockbuster *The Beach*, starring a young Leonardo DiCaprio). Yet while classic ethnographic filmmakers like Rouch have explicitly avoided classifying some films as ethnographic and others as not, some contemporary anthropologists working in an age of pop television documentaries and Baudrilliardian simulacra have urged colleagues to think carefully about the "intent, event, and reaction" of a film before labeling them as ethnographic (Banks 1992:117). While we have not engaged in this type of semantics, the films on ATIG's list largely adhere to filmmaker T. Minh-Ha Trinh's definitions of *ethnography* as "grasping the native's point of view, to realize his vision of the world," and *documentary* as a medium that "takes people and real problems from the real world and *deals* with them. It sets a value on intimate observation, and *assesses its worth* according to how well it succeeds in capturing reality on the run . . . powerful living stories, infinite authentic situations" (1991:33, 65; qtd. in Denzin 1997:72, 75).

As a topic, tourism lends itself extremely well to the genre of ethnographic films. On the one hand, ethnography as a methodology is not that dissimilar from touristic practices: both anthropologist and tourist travel sometimes long distances to engage with Otherness (Picard and Di Giovine 2014), filming and photographing their subjects, in an effort to meaningfully "grasp and then render" (see Geertz 2000:10) their experience with cultural diversity. This is somewhat of a blessing and a curse. It is a blessing in that ethnographic film, like photography, draws on what can be considered "native" practices and worldviews—if by native we also include tourists themselves: it privileges performance (MacCannell 1976; Bruner 2005), as well as the acts of seeing (Urry 2002; Di Giovine 2015), framing (Robinson and Picard 2009), and representing through symbols and imaginaries that are produced (Salazar and Graburn 2014). The taking of pictures—still and moving—has become a veritable marker of performing one's role as a tourist, as well as a prime tool of the travel industry to create and project seductive visions of the world to consumers (Robinson and Picard 2009:1). In ATIG's list, for example, *Framing the Other* is a striking representation of the ways in which European tourists photograph and engage in framing Ethiopian Mursi people, and how, likewise, the Mursi play to these outsiders' expectations of Otherness; the result is often dissatisfaction and miscommunication. It is reminiscent of O'Rourke's classic film, *Cannibal Tours*—with both visitor and visited consuming the other (economically, politically, and socially). Produced in 1988, *Cannibal Tours* stands as one of the first ethnographic films on tourism and continues to be relevant today.

Yet it is precisely this closeness with traditional touristic practices that makes ethnographic filmmaking on tourism a curse to some, as well. In attempting to separate ethnographic film from touristic productions, Banks emphasizes common stereotypes between the two types of travelers, the tourist and the ethnographic filmmaker: supposedly anthropologists are more fluent in a local language, live longer in a field site, see interconnectedness below the surface, and do more than simply observe like a travel writer "who sees only incidents and social facts in isolation" (1992:121). Of course, the relationships are more complex and less essentialized than that, and younger generations of tourism anthropologists often contest such stereotypes.

On the other hand, studies have shown that, pedagogically, documentary films are highly effective at teaching difficult topics, because through their fusion of visual, audio, narrative, and character elements, they are able to appeal to students' emotions, putting faces on oft-abstracted historical or social concepts, and sometimes creating conflict with preconceived notions they have. In a study of the use of (popular and documentary) films in high schools, Stoddard, Marcus, and Hicks (2017:3–5) found that films are frequently used to cover topics "often marginalized in the . . . curriculum," and which teachers either are not as familiar with or not as comfortable teaching (i.e., rural, white teachers show more films on slavery, while urban teachers show more films on Native Americans). Conversely, experts have also found that some use films to deal with traumatic issues or events that resonate with students but are uncomfortable and hard to acknowledge, such as genocides or continuing racial disparities in the United States (Walsh, Hicks, and van Hover 2017). What these students see may conflict with personal, family/community, or other understandings; such disparities, argue the UK's Historical Association (2007:3), create strong and lasting resonance with students.

Though conceived of as a leisure-time event, and though most people at some point have been tourists, tourism may very well be a "difficult" topic from the social scientific perspective, as it inherently deals with problematic issues of race, gender disparities, sexual diversity and violence, fluid identities and kinship, economic inequality, and neocolonialism. Critical, in-depth examinations of tourism often reveal its dark underbelly and may create discomfort in students who recognize problematic behaviors, imaginaries, and stereotypes in their own touristic practices (I always seem to have a student or two who say that my tourism class "ruined" tourism for them!). Tourism, for example, is predicated on racial, sexual, cultural, and economic Otherness (Picard and Di Giovine 2014); Walsh, Hicks, and van Hover (2017) found in particular that films are the preferred method of teaching Otherness, especially when difficult or critical of taken-for-granted, ethnocentric notions of difference are the subjects. Race and identity are problematized in the classic film, *Roots*, which documents African American Alex Haley's visit to Africa through an exploration of the slave trade, while in *Refugee*, an adopted Khmer-American returns to his biological father in Cambodia and faces difficulty in connecting with the people and places he left behind. The several films on sex tourism, such as *Cowboys in Paradise* and *My Boyfriend, the Sex Tourist*, complicate sexual commodification, gender issues, and common ideas concerning the sex trade. Chinese tourism laborers in *Up the Yangtze* and Muslim Kenyan youths in *Edge of Islam* both struggle with difficult social, economic and religious pressures as they weigh the options to embrace work in the tourism industry; seemingly well-intentioned volunteer tourism is critiqued in *Can't Do It in Europe*; and the dubious benefits of tourism development are made clear in a number of films such as *Paraíso for Sale* and *Destination: Tourism*. These and other films tracing unchecked mass tourism, such as *Gringo Trails* and *Bye Bye Barcelona*, ask students to contemplate the benefits as well as the pressures of tourism and cultural change.

Through their poignant narratives and sensitive focus on the lived experiences of the many diverse stakeholders who are affected by tourist interactions—from indigenous peoples to industry works to different types of tourists themselves—films often complement the critical and theoretical analyses that can be assigned readings in anthropology of tourism syllabi, and have cultivated productively affective responses in students. Available with their descriptions, links, and some reviews at ATIG's website, the ethnographic films are listed by ATIG members because they have proven to be useful instruments for teaching tourism, and ATIG encourages students and instructors to visit the interactive web page and add their own favorites: http://atig.americananthro.org/films-for-teaching-the-anthropology-of-tourism/.

References Cited

Banks, Marcus. 1992. "Which Films are Ethnographic Films?" in *Film as Ethnography*, eds. Peter Ian Crawford and David Turton, pp. 116–129. Manchester: Manchester University.

Birdwhistell, Ray. 1970. *Kinesics and Context*. Philadelphia: University of Pennsylvania Press.

Bruner, Ed. 2005. *Culture on Tour*. Chicago: University of Chicago Press.

Clifford, James, and George E. Marcus. 1986. *Writing Culture: The Poetics and Politics of Ethnography*. Berkeley: University of California Press.

Collier, John. 1975. "Photography and Visual Anthropology," in *Visual Anthropology*, ed. Paul Hockings, pp. 211–230. The Hague: Mouton and Co.

de Brigard, Emilie. 1975. "The History of Ethnographic Film," in *Visual Anthropology*, ed. Paul Hockings, pp. 13–43. The Hague: Mouton and Co.

Denzin, Norman K. 1997. *Interpretative Ethnography*. Thousand Oaks, CA: Sage.

Di Giovine, Michael A. 2015. "When Popular Religion Becomes Elite Heritage: Tensions and Transformations at the Shrine of St. Padre Pio of Pietrelcina," in *Encounters with Popular Pasts*, eds. Mike Robinson and Helaine Silverman, pp. 31–47. New York: Springer.

Disney, Walt. 1954. "Educational Values in Factual Nature Pictures." *Educational Horizons* 33(2): 82–84.

Geertz, Clifford. 2000. *The Interpretation of Cultures*. New York: Basic Books.

Grimshaw, Anne. 2001. *The Ethnographic Eye: Ways of Seeing in Anthropology*. Cambridge: Cambridge University Press.

Hall, Edward. 1966. *The hidden dimension*. NY: Anchor Books.

Hastrup, Kristen (1992). "Anthropological Visions: Some Notes on Visual and Textual Authority," in *Film as Ethnography*, eds. Peter Ian Crawford and David Turton, pp. 8–25. Manchester: Manchester University Press.

Historical Association. 2007. "T. E. A. C. H. Teaching Emotive and Controversial History." London: The Historical Association, pp. 3-19. www.history.org.uk/resources/recourse_780.html (accessed July 20, 2017).

Lomax, Alan. 1968. *Folk Song Style and Culture: A Staff Report on Cantometrics,* vol. 88. Washington, DC: American Association for the Advancement of Science.

MacCannell, Dean. 1976. *The Tourist*. Berkeley: University of California Press.

Meade, Margaret. 1975. "Introduction: Visual Anthropology in a Discipline of Words," in *Visual Anthropology*, ed. Paul Hockings, pp. 3–10. The Hague: Mouton and Co.

Picard, David, and Michael A. Di Giovine (eds.). 2014. *Tourism and the Power of Otherness: Seductions of Difference*. Bristol: Channel View.

Regnault, Félix-Louis. 1931. "Le rôle du cinéma en ethnographie." *La Nature* 59:304–306.

Robinson, Mike, and David Picard (eds.). 2009. *The Framed World*. Farnham: Ashgate.

Rouch, Jean. 1975. "The Camera and Man," in *Visual Anthropology*, ed. Paul Hockings, pp. 83–102. The Hague: Mouton and Co.

Salazar, Noel, and Nelson Graburn. 2014. *Tourism Imaginaries: Anthropological Approaches*. Oxford: Berghahn.

Stoddard, Jeremy, Alan S. Marcus, and David Hicks. 2017. "Using Film to Teach Difficult Histories," in *Teaching Difficult History through Film*, eds. Jeremy Stoddard, Alan S. Marcus, and David Hicks, pp. 3–16. New York: Routledge.

Trinh, T. M-ha. 1991. *When the Moon Waxes Red: Representation, Gender and Cultural Politics*. New York: Routledge.

Urry, John. 2002. *The Tourist Gaze*, 2nd ed. Thousand Oaks, CA: Sage.

Walsh, Ben, David Hicks, and Stephanie van Hover. 2017. "Difficult History Means Difficult Questions: Using Film to Reveal the Perspective of 'The Other' in Difficult History Topics," in *Teaching Difficult History through Film*, eds. Jeremy Stoddard, Alan S. Marcus, and David Hicks, pp. 17–36. New York: Routledge.

Young, Eric. 2015. How Millennials Get News: Inside the Habits of America's First Digital Generation. *American Press Institute associated Press-NORC Centre for Public Affairs Research*. www.mediainsight.org/PDFs/Millennials/Millennials%20Report%20FINAL.pdf (accessed July 19, 2017).

Appendix B

Contributors

Lisa Beth Anderson is a photographer and MA Migration Studies candidate at the University of San Francisco. Her photographic work has been featured in print and online publications around the world. Lisa runs In Good Company, a studio specializing in the creation of photographic narratives for nonprofits. Her work explores gender, power, and efforts to make the world a more humane place.

Denise Brennan is Professor and Chair of the Department of Anthropology at Georgetown University. She is the author of *Life Interrupted: Trafficking into Forced Labor in the United States* (2014), which follows the lives of the first trafficking survivors in the United States, and *What's Love Got to Do with It? Transnational Desires and Sex Tourism in the Dominican Republic* (2004), which explores how Dominican women strategically use the sex sector to meet tourists, feign love, and legally migrate off the island through marriage.

Edward M. Bruner is Professor Emeritus of Anthropology and Professor Emeritus of Criticism and Interpretive Theory at the University of Illinois. He was past president of the American Ethnological Society and the Society for Humanistic Anthropology. He became interested in tourism in the mid-1980s while leading a student group on a round-the-world year abroad program, where he realized that anthropologists and tourists are found together, everywhere. "Tourism haunts the anthropological enterprise," he says. His edited volumes include *Text, Play, and Story* (1984) and *The Anthropology of Experience* (1986). His most recent book is *Culture on Tour: Ethnographies of Travel* (2004).

Ralf Buckley holds the International Chair in Ecotourism Research at Griffith University, Australia, and is a Distinguished Professor at the Chinese Academy of Sciences. He has written a dozen books and two hundred journal articles, and has over ten thousand citations (calculated in H index53). His interests are in links between adventure and ecotourism, biodiversity and conservation, and human health and culture.

Michael A. Di Giovine is Assistant Professor of Anthropology at West Chester University of Pennsylvania and Honorary Fellow in the Department of Anthropology at the University of Wisconsin-Madison. A former tour operator, he is the Convenor of the AAA's Anthropology of Tourism Interest Group and co-editor (with Noel Salazar) of Lexington Books' series, *The Anthropology of Tourism:*

Heritage, Mobility, and Society. His latest book is *Tourism: Anthropological Insights* (2018).

Tim Edensor is a Senior Lecturer in Cultural Studies at Staffordshire University. He is author of *Tourists at the Taj* (1998), editor of *Reclaiming Stoke-on-Trent: Leisure, Space and Identity in the Potteries* (2000), and has written on walking in the countryside and the town, football in Mauritius, and *Braveheart* and Scottish identity. He is presently completing a book entitled *National Identity, Popular Culture and Everyday Life*, and is carrying out research into industrial ruins.

Elizabeth Garland is a Senior Program Director at the international fair labor NGO Verité (www.verite.org), where she leads the organization's Africa region programming and oversees initiatives to improve labor practices within the raw materials supply chains of multinational corporations. Before leaving academia to join Verité, she taught Anthropology, and African Studies as a visiting lecturer at Smith College and Dartmouth College, and as an Assistant Professor at Union College.

Chris Gibson is Professor of Human Geography at the University of Wollongong, Australia, and Editor-in-Chief, *Australian Geographer*. His research critically examines the nexus between creative industries, tourism, and place, with a focus on embodied encounters and livelihoods. His books include *Creativity in Peripheral Places: Redefining the Creative Industries* (2012), *Surfing Places, Surfboard-Makers* (2014, with Andrew Warren), and with long-time collaborator John Connell, *Sound Tracks: Popular Music, Identity and Place* (2003), *Music and Tourism* (2005), *Festival Places* (2011), *Music Festivals and Regional Development in Australia* (2012), and *Outback Elvis* (2017).

Alex Gillespie is Associate Professor of Social Psychology in the Department of Psychological and Behavioural Science at the London School of Economics and an editor of *Journal for the Theory of Social Behaviour*. He is an expert on communication, divergences of perspective, misunderstandings, trust, and listening. He is particularly interested in what people can learn from listening to each other and why people often fail to understand, or actively ignore, points of view that are different or challenging.

George Gmelch is Professor of Anthropology at the University of San Francisco and Union College. He is the author of fourteen books, including two memoirs: *Playing with Tigers: A Minor-League Chronicle of the Sixties* (2016) and, with Sharon Bohn Gmelch, *In the Field: Life and Work in Cultural Anthropology* (2018). The latter describes their field research among Irish Travellers, English Gypsies, Alaskan Natives, Caribbean villagers and tourism workers, professional baseball players, Newfoundland oil rig and tankermen, among others. He did his undergraduate work at Stanford and his PhD at the University of California, Santa Barbara.

Sharon Bohn Gmelch is Professor of Anthropology at the University of San Francisco and Union College. She is the author or editor of ten books, including *Nan: The Life of an Irish Travelling Woman* (1986), *The Tlingit Encounter with Photography* (2008), *Tasting the Good Life: Wine Tourism in the Napa Valley*

(2011), and *Irish Travelllers: The Unsettled Life* (2014)—the latter two with George Gmelch. She is currently working on a cross-cultural study of tour guides.

Nelson Graburn was educated in Classics at King's, Canterbury, and in Natural Sciences and Anthropology at Cambridge, McGill, and University of Chicago. He has carried out ethnographic research with the Inuit (and Naskapi) of Canada (and Alaska and Greenland) since 1959, in Japan (and East and Southeast Asia) since 1974, and China since 1991. His areas of interest are ethnic arts, tourism, heritage, museums; multiculturalism, Inuit, Circumpolar peoples, China, and Japan.

Lynn Horton is an Associate Professor of Sociology at Chapman University. She works on issues of sustainable development, social movements, and gender equality with a focus on Latin America. She is author of *Peasants in Arms: War and Peace in the Mountains of Nicaragua* (1999), *Grassroots Struggles for Sustainability in Central America* (2007) and most recently, *Women and Microfinance in the Global South* (2017).

Rami Isaac was born in Palestine and studied in The Netherlands and the UK. He is a Senior Lecturer in tourism at the NHTV Breda University of Applied Sciences in The Netherlands, and an Assistant Professor of Tourism and Hotel Management at Bethlehem University, Palestine. His research focuses on tourism development and management, critical theory, and political aspects of tourism. He has published widely on tourism and political (in)stability, occupation, tourism and war, dark tourism, violence, and transformational tourism.

Adam Kaul is an Associate Professor of Anthropology at Augustana College. He is the author of *Turning the Tune* (2009) and several articles and book chapters about traditional music, tourism, and the economics of musical performance in the West of Ireland.

Seung Hwan (Danny) Kim serves as the Assistant Director of International Student Life at Augustana College. He studied Psychology and Broadcasting & Digital Media at Cedarville University and he obtained his M.A. from The Ohio State University in Higher Education & Student Affairs. As a former international student hailing from Paraguay and South Korea, his passion is positioning international students for leadership and development.

Ross A. Klein is Professor of Social Work at the Memorial University of Newfoundland, Canada and an international authority on the cruise industry and cruise tourism. He is the author of ten books and monographs, many articles and book chapters, and has testified four times before the U.S. Congress. He is founder of www.cruisejunkie.com

Tamara Kohn is Associate Professor of Anthropology at the University of Melbourne. She has conducted fieldwork in the Scottish Hebrides, Nepal, Japan, and the U.S., and she held research and teaching positions in Oxford and Durham before moving Down Under. She publishes on identity, transcultural communities of practice, leisure and mobility, death studies, the body and senses, and methods and ethics in anthropology.

Dean MacCannell is Professor Emeritus of Environmental Design and Landscape Architecture at the University of California at Davis. His book, *The Tourist: A New Theory of the Leisure Class* (1976), was one of the earliest contributions to tourist studies. He was a founding member of the International Tourism Research Academy and Research Group 50 (the sociology of tourism) of the International Sociological Association. He has recently taught seminars on tourism theory at A.I.L.U.N. in Italy and at Colombia National University in Bogotá. His newest book is *The Ethics of Sightseeing* (2011).

Heather Montgomery is Reader in the Anthropology of Childhood at the Open University in the UK. Her PhD, which she received from Cambridge University, was an ethnographic study of the lives and experiences of young prostitutes in Thailand. She is the author of *Modern Babylon? Prostituting Children in Thailand* (2001) and *An Introduction to Childhood: Anthropological Perspectives on Children's Lives* (2008). Her research interests are children and sexuality, child labor, and children's rights.

David Picard holds a PhD in anthropology (2001) from the University of La Réunion, Indian Ocean, and is currently working at the Centre for Research in Anthropology (CRIA) at the New University of Lisbon, Portugal. He is the author of *Tourism, Magic and Modernity: Cultivating the Human Garden* (2011).

Noel B. Salazar is Research Professor in Anthropology at the University of Leuven, Belgium. He is Vice President of the International Union of Anthropological and Ethnological Sciences, Chair of the IUAES Commission on the Anthropology of Tourism, and Past President of the European Association of Social Anthropologists. In addition, he is on UNESCO's and UNWTO's official roster of consultants and an expert member of the ICOMOS International Cultural Tourism Committee and the UNESCO-UNITWIN Network "Culture, Tourism and Development."

Amit Sengupta is trained in medicine. His main interests are public health issues, pharmaceuticals policy, and other science and technology-related policy issues like intellectual property rights. He is associated with the Peoples Science and the Peoples Health Movements in India and at the global level. Currently, Dr. Sengupta is the Associate Global Coordinator of the Peoples Health Movement (PHM) and the Managing Editor of Global Health Watch.

Dallen J. Timothy is Professor of Community Resources and Development at Arizona State University and holds visiting professorships in China, Italy, and Spain. He is the editor of the *Journal of Heritage Tourism*, serves on the editorial boards of 20 international journals, and is commissioning editor for five book series by Routledge and Channel View Publications. His tourism research interests include all aspects of heritage, globalization, pilgrimage, geopolitics, and cultural change. Professor Timothy has ongoing research projects in the Middle East, Asia, North America, and Western Europe.